OVER
THERE

The Man Who Presumed:
A Biography of Henry Morton Stanley

Burton: A Biography of Sir Richard Francis Burton

Prisoners of the Mahdi

Queen Victoria's Little Wars

The Great Anglo-Boer War

Mr. Kipling's Army

The Gurkhas

Eminent Victorian Soldiers: Seekers of Glory

The Great War in Africa, 1914–1918

Armies of the Raj:
From the Mutiny to Independence, 1858–1947

Balls Bluff: A Small Battle and Its Long Shadow

Stonewall: A Biography of General
Thomas J. Jackson

OVER THERE

THE UNITED STATES IN THE GREAT WAR

1917–1918

BYRON FARWELL

W. W. NORTON & COMPANY

NEW YORK • LONDON

Copyright © 1999 by Byron Farwell

Maps on pages 55, 119, 162, 207, and 319 are from Leonard P. Ayres,
The War With Germany: A Statistical Summary (Washington, D.C.:
Government Printing Office, 1919), pages 28, 108, 106, 110, and 214. Map
on page 279 is from American Battle Monuments Commission, *American
Armies and Battlefields in Europe: A History, Guide, and Reference Book*
(Washington, D.C.: Government Printing Office, 1938), page 432.

For information about permission to reproduce selections from this book,
write to Permissions, W. W. Norton & Company, Inc.,
500 Fifth Avenue, New York, NY 10110.

The text of this book is composed in Electra
with the display set in Belwe
Desktop composition by Tom Ernst
Manufacturing by Quebecor Printing, Fairfield, Inc.
Book design by JAM Design

Library of Congress Cataloging-in-Publication Data

Farwell, Byron.
Over there : the United States in the Great War, 1917–1918 / by Byron Farwell.
p.   cm.
Includes bibliographical references and index.
ISBN 0-393-04698-2
1. World War, 1914–1918—United States.   2. United States—
History—1913–1921.   I. Title.
D570.F37   1999
940.4'0973—dc21   98-35705
CIP

ISBN 0-393-32028-6 pbk.

W. W. Norton & Company, Inc., 500 Fifth Avenue, New York, N.Y. 10110
www.wwnorton.com

W. W. Norton & Company Ltd., 10 Coptic Street, London WC1A 1PU

2   3   4   5   6   7   8   9   0

FOR RUTH

CONTENTS

Illustrations follow pages 126 and 228

ACKNOWLEDGMENTS

I WANT TO acknowledge the help I have received on medical and surgical matters from Dr. Robert J. T. Joy, professor emeritus and former chairman of the department of Medical History at the Uniformed Services University of the Health Sciences, F. Hébert School of Medicine. I also wish to thank William Carey, Esq., of Berkeley Springs, West Virginia, for his help. Above all I wish to thank my wife, Ruth, whose sure eye for the wrong word and talent for finding the right one, have much improved the readablility of this book. Errors, of course, are my own.

PROLOGUE

IT WAS SEVEN months after the United States declared war on Germany before American troops were placed in harm's way on the Western Front. Among the first were the men of the 2nd Battalion, 16th Infantry, who moved into trenches in the Sommerviller sector near Bathelémont on the cold, rainy, miserable evening of 2 November 1917. This part of Artois was regarded as a quiet sector, as it had seen no serious fighting since October 1915. But at about 3:30 A.M. on 3 November, the new arrivals were stormed by a German raiding party, 213 officers and men of the 7th Bavarian Landwehr. Eleven men were captured and three young men in Company F were killed: Corporal James Bethel Gresham from Evansville, Indiana; Private Merle D. Hay, from Glidden, Illinois; and Private Thomas F. Enright from Pittsburgh, Pennsylvania, the first three enlisted men to be killed by enemy action on the Western Front.

Their throats had been cut, their heads nearly severed, presumably by trench knives, a detail not reported in the press. A buddy saw Merle Hay's body "in the mud, all mussed up very badly."

Private Hay, a husky twenty-one-year-old, six feet tall, had been the eldest of three children. In May he had quit his job repairing equipment at a farm near Coon Rapids, Iowa, and with some friends had gone to Des Moines to enlist. Although he had flat feet, he was readily accepted and, although he had volunteered for the Coast Artillery, he soon found himself in the 16th Infantry in France.

A newspaper reporter broke the news of his death to his parents. By the time a second reporter called from the county newspaper, his father,

Daniel Hay, was collected enough to say: "I'm proud of my boy if he has given up his life for his country. He had my consent to go and I am not sorry." His mother, Carrie, later tried to describe him: "He was," she said, "a lamb. You would never have thought he could get angry enough to go to war."

Private Tom Enright, who became Merle's friend, was a mild young man who neither drank nor smoked and had seldom been known to go out with a woman. His brother-in-law, Charlie Trunzer, thought him "one of the quietest men I'd ever known." His father, an Irish-born laborer, had died when he was a boy. After eight years in a Catholic school in Pittsburgh, he joined the army and had seen service on the Mexican border. At the time of the raid he was serving his third hitch. "I kind of like the army," he once told his sister.

Corporal James Bethel Gresham, called Bethel, was born in Henderson, Kentucky, where he lost his father, a Confederate veteran, when he was seven. A grave, well-behaved boy, he stuttered when excited. In 1901 his mother moved the family of three boys and two girls to Evansville, Indiana, where they settled in a rough section of town called Cotton Mill. In 1904 she married another Confederate veteran. Leaving school at the age of fourteen, Bethel found work driving wagon teams. After an argument with his stepfather, he joined the army in 1914, and had served in Mexico before being shipped to Europe.

A reporter, a young woman from the Evansville *Press*, broke the news of his death to his mother as she was bending over her washtubs. She found it hard to respond to the reporter's persistent questions.

"Don't you think any mother would be proud to have her boy give his life for a cause like that?"

"It's awfully hard to have him gone. God help me to endure."

"But you are the mother of a hero."

"Yes, he's a hero, and for his sake I ought to be brave. But I'm not a hero. I'm just a mother."

Later in the week she received a government check for $45 — $20 of her son's pay and $25 insurance money.

The three young men were buried with considerable ceremony on a little rise of pasturage near Bathelémont-Bauzemont, Meurthe-et-Moselle. The French provided a guard of honor and a French general, Paul Bordeaux, spoke at some length. The one woman present, Countess Daisy Polk de Burger, an American married to a Frenchman, thoughtfully wrote to the families, describing the ceremony. The French government conferred the *Croix de Guerre* posthumously upon the three and later a small monument was raised with the inscription: "Here lie the First Soldiers of the Great Republic of the United States who died on the soil of France for Justice and Liberty." General Pershing visited the graves and stood for a moment bareheaded.

Across America people took notice. The war had finally struck home. There were American dead. "Our playing at war is over," announced the New York *Tribune*.

INTRODUCTION

AT THE TURN of the century a British subaltern, writing home from South Africa where he was fighting Afrikaner farmers, quipped that the war he was engaged in was like every other war in that it was different from every other war. The same could be said with greater emphasis of the war that erupted a dozen years later in Europe.

The First World War—the Great War—was the first general European war since the defeat of Napoleon in 1815 and it created one of the most massive social and political upheavals in history. Waged in ways vastly different from anything seen before or since, it involved some seventy million combatants and in a period of little more than four years resulted in the death of from nine to twelve million people.

Although the war was fought in many places—in Africa, Asia, the Middle East, and in the Atlantic, Pacific and Indian Oceans—the principal action took place in Europe. Not counting the war in northern Russia and Siberia, there were four European fronts or seats of war—Italian, Macedonian, Eastern, and Western—but the war was won and lost on Germany's Western Front, so called even though most of the action was between armies facing north and south. It was on this front that most American soldiers fought. In time it stretched in a great arc from the English Channel to Switzerland, a flankless line of battle, but the main killing grounds lay in a 475-mile section in northern France and southern Belgium, a land of familiar battlefield sites since Agincourt 500 years earlier.

The era in which the war was fought was one of unprecedented rapid social and technical change difficult to absorb. Never before had so much innovation taken place in so short a period of time. In no previous war had there been so many changes in the nature of warfare itself and in the equipment with which it was waged. Military aircraft, submarines, internal combustion engines, wireless telegraphy, chemical warfare, automatic rifles and machine guns, tanks, flame throwers, and quick-firing artillery were all new to the battlefield or the war at sea. It was also, particularly for the army, an era of enormous logistical problems and complex administrative detail.

The war aims of the contending Allied countries varied, and there were major differences between the United States and the Allies. Britain sought to preserve her empire and her dominance of the seas; France sought the return of Alsace-Lorraine, lost to Germany in the Franco-Prussian War, and the permanent crippling of Germany; Italy wanted Trieste and other Austrian territories; Japan wanted an expansion of her territory on the Asian continent; and China wanted to regain the German enclave, territory lost after the Boxer Rebellion. The United States alone had no territorial ambitions. American goals, as outlined by President Wilson, were visionary, "to make the world safe for democracy." The Allies, while recognizing the propaganda value of Wilson's ideals, did not take them seriously.

The Great War was the only major war ever fought without voice control on the battlefield. Generals could no longer give effective commands in the course of a battle; once their troops were committed, they lost almost all control of the action. They were much criticized after the war for stationing themselves in chateaux behind the lines instead of in the front line trenches with their men, but as French General Charles Mangin, one of the most front-line, hands-on generals of the war noted: "If I walked about the front line I would command only one or two companies." Communication was a problem throughout the war.

It was not the kind of war anyone wanted to fight, least of all the soldiers. The generals on both sides envisioned a war of maneuver. And so it was for a short time when the war began in early August 1914. But by the end of September machine guns and the new quick-firing artillery had driven everyone into the ground. The first of those thousands of miles of trenches had been dug, and from September 1914 for three and one-half years—until March 1917—there followed an ebb and flow of battle in which, despite furious bloody fighting, the range of advance and retreat never reached ten miles in either direction. Gone were the flags, trumpets, and drums, the flashing sabres and the trampling horses. Little glory could be found living in filthy ditches wearing gas masks.

Even the generals found it a bad war. There were no flanks to attack or turn. No room for cavalry charges. Strategy was largely replaced by logistics and battles were fought with strange, unfamiliar weapons of previously unimagined frightfulness.

The small Belgian army held the line from the English Channel to Dixmunde, twenty miles southwest of Brugge, where floods prevented any serious infantry fighting. A small French sector followed running about four miles north of Ypres. From there the Flemish plain as far as Givenchy was defended by the British. The remainder of the line east and south was held by the French until the summer of 1918 when the Americans began to take their place in the line of battle. The closest the Germans ever came to Paris was Noyon, sixty miles away.

There were a few major battles at sea—at Jutland and off the Falkland Islands—but the war primarily was fought on land. Although military commanders on both sides wanted a war of maneuver, all their efforts were bent and hundreds of thousands of lives lost to prevent this from happening. As soon as it did become possible, the war ended.

Once armies were driven into the ground, there were no battles in the conventional sense. Although men were killed or maimed every day for nearly four years, the battlefield itself was mostly bare. Airmen flying over the lines rarely saw signs of life. Machine guns and quick-firing artillery made any movement above ground hazardous. Between the opposing trenches lay always an empty stretch of ground appositely named no-man's-land. No trees grew. No structure remained unscathed. It was siege warfare, except that nothing and no one was truly besieged.

Attempts to break through the lines of trenches and barbed wire created bulges, called salients, in the battle lines. Both sides then endeavored to eliminate the salient; the side that created it attempted to straighten it by expanding it into a new line, their opponents by pinching it off or driving it in. Battles, called offensives when large numbers of men were involved, occurred when the troops on one side left their trenches, and went "over the top," to create or remove a salient. Smaller actions—raids, usually to obtain prisoners for interrogation—ordinarily occurred at night. It was only at such times and when men went "over the top" that the enemy actually was seen.

The long lines of trenches and barbed wire were artificially divided into sectors of various sizes and assigned to specific military units to defend and develop. Opposing sides sought to determine their exact boundaries, for the point at which, say, a French unit abutted an American unit or Germans abutted Hungarians, might be a good place to center an attack, since there were likely to be communications problems and confusion over who was responsible for doing what.

All armies were divided into smaller units bearing similar names. The smallest administrative unit was the company (*compagnie* in French; *Kompanie* in German) usually commanded by a captain (*Hauptmann* in German). The equivalent unit of artillery was the battery and, in the cavalry, the troop. Companies, batteries, and troops were identified by alphabetical letters, except in the United States Marines and the British army, and were usually divided into platoons, which were in turn divided into sections or squads, the latter commanded by noncommissioned officers. The size of a captain's command varied, depending upon the arm or service within each national army. A company of infantry in the American army at full strength during the war was originally 250, later reduced to 175. German companies at full strength were somewhat larger.

The smallest unit containing all arms and services* was the division. An American division, as defined by the *Field Service Regulations* (1914), was "a self-contained unit made up of all necessary arms and services, and complete in itself with every requirement for independent action incident to its operation." It could be either infantry or cavalry, but contained units of ordnance, engineers, quartermasters, et al. It was commanded by a major general in the American service; its major units, brigades of infantry, cavalry or artillery, were commanded by brigadier generals. An American infantry division contained about 28,000 men and was about twice the size of a European division. The brigades of an American infantry division contained two or more regiments, which were divided into two or more battalions, each of which contained two or more companies. In the American army divisions were assigned numbers, but most had unofficial names, for example, the 42nd Division was also known as the Rainbow Division.

The word *army* has two different specific meanings. It can encompass the entire land forces of a nation or a unit of a national army consisting of two or more corps, each including two or more divisions with supporting

---

*Arms are the combat units such as infantry and artillery; services are ordnance, transport, quartermaster, et. al.

troops. When these are field armies they usually are named after some geographical or political feature, as was done in the American Civil War, or numbered, as in the Great War. When numbered the number is usually written out and capitalized, for example, Second Army. Army corps are by convention designated by Roman numerals, for example, IV Corps. The American Expeditionary Force sent to fight in France became first a single field army. Later as more and more troops arrived, Pershing divided his forces into two armies, designated First Army and Second Army. In November 1918 he created the Third Army that became the American army of occupation in Germany.

When the war began, the American army, thanks to a lack of interest by its people and the parsimony of its government, had not even a single division; many of its soldiers had never seen even an entire regiment in one place. It lacked not only enlisted men, but the officers and noncommissioned officers to train them. It was badly in need of arms and equipment, but American industries lacked the skills to produce in quantity the materials for a modern European war. It was awareness of these facts that initially led Germany to discount any threat of American entry into the war.

What the United States accomplished in its nineteen months of war in raising an army and navy of nearly four million men, clothing and equipping them, was nearly incredible, but its armed forces retained all the marks of a hastily put together, partially trained, amateur affair, poor in almost everything except enthusiasm, for although President Wilson had been reelected on a platform which boasted that "he kept us out of war," the war, once declared, was embarked upon with gusto.

The American Expeditionary Force (AEF) saw only 150 days of combat, but in that time it seized 485,000 square miles of enemy-held territory and captured 63,000 prisoners, 1,300 artillery pieces, and 10,000 mortars and machine guns. The United States did not by itself win the war, but it did make a significant contribution to the Allied victory.

Winston Churchill described the effect of the arrival of the first American soldiers on the French:

> The impression made upon the hard-pressed French by this seemingly inexhaustible flood of gleaming youth in its first maturity of health and vigour was prodigious. . . . As crammed in their lorries they clattered along the roads singing the songs of a new world at the top of their voices, burning to reach the bloody field, the French Headquarters were thrilled with the impulse of new life. . . . Half trained, half organized,

with only their courage and their numbers and their magnificent youth behind their weapons, they were to buy their experience at a bitter price. But this they were quite ready to do.

The élan of the Americans counted for much, for although they faced German soldiers more skilled and experienced, the still formidable German army of 1918 was not the well-oiled war machine of 1914 and the German soldiers were not the well-trained troops who had so confidently marched through Belgium. Among them now were those too young or too old for hard service.

The criticisms of the French and British officers—that the Americans' logistical arrangements left much to be desired, that they failed to control their transportation requirements and caused appalling road jams behind the lines, and that although they succeeded in their objectives, they paid too high a price because they lacked battlefield skills—were all true, but they failed to recognize that they themselves had demanded that the Americans be pushed into action before they were fully trained and that it was the increasing presence of these amateur soldiers in the battle line that in fact led to victory in 1918.

1

☆

EDGING TOWARD WAR

IN THE NINETEENTH century Bismarck predicted that "some damned thing in the Balkans" might someday plunge Europe into total war. He was right. In 1908 Austria annexed Bosnia and Herzegovina, so incensing the Serbs that when the Archduke Franz Ferdinand of Austria was assassinated by a young Serb at Sarajevo on 24 June 1914, the Austrians, suspecting Serbian complicity, delivered an unacceptable ultimatum and marched into Serbia.

A network of treaties insured that Europe had become, in the words of Albert Marrin, "a fireworks warehouse guarded by careless watchmen." The Austrian attack on Serbia brought Russia into the conflict, for it had a treaty with Serbia. A treaty between France and Russia brought in France. Germany, brought into the war by its pact with Austria, faced a two-front war, and when Italy sided with France, Austria, too, faced a war on two fronts.

Germany's strategy was first to knock France out of the conflict and then defeat Russia. Such a war had long been anticipated by the German Great General Staff and its chief at the turn of the century, General Alfred von Schlieffen. His plan called for German armies to swing through Belgium and Luxembourg to attack France from the north, while simply holding the Western Front facing France. Chancellor Bethmann-Hollweg explained abrogation of the pact that ensured the neutrality of Belgium by saying that the invasion was "a matter of military necessity, and necessity knows no law." This brought Britain, a guarantor of Belgian neutrality, into the war.

Now the antagonists were evenly matched; neither could outreach the other. By 1917, after more than two years of war, the Allies and the Central Powers were locked on land in a hopeless, bloody, fruitless, seemingly endless conflict. There was valor aplenty on both sides; courage had not been wanting. But each new effort stagnated; battlefields became immobile killing grounds. In a war of attrition hundreds of thousands had fallen on both sides for negligible gains. On the Italian Front the Italian army, after five bloody, unimaginative offensives that resulted in 273,000 casualties, sought help from Britain and France. The Austrians had lost 184,000 and begged Berlin for aid. On the Salonika Front, where the French, British, and Serbians had suffered 50,000 casualties in a failed offensive, the survivors were being felled by malaria. General Erich Ludendorff sneered that Salonika was his biggest prison camp. Russia, after losing more than a million men, was on the verge of total collapse.

Shortly before he was killed in 1914, a French officer, Alfred Joubaire, scribbled in his diary: "Humanity is mad! It must be mad to do what it is doing. What a massacre! What bloody scenes of horror! Hell cannot be so terrible. Men are mad!"

So it seemed. Eventually, Bulgaria, Rumania, Japan, Italy, and even impotent South American countries, were drawn into the war's vortex. And so eventually was the United States.

In the first eight months of the war in Europe sentiment in the United States was mixed. The *Literary Digest*, having polled 367 writers and editors, announced that 105 favored the Allies, 20 favored the Central Powers, and 242 favored neutrality, but as the war progressed partiality for the Allied cause was encouraged by a barrage of expert British propaganda. The Central Powers found themselves powerless to compete, for Britannia, ruler of the waves, cut the cable between Germany and the United States.

American wrath was roused by the devastation wrought by German U-boats (*Unterseeboots*), by the execution of Nurse Edith Cavell,* the destruction of the beautiful cathedral at Rheims and the burning of the famous library at Louvain. British politicians and even poets played up the beastliness of the Germans in Belgium and Thomas Hardy in December 1914 wrote a poem: "An Appeal to America on Behalf of the Belgian Destitute." Atrocity stories, widely credited, fed the flames. It was said that German soldiers had crucified Belgian officers on barn doors, and amputated the hands of Belgian boys and the breasts of Belgian

---

*A British Red Cross nurse in Brussels, who helped some 200 Allied soldiers to escape through the Netherlands.

women. The New York *Herald* ran a story under the headline: TOURIST
SAW SOLDIER WITH BAGFUL OF EARS.

Herbert Hoover, forty years old in 1915, and in charge of Belgian relief
efforts, had no trouble raising money and goods. "Women all over the
world started knitting clothing," Hoover recalled. "They were mostly
sweaters. The Belgian women carefully unraveled them and knitted them
over again into shawls—which was their idea of a knitted garment."

Above all, it was the sinking by the U-20 of the British passenger liner
Lusitania, the most luxurious ship afloat, on 7 May 1915, which rallied
most Americans to the Allied side.

The ship had been designed for the Cunard Line by Leonard Peskett,
following certain guidelines established by the British Admiralty, which
subsidized its cost. Displacing 45,000 tons, it was 785 feet long, the
biggest and at 25.88 knots the fastest ship afloat; capable of carrying about
2,000 passengers and a crew of nearly 900. The New York *Times* declared
that it was "as unsinkable as a ship can be."

Launched at Clydebank on 7 June 1906, it made the first of many voyages from Liverpool to New York on 7 September 1907. In May 1913 it
was drydocked to be fitted with posts that could house artillery. The Great
War began on 4 August 1914 and on 14 September the Admiralty
informed Cunard that the *Lusitania* must carry war material, although
this was a clear violation of the Cruiser Laws—traditional naval laws
regarding warfare at sea established by Henry VIII in 1512. Thereafter,
mounting twelve six-inch guns and classed by the Admiralty as an auxiliary cruiser the *Lusitania* carried war material as well as passengers
unaware of their danger.

The *Lusitania*'s captain, fifty-nine-year-old William Turner, who had
two sons on the Western Front, had been a seaman since the age of thirteen. He had so little fear of submarines that he refused to zigzag, a
maneuver which would use more coal and make his voyages more expensive. He could outrun or ram them, he said.*

On 26 April 1915 the German government informed the American
Secretary of State William Jennings Bryan that on its next voyage the
Lusitania would sail from New York carrying six million rounds of .303
rifle ammunition manufactured by Remington for British Enfield rifles.

---

*When British merchant ships were ordered to attempt to ram submarines the German
rules of engagement changed, for such a practice was against the Cruiser Laws. German
submarine commanders had observed them, but with the ramming order merchant ships
became fair game.

Permission was requested to print a warning to the American public. Cleared by Bryan, it appeared bordered in black in New York newspapers on 1 May 1915, sharing a page with Cunard's announcement of the scheduled departure of the ship for its 202nd crossing. Still, Cunard reported no more than the usual number of last-minute cancellations.

In addition to the ten and one-half tons of rifle cartridges in 4,200 boxes, the *Lusitania* sailed with fifty-one tons of shrapnel shells, and an unknown quantity of guncotton of the kind used in mines manufactured to explode when exposed to water, all a part of the billion dollars worth of war material the United States sold to the Allies. Some extra cargo, including 200 additional tons of ammunition, and sixty-seven soldiers of the 6th Winnipeg Rifles, was taken on from the mechanically distressed SS *Queen Margaret*. Carrying both British troops and contraband ammunition, the *Lusitania* was thus a legitimate target for any German submarine.

This was not the first time the British had recklessly endangered the lives of peaceful civilians by mixing war material and passengers. On 16 January 1915 the Cunard liner *Orduna* sailed from New York with 155 civilian passengers and two fourteen-inch guns consigned to Liverpool lashed down on her forward deck.

Of the 1,257 passengers on the *Lusitania*, 159 were Americans, of whom 124 perished including the multimillionaire Alfred Vanderbilt, thirty-eight, one of the world's most eligible bachelors; theatrical impresario Charles Frohman; and the flamboyant Elbert Hubbard, the "Sage of East Aurora," best known as the author of A *Message to Garcia*, and publisher of the journal, *The Philistine*. Hubbard was on his way to Germany in the hope of interviewing Kaiser Wilhelm.

When Kapitänleutnant Walther Schwieger, the handsome thirty-two-year-old commander of the U-20, sighted the *Lusitania* off the coast of Ireland by the Old Head of Kinsale, he had only two torpedoes left. One was enough. He fired it at 1:35 P.M. Greenwich Mean Time and it struck the liner just forward of the bridge on the starboard side. The largest ship afloat sank in 18 minutes in 300 feet of water. Only 764 survived. Of the 1,959 passengers and crew, 1,195 perished. Of the 129 children on board, 95 were lost. A photograph of Mrs. Paul Crompton of Philadelphia and her six children was later widely published. All were lost.

American newspapers heralded their outrage and indignation. The Des Moines *Register and Leader* declared the sinking "deliberate murder." The New York *Herald* pronounced it "premeditated murder." The New York *Times*, putting history to one side, thundered "in the history of wars there is no single deed comparable in its inhumanity and its horror." Theodore Roosevelt called it "piracy on a grander scale than any old-time pirate ever practiced" and, ever the fire-eater, demanded that the United States declare war at once. Walter Hines Page, the Anglophile American ambassador in London, agreed and cabled: "We must declare war at once or forfeit European respect."

Secretary of State William Jennings Bryan was one of the few who viewed the disaster realistically: "Germany," he said, "has a right to prevent contraband going to the Allies and a ship carrying contraband should not rely upon passengers to prevent her from attack." Few chose to regard the disaster in this light.

President Woodrow Wilson, elected in 1912, and reelected in 1916 on the slogan that "he kept us out of war," opposed any military preparations. However, he pronounced the sinking of the *Lusitania* "unlawful and inhuman," and he demanded reparations. The tone of his notes to the German government shocked Secretary Bryan, who on 9 May, after United States Customs had confirmed that the *Lusitania* carried contraband, wrote to Wilson recommending that passenger ships be prohibited from carrying war matériel: "A ship carrying contraband should not rely upon passengers to protect her from attack—it would be like putting women and children in front of an army." True enough, but the country, including Wilson, placed the blame not on the provocative and reprehensible policy of the British Admiralty but upon German submarine rules of engagement, and on 9 June, after Wilson dispatched still another sharp note, Bryan resigned in protest.

In vain the Germans pointed out that the *Lusitania* had been built with Admiralty funds and was officially classed as an auxiliary cruiser, that it was armed, carrying contraband ammunition, and was sunk in the war zone. In February 1916 German authorities even agreed to pay some reparation to Americans, but Wilson considered the sum they named inadequate. The matter smoldered until it became moot with America's entry into the war.

The sinking of the *Lusitania* brought home the new realities of the war. Almost from the beginning there occurred a breakdown of all traditional attempts to shield noncombatants from war's traumas. They were to suffer not only from blockades, but from the bombing of cities, the destruction of crops and livestock, and the leveling of villages.

The fate of the great ship gave new momentum to the clamor of those who demanded immediate entry into the war. But Wilson had no intention of going to war; on 10 May, three days after the sinking, in a talk in

Philadelphia to 4,000 newly made citizens he said, "There is such a thing as a man being too proud to fight." This was too much for the fire-eaters. Theodore Roosevelt raged against "Flubdubs and Molycoddles!," ignoring the incontrovertible fact that the country was unprepared to fight. In 1914 the Army War College had begun work on what was to be entitled "A Statement of a Proper Military Policy for the United States." Completed, it demonstrated that some thinking officers had a clear-eyed view of modern warfare: "The safeguard of isolation no longer exists. The oceans, once barriers, are now easy avenues of approach by reason of the number, speed and carrying capacity of ocean-going vessels. The increasing radii of action of the submarine, the aeroplane, and wireless telegraphy, all supplement ocean transport in placing both our Atlantic and Pacific coasts within the sphere of hostile activities of overseas nations.

"The great mass of the public does not yet realize the effect of these changed conditions upon our scheme of defense."

War College analysts estimated that the country needed a standing army of at least 500,000 backed by a fully equipped reserve of equal strength, that it would take from eighteen to twenty-four months just to arm and equip such a force, and that, above all, trained manpower would be essential.

One small step already had been taken. In 1913 General Leonard Wood, a medical doctor turned professional soldier, brave, egotistical, flamboyant, ambitious, and short-tempered—Walter Lippmann said he had an "apoplectic soul"—was the senior officer in the army and commander of the Department of the East. Convinced that war was in the offing, he acted on a suggestion of Grenville Clark, a New York lawyer, and established a military training camp at Plattsburg, New York. There, largely at their own expense, Clark and other professionals and businessmen, many of whom were socially prominent, were trained to be reserve officers in a five-week course given by regular army personnel. General Wood adopted preparedness as a crusade, calling Plattsburg "a voice to the slumbering people of the country," and, thanks to financial aid provided by financier Bernard Baruch and his wealthy friends, the movement expanded to other eastern cities. More camps were established and some 16,000 young business and professional men received some training.

Wood was well aware that the main value of the camps was political. "We do not expect," he said, "to accomplish much in the way of detailed military instruction, . . . but we do believe a great deal can be done in the implementing of a sound military policy."

Wood himself, an indefatigable lecturer, cultivator of the press, and attender of dinner parties of the nation's movers and shakers, "talked preparedness day and night to whomever would listen." An early supporter of the Plattsburg Movement, as it came to be called, was Wood's good friend, the aging lion, Theodore Roosevelt, who managed to undermine Wood's relationship with the Wilson administration and alienate a considerable number of conservatives by delivering at Plattsburg a fiery antipacifist, anti-Wilson speech. To reporters there he pointed out a dog that had rolled over on its back to have its stomach scratched. "A very nice dog," said Roosevelt, "His present attitude is strictly one of neutrality."

In 1916 Wilson's then secretary of war, Lindley M. Garrison, and his assistant, Henry Breckinridge, drew up a national defense plan supported by Wilson, calling for the establishment over a three-year period of a large volunteer federal reserve, a so-called Continental Army. When this created a stir in Congress, Wilson withdrew his support and Garrison and Breckinridge resigned. However, in June Congress passed the National Defense Act, authorizing the president to commandeer factories and to establish a government nitrate plant, and authorizing the army to double its strength by adding 11,450 officers and 223,580 enlisted men in annual increments over five years. The militia, identified as the National Guard, was authorized to expand to 17,000 officers and 440,000 men; reserve officer recruitment was restricted to existing sources, giving a near-death blow to the Plattsburg Movement and pleasing the politicized National Guard, whose officers saw the movement as a back door to army commissions for a privileged northeastern elite and a threat to their interests.

On 30 July 1916 the United States came a bit closer to the war when on Black Tom Island, a man-made promontory jutting into New York Harbor from New Jersey, an ammunition dump holding over two million pounds of explosives blew up, raining shards upon Ellis Island, damaging the Statue of Liberty, and blowing out windows in Brooklyn. There were, surprisingly, only seven fatalities. Although the explosion was widely believed to be the work of German agents, it was not until after World War II that incontrovertible evidence was found linking it to the German government.

In August 1916 Congress created a Council of National Defense to integrate economic and military power. The Council included Dr. Hollis Godfrey, president of the Drexel Institute in Philadelphia, and eminent zoologist Dr. Harry Edward Crampton of Columbia University, as well as six cabinet ministers and an advisory commission of labor leaders and professors. It accomplished little.

Such feeble measures demonstrated a clear lack of understanding of the requirements for waging modern war. Historian B. H. Liddell Hart was later to describe the United States as "a giant armed with a penknife." An exception was the Industrial Preparedness Committee formed by Howard E. Coffin, a wealthy engineer and a vice president of the Hudson Motor Car Company, who wrote: "Twentieth century warfare demands that the blood of the soldier must be mingled three to five parts with the sweat of the man in the factories, mills, mines and fields of the nation in arms." His committee surveyed the country's industries and by September 1916 some 200,000 plants had reported what they might be capable of doing in case of war.

While the government waffled, numerous Americans took matters in their own hands and joined organizations providing aid to Allied troops and to refugees. Writers such as Edith Wharton and Henry James threw themselves into war work, aiding refugees and sick and wounded soldiers. Many Americans, like Wharton, believed that a German victory would be "the crash of civilization." Some men volunteered as ambulance drivers, the most glamorous of these services, a wealthy few even offering their own automobiles, for when the Great War began the French army had only forty motorized ambulances and those capable of driving motorized vehicles and maintaining them were thin on the ground.

Many of the drivers were recruited from eastern prep schools and Ivy League universities. Among them were future luminaries such as Walt Disney, John Dos Passos, E. E. Cummings, Archibald Macleish, Louis Bromfield, Charles B. Nordhoff, and Malcolm Cowley, although the driving career of many was brief. Ernest Hemingway's active service in Italy lasted only from 4 June until 8 July 1918.

Most Americans who served in ambulance corps in France were members of one of the three major volunteer organizations. The first, the Harjes Formation, was founded by thirty-nine-year-old H. Herman Harjes, a senior partner of the Morgan-Harjes Bank in Paris, who provided it with five Packards. A second, the Anglo-American Volunteer Motor-Ambulance Corps initially sponsored by the British Red Cross and the St. John Ambulance association, was founded by forty-two-year-old Richard Norton, the son of Harvard's distinguished professor of art history, Charles Eliot Norton. In 1916 the Norton and Harjes organizations amalgamated and became known as the Norton-Harjes Sections. By the time the United States declared war in April 1917 the Norton-Harjes group had increased in size from a handful of automobiles and drivers to more than 100 vehicles and some 200 personnel.

Still another unit was operated by forty-one-year-old Abram Piatt Andrew, a bachelor and Princeton graduate (1893) from Gloucester, Massachusetts, who had served as an economics professor at Harvard, as director of the United States Mint, and as assistant secretary of the Treasury. At first an ambulance driver for the American Ambulance (military hospital) at Neuilly, he soon became its director and expanded the operation enormously.

Numerous smaller, volunteer organizations provided goods and services for sick and wounded soldiers. For a time Gertrude Stein and her companion, Alice B. Toklas, drove for the American Fund for French Wounded. Their Model T Ford, christened "Aunt Pauline," was provided by Miss Stein who had written to her cousin, Fred Stein, in America asking him to send her one. While waiting for it she prudently prepared herself by taking driving lessons from a Paris taxi driver. When the car finally arrived early in 1917, it was taken to a workshop where a truck body was fitted to it. All work completed, the two ladies confidently set off; however, within a few blocks, they found themselves wedged between two Paris street cars bearing down in opposite directions. Undeterred, the next day they began what was known as jitney work, delivering donated supplies to military hospitals.

Neither Stein nor Toklas knew much about repairing or maintaining their vehicle. Miss Stein once attempted to repair a broken fan belt with a hairpin. Stopped at the side of the road one day, frightened because Aunt Pauline was making a strange noise, they were befriended by two American soldiers. Miss Toklas later told how "they got down on their knees and before you knew it they had taken the engine down, looked it over, brushed all the parts and put them back again. This did not take them any time at all. Gertrude and I were astonished." Aunt Pauline saw hard service and when a friend unkindly remarked that it "resembled a second-class hearse," Miss Stein simply bought another and they went on with their work.

The Model T, manufactured with few changes since 1908, became the ambulance of choice in France. In 1916 one could be purchased for $360 FOB (Freight on Board) Detroit. Shipped to France, it was modified to carry three stretchers or four walking wounded, although they often carried more. Originally the body was covered with a canvas, but this proved difficult to clean and disinfect so early in 1916 the canvas was replaced by wood. A number of attached boxes held spare parts and tools and room was found for cans of gas and water as well as a can of oil and one of kerosene. At least twenty areas required regular greasing or oiling and drivers were expected to be skilled in car maintenance and repair.

Learning to drive the Fords with their gearless transmissions was not easy, involving as it did maneuvering three foot pedals and a hand lever with three positions. Orchestrating them, wrote one driver, "was an acquired art, rather like playing the organ. The whole body was engaged." E. B. White once described the Ford planetary transmission as "half metaphysics and half sheer fiction."

Drivers came face to face with war's realities. Jack Edwards wrote back to Bowdoin College, his alma mater: "Americans don't know what war means, filth, mud, sickness, ruins and rain."

In all about 15,000 young Americans, lured by a spirit of adventure, inspired by humanitarian motives, or convinced of the righteousness of the Allied cause, went to war before the United States was involved, many in combat roles. On 5 September 1914 Winston Churchill, then First Lord of the Admiralty, eager to enlist Americans into the war, wrote to War Minister Lord Kitchener and to Prime Minister Edward Grey, stating his belief that a division could be raised in Canada composed of American volunteers: "Nothing will bring along American sympathy with us so much as American blood shed in the field," he added.

As Churchill had predicted, so many young men crossed to Canada to enlist that the 97th Battalion of the Canadian Expeditionary Force was officially named the "American Legion." A number of its officers were West Pointers.

Poet Alan Seeger and eighty-nine other Americans joined the French Foreign Legion. From the Aisne sector of the Western Front he wrote his mother: "Everybody should take part in this struggle which is to have so decisive an effect, not only on the nations engaged but on all humanity. There should be no neutrals . . . death is nothing terrible after all. It may mean something even more than life." Seeger, at the age of twenty-nine, had his "rendezvous with death" on 4 July 1916 near Belloy-en-Santerre on the fourth day of the French offensive on the Somme.

Casper Henry Burton, Jr., of Cincinnati, who had been a medical student at Harvard, served with the British. In a letter to his mother he wrote: "Death doesn't seem as dreadful to me as failure to do whatever job you are given. For each little failure prolongs the war, each little failure strengthens Prussian power." He did not survive the war.

2

☆

THE UNITED STATES
ENTERS THE WAR

FIVE WEEKS BEFORE urging Congress to declare war upon Germany Wilson said of the war in Europe: "It is a war with which we have nothing to do," he said, "whose causes cannot touch us." But they did. He perhaps overlooked the war at sea, which could and did involve Americans.

When on 24 March 1916 a German submarine attacked an unarmed British passenger steamer, the *Sussex*, it was probably a case of mistaken identity on the part of the U-boat commander. Although the ship did not sink, about eighty people were killed and many more injured, some of them Americans. There had been no warning.

When the American steamer *Aztec* was torpedoed on the night of 1 April 1916 John I. Eopolucci of Washington, D.C., one of the ship's gun crew, became the first American in the armed forces to lose his life in the war. (Before the end of the war 384 merchant vessels made 1,832 crossings with naval gunners on board to man the guns. Twenty-nine were torpedoed and two were sunk by shell fire.)

On 18 April Wilson sent a message to the German government, which he made public, demanding that submarines refrain from attacking all "passenger and freight-carrying vessels" or the United States would "sever diplomatic relations." German Chancellor Bethmann-Hollweg, anxious to keep the United States out of the war, fought a factional battle with the German admirals and promised that merchant ships subject to search for contraband within and without the war zone would "not be sunk without warning and without saving human lives unless such ships attempt to escape or offer resistance." This became known as the *Sussex* pledge.

On 9 January 1917 the Kaiser, over the objections of his chancellor, was persuaded by Field Marshal Paul von Beneckendorff und Hindenburg and General Erich Ludendorff, now probably the two most powerful men in Germany, to renounce the *Sussex* pledge and to engage in unrestricted submarine warfare, which his admirals assured him would force Britain to sue for peace within five months. Count Bernstorff, the German ambassador, learned of the policy change on 19 January. As instructed, however, he delayed informing Secretary of State Robert Lansing that the new German policy would come into effect on 1 February until 4:10 in the afternoon of 31 January. "He did not smile with his customary assurance," Secretary Lansing recalled.

Lansing immediately telephoned the president, but Wilson was out so he despatched the German note to the White House. There it was mixed with less important papers and was not seen by Wilson until 8:00 that evening—only four hours before the new policy came into effect.

On 22 January, in a speech to the Senate, Wilson called for "a peace without victory." Seemingly, the humanitarian dreamer had completely lost touch with reality. While Germany built submarines, Wilson dreamed of world peace without victory and of a union of nations working together. Some of his advisors began to doubt the ability of their leader to deal with this crisis. Secretary of the Interior Franklin Lane thought that his patriotism was "covered over with a film of philosophic humanitarianism that certainly doesn't make for punch at a time like this."

On 3 February the United States severed relations with Germany. Several Latin American nations joined the protest, including Peru, Bolivia, and Brazil. On 14 March China also protested. All such protests by impotent states were ignored. Although German authorities recognized that unrestricted submarine warfare might bring the United States into the war on the Allied side, it was believed that the war would be over before the Americans would be able to take effective action. The policy nearly succeeded.

Germany had already demonstrated that its submarines could reach America's shores and that the long Atlantic coastline was open to attack. On Sunday, 9 July 1916, the German "mercantile submarine" *Deutschland*, 213 feet long with a submerged displacement of 2,200 tons, had broken the surface in Chesapeake Bay, having eluded the British cruisers just outside. In a few hours it had docked in Baltimore. With a surface speed of up to 14 knots and an underwater speed of 7.5 knots it was an impressive vessel.

In November it returned, appearing this time at New London,

Connecticut, paying a visit that set off a wrangle and ended in a disaster. The German captain, insisting on employing only black stevedores, enraged the white stevedores and in a bar fight a German crewman stabbed a bartender. When, after a series of bureaucratic delays, the *Deutschland* finally got underway it rammed a tug in Long Island Sound, killing all five of the tug's crew. (On its return on 10 December 1918 it was armed and had become the U-155, one of the submarines sent to sink shipping in American waters.)

Even more ominous was the visit of the U-53, almost as large as the *Deutschland* and a fully armed German man-of-war. It appeared at Newport, Rhode Island, on 7 October 1916 and asked to be assigned a berth. Its commander, Kapitänleutnant Hans Rose, in full uniform, called on the commandant of the naval station to pay his respects and courteously invited officers to visit his ship.

The U-53 was careful to observe neutrality regulations, but when it left port it sank two British steamships just outside the three-mile limit, within sight of the Nantucket lightship. Soon afterward it sank another British ship, a Dutch ship, and a Norwegian ship, all close to American shores. Crews and passengers were rescued by American destroyers. Cries of indignation were raised throughout the land, but such handwringing had no effect. German submarines were sinking one in four ships sailing to Britain.

On 26 February 1917 Wilson asked Congress for extraordinary powers to maintain an "armed neutrality," and to permit armed merchant ships. The House approved but it was successfully filibustered in the Senate by what Wilson called "a little group of willful men." But when a German submarine sank the *Algonquin*, an American merchant ship, on 12 March 1917, Wilson found excuses to bypass Congressional approval and announced that vessels passing through the war zone would henceforth be armed. The navy was instructed to mount guns on merchant ships and supply gun crews for them.

On 18 March, three more American merchant ships were sunk, all without warning. One of these was the *Lincoln*, a homeward-bound oil tanker sunk in the English Channel. It had been flying two American flags and on its side in large letters was painted "U.S.A." It seemed a deliberate insult.

On 1 March President Wilson revealed the "Zimmermann note" to the press. On 19 January 1917 Alfred Zimmermann, German foreign secretary, sent a coded message to von Eckhardt, the German minister to

Mexico, proposing a defensive alliance with Mexico in case of war between the United States and Germany. It contained the proviso that "Mexico is to reconquer the lost territory in New Mexico, Texas and Arizona," and further suggested that Mexico urge Japan to join the Central Powers, which then consisted of Germany, Austria-Hungary, Bulgaria, and Turkey.

British naval intelligence intercepted and decoded the message and on 24 February had given a copy to Ambassador Walter Hines Page, who turned it over to the State Department. United States intelligence later verified its authenticity. Released to the public, it created a storm of outrage.

Many now felt that war with Germany was inevitable. On 31 March when Secretary of the Interior Lane wrote, "We can stand Germany's arrogance no longer," he reflected a growing sentiment. Although on this day socialists in St. Paul, Minnesota, held a mass meeting to "oppose the present threatened war," elsewhere the mood was generally, although not universally, growing increasingly bellicose. Boston Mayor James M. Curley proclaimed to a mob of war enthusiasts: "We love liberty more than peace!" Senator Hiram Johnson of California addressed a large gathering of militants in Independence Square, Philadelphia, and in New York City Plattsburg reservists formed a "broomstick brigade" and marched on Broadway chanting: "A rifle for every American . . . universal compulsory military training!"

The next day, Palm Sunday, "women suffragetists" picketed the White House, and pacifists and antipacifists descended upon Washington. Cavalry from Fort Myer, across the Potomac from Washington in Virginia, was sent to help keep order in an increasingly agitated city.

That evening the President sat with his friend Frank Cobb of the New York World, and Cobb later reported that he had "never seen him so worn down." If the country went to war, he told Cobb, Americans would forget tolerance: "To fight you must be brutal and ruthless. The spirit of ruthless brutality will enter into the very fiber of our national life, infecting Congress, the courts, the policeman on the beat, the man in the street. Conformity will be the only virtue. And every man who refuses to conform must pay the penalty." President Wilson was never more prescient.

On Monday, 2 April, Congressman Frank Stanley, the only Civil War veteran in the House of Representatives, declared he was willing "to go again if needed." Senator Henry Cabot Lodge, sixty-seven, knocked down a man who called him a coward. At Jackson Place, across from the White

House, a mob broke into the offices of the Emergency Peace Federation, wrecking furniture, strewing papers, and smearing the premises with yellow paint.

That evening, warm and rainy, Wilson rode through mostly cheering throngs from the White House to the Capitol surrounded by cavalrymen with drawn sabers. Armed soldiers and marines were posted on rooftops and hidden in windows behind curtains, but the president arrived without incident and at 8:40 entered the floodlit Capitol. Inside were waiting senators and representatives, several ambassadors, and, for the first time on such an occasion, the members of the Supreme Court. Wilson adjusted his steel-rimmed spectacles and took from his pocket the speech he had himself typed on his portable typewriter while Mrs. Wilson supplied him with crackers and milk. There were no microphones and he delivered a thirty-two-minute war message in his distinct professorial manner until, raising his voice, he declared, "There is one choice we cannot make; we are incapable of making. We will not chose the path of submission!" The assembly rose to its feet, clapping and cheering. Chief Justice Edward White, seventy-two, a Confederate veteran, stood cheering, tears streaming down his face. Wilson called upon the nation to "accept the status of belligerent which has . . . been thrust upon it; and . . . take immediate steps not only to put the country in a more thorough state of defense but also to exert all its power and employ all its resources to bring the Government of the German Empire to terms and end the war." The United States must fight, he said, "for the ultimate peace of the world and the liberation of its people. . . . The world must be made safe for democracy." It was the greatest speech of his life.

At about 10:00, when the president returned to the White House, he and his wife had dinner with friends, after which Wilson wandered into the empty cabinet room. His secretary, Joseph Tumulty, found him there: "Think what it was they were applauding," he said to Tumulty. "My message today was a message of death for our young men. How strange it seems to applaud that." He put his head down on the table in the Cabinet Room, and sobbed.

There appears to have been no examination or comprehension by Wilson or any other American politician of the difference between the political decision to declare war and the nation's ability to fight one. Three days after Wilson's call to arms the Senate voted for war by a vote of 82 to 6. On 6 April the House followed by a 373 to 50 vote—one of the no votes coming from Miss Jeannette Rankin of Montana, the first and

then the only woman in Congress—and the United States declared war
on Germany. It did not at this time declare war on the other Central
Powers. (War was not declared on the Austro-Hungarian Empire until 7
December 1917—eight months later.)

At 1:18 P.M. President Wilson signed the declaration of war. A buzzer
sounded in Secretary Daniel's office and immediately Lieutenant Byron
McCandless, Daniel's personal aide ran out on the White House lawn and
semaphored to a watching officer in the Navy Department across the street.
The signal was quickly passed on to every ship and station: W . . . A . . . R.

The news was relayed in newspaper extras and throughout the land
everyone was soon aware that the country was at war. In Great Neck,
Long Island, the news inspired actor, playwright, and songwriter George
M. Cohan to go to his piano and compose "Over There," a cocksure song
with a swinging tune:

> Over there, over there,
> Send the word, send the word, over there
> That the Yanks are coming, the Yanks are coming,
> The drums rum-tumming everywhere.
> So prepare, say a pray'r
> Send the word, send the word to beware,
> We'll be over, we're coming over,
> And we won't be back till it's over over there.

Cohan carried his song to Nora Bayes, a popular vaudeville performer,
who that night sang it with many encores to a wildly cheering audience.
Soon available on Victrola records and in sheet music, it was to be the
most popular song of the war.

From a pacifist, tolerant nation, the United States became, as Wilson
had foreseen, a brutal one. In a saloon in Thermopolis, Wyoming, a mining town on the Big Horn River, a customer who brashly proposed a toast
to the Kaiser was promptly strung up, revived with cold water, forced to
kiss the American flag, and run out of town.

A few days after the declaration of war Senator Thomas S. Martin,
chairman of the powerful Senate Appropriations Committee, announced
that "Congress will not permit American soldiers to be sent to Europe."
Indeed, it had not occurred to President Wilson until perhaps the last
days of March that troops would be sent to France. It was his notion that
the United States would cooperate with the French on land and the

British at sea. He envisioned providing supplies to the Allies and using the navy to help Britain; he had not imagined sending a huge army to Europe. But it was American bodies in trenches on the Western Front which the Allies most needed.

On 22 April a British delegation headed by Foreign Secretary Arthur J. Balfour arrived in Washington and three days later a similar delegation, including Marshal Joseph Joffre, the "Hero of the Marne," arrived from France. Each described the perilous situation in which the Allies found themselves and explained their needs. Above all, Joffre insisted, "We want men, men, men." On 2 May he called on President Wilson and urged that at least one American division be dispatched for France at once, but this was impossible. The United States did not have a division. Not a single formed and equipped American regular combat division existed.

This was the nadir of the war for the Allies. Already the six great European nations—France, Britain, Russia, Italy, Germany, and Austria-Hungary—had among them suffered perhaps four million casualties (estimates run from a high of 4,174,000 to a low of not less than 3,742,000), of whom about a quarter were dead. In spite of these terrible losses there had been no apparent gain by either side. On 1 November 1916 Prime Minister Lloyd George, in a moment of despair, remarked ". . . better make peace than repeat the experience of 1916." It had indeed been a horrific year. Captain Cyril Falls named it "the year of killing." Furthermore, to the war of attrition then in progress there appeared to be no end in sight.

There had been general elation in France and Britain when the United States declared war; here was a fresh and powerful ally. But elation soon turned to dismay when it was learned how utterly unprepared the country was.

Although European officers recognized the potential value of America's manpower, raw materials, and technology, they uniformly agreed that its army was unprepared for war as it was being fought in Europe, and that it lacked trained enlisted men, junior officers, experienced commanders, and trained staff. Among the armies of the world, that of the United States ranked sixteenth, just behind Portugal. The punitive expedition of regulars and ill-trained and ill-equipped National Guardsmen led by Brigadier General John Pershing against Francisco ("Pancho") Villa in 1916 had learned little that could be of value to them on the Western Front and their stumbling about south of the border illustrated all too starkly how unprepared the country was to fight a modern war. It had not even been able to suppress a Mexican bandit.

But the Americans were willing to start almost from scratch. In fact, there was little else they could do. In spite of the National Defense Act, which had authorized an increase in strength, the army had been unable to recruit up to the authorized strength. On 1 April 1917 the regular army consisted of only 5,791 officers and 121,797 enlisted men. There were 66,594 National Guardsmen in federal service (most serving on the Mexican border) and 101,174 National Guardsmen still under state control, but none of these troops was organized or equipped for service in Europe. Despite a desperate shortage of machine guns, the War Department was still debating which make and model to select. The army remained, as six years earlier Secretary of War Henry L. Stimson had characterized it, "a profoundly peaceful army."

It had always been assumed that the United States was a peace loving nation, and that any war it fought would be a defensive one. The basis of this assumption is unclear. Since independence, every war the country had fought had been aggressive. American wars with Spain and Mexico had been offensive operations, as had been the suppression of the Philippine patriots, American Indians, and the Chinese boxers. So, too, were American interventions into Central and South American countries. Even in the War of 1812 Americans attempted to invade and annex Canada.

The idea that the United States did not need a standing army had been generally accepted; militia and state forces, it was believed, could handle any emergency. In 1914 Secretary of State William Jennings Bryan boasted that, "The President knows that if this country needed a million men, and needed them in a day, the call would go out at sunrise and the sun would go down on a million men in arms." Though many believed it, this was utter nonsense. Americans no longer shot their dinners and no longer could a man take down the flintlock from above his hearth and go to war. Weapons had grown complex and more deadly. Advancing technology made it imperative that soldiers be trained for the new types of warfare thrust upon them.

On 14 June in an official report, "Forecast of the Arrival of American Land Forces in France," British Major General Tom Bridges, the military representative of the British mission to the United States, informed the War Cabinet that, "It seems probable that America can have an army of 120,000–150,000 men in France by 1st January 1918, and 500,000 men by the end of 1918." The Cabinet, optimistically expecting one million men in short order, was shocked. One member described Bridges' message as "the most depressing statement that the Cabinet had received for a long time."

Although the country was remarkably quick to mobilize, and nearly four million men were eventually raised for the forces, it lacked the arms, equipment, and the organization to train them and the ships to transport them to the European battlefields. Ten months after declaring war the United States had only one division in the line of battle in France. Two months later it had only one more.

The man selected to command this gathering host was John Joseph Pershing. This came as a surprise to most people who had assumed that the command would be given to the senior general in the army, General Leonard Wood. Wood, who had preached the need to be prepared for war, now paid the penalty many pay for being right. It did not help that, overzealous in his cause, he had hitched his political star to Theodore Roosevelt and had publicly denounced some of Wilson's policies, making himself anathema to the Wilson administration. In January 1917 President Wilson, speaking to the Secretary of War, said: "Personally, I have no confidence either in General Wood's discretion or in his loyalty to his superiors." Secretary Baker considered him "the most insubordinate general in the entire army."

Pershing, born in 1860 at Laclede, Missouri, grew up on a farm. As a teenager he taught in a black school and saved enough money to enter Kirksville Normal School. In May 1882 he passed an examination and entered West Point, not because he wanted to be a soldier but because he wanted a good, free formal education. He was twenty-two years old then and just above the age limit, but he shaved a few months off his age to qualify. Although academically he ranked thirtieth in a class of seventy-six, he was named first captain and voted class president. One of his West Point professors, describing his command style said it was "of a nature peculiarly impersonal, dispassionate, hard and firm. . . . His manner carried . . . the conviction of unquestionable right to obedience. There was no shadow of doubt about it."

In June 1886, after graduating, he was commissioned in the 6th Cavalry, and he fought Indians in the West until in 1891 he was appointed commandant of cadets at the University of Nebraska. While there he earned a law degree and formed an outstanding drill team, the Varsity Rifles, which, after he left, became the Pershing Rifles, now the nationwide honorary military society. In 1896 he was appointed aide to General Nelson A. Miles and in June 1897 he became a tactical instructor at West Point.

During the Spanish-American War he served as quartermaster of the

10th Cavalry and fought at El Caney and San Juan Hill, leading his troopers in the charge beside Roosevelt's Rough Riders. His colonel said of him: "I have been in many fights through the Civil War, but Captain Pershing is the coolest man under fire I ever saw in my life." In 1899 he was sent to the Philippines, where he served in northern Mindanao and then pacified the Moros around Lake Lanao (Lake Sultan). It was trying work. General Benjamin Foulois once said, "Anybody who lived through the fighting in the Philippines could live through anything."

In 1903 Pershing returned to the United States and in 1905 he married Helen Frances Warren, daughter of Senator Francis E. Warren of Wyoming. Six weeks later he was appointed military attaché in Japan. There he was an observer of the Russo-Japanese War. On 20 September 1906 the impetuous President Theodore Roosevelt gave him a most extraordinary promotion from captain to brigadier general, youngest in the army, over the heads of 862 more senior officers. That his father-in-law was chairman of the Senate Military Affairs Committee helped. Returning to the Philippines, he commanded a brigade and directed several campaigns against Moro rebels.

In 1915, newly appointed commanding general at Fort Bliss, Texas, he learned that his wife and three daughters had perished in a fire on 27 August at the Presidio in San Francisco, California. A six-year-old son, Warren, survived. Although later Pershing had love affairs, including one with the woman who was to become Douglas MacArthur's first wife, he allowed none of them to distract him from his profession, to which he devoted all his energy.

Following Pancho Villa's raid on Columbus, New Mexico, on 9 March 1916, he was sent to the Mexican border with orders to capture Villa. For nearly ten months he pursued Villa with 4,800 men, and, although he failed to capture him, he did fragment his band.

He was ordered home on 27 January 1917 and on 10 May reported in Washington to Secretary of War Newton D. Baker, who had been mayor of Cleveland and had been associated with several pacifist organizations. Baker had seemed a strange choice to be Secretary of War. He had never evinced an interest in military affairs and confessed that as a boy he "had never played even with tin soldiers." But he had a keen mind and proved himself one of Wilson's best appointees.

Baker informed Pershing that he had been selected to command a division that was to be organized and sent to France. Two days later, he was appointed to command of the entire American Expeditionary Force

(AEF). In his memoirs Pershing wrote, "I had scarcely given a thought to the possibility of my being chosen commander-in-chief." Perhaps his memory failed him, for in February, while still in Texas, he had talked to journalists about the possibility of an expeditionary force being sent to France and had confessed his desire to command it.

Pershing was the junior major general, having been promoted to that rank, then the highest in the army, only a month before the war. He was also, at the age of fifty-seven, the second youngest, General Leonard Wood being about six months younger. Before the end of his first year in France he was promoted a full four-star general in the National Army (the equivalent of the World War II Army of the United States [AUS]). Only Grant, Sherman, and Sheridan had ever before held this rank.

For his AEF chief of staff Pershing selected fifty-one-year-old James Guthrie Harbord, who had had a remarkable military career. After graduation from Kansas State Agricultural College and after trying unsuccessfully to obtain an appointment for West Point, he enlisted as a private in 1889. In July 1891 he was commissioned a second lieutenant in the cavalry. When the United States declared war he was a major attending the Army War College. He had served in the Spanish American War and spent twelve years in the Philippines. Pershing said of him: "Entirely unselfish, he labored incessantly for what he believed to be the best interest of our armies. His ability, his resourcefulness, his faculty for organization, and above all his loyalty, were outstanding qualities, and these together with his compelling personality made him invaluable to the nation in this important position."

Although Pershing was to refuse to have around him officers who might be a challenge to his authority, one of his most outstanding qualities was his ability to select good subordinates for his staff and, generally speaking, good subordinate commanders. In France he would need all of the best help he could get.

3

☆

THE TOOLS AND ENGINES

OF DESTRUCTION

FIVE MAJOR DEVELOPMENTS in weaponry differentiated the land battles fought by Wellington and Napoleon from those fought one hundred years later by Foch, Haig, Cadorna, and Pershing in the Great War: the breech loading rifle, the machine gun, quick-firing artillery, chemical weapons, and smokeless powder, which had first shown its effectiveness in the Second Anglo-Boer War. One might be tempted to include aircraft and tanks, but these innovations had little effect upon the Western Front and the number of casualties they accounted for was relatively minuscule.

At sea the changes had been greater in the days since Nelson fought at Trafalgar. There now were steam-driven steel ships with much heavier and more accurate guns, submarines with powered torpedoes, and potent, deadly mines.

As the war progressed—if that is the right verb—the means by which men could destroy each other became ever more hideous. Poison gas was first used by the Germans against the Russians in January 1915. On 22 April 1915 it was introduced on the Western Front near Ypres when German troops opened 6,000 cylinders of chlorine gas along an eight-kilometer front, which drifted on the wind, killing or suffocating French and Algerian troops. Thus began a five-week-long struggle called the Second Battle of Ypres. The new weapon had a devastating psychological effect, for until respirators were developed there was no defense. On 24 April Canadian troops were gassed. In early May there were three gas attacks on British troops; in one the wind changed direction and both sides suffered casualties.

It was not long before the Allies, too, resorted to using gas and soon the risky business of dispensing it by container was replaced by gas artillery shells. By 1918 nearly one shell in four was a chemical shell. Ever more frightful gasses were invented. Chlorine was replaced by the more lethal phosgene; then mustard gas was introduced. This burned out the lungs if breathed and raised huge, painful blisters on exposed skin; many were blinded by it.

The flamethrower (*Flammenwerfer*), introduced by the French in the Argonne Forest in the fall of 1914 and perfected by the Germans, offered instant cremation. Britain, France, and Germany used the weapon; the Americans mostly relied upon others, mainly the French, for flamethrower support.

It was the machine gun that dominated no-man's-land. The first practical model was a crank-operated weapon invented by Richard Jourdon Gatling, an American who was issued a patent on 4 November 1862. Although the French developed an improved model, all were operated by rotating barrels with a crank and all were heavy and cumbersome. It was not until 1869 that Hiram Maxim, an American, developed the first truly automatic gun in which the power of the recoil was used to load, fire, and extract the cartridge case.

There were objections to their use, not on humanitarian grounds, but because their rapid rate of fire made them so expensive to operate. General Haig, who rose to command the British Expeditionary Force, declared them to be a much overrated weapon; "two per battalion is more than sufficient." Vickers, the sole British supplier in the decade before the war, manufactured them at the leisurely rate of eleven *per year*. Production rate of the gun increased rapidly, but on 15 February 1915, when the Great War was well underway, 890 British machine guns sat idle in French warehouses because not enough men had been trained to use them. France began the war with 2,500 machine guns; by the Armistice it had built and deployed 314,000.

The Germans trained the best machine gun crews and proved throughout the war the most skillful in deploying them. Their superiority was dramatically demonstrated on the Western Front at Loos on 26 September 1915 when twelve British infantry battalions, about 10,000 men, left their trenches—went "over the top," as the expression went—and attacked well-entrenched and wired German positions which had been unaffected by a twenty-minute artillery barrage. When three and one-half hours later the remnants of the force stumbled back, they left on

the ground or draped on the uncut wire 385 officers and 7,861 other
ranks—almost all shot down by well-directed machine gun fire. The
Germans did not lose a single soldier.

The invention of a breach-loading cannon with an effective recoil
mechanism revolutionized the use of artillery and made it a highly efficient, quick-firing engine of destruction. In no major war had the artillery
ever before been so dominant. The archetype of field guns was the
famous "French 75," kept secret by the French for as long as possible. A
75 mm gun with a Nordenfeldt eccentric screw-type breach block and a
superior recoil mechanism was so superior that all other guns came to be
modeled on it. The new recoil mechanism enabled it to sustain a rapid
rate of fire, for it was no longer necessary to re-lay it after each shot. In
fact, an experienced gunner could "ride the gun": sitting on a small
metal stool attached to the carriage and facing the tube, he could hook
the tip of his right foot under the carriage's axle and, leaning back, throw
open the breech and eject the empty shell case before the barrel returned
to battery, ready to fire again. The breech, left open, was instantly ready
to receive a fresh round.

The "75" was produced in such quantities that there were sufficient to
supply the entire American Expeditionary Force. However, Allied
artillery was deficient in howitzers and large caliber weapons such as
those which Krupp and Skoda supplied to the German army. Each
German army corps was provided with a dozen 150 mm heavy howitzers;
in 1914 the French had only 300 and the British even fewer.

Artillery proved to be the greatest killer of men. The number of artillery
pieces of all calibers increased enormously until by 11 November 1918
(the day the Armistice was signed) the Allies had 21,668 guns on the
Western Front and the Germans 16,181, a somewhat misleading figure as
in the three months preceding the Armistice the Allies had captured 6,615
guns; it is probably fair to say that each side had approximately the same
number on the Western Front in the course of the war.

Artillery was used to cut wire, destroy enemy strong points, wipe out
machine gun nests, and trench mortar emplacements. It could "soften
up" the enemy before an attack, provide a smoke screen, and cripple
attacking forces. Basically, there were three types of shells: chemical
shells for delivering gas or smoke, fragmentation or high explosive shells,
and shrapnel.

High explosive (HE) shells broke into jagged hunks of steel that flew
off in all directions. Their fuses could be set to explode upon impact—as

would be needed to cut the enemy's wire—or for delayed action if the aim was to penetrate enemy dugouts.

Because of the misuse of the word "shrapnel" by several generations of ignorant journalists, many readers of World War I literature assume that the word "shrapnel" meant shell fragments. But this was not the case. Shrapnel, invented by Major Henry Shrapnel (1761–1842) of the British Royal Artillery, was first used in 1804. It was, of course, much improved when used 110 years later on the Western Front. An antipersonnel shell, it consisted of a cylinder holding dozens of small lead balls, each the size of a small marble and was fused to explode in mid-air on the downward arc of its trajectory. Its effect was that of a large shotgun.

Shrapnel wounds were unlike any other. Dr. William W. van Dolsen, a surgeon in the Rainbow Division, described them in a letter to his mother: "Shrapnel wounds are queer things. When you see the men undressed you would think they had been hit by a charge from a shotgun. Just small holes here and there but you see they have great power of penetration and go way down deep and are apt to carry lots of clothing and gas forming bacillus. You have to cut down deep and open them wide taking out all of the damaged tissue."

Few anticipated the enormous amount of ammunition of all types that the quick-firing guns would expend. Certainly the British did not, and in 1915 the British Expeditionary Force in France experienced a severe ammunition shortage. In 1916 the amount of ammunition being manufactured in Britain and the United States increased enormously, but the quality of the British shells was poor and that of the Americans was worse. The French and Germans were better prepared and their shells were more effective. At Verdun between 21 February and 15 July 1916, about five months, the Germans and French fired twenty-three million shells at each other.

The usual heavy and lengthy bombardments before an infantry attack cost the attacker the element of surprise, but they were usually essential. Eventually the artillery developed a "creeping" or "rolling" barrage behind which the infantry advanced. It was risky business, for "shorts" fell among one's own troops and fast-moving infantry sometimes ran into its own barrage.

Subjected to an artillery bombardment the poor infantryman could make no response; he could only cower in his trenches and hope to survive. Men soon learned to distinguish enemy shells. The heavy German 150 mm shells filled with high explosives created violent explosions and clouds of black smoke. British and Americans came to call them "Jack Johnsons," after the black American boxer who was heavyweight champion from 1908 until 1915.

The trench mortar, a simple but destructive weapon that fired a shell at a very high angle, was basically a pipe down which a shell was slid from the muzzle to hit a pin at the end. Its range was short but it could be fired from trench to trench across no-man's-land (which varied from a half-mile to a few yards in width). The German mortar, the *Minnenwerfer*, fired a large metal canister filled with scrap metal that sometimes left its victims with wounds from which parts of garden hoes or old clocks protruded.

In the British army 58.51 percent of all battle casualties were caused by enemy artillery and mortar fire; rifle and machine gun fire accounted for 38.98 percent. Percentages were roughly the same in other armies. Wounds from bayonets, sabers, lances, and other edged weapons probably accounted for less than 1 percent. Most of the remaining casualties came from hand grenades or, as they were then often called, bombs, weapons for which no training was given in the United States.

One of the newest weapons (and the least effective) to take its place in the arsenal of armies was the airplane. It is safe to say that although by 1918 the Allies had achieved aerial superiority on the Western Front, its benefits were few, its overall effect upon the fighting below slight. Marshal Foch, the horse artilleryman who led the Allied armies to eventual victory, pronounced its value in war to be "zero." Fighter planes (then called pursuit planes), the most glamorous of weapons, accomplished little of value. Bombers were too clumsy and their bombs too small (and too often dropped inaccurately) to cause much damage, although the Germans did score one huge success when a bomb managed to hit and destroy 9,000 tons of high explosives on 20 July 1916. Aerial photography, which made giant strides in the course of the war, proved to be the airplane's most valuable contribution.

Tanks appeared on the battlefield for the first time. Tractors had been used as early as the Crimean War in 1854–55, and it had been suggested then that if they were armed and armored they might be useful, but the notion was not pursued. In 1892 Dr. Rudolph Diesel patented his remarkable diesel engine, which the military ignored. In 1900 the Simms war car, mounting a 1.5-pounder gun and capable of traveling at nine miles per hour, was successfully demonstrated, but the British army rejected it out of hand. It was Winston Churchill at the British Admiralty who began the secret development of what were called, to mislead enemy ears, "tanks." In July 1918 he optimistically placed an order in the United States for 10,000 "cross-country caterpillar vehicles" for full delivery in the spring of 1919.

In fact, only seventy-nine tanks were manufactured in the United States in the entire course of the war and only fifteen ever reached France. The first, a two-man 2.5-tonner, arrived on the Western Front in October 1918—just before the Armistice.

One of the abiding myths about the use of tanks on the Western Front accuses the Allied generals of being too stupid to use them in mass and sending them out instead in "penny packets" (groups too small to be effective). Lloyd George damned his generals in his memoirs, saying, "So the great secret was sold for the battered ruin of a little hamlet on the Somme, which was not worth capturing." In truth, these early pioneer tanks were sent forward in penny packets because only penny packets were to be had. For the great British attack launched on the Somme on 15 September 1916 only forty-nine tanks were available. And these were not great performers. Only thirty-two were able actually to reach their starting point and to take any part in the action.

The much-maligned General Douglas Haig made repeated requests for more tanks and 1,000 were on order, but by the Battle of Arras, six months later, only sixty were on hand and some of these were patched up affairs salvaged from the Somme. Not until the Battle of Cambrai that began on 20 November 1917 were tanks used en masse. There the entire British Royal Tank Corps, 324 Mark IV fighting tanks with fifty-four in reserve plus a few specialized tanks, was thrown into battle. They proved their usefulness in breaking into the enemy's defenses, although they had yet to prove that they could go through them.

Clumsy and lumbering, subject to frequent breakdowns, tanks in the Great War were not war-winners. The maximum speed of the 1918 British heavy tank, the Mark V, was 4.6 mph. A "male" was equipped with two 6-pounder guns; the "female" with five Hotchkiss or Lewis machine guns. The medium sized Whippet, or Mark A, could travel 8.3 mph on a good road, but could scarcely make 2 mph on a cratered battlefield.

The Germans never used more than thirteen tanks on a single occasion. The first (and only occasion in this war) in which tank fought against tank occurred on 24 April 1918 when Australians threw back a German attack upon Villers-Bretonneaux ridge, the final ridge from which the city of Amiens is distantly visible. In the battle three or four tanks on each side briefly exchanged fire.

Not all weapons on the battlefield were high tech. Infantry were armed with more accurate, magazine-fed rifles to which bayonets could be attached. Officers, artillerymen, and some others carried pistols, usually automatics. Grenades, much used in the war, were ancient weapons that for obscure reasons had fallen out of use. At the beginning of the war the British had none, although they had grenadiers, elite units of tall soldiers once trained to throw them. When the Allies reintroduced them on the Western Front the men who threw them were called bombers. They soon became indispensable weapons in trench warfare. From the beginning grenades were standard issue in the German army.

Steel helmets, a progeny of medieval armor, also were revived. The British sold 1.5 million to the United States. They were badly designed but at least were better than cloth headgear. The German helmets, well designed, were similar to those now worn by American soldiers.

Although barbed wire was widely known, its uses myriad—by 1900 the United States was manufacturing 200,000 tons annually—its value in static defense was not readily apparent to military tacticians. First used militarily in the 1890s by the Spanish in Cuba, the wire defenses so impressed Brigadier General Joseph Wheeler when he rode into Santiago soon after its surrender that he reported: "They were not merely lines of wire, but pieces running perpendicularly, diagonally, horizontally and in every other direction, resembling nothing so much as a huge thick spider's web with an enormous mass in the center."

In the Second Anglo-Boer War the Boers, not bound by military traditions, used it to protect their trenches before Magersfontein; the Japanese used it in Manchuria. Yet, in the intervening years no thought had been given by any of the European Allies or the Americans as to how, when, and where it could or should be employed, for this was a protective device and its use ran contrary to the admired and desired offensive spirit. That a well-armed, entrenched enemy, protected by barbed wire, could devastate attackers was not envisioned. That three men and a machine gun could wipe out a battalion of heroes seemed unimaginable. The doctrine of the offensive prevailed.

It seems not to have occurred to any general on either side that in a war of attrition the advantage lay with the defensive, that the attacker lost more men than the defender. It was a lesson never learned.

4

☆

FINDING THE MEN AND TOOLS

IN NEW YORK on 27 January 1916 President Wilson spoke vaguely of the need for military and industrial preparedness and for a half-million trained "citizens" who would serve "under conditions of danger." But this was mere lip service—or ignorance. Wilson, a man engaged in the pursuits of peace and humanity, with little interest in and less understanding of what was required to make war, cherished the curious notion that neutrality forbade preparedness. Although he had some interest in ships and naval affairs, soldiers and their profession were beyond his ken. He was willing, he said, "to follow experts in a war of experts"—a precept he did not always heed.

By April 1917 much of the magnificent German army had perished, but it still displayed considerable initiative, an enduring courage, and a tough efficiency that made it a danger to its foes. The American entry into the war could not have come at a more apposite moment, for Allied morale was sagging badly. But an American army had yet to come into being. It had to be trained, armed, and equipped, transported to France, and put in the line of battle. And there was no assurance that this could be done. American lack of preparedness suddenly became a major problem.

On 10 May 1917, the same day that Pershing was told he had been selected to lead a division to France, the War College Division of the General Staff, unaware that a decision had already been made by the president, drew up a consideration of an expeditionary force. It concluded that "the early dispatch of any expeditionary force to France is inadvisable because of lack of organization and training."

Belatedly, some important preparation for creating a wartime army had begun. In February 1917, after the diplomatic break with Germany, Chief of Staff General Hugh Scott and Secretary of War Newton D. Baker (a pacifist who had been a spokesman for the League to Enforce Peace) recommended and Wilson approved the drawing up of a conscription bill. This was done by Judge Advocate General Enoch H. Crowder, a stony-faced, cadaverous lawyer known for his remarkable "capacity for sustained labor." Although Crowder was against conscription, feeling that it was "not in harmony with the spirit of our people," he had a draft of a bill ready for the president within twenty-four hours.

Although then on the edge of war, "I Didn't Raise My Boy to Be a Soldier" was the most popular song in Tin Pan Alley, which then so often expressed popular opinion. Pacifists were vociferous in their objections to conscription. Some prophesied widespread rioting. Upton Sinclair, an apostate socialist, predicted a reign of terror and anarchist Emma Goldman anticipated "almost civil war." In an acrimonious debate in Congress Senator James Reed from Missouri predicted that if the bill passed the streets of St. Louis would "run red with blood." Champ Clark, the influential Speaker of the House, also from Missouri, declaimed: "I protest with all my heart and mind and soul against having the slur of being a conscript placed upon any men of Missouri; in the estimation of Missourians there is precious little difference between a conscript and a convict." Other Congressmen predicted that the bill would produce only "a sulky, unwilling, indifferent army" or would "Prussianize America." One came close to the truth when he feared, "It will destroy democracy at home while fighting for it abroad." Nevertheless, the Selective Service Act was passed, and on 18 May 1917 President Wilson signed it into law.

Blood did not stain the streets of St. Louis or of any other city or town, and the conscripts, euphemistically dubbed "draftees" or "selectees," failed to protest. By the end of the September some half-million men were in training.

The new act differed significantly from the Civil War draft law; it was the brilliant inspiration of Secretary Baker that the actual conscription was to be administered by civilians. State governors appointed "boards of responsible citizens" in the nation's 155 federal judicial districts. These state and district boards provided an administrative skeleton for 4,648 local boards composed of county clerks, local lawyers, doctors, and "community leaders." Thus, "friends and neighbors," not military officers, would select who was to serve.

All males between the ages of twenty-one and thirty-one were required to register on 5 June 1917 and more than nine million did; eventually twenty-four million men were registered. Famed evangelist Billy Sunday made impassioned speeches as he toured New York City. Leaping up and down and waving his hat, he called upon God to "strike down in his tracks" any man who failed to register. "If hell could be turned upside down," he stormed, "you would find stamped on its bottom 'Made in Germany!' "

On 20 July the "great national lottery" began when a blindfolded Baker drew the first number (258) from a large glass jar. Men holding this number in each local board were called up for military service. In Chicago Alfred A. Primeau, who held number 258, told reporters, "It is more honor than I have ever had before." In Greenville, Mississippi, when George M. Bradshaw saw that he had the number he rushed to the telegraph office to wire Secretary Baker: "Thanks for drawing 258. That's me." For the next 16 hours and 45 minutes the drawing continued in the Senate Office Building until 10,500 numbers were drawn, that being the largest number of men registered in any one board.

Once registered, men were divided into five categories. The first was made up of fit unmarried males without dependents who were not employed in an essential occupation; the fifth comprised of those regarded as permanently unavailable for service. One of three called by the draft board proved physically unfit. Those from rural areas were more healthy than those from cities; whites were more fit than blacks; and native-born men more fit than immigrants. General James G. Harbord, when chief of staff of the AEF, contended that: "The majority of our World War recruits were narrow chested, awkward, and under weight in proportion to height." Although the minimum was five feet one inch (this height requirement was lowered by an inch in January 1918), the average recruit stood five feet nine inches in his stocking feet; he wore a size seven hat, had a collar size of fifteen and one-half inches, a thirty-seven-inch chest, a thirty-four-inch waist, wore a size 9C shoe, and weighed 141.5 pounds (four and one-half pounds heavier than those who served in Union armies during the Civil War). Most were single in their early twenties. Foreign-born soldiers and blacks were overdrafted, for the draft tended to sweep up those in the lowest socioeconomic classes.

With the outbreak of war young men became the nation's most valuable resource, their fitness a national issue, but many were weeded out in physical examinations. Of those called up, 51.4 percent were found to have some physical defect and 27.4 percent were rejected outright.

Actor John Barrymore was rejected for varicose veins. Cartoonist James Thurber, then a student at Ohio State University, blind in one eye and shortsighted in the other, had trouble explaining his problem, and was twice called to appear before medical examiners. Told to take off his glasses he confessed to the examining doctor, "You're just a blur to me."

"You're absolutely nothing to me," the doctor snapped back.

It was only after he had stripped and taken the entire examination that he was told, "Why, you couldn't get into the service with sight like that!"

"I know," said Thurber.

A study of nearly a million conscripts showed that 5.6 percent were infected with a venereal disease, of which about 90 percent, probably those with gonorrhea, were accepted and treated. Rates were highest in the south and increased in proportion to the number of blacks in the population. Soldiers who were mentally, physically, or morally incapable of performing their duties were eventually transferred into Special Development battalions for "unfit and venereal soldiers."

An enthusiasm for the war swept the country. Most men readily accepted induction and were eager to go "over there." Some of the less zealous rushed their sweethearts to the altar, but Washington decreed that marriages after 6 April would not affect a man's draft status. Canada cooperated by closing its borders to all Americans of draft age. Organized opposition to the war for religious or political reasons was never a serious problem. Some 64,693 men applied for noncombatant status and nearly 57,000 were granted, usually for religious reasons. Fewer than 1,700 claimed to be "conscientious objectors" for other than religious reasons, arguing that one need not be religious to have a conscience, and, surprisingly, given the patriotic fervor of the country, draft boards allowed about 1,500 of these.

General Crowder, appointed Provost Marshal General, divided those who resisted the draft into three categories: "slackers"* who failed to register; "delinquents" who registered but refused to submit to the authority of the local draft boards; and "deserters" who, when called to the service, failed to report for duty. Although the armed services obtained all the men they needed—indeed, initially more than they could handle—in the course of the war 337,649 refused to report for military service when ordered. About 170,000 had still not been apprehended in 1920.

---

*"Slacker" was a new word, first used by the British as a term for male British subjects in the United States who refused to come home and fight.

Of the conscientious objectors who were inducted, 16,000, like Alvin York in Tennessee, changed their minds and served. Secretary Baker, who met with some at Camp Meade, Maryland, found, "Only two of those with whom I talked seemed quite normal mentally." He ordered that conscientious objectors be treated with "kindly consideration," but Theodore Roosevelt expressed the majority view: "The bulk of them are slackers, pure and simple, or else traitorous pro-Germans." In spite of all persuasions 3,989 refused to serve as combatants, but 2,599 accepted alternative noncombat roles. In spite of Baker's instructions, those inducted who absolutely refused any service were taunted, abused, and threatened with court-martial if they did not see their "patriotic duty." Future novelist Lieutenant F. Scott Fitzgerald forced one man to drill by pointing his pistol at him.

The worst cases of abuse occurred in Camp Funston and Camp Riley, both under the command of General Leonard Wood, who pronounced all conscientious objectors "enemies of the Republic, fakers and active agents of the enemy." Private Otto Gottschalk, doubtless suffering from his German name as well as his pacifist beliefs, was dragged from his tent, stripped, thrown in a ditch, forced to swallow mired water, and then badly beaten.

Of the 504 "absolutists" actually court-martialed, 17 were sentenced to death, 142 to life imprisonment, and 345 to terms averaging 16.5 years. In the event, none was executed; after the war many had their sentences reduced and by the end of 1920 most were freed, but not until 1933 were the last pardoned by President Franklin D. Roosevelt. At least 17 died in prison as a result of physical abuse or prison conditions; one committed suicide.

In the course of the war the army grew from its 1917 strength of 208,034 men, including National Guardsmen in federal service, to 3,685,458 on 11 November 1918. Of this number 2,180,296 were conscripts inducted under the Selective Service Act 1917 and a supplementary measure in 1918 that expanded the age limits to men as young as eighteen and as old as forty-five. By the summer of 1918 the first enthusiasm had waned. Military intelligence reported that many men now regarded induction as "an unpleasant necessity rather than an opportunity to serve." Draft evasion became a problem, but the war ended before the army suffered a shortage of men.

The American call upon its manpower never compared with that of European countries. By the war's end some 24,234,021 American men had been registered and a total of 3,099,000, or roughly three percent of the total population, were in uniform, of whom all but 8,000 were in the army. By contrast, in the American Civil War eight percent of the population served. France in the course of the war called up 7,800,000 men, one-fifth of her total population. Britain by voluntary recruitment or conscription called up 5,704,416, ten percent of its population. The British Empire assembled and prepared 8,654,467 for war.

Although the draft supplied the men, they had to be housed, clothed, armed, equipped, and trained. When war was declared in April the army possessed housing for only 124,000 officers and men. Although it had requested a 687,000 increase in strength, it was soon obvious that it was unprepared to quarter and equip that many. A Cantonment Division was created in the Quartermaster Corps under Colonel Isaac W. Littell and in July 50,000 carpenters and 150,000 other workmen went to work. Existing military installations were expanded and sixteen tent camps were built for the National Guard in the south and sixteen wooden barracks for the National Army (conscripts and volunteers) in the north.

By December Colonel Littell had built or expanded facilities to quarter 1.5 million men. It had been a massive undertaking. In the north each of the new cantonments required an average of twenty-five million board feet of lumber, 37,000 window sashes, 4,665 casks of cement, 7,000 kegs of nails, and enormous quantities of other materials. Twenty-six boxcars were needed just to transport the cooking stoves; heating stoves required an additional 156 cars.

Once in camp men had to be clothed and from the beginning of the war until the end of May 1918 the army took delivery of 131.8 million pairs of stockings, 8.3 million overcoats, 83.6 million underdrawers, and, curiously, 85.2 million undershirts. The army thought it knew roughly the range and number of each size needed, but the draft brought in more men taller and shorter, smaller and larger than expected. Hugh Johnson, a cavalry captain and assistant to General Crowder at the beginning of the war and a general at the end, wrote: "The supply situation was as nearly a perfect mess as can be imagined." Many had to wait for their full allotment of clothing and equipment. Private Clayton K. Slack later remembered, "It was two months or so before I looked really like a soldier."

Special optical, radio, photographic, bridging, arms, ammunition, and other specifically military items had to be provided. And the army needed more than 15,000 pigeons to be trained as message carriers. It was soon discovered that some companies had signed contracts to provide items in quantities they could not produce. Among other problems were those ini-

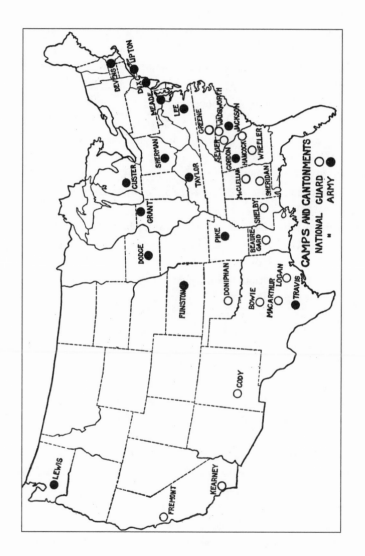

Camps and cantonments
CREDIT: *The War With Germany*

tiated by the French who, unwilling to release patents and drawings for aircraft and weapons, demanded royalties in advance. Many Americans, understandably, wondered why they should pay the French a license fee for materials needed to save France. Production was only one of many supply problems.

The government, which had always maintained a laissez-faire attitude toward business and industry, now became intrusive. In many instances the army took control of all stages of the manufacturing process from finding raw material to inspecting finished products. A Food Administration under Herbert Hoover regulated the supply and consumption of food. All retailers whose gross sales exceeded $100,000 were required to have a license to trade and this could be revoked for any infringement of government regulations. For months before the Armistice the War Department owned all the wool in the country. There were in total more than 30,000 categories of commercial products purchased by the army.

On the same day that General March became chief of staff, multimillionaire Bernard Mannes Baruch, who had long been an advocate for preparedness, became chairman of the War Industries Board with broad powers to control production and supplies. As a hugely successful Wall Street speculator, primarily in metals and railroad stock, Baruch had no ties to any particular company, institution, or individual. On his appointment, President Wilson, assured him: "I won't overrule you."

The Board immediately set about surveying all the nation's resources and industries that would be useful in war, identifying 35,000 firms that could manufacture war material. Baruch believed that the secret to controlling war production was to exercise dictatorial power, or, as he called it, "priority," which he defined as "the power to determine who gets what and when." In his memoirs he wrote: "Priority enabled us to allocate scarce materials where they were needed most, to curtail less essential production, to break bottlenecks, to end reckless and chaotic competition, to conserve fuel, to save shipping space, to pool and ration."

There were serious shortages. Aside from arms in the hands of troops, the army in 1917 had only 400 light field guns and 150 heavy field guns. It had only 1,500 machine guns and these were of four different types. Senator Henry Cabot Lodge was outraged by what he regarded as a machine gun scandal and wrote to Theodore Roosevelt about the decision to drop the Lewis gun: "They took months to consider a new gun, and then that expert ordnance officer, the Secretary of War, decided on the Browning gun, which never had a field test and of which there is only one in existence—the model. After deciding on their gun, they have made none."

It sometimes proved impossible for officers to break with old habits and the slow and deliberate methods of an army in times of peace. Each of the army service bureaus—ordnance, engineer, quartermaster, medical, and signal—had its own supply system and there was virtually no coordination among them. Congress, its attention drawn to the lack of munitions, requested an explanation from General William Crozier, who had been chief of ordnance since 1901. He first blamed Congress, but when this turned out to be a bad idea, he blamed Secretary Baker. This, too, was not a career-enhancing maneuver. Crozier was a crusty general who believed that he and his experts knew what ordnance items combatants should have and usually ignored the opinions of those who were to use them. When asked by Joseph E. Kuhn, chief of the War College Division of the General Staff, how long it would take to supply ordnance for an army of a million men, he replied that it would take eighteen months to supply machine guns and up to two and one-half years to supply a number of other critical items. Soon after he was replaced by General Clarence C. Williams, who had a different philosophy, believing, "If the fighting men want elephants, we get them elephants."

However, most weapons required long lead times, making it difficult to produce them in quantity and in a timely fashion. The service rifle was the 1903 Springfield, a fine bolt action weapon, but only 600,000 were on hand along with some 200,000 of the older Krag-Jörgensens. Production of Springfields could only be increased to one thousand per day. However, as Remington and Winchester were making Enfield rifles for the British it was decided to redesign the British Enfield. The American Enfield Model 1917 was chambered for the then standard .30-06 round and incorporated a five-round, in-line, fixed-box magazine. This was a satisfactory solution but it caused a delay until the redesigned weapon could be put into production. By the end of the war more than 2.5 million rifles of all makes had been produced.

Three months into the war Secretary Baker thought things "seemed to be getting forward fairly well. . . . There are many who are criticizing; but most of them have . . . no real comprehension of how hard it is to expand industrially an unmilitary country into any sort of adequate response to such an emergency as we are now facing."

It was not until eighteen months after declaring war that the United

States was able effectively to engage in the fighting in Europe, and then only because the Allies, principally France and Britain, supplied—for a price and often grudgingly—weapons, ammunition, transportation, and equipment. Most of the troops were transported to Europe in British ships, carried to the front in French trains or British and French trucks, and supplied with most of their tools of the trade by the Allies. Of the 3,499 pieces of field artillery used by the AEF in battle, only 130 were American-made; of the 8,116,000 rounds of artillery expended in battle, only 8,400 were made in the United States. In return, the United States could, for the most part, only supply steel, copper, and other raw materials. In short, the Allies could not have won the war, at least not in 1918, without American troops, but the United States could not have fought the war without the matériel supplied by the Allies.

By 1918 the United States was making a greater contribution: the American production of smokeless powder was 45 percent greater than French and British production combined, and American production of high explosives was 40 percent of Great Britain's and nearly double that of France. The United States also produced 10,000 tons of poison gas, much of it used by the Allies. American factories finally managed to produce an airplane engine, the Liberty, but failed to produce a complete airplane suitable for combat, and in the land of the motor car, the automobile industry failed to produce enough cars and trucks.

When Pershing arrived in Washington in May he was "chagrined" to discover that even weeks after the declaration of war so little had been done. Wilson, who had equated unpreparedness with neutrality, was primarily responsible, but Pershing blamed the War Department, which he condemned for "our inexcusable failure to do what common sense long before our entry into the war plainly indicated what should have been done." Even after the war Pershing failed to understand the impotence of a War Department forced to abide by Wilson's policies. The War Department, he wrote in his memoirs "seemed to be suffering from a kind of inertia."

One of the greatest deficiencies of the army was the absence of a properly organized and manned general staff. The American general staff, limited by law to eighteen members, fell ludicrously short of the superb Great General Staff of Germany, which had begun the war with 650 highly selected officers, or even the Imperial Staff of Britain, which entered the war with 232. The American staff, to which officers were detailed for four years of duty, was denied the influence and authority of its European counterparts. It was not authorized to administer the bureau chiefs, who occupied their own little fiefdoms. The chief of staff spoke in the name of the secretary of war; he did not command. Incredibly, the country entered the war with an intelligence section of two officers and two clerks. In May emergency legislation increased the staff to fifty-four but, apparently fearing their influence, decreed that no more than half should be stationed in Washington. Their numbers were later increased to ninety-one. By the end of the war there were 1,072 general staff officers in Washington alone.

When Baker wanted a new chief of staff he asked Pershing's advice and Pershing recommended as his first choice General John Biddle, who had twice for brief periods been acting chief of staff. As second choice he nominated General Peyton C. March, of whom he said: "I have always had a high opinion of March and have often thought of him as timber for Chief of Staff. . . . I think March is a strong man and that he would be of great assistance to you." Baker chose March, who was appointed in March 1918, but he proved to be a stronger man than Pershing wished and their ideas frequently clashed.

It was unclear whether the army was controlled by the chief of staff or the commander of the American Expeditionary Force. On 22 September 1917, in his last annual report as chief of staff, General Hugh Scott wrote: "There should be one and only one organ through which the Secretary of War commands the Army—the Chief of Staff . . . [who] should be the medium of recommendation to the Secretary and the execution of his orders. He should have ample authority for securing the coordination of all of the activity of the military establishment." This was also March's understanding of his position, and eventually Baker agreed, but Pershing maintained that he was responsible only to the president and the General Staff was there merely to assist him. These divergent views were a source of much confusion, many misunderstandings, and considerable ill-feeling in high places. It remained a knotty kink in the high command that was not entirely unravelled until after the war when Pershing himself became chief of staff. He then, not surprisingly, acknowledged that the chief of staff should command the army.

5

☆

TRAINING IN THE
UNITED STATES

AS THE ARMY began training America's young men for war it discovered that it needed to educate them in more ways than had been anticipated. In 1917 the American melting pot was still boiling. A third of the population of about one hundred million people were "hyphenated Americans," sometimes called simply "hyphenates," the foreign-born or those with a foreign-born parent. Eighteen percent of the white recruits were foreign-born, most from southern and eastern Europe with Catholic or Jewish backgrounds, and seventy percent of these had been in the United States for fewer than ten years, thirty percent for fewer than five years. About eight million were German-Americans, many of whom still held warm feelings for the Fatherland, and more than four million were Irish-Americans who retained their hatred of Great Britain. About eleven percent of those who registered with their draft board were not citizens, being aliens or reservation Indians.

In June 1918 the Army formed a Military Morale Section within the Military Intelligence Division of the War Department. Its mission was to concentrate on "stimulating and maintaining the morale of the army, not only as a whole but with special references to the various races" (nationalities). A Foreign-Speaking Soldier Sub-Section concentrated on organizing units by their nationality, creating ethnic-specific "Foreign Legion" companies.

Whenever possible the services complied with requests for special consideration. The Jewish Welfare Board successfully petitioned the War Department that furloughs be granted Jewish soldiers for Yom Kipper,

Rosh Hashanah, and the Passover, and that the graves of Jewish soldiers be marked with a Star of David. Italian associations protested the absence of Italian flags in places where Allied flags were displayed and an effort was made to correct this oversight. Somewhat less attention was given to European ethnic prejudices—soldiers of Rumanian and Czech stock objected to being in the same unit with Hungarians of Magyar stock—but there was at least a recognition that such problems existed.

Some thought that service in the army provided a good time and place to Americanize the unwashed masses. To an extent this was true and efforts were made to Americanize non-English speakers and to implant or reinforce the middle-class virtues of personal hygiene, efficiency, chastity, sobriety, and patriotism. "These men of many nations," said Henry Ford, "must be taught American ways, the English language and the right way to live." The New York *Times* agreed and opined that the Selective Service Act "gives a long and sorely needed means of disciplining a certain insolent foreign element in this nation."

As early as 1913 the navy had instituted an educational program to be carried out on every ship. In addition to technical subjects, officers taught their men reading, writing, mathematics, geography, and history. The pattern set by the navy was adopted in part by the army.

In February 1918, 14,249 soldiers were enrolled in English classes in camps. Some propaganda came with the lessons. A Princeton English professor prepared a little book, *Camp Reader for American Soldiers*, incorporating such lines as "A good soldier keeps his gun cleaned" and "I will write a letter to my brother Jack. I will tell him how proud I am to be an American soldier."

It was not only immigrant soldiers who needed help. About 25 percent of native-born Americans were illiterate, unable to read a newspaper or write a letter. Many of these came from the rural south. When the 165th Infantry, originally a New York National Guard regiment, received an influx of replacements from southern states, it was found that about two hundred could not sign their names to the payroll. A third of all conscripts had less than the six years of schooling which the War Department initially thought necessary for a man to function as a soldier. Only 14.5 percent of the population were high school graduates.

The first man appointed chief of the training and instruction branch of the General Staff, Major General John F. Morrison, believed the best recruits came from "small towns and rural districts" rather than from "the slums of the big cities." As about half of all Americans lived in rural areas most of the conscripts were country boys. In 1919 a sample of 592,854 men, mostly combat veterans, gave this rough breakdown of their civilian occupations:

Farmers: 112,523
"Horsemen": 40,000
Clerical workers: 40,000
Laborers: 38,000
Mechanics and machinists: 26,000
Chauffeurs [apparently meaning men who worked driving a motor
    vehicle]: 26,000
Factory Workers: 16,000

Farm boys may have made the best soldiers, but as they tended to have had the least education, they required the longest training period. It came as a surprise to army recreational directors that so many young men did not know how to play any game; some did not even understand the concept of play.

The experience of most recruits, ill-educated and unsophisticated, involved leaving home and familiar surroundings for the first time. Some had no conception of the size and diversity of the world. One young Virginia mountaineer riding a train speeding west marvelled, "Bud, if this old world is as big the other way as she is this, she's a hell-buster for sartin."

Private John Dombrocuski, son of a German immigrant, found it hard to leave his home on a Wisconsin farm to join the 109th Infantry in the 28th Division. He later recalled that he was "very frightened and uncertain with a major World War on, and leaving family and home for the first time." He was worried too that he might be shooting at his own relatives.

Conscripts in many towns were sent off in style with bands and speeches from local politicians. Some were uncertain as to what clothes to wear when called off for the army. Many recruits put on their best. John L. Barkley of Holden, Missouri, who did not, said he "felt like a fool" because he wore overalls. He felt better when thirteen months later he returned from the war in uniform with the Medal of Honor on his chest.

For many conscripts the trip from home to the army was a long one. Wesley Fieldon, raised on a farm, began his trip to war riding in a familiar buckboard wagon, progressed to a boat on the Barren and Green rivers, and finally arrived at Camp Taylor, Kentucky, in the luxury of a passenger coach of the L & N Railroad.

Some thought it would be grand to have a good last drunk on the way to war. A train load of conscripts from Arizona, a mix of cowboys, miners, and Indians, became not just drunk but "extravagantly drunk." They looted a bar at one station and threw a porter off the moving train. During a stop at Trinidad, Colorado, they lassoed a number of citizens and staged a fight among a bulldog, a goat, and a tame wildcat—all being pets brought along to keep them company in the army.

By early September conscripts began to arrive at the partially built training camps. The army did not have separate camps for basic training. Recruits were at once assigned to units and were trained in the divisions in which it was expected that they would serve, but most divisions were gutted and their training schedules ruined in the search for instructors, mechanics, typists, teamsters, and other specialists. Even when divisions at full strength were sent to France, no provision was made to replace casualties.

The camps usually sat on bare, unprepossessing landscapes. A soldier in Battery A, 306th Field Artillery described his camp as "a desolate wilderness of sand and scrub oak and famous for nothing but our great national bird, the mosquito." Lieutenant Harry S. Truman, in training with his National Guard Unit in January 1918, at Camp Doniphan, adjacent to Fort Sill, Oklahoma, said the camp "just sticks up high enough to catch every misting air current that goes from the Arctic to fill the holes in the Gulf of Mexico. In summer it catches all the dust in the whole of North America."

Still, for many country boys, and even some from the cities, the barracks, crude as they were, held hitherto unseen amenities such as indoor plumbing with showers and flush toilets.

One recruit described his first days in the army: "First we were physically examined, vaccinated, inoculated, berated, carbolated, blockaded and mustered in. Sounds like a hard day's work, but we had nothing to do but just 'be there.' "

Many were surprised by the quantity of food served. American soldiers were given more meat and more calories (4,761 daily) than soldiers in any other army. Private Clinton Harbison assured those at home: "They are feeding us here like lords." Some of the food seemed strange to many and one recruit described his breakfast: "We had coffee, bread, butter, scrambled eggs, potatoes, corn flakes and some damn wild oranges so sour you couldn't touch 'em." The "wild oranges" were grapefruit.

Psychological tests were used for the first time to classify men, afford-

ing psychologists a chance to test their theories on an imposing sampling.
Dr. Robert Mearnes Yerkes, president of the American Psychological
Association, took charge of a team which designed intelligence tests: an
alpha test for those who could read English and a *beta* test for some of
the 100,000 men who could not. Between April 1918 and January 1919,
1.5 million enlisted men and 33,000 officers took the tests. More than a
quarter had to take the *beta* test for illiterates and about one-third proved
to have a low standard of literacy. The results were the source of controversy for years to come.

By modern standards the tests were badly flawed, measuring not intelligence but the educational level and social background of those tested. Yet,
in a rough way they seemed to work: Corporals generally scored higher
than privates, sergeants higher than corporals, and officers higher than
sergeants. One study of results, comparing 660 officers having only eighth
grade educations with a similar number of enlisted men with high school
or college educations, found the officers scored about ten percent higher.

Pershing and General March at the War Department disagreed on the
type of instruction recruits should be given and on the length of time
needed to make a soldier of a civilian. Although the war was being fought
on the Western Front from trenches, Pershing considered trench warfare
defeatist; he called for training in offensive, open warfare and individual
marksmanship. He published his views in a small booklet in which
trench warfare was never discussed. In his memoirs he wrote: "The
instruction of our troops at home at this time [1917] was far from being
satisfactory, tests of newly-arrived units having shown that their work was
not up to our standards. It was evident that my recommendations were
being disregarded. This threw the extra burden upon us of training officers and men after their arrival." Although machine guns and artillery
were the main killing machines, he was particularly disturbed that the
trainers in the United States were not "emphasizing the rifle and bayonet
as the supreme weapons of the infantry soldier. . . ."

Finding enough instructors was a major problem. The Allies con-
tributed a few: 261 British and 286 French officers and 226 British noncommissioned officers were sent to the United States, but lack of time,
lack of proper equipment, language barriers, and administrative duties
kept these from being as helpful as they might have been.

Lack of time was another major problem. The army emphasized discipline, which it defined as "the habit of instantaneous obedience under
any and all circumstances," but instilling discipline required time that

was not available. It was believed that a recruit should undergo a systematic, well-planned program of physical education, but there was not time for this either.

Most soldiers scarcely had time to learn the school of the soldier — close order drill, personal hygiene, care of arms and equipment, military courtesies, mounting guard, et al. — before they were shipped off to France. Some of the simplest things had to be taught. As one soldier wrote home: "I didn't know there were so many people on earth who didn't know their right hand from their left." Many arrived in France without ever having fired their weapon. The situation did not improve. When the 90th Division shipped out in June 1918 only 35 percent of its personnel had received more than four weeks of formal instruction.

Still, time was found for propaganda talks by officers using notes supplied by the army. Lecture 22, "Why We Are at War," took up German atrocities: "We know that in certain Belgian towns young girls were dragged from their homes into the streets and publicly violated by . . . German beasts. We know that Belgian children clinging to their parents had their hands cut off and their parents murdered before their eyes. We know that the German soldier commonly cut off the breasts of the women he or some one else had violated and murdered. He wanted them as souvenirs. . . . We know that wounded men have been mutilated and in at least one instance crucified." That none of this was true did not reduce its effectiveness.

March believed that "entirely too much time was spent on the training considered necessary by General Pershing." He argued that while in peacetime it was assumed that it would take one to three years to train a soldier, depending upon his branch of the service, the average conscript or volunteer was "well above the average citizen of the United States mentally, morally and physically." They did not join the army because they were out of a job or were social misfits; they were young men "full of enthusiasm for what they regarded as a righteous cause" and "threw themselves into training with a zeal and enthusiasm which produced results in a very short time." Under these conditions he considered three months was sufficient to make a soldier.

The training experience was different in different ways for nearly all the recruits. Many rural men were excellent shots, but had never driven — some had never seen — a truck, and many city toughs were unnerved by a night in a forest. For all there was much to learn.

Although the bayonet was an almost useless weapon, bayonet training was regarded as essential to instill the warrior spirit and honed aggressive instincts. Twelve hours' instruction in its use were taken up in the first four weeks of a recruit's training. Instructors exhorted their charges: "Bring the liver out on the bayonet. Bring the kidney out. Bring his breakfast out." To free a stuck bayonet, "fire a slug." Samuel M. Wilson, a Kentucky lawyer who, although nearly forty-six years old, managed to volunteer, wrote: "We drilled and fought dummies with bayonets until we couldn't see straight."

Even would-be officers had to submit to bayonet exercises. Frederick T. Edwards, a recent seminarian who became an officer candidate, discovered that "getting ready for war isn't all brass bands and cheering." He wrote his father: "Two weeks ago I was studying Aristotle and Christian ethics; this afternoon I have been learning to use a bayonet—just how to jab a man—to aim for his stomach first and always to twist the bayonet before pulling it out."

Impatient to get to France and fight the Hun, many soldiers found the time spent on bayonet drill, gas mask drill, close order drill, grenade throwing, and lectures on first aid, hygiene, and German atrocities was long enough. Outside one camp a touring evangelist hung out a sign: "WHERE WILL YOU SPEND ETERNITY?" A wit wrote under it: "At Camp McClellan."

Although many untrained soldiers were sent to France, the War Department maintained after the war that the average American soldier received six months' training in the United States, two months' training in France, followed by one month in a quiet sector of the Western Front, before being exposed to hard fighting. This at least was the goal.

Originally the army remained divided into Regular Army, National Guard, and National Army (conscript) divisions, each wearing distinctive insignia, but all divisions were soon filled with conscripts. There was some friction between the various categories until on 7 August 1918 General Peyton C. March, then chief of staff, consolidated them into one army without differentiation.

In National Guard units officers and men, many equally green, trained together. Before the war Harry S. Truman had served a hitch in a battery of artillery in the Missouri National Guard and had risen to the rank of corporal. In 1917, when the Missouri National Guard was called into federal service as part of the 35th Division, he had energetically recruited for his battery. Many National Guard units elected their officers and noncommissioned officers and Truman had hoped to be elected sergeant;

instead he was voted first lieutenant of Battery D, 129th Field Artillery, 35th Division, and in late September 1917 went off with his division to train at Camp Doniphan. From here he wrote to his fiancée, Bess Wallace.

He was, he said, "working like a nigger." "They are most certainly giving us an intensive course of training. We study drill regulations all week and take an examination on Saturday. . . . I have also been teaching school for noncommissioned officers most every night until nine-thirty. . . ." Private Harry R. Richmond, writing from a camp in New Mexico, told those at home: "The rookie is expected now to learn in three weeks what his fellow soldiers acquired a year ago in three months. We are drilled nearly 7 or 8 hours per day." Private Rex H. Thurston wrote home from Camp Travis in Texas: "We were drilled on all movements of marching without rifles and are now learning all over again with rifles, and a man sure finds out how awkward he is when he starts it. We are being drilled a little harder every day . . ."

On many nights there were lectures. Harry S. Truman told his Bess: "We heard a lecture by an English colonel from the Western Front and it sure put the pep into us. . . . I wouldn't be left out of the greatest history-making epoch the world has ever seen for all there is to live for."

Like most National Guard officers, he complained of his regular army superiors. "They are always hunting for some good excuse to rim a N.G. officer," he said. His antipathy increased, and later from France he wrote that he was considering running for Congress so that he could sit on the Military Affairs Committee and "consign all regular army colonels to damnation."

In addition to the camps for organized units, sixteen officer training camps were established at thirteen army posts, giving three months' training to aspiring officers. The chief of artillery, Major General William J. Snow, later said: "The only uniformity among them was that each was distinguished for its wholly inadequate course of instruction, its incompetent instructors, and its insufficient equipment."

Chester V. Easum, a Rhodes scholar who hurried home from Oxford to be trained as an officer at Fort Sheridan, remembered: "We had to dig and live in trenches for a week near the end of the course. We couldn't drain them so we sloshed in the mud in the cold weather." He considered that "For sheer hardship this surpassed the trenches in France."

At Fort Benjamin Harrison, Indiana, twenty-two-year-old Second Lieutenant Charles L. Bolté, who had been to three summer Reserve

Officer Training Corps (ROTC) camps before his recent graduation from Armour Institute of Technology, struggled to teach students to strip, clean, and reassemble a Colt .45 automatic pistol: "I had to sit up all night long with a manual just learning how you took it apart and put it together again so the next day I could sit down as if I knew all about it and try to teach this company how to do this very complicated task. It was the blind leading the blind."

Nevertheless, nearly half of the army's officers were products of these camps and more than two-thirds served in combatant roles. Until a school for blacks was established at Des Moines, Iowa, in June 1917, only white candidates were accepted.

After all the prodding and testing and such training as could be provided ended, the troops were shipped from their dreary training camps to ports of embarkation. Many found the trip joyous. Private C. W. Stubbs described the five-day journey from Texas: "Yes, it was a great trip. I waved to all the girls from El Paso to Camp Dix." The newly minted soldiers now had to be transported across the perilous, submarine-infested Atlantic to Europe, where wine, women, and war awaited them. But it was not readily apparent where the ships to transport them could be found.

6

☆

THE WAR AT SEA:

THE ANTI-SUBMARINE CAMPAIGN

IN HIS ANNUAL message to Congress in December 1914 President Wilson announced: "We shall take leave to be strong upon the seas," and in the next two years the navy busily prepared for war. On 15 May 1915 Admiral George Dewey, seventy-eight, the aging "Hero of Manila Bay," assured the president: "I can say with absolute confidence that the efficiency of the fleet has steadily progressed, and has never been so high as it is today."

On 29 August 1916 Congress authorized the construction of 157 warships, including ten battleships of the largest type, six of the largest and fastest cruisers in existence, ten scout cruisers, fifty destroyers, fifty-nine submarines, and seven other ships, the largest appropriation ($312,678,000) ever made for naval purposes in time of peace. The navy acted swiftly, enabling Secretary of the Navy Josephus Daniels to claim that by the end of the year the United States had "entered upon the biggest shipbuilding program ever undertaken by any navy at one time." Unfortunately, the money spent on building dreadnoughts and cruisers would have been better spent on more destroyers, the most effective surface vessels against submarines. As late as November 1915 Admiral Dewey wrote: "[T]he submarine is not an instrument fitted to dominate naval warfare. . . . the battleship is still the principal reliance of navies, as it has been in the past." He was a poor prophet. The war against German submarines was the prime concern of the Allies in the war at sea, for the German submarine campaign of 1917 brought them closer to defeat than any military operation of the war.

At the end of March 1917 Rear Admiral Charles P. Plunkett,

Director of Gunnery Exercises, announced that "gunnery was in the highest state of efficiency that it has been in the history of the American Navy," and on 1 April Admiral Henry T. Mayo, commanding the Atlantic Fleet, pronounced the navy to be "in the best state of preparedness that it has ever been." By the time war was declared it had become the third largest navy in the world, with 151 fighting ships and a total of 360 of all categories. Lamentably, two-thirds needed repairs and ninety percent were undermanned.

More manpower was desperately needed. To the peacetime strength of 64,680 enlisted men and 4,376 commissioned and warrant officers about 22,000 militia and reserves were added and about 4,000 Coast Guard were placed under the navy's control—in all, about 95,000 men. Moreover, Congress voted an increase in the strength of the navy, including the Marine Corps; the Naval Reserve, instituted in 1915, was permitted unlimited numbers. In the course of the war the navy was to train 33,000 officers and 500,000 enlisted men, mostly volunteers, one thousand miles from the sea at the Great Lakes Naval Training Station near Chicago, which grew to be the largest naval training station in the world. It was there that Reserve Lieutenant John Philip Sousa trained 1,500 musicians.

The Marine Corps grew from 511 commissioned and warrant officers and 13,214 enlisted men to 2,174 commissioned officers, 288 warrant officers, 65,000 enlisted regulars, 6,704 reserves, and 269 (later increased to 305) female reservists (uniformed in long green skirts), who served in clerical positions. By the end of the war, 73,000 marines were on active service, 24,555 of them in France fighting as an infantry brigade in the Army's 2nd Division.

Charged with the responsibly for the wartime navy were Secretary of the Navy Josephus Daniels, a pacifist and former North Carolina newspaper editor who knew little about the service, and his assistant secretary, Franklin Delano Roosevelt, a young New York aristocrat. Rear Admiral William S. Benson, the chief of naval operations, the first to hold that position, assumed office on 10 May 1915—three days after the sinking of the *Lusitania*—and was charged with responsibility for "the operation of the fleet and its readiness for war." He was not, it seems, one of the navy's luminaries. Walter Long, First Lord of the Admiralty, found him "not very quick to grasp any ideas other than his own."

In the last week of March 1917 Wilson decided on active collaboration with the Royal Navy. He wrote Secretary Daniels: "The main thing, no doubt, is to get into immediate communication with the Admiralty on the other side (through confidential channels until Congress has acted) and work out the scheme of cooperation."

Rear Admiral William Sowden Sims, fifty-nine, who had made his reputation as a naval gunner and had invented a system for aiming the guns on battleships, was selected to open the talks. Blue-eyed and white-bearded, he was described by British Admiral Arthur Pollen, also a pioneer in the development of naval fire control, as "preposterously good looking." Wearing mufti and under the assumed name of Mr. S. W. Dawson, he boarded the *New York*, a liner bound for England, on the last day of March 1917. By the time the ship docked on 9 April the need for secrecy had passed; the United States was at war.

Sims was an Anglophile who had been reprimanded and had drawn down the wrath of President Taft for exceeding his authority in a 1910 speech he had delivered at the Guildhall in London in which he remarked: "If the time ever comes when the British Empire is seriously menaced by an external enemy, it is my opinion that you may count upon every man, every dollar, every drop of blood of your kindred across the sea." In appointing him to the London post Secretary Daniels cautioned: "You have been selected for this mission not because of your Guildhall speech, but in spite of it."

In London on the day after landing, Sims met with Admiral Sir John Jellicoe, Britain's First Sea Lord, and Jellicoe revealed what the British public had not been told: In the first three months of unrestricted submarine warfare German submarines had sunk 844 Allied ships for a loss of only ten submarines out of an estimated fleet of ninety. In the first four months 2.7 million tons of shipping had been sunk. In the previous two months the Germans had sunk more than a million tons. By the end of the month that figure would double. Many British merchant seamen and sailors from neutral countries were refusing to sail. The country was "within measurable distance of strangulation" and it was reliably estimated that Britain could not hold out past 1 November.

Jellicoe told Sims: "It is impossible to go on with the war if losses like this continue." Germany, he said, would win unless such losses could be stopped, and stopped soon. Sims asked if there was any solution.

"Absolutely none that we can see now," Jellicoe said grimly.

Sims was jolted. In his first cable on 14 April he informed Secretary Daniels: "The amount of British neutral and Allied shipping lost in February was 536,000 tons, in March 571,000 and in the first ten days of

April 205,000 tons. With short nights and better weather these losses are increasing."

Sims strongly recommended and Lloyd George agreed, that a convoy system — merchant ships assembled and traveling together under the protection of destroyers — must be instituted, but the Admiralty rejected the idea out of hand, declaring it to be a waste of cruisers and destroyers. Nevertheless, an experiment was tried: The first transatlantic convoy put to sea on 10 May and proved dramatically successful. Thereafter, all merchantmen crossed in convoy. Sinkings decreased to 200 in July, 184 in August, and 107 in December. During the last months of the war convoys lost only about one percent of their ships and Admiral Sims concluded that, "The important agency in defeating the submarines was the convoy system."

When the war began there was no way in which a submerged submarine could be sunk. Not until 1916 was the depth charge, a 300-pound drum of TNT with a variable-water-pressure fuse, invented by the Royal Navy. The drums were simply rolled off the decks until American inventors developed the "Y gun," a specially devised apparatus which hurled the huge charges with greater accuracy and less risk.

Depth charges, mostly used by destroyers, sank twenty-nine submarines and drove many more to the surface where they could be sunk by gunfire. Two American inventions were particularly helpful, perhaps none greater than a submarine detection device developed by forty-year-old Professor Max Mason, a mathematician then at the University of Wisconsin. It not only could detect the sound of submarines as far as twenty miles away, but also could reveal the direction of the sound.

Second to this was the development by two Americans, Commander S. P. Fullinwider and a civilian, thirty-seven-year-old Ralph Cowan Browne, a roentgenologist, of an electrical system and mechanism that made possible an improved mine. Up to this time mines were all of the "contact type," needing direct contact before they exploded. What was needed was a mine with a much larger radius of danger. The new mines, called Mark VI, loaded with three hundred pounds of TNT, were often called "antenna mines," for a long thin copper cable, suspended just below the surface by a small metal buoy, electronically fired the mine below.

The development and production of these mines was kept a secret, even from Congress, and in February 1918 Rear Admiral Ralph Earle, chief of the navy's Bureau of Ordnance, citing national security, refused to disclose to a congressional committee where the unaccounted millions of dollars were being spent.

On 15 April 1917 the United States Bureau of Ordnance proposed a mine barrier across the North Sea and the English Channel. The new mines made this a practical proposition, but the British claimed that this had been tried and found "quite unfeasible." Although the British Admiralty rejected the idea, and sniffed that the United States could "more profitably concentrate on other work," the American naval administration advanced the scheme again and again.

After six months of cajoling, the plan for the great North Sea Mine Barrage was at last adopted on 2 November 1917, but even though Prime Minister Lloyd George supported the scheme, the British Admiralty continued to drag its feet.

President Wilson, addressing a group of American naval officers on 11 August 1917 from the quarterdeck of the USS *Pennsylvania*, urged them to ignore the example of the Royal Navy and "throw tradition to the winds." "Every time we have suggested anything to the British Admiralty," he said, "the reply has come back that virtually amounted to this, that it had never been done that way, and I felt like saying, 'Well, nothing was ever done so systematically as nothing is being done now.' Therefore, I should like to see something unusual happen. . . ."

It was 8 June 1918 before the first mines were finally laid. Under the command of Rear Admiral Joseph Strauss, 135 American ships seeded a band roughly 250 miles long and fifteen to thirty-five miles wide in the North Sea from Scapa Flow, off Aberdeen, Scotland, to Norway. In all, 70,165 mines were placed at various depths, some near the surface, others at a depth of 240 feet. At the same time the British laid a barrage across the straits of Dover and by August 1918 this avenue to the Atlantic was sealed.

More than any other single weapon, the mines wreaked havoc with the German submarines. Their actual destruction of submarines was difficult to measure. Seeing oil slicks and bits of jetsam did not count, for a submarine could release them as a ruse, but at least four, probably six, were sunk in the North Sea Barrage and four possibles were claimed; it was believed that seventeen were damaged and forced to return to their base. Secretary Daniels maintained that "there was no one thing that had more influence in breaking the German morale, particularly in the U-boat service, than did the Northern Mine Barrage." Even Admiral Sims, who had initially shared the British skepticism, later admitted that the North Sea Mine Barrage was "one of the wonders of the war."

The first battle between a ship of the United States Navy and a

German submarine was fought in an unlikely place by an unlikely combination. On 4 July 1917 the U-155, formerly the *Deutschland*, surfaced and shelled Ponta Delgada, the chief town of the Azores on the southwest coast of São Miguel Island. The island's antiquated forts offered the town no defense and the citizens were panic stricken. Rescue came from an unexpected source. The USS *Orion*, a lowly naval collier, had put in for repairs on the far side of a point of land jutting out into the harbor. Although her stern had been hoisted out of the water and she could not sail, the crew jumped to her guns and within three minutes returned the fire. With shells from an unknown source landing around them, the Germans beat a retreat.

Lieutenant Commander J. H. Boesch, the *Orion's* captain, found himself the hero of the Azores. Portuguese officials tendered him formal thanks and the ship's crew were plied with gifts. A cigar was named after him and his picture graced its boxes. Popular acclaim could go no further.

Fear of enemy submarines off America's Atlantic coast led to absurd rumors. Some swore that German submarines were landing spies or men to poison wells; sightings of strange boats were reported; flashing lights from shore were thought to be signals to U-boats; and, most bizarre, it was believed by some that German submarines would launch airplanes to bomb New York.

However, some fears became reality soon after the United States entered the war. On 2 June 1918 a German submarine, the U-151, which had left Kiel on 14 April, appeared off the New Jersey coast and sank six ships, including the passenger steamer *Carolina*, en route to New York from Puerto Rico with a crew of 117, carrying 218 passengers. All aboard found places in lifeboats, but six crew members and seven passengers were lost in the night when one capsized during a storm.

Word of the sinking raised an alarm from Cape Cod to Key West; within twenty-four hours 5,000 telegrams, cables, and telephone calls flooded the Navy Department, where the halls and offices were filled with anxious shipowners, shippers, relatives, and the simply curious. Amid the chaos Secretary Daniels did his best to answer the questions shouted by reporters.

The U-151 was to sink six more ships, one of them American, before returning to Germany. In its three-month cruise it had sunk twenty-three vessels totaling 59,000 gross tons. It was not the only German submarine to operate off the American east coast. The U-156 sank nine American steamers in American waters; the largest was the *Winneconne*, weighing 1,869 tons.

The only large American warship sunk off the eastern shore was the USS *San Diego*, an armored cruiser, which struck a mine off Fire Island, New York, at 11:05 A.M. on 19 July 1918. Six men were lost, three of whom were killed by the explosion. Captain H. H. Christy, the last to leave the ship, was cheered by the 1,056 survivors in boats and on rafts, who then passed the time while awaiting rescue by singing "The Star Spangled Banner" and "My Country 'Tis of Thee." A court of inquiry concluded that "the conduct of the Captain, officers and crew was in the highest degree commendable" and that "the remarkably small loss of life was due to the high state of discipline maintained on board."

Patroling the American Atlantic coast could be dangerous. Many fishing vessels were converted into mine sweepers and these were frequently called upon to reinforce coastal patrols or to go to the aid of vessels grounded or in distress. Operating in shipping lanes where vessels ran without lights, they were in danger of being run down or mistaken for enemy craft. Subchaser 209 was shelled and sunk off Fire Island by the American steamship *Felix Taussig*. Two officers and fourteen enlisted men were killed.

The navy introduced subchasers in the summer of 1918. Although originally designed to protect the entrances to harbors and to patrol coasts, they served in the Atlantic and Mediterranean, usually organized into hunting units of three. Dubbed the "Cinderellas of the Fleet," they were called by the men who sailed in them the "Splinter Navy," for they were wooden ships of less than one hundred tons, 110 feet long. Powered by three high-powered gasoline engines, and equipped with the newly invented listening devices, they mounted a three-inch gun forward and elaborate paraphernalia for launching mines aft. Four hundred and forty-one were built and 341 were manned by American sailors. (One hundred were given to the French.) Each carried a crew of two reserve officers, many of them recent college graduates, and twenty-two men.

They particularly distinguished themselves in the crowded waters of the Mediterranean, where both German and Austrian submarines threatened Allied ships. On 2 October 1918 eleven subchasers, under the command of Captain Charles P. ("Juggy") Nelson, a jovial, energetic officer, particularly distinguished themselves in the successful British and Italian attack upon the major Austrian naval base at Durazzo (now Durrës in Albania), just north of the Strait of Otranto, where they acted as a screen for the larger vessels and even sank a submarine with depth charges.

The largest and most seaworthy yachts, including private yachts such as

J. P. Morgan's pleasure boat, *Corsair,* and the *Nokomis,* a yacht built for Horace E. Dodge of Detroit, were stripped of their luxurious fittings, armed, and converted into men-of-war. A special force of these, organized under Rear Admiral William B. Fletcher, sailed for Europe on 8 June 1917. On 21 May 1918 the *Christabel,* smallest of the converted yachts, so damaged one German submarine, the UC-56, that it was barely able to reach Santander, Spain, where it and its crew were interned for the duration of the war.

American warships were credited with making 256 attacks on submarines. One of the most dramatic was the destruction of the U-58 on 17 November 1917. Two American destroyers, the *Fanning* and *Nicholson,* were escorting a convoy when at 4:10 P.M. the sharp eyes of Coxswain David D. Loomis on the *Fanning* spotted a finger telescope, a thin instrument only an inch and one-half in diameter, scarcely larger than a walking stick. It was above the surface for only a few seconds, but Loomis was able to get its direction and bearing—three points off the port bow, 400 yards away. The *Fanning* headed for the spot and dropped a depth bomb. The concussion wrecked the submarine's motors, broke its oil leads, and jammed the diving planes. The *Nicholson* made for the spot as well, and dropped another depth charge. The submarine's bow came up rapidly, but it was down in the stern and obviously damaged. The *Nicholson* fired from her stern gun. The bow gun on the *Fanning* also opened fire and at the third shot the German commander, Kapitänleutnant Gustav Amberger, emerged. Ensign H. W. Dwight Rudd on the *Nicholson* described the scene: "Out came the first Hun I or anybody present had seen in the war. I shall never forget the sight of that man as he ran frantically up and down the deck, his hands over his head. He, anyway, had surrendered; there was little doubt of that. Bees from out a hive had nothing on the crew of that submarine. They simply poured out of those hatches, until the deck was black with them."

Lines were attached in an effort to salvage the submarine, but crew members managed to scuttle it. All on board dived overboard before it sank. Lines were thrown to them and all but one, Franz Glinder, were saved. Two of the *Fanning*'s crew leaped overboard and reached him; he was hauled aboard, but all efforts to resuscitate him failed. The entire action lasted only eighteen minutes.

Amberger, his three officers, and thirty-five crewmen were made prisoner, given coffee, sandwiches, and the loan of warm clothing. The first officer exchanged his Iron Cross for a clean undershirt. As Amberger later said, "The Americans were much nicer and obliging than expected." When the Germans were put in boats to be taken ashore they cheered their captors.

Sims' relations with the Allies was a happy one. He did not attempt to establish an independent American naval command and American-British collaboration was a complete success. American naval policy, in striking contrast to army policy, was to assist the British and, in effect, become a junior partner.

On 24 April 1917 the first American destroyers docked at Queenstown (now Cobh), Ireland, after a stormy crossing. Their commander, thirty-nine-year-old Commander Joseph K. Taussig, immediately reported to British Vice Admiral Sir Lewis Bayley, who gruffly asked how soon his flotilla would be ready for sea duty. Taussig gave the right answer: "I shall be ready when fueled." This, at least, is the legend, and perhaps it is close enough. His actual reply, it seems, was: "We are ready now, sir, that is as soon as we finish fueling. Of course you know how destroyers are—always wanting something done to them. But this is war and we are ready to make the best of things and go to sea immediately." Many of the British destroyers were long overdue for repairs and refitting. The arrival of American destroyers was welcome indeed.

Queenstown became the main American base in the United Kingdom, and by the end of May twenty-eight American destroyers were stationed there. By 5 July seven more arrived and two tenders were added.

In December 1917, when six coal-burning American battleships under Admiral Hugh Rodman arrived in Britain, they joined the British Grand Fleet and operated as its Sixth Battle Squadron under Admiral Sir David Beatty. Rodman told Beatty: "We are here and we put ourselves entirely at your command. We ask no favors or privileges. We want only to be one of you."

Sims, promoted in June to vice admiral and appointed commander of United States naval operations in European waters and naval attaché to Britain, established his headquarters in London, where by the end of the war his staff had expanded to two hundred officers and about one thousand enlisted men and occupied six residences near the United States Embassy. Officers and men were ordered not to criticize the "methods, manners and customs" of the Allies. Sims, not given the independence accorded Pershing, experienced more difficulty with Secretary Daniels and the Navy Department in Washington than from the British. Staff and command responsibilities were muddled. He was told that he was subordinate to the commander of the Atlantic Fleet, headquartered in Yorktown, Virginia, but that he was to continue direct correspondence with the Navy Department in Washington. He was frequently at odds with Admiral Benson and Secretary Daniels. During the course of the war he received not a single operational order from the commander of the Atlantic Fleet.

By the end of the war the United States had sent 373 vessels of all sorts to European waters, including eighty-five destroyers. Although American warships fired comparatively few shells they did accomplish what was, after all, their most important function: Seeing that Pershing's army arrived safely "Over There."

7

☆

THE WAR AT SEA:

GETTING THE ARMY
OVER THERE

IN SEPTEMBER 1917 Captain Willi Brüninghaus of the German Naval Office informed the German leaders that the U-boat war was progressing so well that any American troops arriving in Europe would be "naked so to speak," sans clothing, arms, equipment, or other supplies. He was in many respects correct, but American shortages were unrelated to the activities of U-boats. Blunders and ignorance on both sides of the Atlantic accounted for them.

One ship, which sailed into the harbor of St. Nazaire carrying as ballast three hundred tons of much needed steel, returned with the steel instead of sand in the lower hold. Another docked in New York with sand as ballast and sailed back to France still carrying the sand, leaving behind tons of much needed supplies. Some 14,000 tons of sawdust and shavings were shipped to France to insulate the great cold storage facility at Gièvres, landing not far from where forestry troops and saw mills were operating at top speed. Useless or nonvital material was sent in such quantities that Pershing cabled his recommendation that no further shipments be made of bath bricks, bookcases, spittoons, bathtubs, cabinets for blanks, floor wax, office desks, hose except fire hose, lawn mowers, stepladders, refrigerators, safes except field iron safes, settees, stools, sickles, and window shades.

Cargo ships, which usually had to wait to be fitted into a convoy, averaged seventy days for a round trip. In 1917 and early 1918 a shortage of docking facilities in France caused even longer delays. Pershing's staff officers, working furiously to obtain permissions to create others and then to obtain the needed materials, were blocked by French intransigence. There was a shortage of warehouses, and a shortage of stevedores until a number of black labor battalions landed. Even then it was found that most of their officers knew absolutely nothing about handling cargo.

Much of the confusion and the inefficiency was understandable considering the haste with which everything needed to be done. However, by June 1918, after General James Harbord had been placed in charge of the Services of Supply (SOS) the landing of men and supplies and their movement to the front or elsewhere was vastly improved and an average of 244 ships a week were being discharged.

Even before the submarine menace had abated, the transportation of troops to Europe began, but it was a trickle, for there were not nearly enough American ships. The British were aware of the shortage, for the Americans constantly pleaded for transport, which the Admiralty consistently refused to provide.

In a minute to the War Cabinet on 14 March 1918, Churchill made clear his concern that the Royal Navy and the Mercantile Marine were not devoting enough effort to the transportation of American troops. Addressing not only the military but the political need, he wrote: "Quite apart from the imperious military need, the intermingling of British and American units on the field of battle and their endurance of losses and suffering together may exert an immeasurable effect upon the future destiny of the English-speaking peoples, and will afford us perhaps the only guarantee of safety if Germany emerges stronger from the war than she entered it."

Finally, General William Robertson, Chief of the Imperial General Staff, implied in talks with Americans that more ships could perhaps be provided if the troops transported were assigned to British command. This bit of attempted blackmail revealed that more ships could be made available and they finally were, but not until early 1918. Then, although only a half million men were transported in the first thirteen months, about 1.5 million were transported in the last six months.

Of the 2,079,880 American troops sent to France, 952,581 sailed in American vessels or in seized enemy vessels, 1,006,987 in British ships, 68,246 in British-leased Italian ships, and 52,066 in French, Italian, and other foreign ships. By contract or purchase, other oceangoing ships were eventually acquired from other countries. The number of troops transported to France each month increased until July 1918, when a record 306,350 were transported.

The British, French, and others who supplied ships were not eleemosy-nary; the American government paid for every soldier transported in a for-eign vessel. The French made an attempt to charge for every man sent to fight for them as if he were a prewar passenger on a liner instead of a human sardine on a troopship. When the Americans refused to be gouged the price was reduced from $150 per man to $81.75.

The ninety-one German ships, totaling 592,195 tons, interned in American ports to which they had scurried when war was declared, were seized when the United States entered the war. Later, 40,461 tons of Austrian shipping were acquired. Some of the interned ships were rusty, rat-infested, barnacled hulks of little value, but others, such as the 54,000-ton *Vaterland*, the second largest ship afloat, were great prizes.

The crews of these ships, as instructed, destroyed or damaged much of the machinery, but the damages were repaired within a few months, thanks largely to the new electric welding process. Renamed, they carried 557,788 American troops to Europe. The *Vaterland*, rechristened *Leviathan*, the fastest of the transporters, was capable of sailing at a speed of 22.5 knots and sometimes made the run to France without an escort. In peacetime it had carried about 5,000 passengers and 1,000 crew mem-bers; as a troopship it carried a maximum of 12,000, sleeping them in tiered bunks, six to ten in a section. During the war it made ten trips and carried 96,804 troops; after the Armistice it brought 93,746 men home.

The Germans, capable of deploying only eight or ten submarines at a time in the eastern Atlantic, had to choose between preying upon cargo ships or transporters, equally important strategically. Each type traveled in a different sea lane; cargo ships, being more numerous and slower, sailed in narrower lanes. U-boat commanders found them easier to attack than the heavily guarded troop transporters. This was fortunate for, as General Harbord noted in his diary, if the Germans had succeeded in sinking "a troopship or two" and "a thousand or two American boys are drowned like rats" American enthusiasm for the war might have dissolved.

Most seemed to leave for the seat of war with a light heart. Poet Joyce Kilmer, who sailed with the 165th Infantry of the Rainbow Division wrote that on leaving port as the men "thronged the deck space available and looked at the lights along the fast receding shore, they showed a con-tentment, a mirth that amazed the crew, long accustomed to transport-ing troops."

Yet many must have been homesick. Miss Oleda Joure, a Signal Corps telephone operator, who had grown up in a small Michigan town, later confessed that aboard ship, "I realized that a person can be lonesome and homesick even among hundreds of strangers. At night I used to go up on deck and crawl underneath a lifeboat to cry out loud."

Not every soldier was dry-eyed. Private Donald Carey from Michigan recorded: "As we turned seaward and the land receded, I could not restrain a few tears at leaving the finest country on the globe, to meet a fate God alone could discern." Carey, who survived the war, was a member of the 339th Infantry, which was bound, not for France, but for Northern Russia to fight Russian Bolsheviks, not Germans.

On the night of 29 March 1918 Lieutenant Harry S. Truman sailed from New York on the *George Washington*, a packed troopship converted from a seized German luxury liner that later carried President Wilson to the peace conference. Truman shared a cabin with five other lieutenants. "We play cards awhile then go on deck and hunt submarines awhile and sleep the rest of the time except when we're on guard," he wrote. Laid low by sea sickness, he grumbled in his daily letters to Bess: "I can't see what a man wants to be a sailor for." The *George Washington* formed part of a convoy that safely zigzagged through the submarine danger zone to reach Brest on 13 April 1918.

Captain George C. Marshall, then a staff officer with the 1st Division, sailed on the *Tenadores*. He noticed that his assigned lifeboat, if launched, would pass over a section of the lower deck quartering several hundred black stevedores who in an emergency were expected to use such rafts as might be found in the water. Marshall was not surprised when at the first submarine alert they swarmed onto the upper deck to commandeer lifeboats.

In the spring and summer of 1918 many ships were so crowded that men had to sleep in shifts. Alexander Woollcott, former drama critic of the New York *Times* and now an army enlisted man, said his sleeping quarters at night reminded him of "the opium den scene in 'The Man Who Came Back.' "

An Iowa boy in the 168th Infantry on board the *President Grant* announced at his first sight of its crowded quarters: "I've eaten like a hog and maybe I've lived like one, but I'm damned if I've ever been crated."

Conditions on board the *President Grant* were indeed deplorable. The heads backed up and fresh water was in such short supply that unconscionable sailors sold it to the soldiers. An army medical officer, citing the "colossal ignorance and inefficiency of the naval officers," later declared, "This was, without doubt, the most unsanitary vessel of ancient or modern times." It was perhaps as well that the ship's boilers gave out and it turned back. Its passengers were transferred to a British ship where they briefly rioted when on Thanksgiving they were served the usual English rations.

Food was a source of constant complaint. T. F. Heath described his first breakfast on board: "I never thought such a small place could hold so many horrible smells—it stunk. The food was all steamed as there was no other means of cooking in the necessary quantities. Beans and soup were the only things that were at all edible—except the bread which was always good and fresh. . . ." Sergeant Ira Redlinger of the 1st Division complained that the food was "very bad," being "yellow corn meal and stew mostly." Private Donald Carey, who sailed on board an English ship, recorded: "The steam-cooked unseasoned stuff—rice, meal, potatoes and tripe—prepared by English cooks in their native manner was so unpalatable and sickening that I ate little during the voyage." He found the oatmeal without sugar or cream "particularly nauseating."

The crossing normally took twelve days and there was usually little to keep the troops occupied. However, quarters had to be kept clean, lifeboat drills were held, and soldiers were posted as lookouts for submarines. After the first convoy, which was heavily but unsuccessfully attacked by U-boats, the navy shortened its watches to one-half hour and assigned each lookout a limited area of vision indicated by a dial with orders to keep his eyes only on his segment of the ocean, even if a torpedo was sighted in another. Father Francis Duffy of the largely Irish 165th Infantry heard a ship's officer challenge one of them. "What are you staring at, soldier?"

"Lookin' fer somthin' Oi don't wan ter foind," he replied.

The speedy Leviathan had only one brush with a U-boat. At 12:29 P.M. on 30 May 1918, while on its fourth voyage, a submarine was spotted and fired upon. Soldiers crowded on deck and cheered each shot. The ship's history records that "The Army nurses left their luncheon to take a peek at the 'fun,' and their calmness and enthusiasm were an inspiration to the sailors manning the big guns."

The winter of 1917–18 was exceptionally cold in Europe and stormy on the Atlantic. Sergeant Ira Redlinger wrote that he and many others got "six meals a day—three down and three up." Among the unpleasant duties were "puke details" in which men went about with "a small bucket and a piece of tin . . . scooping up retchings" and emptying the buckets in the ship's coal bins. T. F. Heath wrote "I became violently sea sick and stayed so from two days out, the trip took 14. The whole thing was nothing more than a night mare [*sic*] after that." Everett Scott, an Iowa farmer, wrote home: "We seen a lot of interesting things on our trip, and a lot I never want to see again." Private Clayton K. Slack from Madison, Wisconsin, said, "We'd had all the boat ride we wanted."

Bill Halsey, of later fame in World War II, commanded destroyers escorting troopships and wrote in his diary: "You look at them [the troops] and pity them having to go to the trenches. Suppose they look at you and wonder why anyone is damn fool enough to roll and jump around on a destroyer."

Influenza proved more deadly than submarines; 5,027 sailors died of respiratory diseases—more than twice as many as died from enemy action. On the thirty-eight ships that sailed during the height of the influenza epidemic some 15,000 soldiers were stricken; many developed pneumonia and about 700 died. Crowding on board transports was reduced by ten percent, but troops continued to be shipped out, for death rates in the camps in the United States were as high as those on board ships.

On the afternoon of 29 September 1918 the *Leviathan* sailed from New York carrying 9,000 troops and a crew of 2,500. By morning the entire ship's hospital was full. A troop compartment converted into a hospital with two hundred cots was immediately filled. Two more compartments, holding four hundred cots each, were opened. The eleven doctors on board could do little. On the third day out the first death occurred.

Infected men were scattered throughout the ship and it was impossible to quarantine them. An officer reported the scene below decks on the night of 1 October: "Men in upper bunks would lean over the edge and spit or vomit without restraint, the ejected matter usually covering the men in the bunks below. Pools of blood . . . were scattered throughout the compartment, and the attendants were powerless to escape tracking through this mess because of the narrow passages between bunks. Everyone called for water and lemons or oranges." There was plenty of fruit, but "within a few minutes . . . the skins and pulp were added to the blood and vomit upon the decks. The decks became wet and slippery; the filth clung to the clothing of the attendants; groans and cries of the terrified sick added to the confusion of the applicants clamoring for treatment, and altogether a true inferno reigned supreme."

The troops on board, most of whom came from the mountain regions of Tennessee, had been in the army only a short time and were undisciplined. The healthy adamantly refused to enter the holds to clean up the mess or even to remove the sick, leaving these unpleasant tasks to the crew. The death rate climbed steadily until ninety-one deaths were recorded; others died soon after being carried off at Brest.

Bad as conditions were on the troopships, they were infinitely worse on board the ships carrying horses and mules. A sergeant in the 42nd Division left a record of his experience on board a ship out of Norfolk, Virginia, carrying 1,600 horses and mules. The ship encountered rough weather: "The mountainous waves rolled us around like a ball. The horses in housings on the top deck were thrown all over the deck. . . . The screaming and yelling of the animals was pitiful. . . . There were 250 dead animals lying around. We tossed them over the side. . . . When we arrived at Saint-Nazaire [and] started to unload our animals it was just a little more than some of them could take. They went down the gangplank onto the dock, let out a heehaw, and dropped dead."

Nearly eighty-three percent of the escort vessels for the transporters were American. Most troopships were guarded by the Cruiser and Transport Force commanded by Vice Admiral Albert Gleaves, sixty years old when the war ended. His proud boast was that no American soldier had been killed by enemy action while under the protection of his ships and that there had been no unfortunate accidents. The crews, he said, had to be as familiar with safety regulations "as with the Lord's Prayer."

There were losses at sea, however, although not on Admiral Gleaves' watch. Although every soldier who crossed "the big pond" experienced a submarine scare, no outward-bound troopships were sunk. Returning ships were not so lucky. The first such loss was the transport *Antilles*, torpedoed on its return voyage on 17 October 1917. Sixty-seven men were killed, including sixteen army enlisted men; the *Tuscania* went down on 5 February 1918 off the coast of Ireland with a loss of 113 lives, including thirteen men of the 32nd Division; fifty-six men of the 4th Division were killed when the *Moldavia* was hit; 215 soldiers and sailors went down in the animal transporter *Ticonderoga*. Overall, fewer than 700 casualties were due to enemy submarines.

On 31 May 1918 the *President Lincoln*, 500 miles from land on its return voyage, was sunk by the U-90 with a loss of three officers and twenty-three enlisted men. The submarine surfaced and picked up Lieutenant Edouard Victor M. Isaacs as a prisoner, leaving his fellow survivors floating on rafts and lifeboats, singing popular favorites: "Over There," "Keep the Home Fires Burning," "Hail, Hail, the Gang's All Here," "Where Do We Go From Here, Boys," to keep up their spirits. At 11 P.M. two destroyers arrived to rescue them and carry them to Brest. On the way the U-90 was spotted and twenty-two depth charges were dropped, five exploding near it. Lieutenant Isaacs, the unwilling passenger, found that he harbored mixed feelings.

Isaacs was treated well on board the U-90, but at Wilhelmshaven he was turned over to the army and taken to Karlsruhe and later to Villingen. He tried several times to escape, once throwing himself from a speeding train, for which he was given two weeks' solitary confinement. It was not until October that he was successful and after many trials and terrors finally swam across the Rhine to Switzerland. A few days later he was giving details of what he had learned about German submarines to intelligence officers when the Armistice was signed. Four weeks after his escape he was in Washington, where he received the personal congratulations of Secretary Daniels.

8

☆

THE AEF ARRIVES OVER THERE

ON 24 MAY 1917, just before General Pershing sailed for France, Secretary Baker took him to the White House for his only meeting with President Wilson during the course of the war. Pershing anticipated a discussion of such major problems as to whether or not American units should be or could be amalgamated with Allied forces, but Wilson simply said, "You shall have my full support." In the event, Wilson's support consisted of not interfering with Pershing and not sacking him as the Allies pressured him to do.

Pershing and General Harbord, his chief of staff, drew up some general instructions regarding their mission. These were approved, but just before sailing, Pershing received from Baker a more detailed set of orders. Wilson, who never considered the United States one of the Allies, always referred to Britain, France, Italy, and Japan as "associates." In line with this thinking, Pershing was now specifically directed to maintain a separate independent army: "In military operations against the Imperial German Government you are directed to co-operate with the forces of the other countries employed against the enemy; but in so doing the underlying idea must be kept in view that the forces of the United States are separate and distinct components of the combined forces, the identity of which must be preserved. This fundamental rule is subject to such minor exceptions as particular circumstances or your judgment may approve. The action is confided in you and you will exercise full discretion in determining the manner of co-operation."

On 28 May Pershing, with his staff and headquarters personnel, boarded tugs that took them to the *Baltic*, a British White Star liner. All 187 were in mufti except thirty who had not got the word. It scarcely mattered. The attempt at secrecy was a failure, much to Pershing's annoyance. For two days boxes plainly marked "General Pershing's Headquarters" sat on Pier 60 in New York for all to see, and now, as they were leaving, an artillery salute was fired from Governor's Island.

Among Pershing's entourage were forty regular army officers, including First Lieutenant George S. Patton, Jr., whose sister, Anne ("Nita") Patton, was then Pershing's fiancée; there were seventeen reserve officers and sixty-seven enlisted men, including a famous automobile racer Sergeant Edward V. Rickenbacker (his name newly anglicized from Reichenbacher), who was now Pershing's chauffeur. The remainder were civilians, clerks, and interpreters. Three newsmen were aboard, one of whom was Frederick Palmer, whom Teddy Roosevelt had called "our best war correspondent." Pershing soon persuaded Palmer to exchange his reporter's pencil for a blue one, and he donned a uniform as a major to serve as a press censor. Pershing and his staff made up most of the passenger list, but also on board were an opera star and two or three actresses from a British theatrical company who in the evenings sometimes entertained their fellow passengers.

They were vaccinated on board and during the day the staff studied French, discussed their coming duties with Pershing, and lectured to each other. British Colonel F. K. Puckle of the Army Service Corps was on board and spoke of logistical problems. Dr. Hugh Young, a former professor at Johns Hopkins and a specialist in venereal diseases, gave what General Harbord described as "several rather terrifying lectures on his specialty." Being an old soldier had its disadvantages Harbord noted in his diary: "Officers whose lives have been spent in trying to avoid spending fifteen cents of Government money now confront the necessity of spending fifteen millions of dollars—and on their intellectual and professional expansion depends their avoidance of the scrap heap."

After ten days at sea the *Baltic* docked in England. Reporters were not allowed to mention the name of the port, but Floyd Gibbons of the Chicago *Tribune* cabled that Pershing was given a "hearty welcome by the Mayor of Liverpool." They were greeted by the 3rd Battalion of the Royal Welch Fusiliers and their mascot, a goat, and were reminded that the regiment had fought against the Americans at Bunker Hill and Yorktown and had fought by their side in China during the Boxer Rebellion.

Pershing and his party boarded a train to London and as he stepped from it at Euston Station reporter Heywood Broun thought that, "No man ever looked more the ordained leader of fighting men." The Americans stayed at the Savoy. There were briefings, teas, a play one evening, and church services on Sunday at Westminster Abbey. Pershing met King George V, David Lloyd George, General Sir John French, General Jan Smuts, Field Marshal Sir William Robertson, and a host of other luminaries. The young minister of munitions, Winston Churchill, impressed him as being "unusually well informed on American affairs."

From Admiral Sims, he learned of the perilous conditions on the high seas and of Britain's refusal to supply enough ships to transport the AEF to France. Shipping was that without which nothing else was possible, but if the rate of losses could not be reduced, the war would be lost before an American soldier could fire a shot. Without British aid it would take two and one-half years for existing American ships to bring over 900,000 men.

On 13 June Pershing and his party were off to France, where their first greeting came from a small boy wearing a red liberty hat and wooden shoes who, from the outer edge of a breakwater at Boulogne shouted, "Vive l'Amérique!" Pershing, standing on deck, raised his hand to his hat.

Again they were met by dignitaries, then whisked by train to Paris where they were overwhelmed by cheering crowds throwing flowers. Pershing saw it as "a spontaneous outburst of joy over the evidence of support from a nation whose traditional friendship was sincere and unselfish." But he knew that the handful of soldiers he brought was far from being an American army, which had yet to be raised.

In Paris Pershing, with his inspector general, chief of staff, adjutant general, and personal aides, stayed at a magnificent mansion of more than forty rooms at 73 rue de Varenne turned over for their use by Mr. Ogden Mills, a rich American lawyer who was to become secretary of the treasury in 1932–33.

Pershing's first days in the city were filled with social engagements, meetings with political and military leaders, and ceremonial visits to the Senate, the Chamber of Deputies, and the tombs of Lafayette and Napoleon. At Les Invalides an old veteran in charge of Napoleon's personal effects held out the emperor's sword for him to touch. Pershing hesitated a moment and then, bending from the waist, kissed the revered relic. Thought stiff and cold by many, he had a sense of high drama. As Harbord recorded: "The story was told in every bivouac and barracks in France, and ran through the drawing-rooms of the capital like a bulletin from the Grande Armée."

He was soon giving and receiving warmer kisses. On the day of his arrival in Paris he was introduced to Micheline Resco, a twenty-three-year-old Rumanian-born, naturalized French citizen and a talented artist whom the French government had commissioned to paint portraits of war heros and leaders. She had already painted Admiral Sims, and had now been asked to paint Pershing. He consented and soon his engagement to Nita Patton was forgotten. By July he was writing "Michette" affectionate letters; by September they were lovers.

On 16 June Pershing and members of his staff visited the French General Headquarters at Compiégne where, peering through a telescope from an artillery observation post two miles behind the lines, he saw a portion of the Western Front opposite St. Quentin. He made no comment. On the same day he met General Henri Philippe Pétain who, while welcoming him, gloomily remarked, "I hope it is not too late."

Indeed, the situation in Europe was cause for gloom. The Russian revolution, presager of the end of Tsarist rule and the collapse of Russian armies facing Germany, had erupted. Except at Verdun, every German offensive had been successful. The Austrians, with German help, saw promise of defeating Italy, and German submarines seemed likely to bring Britain to her knees.

Overoptimistic hopes had been placed upon an offensive planned by French General Robert Nivelle, who had succeeded Joffre as Commander-in-Chief of the French Armies of the North and Northeast. Nivelle had boasted that, "We shall break the German front at will, provided we do not attack it at its strongest point, and provided that we carry out our operations by means of surprise and sudden attack, in from twenty-four to forty-eight hours."

The offensive was not a complete failure. In ten days (16–25 April) the French took some seventy square miles of territory, captured 28,815 prisoners and 183 guns at a cost of about 187,000 casualties, but they did not effect the war-winning breakthrough that Nivelle had so vaingloriously promised. Indeed, their modest gains were such a far cry from the glorious victory soldiers and civilians had been led to expect that French morale, ever volatile, plummeted. Indeed, most of the French army mutinied.

Nivelle was replaced by Henri Philippe Pétain, the hero of Verdun and France's most popular soldier—but not soon enough. The French army was broken and fast disintegrating as a fighting force. On 5 May soldiers of a French division ordered into the line refused to march. Their desperate officers finally rallied them and they fought without discredit, but as Churchill said, "It was the first drop before the downpour."

Throughout May and June of 1917 there were widespread breakdowns of discipline. Mutinies flared in sixteen army corps, drawing into them some of the finest troops. Of the French army's 112 divisions, sixty-eight were mutinous—or as the French preferred to say, suffered from "collective indiscipline"—and on the front from Soissons to Rheims only two divisions could be considered trustworthy. In some divisions soldiers, emulating the Bolsheviks, formed councils. Some regiments marched off toward Paris. Trains were burned, trucks were overturned. Desertions increased. In 1916 only 8,924 men had deserted; by mid-June 1917, a forecast of 30,000 was made.

As British historian John Terraine has pointed out, "The mutinies were not against the war; they were not a rejection of the necessity of fighting Germany. They were a passionate protest against stupidity, incompetence and indifference, against bad food, sour wine, miserable pay, inadequate leave, dreadful discomfort, shirkers and profiteers, against fire-eating generals who threw away lives in futile 'stunts' for the sake of *la gloire.*"

Defeatism swept through a significant number of civilians, including politicians, some of whom demanded peace at any price. Pacifist agitation doubled. By the end of June 170 strikes or work stoppages had erupted. By the end of the year this figure rose to 689 and involved 293,000 workers. Street demonstrations were often swelled by deserters. On 6 November President Raymond Poincaré wrote in his diary: "There is everywhere, in the Parisian population, and in the Chambers, a wave of illness. The 'defeatists' win more ground every day . . . suspect miasmas float in the air."

It took the stalwart efforts of Pétain, to calm the mutinies and return the soldiers to their duty. He visited ninety of his divisions by car. Often standing on the hood, he gathered men about him, and spoke to them, promising more furloughs, better living conditions, the construction of rest camps, and the dismissal of incompetent officers. He followed through on his promises and he issued a series of "trench pamphlets" to counter the leftist literature which was being distributed to the troops.

The government clamped a strict censorship on the press, suppressing some journals; 1,700 troublemakers were jailed. Of the more than 100,000 soldiers involved in the mutiny, 23,385 were tried and convicted of "grave collective indiscipline"; 412 were condemned to death. Only twenty-three are known to have been executed by firing squads; others were believed to have been shot out of hand.

In the spring of 1916 Russia had agreed to send 400,000 troops to France to fight on the Western Front, but the revolution cut short this venture and only about 10,000 arrived. Badly treated by the French and influenced by the events at home, they became aggressively Bolshevik. The French threatened to turn their artillery on them, disarm them, and place them under guard behind the French lines.

Curiously, German intelligence failed to discover French vulnerability. In the United States Secretary Baker and senior American officers were aware of the mutinies, but the extent of their information is unknown. The American public was kept in the dark.

The first substantial American units to arrive in France were the 1st and 2nd divisions. Although these were supposed to be regular army units, both were composed largely of volunteers and conscripts. The 1st Division, formed in late May 1916 from regular army units sent to the Mexican border, had been gutted and its training schedules ruined in the search for instructors, mechanics, typists, teamsters, and other specialists. Its regiments, which at that time contained only about 700 men, were reduced to half this number as trained men were siphoned off to train others; their numbers were then raised to 2,000 by adding recruits. In mid-July 1917 the division's commander, Major General William Seibert, reported to Pershing: "Over fifty percent of the soldiers in the division are recruits almost without training." Although it had a few good and experienced staff officers, most of its captains, lieutenants, and junior noncommissioned officers had seen at most one or two years' service, and many considerably less.

On 26 June 1917, some 15,000 men of the 1st Division began disembarking from passenger liners and "banana boats" at St. Nazaire, France. Untrained, unsophisticated, undisciplined, and boastful they arrived singing:

> Good-bye Maw! Good-bye Pa!
> Good-bye mule with yer old hee-haw . . .
> I'll bring you a Turk an' a Kaiser too,
> And that's about all one feller can do . . .

Henry Russell Miller, who served in the division's ranks, later summed it up: "Physically it was less impressive than any other outfit I have ever seen. In intelligence it was probably a little below the American average, in education certainly. It spoke a dozen languages and, I have no doubt, maltreated all as sadly as it did its own. Its manners were atrocious, its mode of speech appalling, its appetite enormous, its notions of why we were at war rudimentary."

Describing the landing of the 2nd Battalion of the 16th Infantry, Wilbur Forest of the United Press reported: "Before the troops had been formed into companies and marched to a prepared camp of tents and barracks on the outskirts of the port, they had flirted with every bit of femininity, staged impromptu crap games on the sidewalks surrounded by puzzled natives, and investigated every shop and café."

They were "not soldiers," he wrote. Their uniforms "shrieked of newness. Tunics wrinkled over the chest, trousers were ill-fitting, and puttees showed a lack of skill in winding." They were, however, young, strong, and healthy. Pershing called them "sturdy rookies."

Raw and unsightly though they were, Pershing ordered that some be sent to Paris for a parade on the 4th of July. Although their marching left much to be desired, three companies and the regimental band of the 16th Infantry were selected and after a cramped fifteen-hour overnight train ride arrived at the Gare d'Austerlitz. There was no time for breakfast or a wash, but young French Red Cross women poured them hot coffee with rum and they marched off to a tumultuous welcome. Major Frederick Palmer observed that "they did not know how to keep step and which is the business end of a rifle and that when you march in a column of fours this does not mean three's and two's." One bystander snorted, "If this is what we may expect from America, the war is lost." Nevertheless, the regimental band, joined by the band of the French 230th Territorial Regiment at the Place de la Concorde, played lively tunes and the men wended their way through cheering, flower-throwing throngs composed mostly of women, children, and old men who seemed to care little for marching abilities. One old first sergeant, a veteran of the Spanish-American War, boasted that he had been kissed by "five thousand of the handsomest dames I ever saw." They were, as one reporter put it, "engulfed in a sea of ecstasy."

They marched—or at least progressed—from Les Invalides to Picpus Cemetery, where the Marquis de Lafayette lies buried. Will Irwin, correspondent for the *Saturday Evening Post*, found himself "arm in arm with a stolid Indian of the 16th Infantry." Along both edges of the flower bedecked column, he reported, "a benevolent riot was proceeding." Pershing wrote: "With wreaths around their necks and bouquets in their hats and rifles, the column looked like a moving flower garden." At the cemetery, Charles E. Stanton, a quartermaster lieutenant colonel, who was, as Pershing said, "somewhat of an orator," announced, "Lafayette, we are here!" words later attributed to Pershing himself, who called it a "striking utterance" and one he wished had been his.

When the parade was over, Private Merle Hay, unlike most of his comrades, did not set out to explore the delights of Paris but returned to that portion of the old Pipincerie Barracks assigned to the Americans. There he found that his battalion had been given a lion cub as a mascot; a company cook was feeding it and "stroking it like a kitten." Hay did not know how to describe the great parade, the speeches, the cheering crowds, but writing laboriously in pencil, he sat on his bunk and told his mother about the lion cub.

On 10 July the men of the 1st Division moved by train to a training area near Gondrecourt-le-Château, a village eighteen miles south-south-west of Commercy, making their first acquaintance with the small French boxcars all marked *Hommes 40, Chevaux 8*, indicating that they could carry forty men or eight horses. Passing through the towns and villages some noted the many women in mourning and the few unwounded men. Arrived at their destination, they found, in place of the unprepossessing but clean barracks with flush toilets and showers they had known at home, equally unprepossessing but dirty French barracks offering holes in the floor for toilets. With not enough room for all, the men were scattered about, as one complained, "in hay lofts, cow barns, chicken coops, etc. Dirty lousy men. Every night it seemed as though a thousand chicken lice were crawling over me." Men shared a near-universal conviction that the French were a filthy people who lived amid manure piles and relieved themselves in public. An ambulance driver arriving at Brest and seeing the *pissoirs* wrote of "our shocked horror at the frankness of its public sanitary conveniences."

When the 2nd Division landed, it proved no better trained and equipped than the 1st. It was unique in that its infantry was composed of half regular soldiers and half marines, but 87.2 percent of the soldiers and 74.3 percent of the marines were recruits with less than one year's service.

Leo J. Bailed, a private in Company M, 9th Infantry debarked in early September 1917. He, like the rest of his company, had never fired a Springfield rifle. Few had ever fired a firearm of any description. As he had no scabbard, Bailed's bayonet was wrapped in newspaper. He had been issued ten rounds of ammunition and was eager to fight the Germans, but as he later wrote, "To have sent us to the front at that time would have been murder; but we were all willing to go. We were woefully ignorant of the basic principles of a soldier."

By the end of the war the 2nd Division was to suffer the most killed (2,419), the most wounded (20,657), and to have made the most captures (12,026).

On 6 September Pershing moved out of Paris and made his headquarters in a large old four-storied barracks at Chaumont, a town with a population of about 15,000 in northeastern France 140 miles east-southeast of Paris, at the confluence of the Marne and Suize rivers. In 1814 the victorious great powers had met here; now Pershing's staff made the room in which the fate of Napoleon had been decided their officers' club.

Wherever they were, American soldiers made friends with the local children, who begged for "biskwee" (hardtack) and were introduced to chewing gum. Private Ben H. Bernheisel remembered, "The small French children about our quarters had learned our drill quite well. . . . Their leader would give the commands in fine English, not omitting the profane. It was really a show to watch them."

At Christmastime, at the suggestion of Lieutenant Colonel Benjamin F. Cheatham, a collection was taken up and 35,000 francs were raised. A committee was sent to Paris to "buy out the town" and the doughboys gave the children of Gondrecourt and of the surrounding villages in which they were quartered an American Christmas, complete with Christmas trees, a Santa Claus, fruit, nuts, candy, and toys. Some three hundred French and Belgian refugee children were each given a complete outfit of clothing.

Newsman Floyd Gibbons watched the soldiers passing out gifts to the children of St. Thiébault and rhapsodized: "Our men learned to love the French people. The French people learned to love us." If it was so, it was a short affair and quickly dissipated. Men were soon complaining that cafe owners were overcharging them and selling them polluted wine at high prices. Lieutenant Harry S. Truman grumbled that French merchants "skin us alive. Our dinners cost us 10 francs apiece, about $1.80 so you see that things are not so cheap."

The first National Guard units to be sent to France were the 26th and 42nd divisions. The 26th, originally from New England and known as the "Yankee" Division, began to arrive in late September 1917 but it did not complete its movement until 2 January 1918. Initially filled with "skilled mechanics and office men" who were "acquaintances and friends," it had been, like all divisions, filled up with volunteers and conscripts. It was a division generally contemptuous of the regular army. Its commander, Major General Clarence R. Edwards, although a West Pointer, was often accused by his colleagues of having adopted too many "National Guard ways."

The 26th was to be one of the most active American divisions on the Western Front, spending more days at the front (205) than any other except the 1st Division (223) and more days in battle (forty-five) than even the 1st (twenty-eight). By the end of the war it had fought in seven major engagements, captured 3,000 prisoners, and liberated 37 kilometers of territory.

The 42nd was a unique division formed to placate senior National Guard officers and governors of states who from the beginning had pestered the War Department to send their troops to France. Formed of units from twenty-six states and the District of Columbia, its four infantry regiments, renumbered the 165th, 166th, 167th, and 168th, came from New York, Iowa, Alabama, and Ohio. Its commanders and higher staff officers were named by the War Department. The first of its four wartime divisional commanders, Major General William A. Mann, a 1876 graduate of the United States Military Academy, had seen service in the Sioux insurrection in 1890–91, the Spanish-American War, the pacification of the Philippines, the Cuba occupation in 1906–07, and service on the Mexican border in 1916.

Numbered among its members were men who were, or were to become, famous: poet Joyce Kilmer; William "Wild Bill" Donovan (the future head of the OSS, and later the CIA); Father Francis Duffy, the war's most famous chaplain; Wilber M. Bruckner (future governor of Ohio); Playwright Charles MacArthur, who later married actress Helen Hayes; Olin Johnson (future governor, later senator from South Carolina); Charles P. Summerall, a future chief of staff; and World War II General of the Army Douglas MacArthur. At a press conference MacArthur, then a major, always a man with a gift for words, compared the division's structure to that of a rainbow spanning the continent. A reporter present dubbed it the "Rainbow Division" and the name stuck.

Strong regional differences, real or perceived, and a pronounced gap between the educated and the uneducated were to ruffle the Rainbow. Unit feuds broke out among soldiers from different parts of the country and from different backgrounds. The 167th Infantry from Alabama and the 165th from New York viewed each other with considerable antipathy. Fights were frequent; in one an Alabama soldier was killed. Father

Francis Duffy, chaplain of the 165th, referred to the melee as "a small family row at Camp Mills."

The 165th Infantry, formerly the 69th New York National Guard, preferred to be known as the "Fighting 69th." It was initially a largely Irish-American regiment from New York City, although, as Father Duffy admitted, many of its men had Polish, Italian, German, or other non-Irish family names: "They were Irish by adoption, Irish by association or Irish by conviction," he said, including Sergeant Abe Blaustein, who won the *Croix de Guerre*. It possessed a peculiar distinction, what Father Duffy called a "board of trustees," civilians at home who collected funds to supply it with luxuries unavailable to other regiments. It had served on the Mexican border, but, like other regiments, by the time it reached France most of its members were conscripted recruits.

The division, the first full-strength National Guard division to arrive in France, left the United States from American and Canadian ports in October 1917. Ironically, the 167th Regiment from Alabama was shipped out on the USS *President Grant*. Made up largely of young men from rural areas who had escaped what were then common childhood diseases, it landed in England with 600 cases of mumps and was at once quarantined.

On 10 November Colonel Fox Conner, G-3 (operations) at AEF Headquarters, issued a memo recommending that the 42nd Division be broken up and used as a replacement division, scattering the men among units suffering losses from wounds and diseases. Throughout the war American replacements were acquired by the inefficient practice of breaking up existing units. The reason is revealing: Early in the war Baker had decided against training centers for replacements because, he later explained, "the country at the outset would have been shocked to discover how large we thought the losses were likely to be."

When the proposed fate of the 42nd Division became known there was an instant furor. General Mann protested to Pershing, telling him that the division "had been a uniting force as the nation mobilized for war." Colonel Douglas MacArthur protested to General Harbord and, not satisfied with that, went over the heads of Pershing and the AEF staff and telegraphed Secretary Newton Baker: PERSHING INTENDS CHOP UP RAINBOW DIVISION FOR REPLACEMENTS STOP MEANS RUIN OF CRACK DIVISION TRAINED TO WORK AS A TEAM AND DESTROY MORALE OF TROOPS PROUD OF BEING RAINBOW MEN STOP PROMPT ACTION TO SAVE THE DIVISION SPONSORED BY PRESIDENT WILSON HIMSELF MACARTHUR. Many of the division's officers, politically connected National Guardsmen, wrote to friends back home and a flood of protest in letters and cables arrived at Chaumont and Washington. The War College advised the army chief of staff not to break up any National Guard divisions, particularly the much publicized 42nd. General Harbord concluded that the "division commander is an inactive man but an active politician." Pershing wisely decided to drop this hot potato, but he resented the affront to his authority, for which he blamed Mann and MacArthur, and he was not a forgiving man. The division retained its identity but found its supplies diverted to other units. On 15 December 1917 he relieved Mann of his command and saw him returned to the United States, where he reverted to his former rank of brigadier general. He was replaced by Major General Charles T. Menoher, a classmate of Pershing's. When MacArthur was recommended for promotion to brigadier general, Pershing disapproved it, but MacArthur's mother so lobbied Washington that General Peyton March, the chief of staff, approved the promotion. MacArthur, willing to think that he owed his promotion to Pershing, wrote him a fulsome letter of thanks.

Inexorably, the 42nd, like all other divisions, was temporarily broken up for training. The artillery, still without serviceable weapons, was sent to Coëtquidan in Brittany. The infantry was sent to Vaucouleurs, about seventy-five miles northeast of Chaumont, where awaiting them were a large number of second lieutenants, most of whom were recently graduated "90-day wonders" from the new officer training schools. Later the infantry was dispatched to a second training area at Rolampont.

The journey to Rolampont was made in the *Hommes 40, Chevaux 8* French boxcars pulled by trains that did not make rest stops. One historian recorded how, "As these troop trains sped through the French towns and countryside the undraped posteriors of soldiers usually shone protruding from open doors with shirttails flapping in the breeze."

Major (later Colonel) "Wild Bill" Donovan, who was the first member of the division actually to fire a shot at the enemy, was exhilarated when on 26 December 1917 he entered a forward French trench and came under "shells and rifle fire for the first time." In his diary he wrote: "Curious but easily became accustomed to it. Got my first shot at a Boche. Missed at 1200 yards. . . . Germans attempted a raid, moonless, cloudless, snow, flashing signals, thundering noise all seen from a little knoll about 1 km away."

9

☆

FRANCE:

FIRST CASUALTIES

THE WINTER OF 1917–18 was the most severe of the war and the snow was unusually heavy in eastern France. In the newly arrived troops of the AEF clothing was in short supply, even boots for marching. Urgent appeals to Washington were rejected "owing to need for supply of troops in the United States." Soldiers at war could not be clothed as long as soldiers at home needed uniforms. This, at least was Pershing's view. Major Frederick Palmer referred to this period as the Valley Forge of the AEF.

Partial relief was found in an issue of British tunics which, while they resembled American issue, bore buttons with British devices. This so incensed the Irish-Americans in the 42nd Division, particularly the men of the 165th Infantry, that they set about burning them. Private First Class Albert Ettinger explained: "You cannot imagine the bitter feeling of the native-born Irish Catholic toward the English in those days; very bitter." Father Duffy was called to calm his charges until an officer could arrive from AEF headquarters with a box of buttons bearing the American eagle.

The marines, although part of an army division, cherished their buttons carrying the anchor, globe, and eagle. As their forest green uniforms wore out and were replaced with army khaki, each man carefully saved and transferred his buttons. As one said, "We kept our fierce self-conceit and pride."

Pershing, believing that discipline and pride were the cornerstones of victory, essential to morale and efficiency, set high standards: "Good discipline . . . in a command is an almost certain index of the character of performance in battle. Likewise, an officer or soldier who takes no pride

in his personal appearance is usually found careless in other respects and
to that extent less reliable in time of stress. It need hardly be added that
those of this class who came under my observation and who did not
immediately respond to suggestion were very soon replaced by others of a
different attitude."

Through his adjutant general he announced that "the standards of the
American Army will be those of West Point. The rigid attention, upright
bearing, attention to detail, uncomplaining obedience to instructions
required of cadets will be required of every officer and soldier of our
Armies in France."

The AEF had a long way to go to reach West Point standards. Captain
George C. Marshall noted a tall, rangy sentinel posted outside General
Sibert's office, his blouse unbuttoned and a watch chain across his chest
who, when a French general appeared and evinced an interest in his rifle,
cheerfully handed it over and sat down.

The French 47th Chasseur Division, known as the Blue Devils, was
assigned to train the raw American infantry and the doughboys got along
well with the "chasers," who taught them the intricacies of trench warfare
and the use of the French weapons they would be employing (Hotchkiss
machine guns and Chauchat automatic rifles). The French-made
Chauchat, Model 1917, which the Americans called "sho-sho," carried a
crescent-shaped magazine that held twenty rounds. It was cheap and easy
to manufacture, but it enjoyed the dubious distinction of being the least
reliable weapon of the war.

Pershing was not enthusiastic about French training. He reminded the
commander of the 42nd Division: "The training of American troops must
remain in the hands of American officers. Neither the French officers
sent to your division nor the French battalion commanders will be permitted by you to dictate methods of training, substitute programs for those
contemplated by these headquarters, or relieve American officers in any
way from the responsibility for the training of their units as prescribed in
the programs of training by these headquarters." His chief of the training
section, in a memo to the AEF chief of staff, reported that the French
were "entirely too dependent upon a powerful artillery support" and that
the British "lacked initiative and resource." A senior training officer concluded that, "An American army cannot be made by Frenchmen or
Englishmen."

Pershing particularly disapproved of the French training for trench
warfare, which he considered to be defeatist. American doctrine was

based upon the 1917 Field Regulations, an only slightly revised version of the 1911 version. Little attention was paid to machine guns or grenades. Fire superiority was to be obtained by accurate rifle fire and infantry rushes, a principle Pershing wholeheartedly endorsed. He believed that "victory could not be won by the costly process of attrition, but must be won by driving the enemy out into the open and engaging him in a war of movement."

Pershing's plan was quickly to burst through the German lines to open country: "All instruction must contemplate the assumption of a vigorous offensive. This purpose will be emphasized in every phase of training until it becomes a settled habit of thought." The Chasseurs were sent packing in September.

Major General Robert Lee Bullard, fifty-six, an 1885 graduate of West Point who had seen service in the Philippines and had written extensively on training and discipline, also had a low opinion of French tactics: "A French soldier never rests until he has dug a hole, and after that he never rests anywhere but in the hole." Nevertheless, until the German line was broken, trench warfare had to be learned.

As disdainful as he was of French training, Pershing lauded the skill of French cooks. Although the American rations were more generous and of better quality than the French or British, American army cooks were amateurs. According to Private First Class Alfred Ettinger of the 165th Infantry: "Our mess sergeant had been appointed because he was an inspector of markets in New York; the first cook had been a veterinarian; the second cook a Wall Street runner; and the third cook a hobo."

Marine Captain John W. Thomason watched French cavalry cooking beside a road. "For your Frenchman never fights without his kitchens and a full meal under his cartridge-pouches. They go into the front line with him, the kitchens and the chow, and there is always the coffee avec rhum and the good hot soup that smells so divinely to the hungry Americans passing empty." One marine grumbled that "them frawgs might at least have the decency to keep their home cookin' where we can't smell it."

The early months of 1917 were devoted not only to training, but to weeding out those senior officers unable to stand up to the hardships and pressures of modern war. General George B. Duncan, a brigade commander in the 1st Division, wrote: "This process of training resulted in the relief of some older officers and placing responsibility upon more ambitious youngsters."

There was also a general shaking up of the general staff and of commanders. It was decreed that every general officer must undergo a physical examination and this resulted in the retirement of several officers, most of whom were men in middle life, among them the brigadier general in charge of the Marine Brigade that included the 5th and 6th Marine Regiments. General James Harbord, although an army officer, was given command in his stead.

Before any more divisions sailed for France Pershing required that divisional commanders with their chiefs of staff be sent over and given a tour of the front to see for themselves the problems they would face. This also gave Pershing an opportunity to see what they were like. "The position of division commanders is so important that the success of this war depends upon them," he told Secretary Baker. Of the first batch to be sent over he declared half to be too old, physically unfit or not sufficiently mentally alert for combat duty. Indeed, some behaved like tourists. Of the thirty-two generals brought to Europe in late 1917 and early 1918, ten were rejected.

Major General Leonard Wood had been the army's most prominent and outspoken officer and was the American general best known to Europeans; many, including Wood himself, thought he should have been given command of the AEF. Instead, he was given a division and so made a one-month visit to Europe beginning in late December 1917. In talks with senior politicians and soldiers in both London and Paris he made disparaging remarks about Pershing and even about President Wilson, whom he called "that rabbit." He voiced grave doubts about Pershing's ability to command and he made much of the AEF's difficulties. General Tasker Bliss, who was in Europe as the military representative of "Colonel" Edward House's mission, cabled Secretary Baker that Wood "has done his best to discredit the United States here in Europe."

Wood seemed blithely unaware of the effect of his reckless talk and when criticized later was indignant. He had, he said, been "most careful to avoid anything which could be interpreted as criticism." Needless to say, he had made himself persona non grata in Pershing's army. Pershing not only pronounced him unfit for divisional command but reported that an earlier head injury had left him "seriously and permanently crippled." Baker called him "the most insubordinate general officer in the entire army."

Wood was stunned to learn that he was not to take his division to

France. General March told him candidly, "General Pershing most positively does not want you in France, and frankly, General Wood, I must state that if I were commanding general in France I should not want you, as I fear you would not be subordinate."

Wood asked for and received an interview with Wilson, but the president refused to become involved. He confided to a friend: "Wherever Wood goes there is controversy and conflict of judgement. . . . I have had a great deal of experience with General Wood. He is a man of unusual ability but apparently absolutely unable to submit his judgement to those who are superior to him in command." Exit General Wood. He sat out the war in the United States, a bitter, angry man.

Among those already in France Pershing weeded out Major General William L. Sibert, who had won distinction as an engineer in the construction of the Panama Canal. He had brought the 1st Division to France but Pershing's assessment of him was devastating: "slow of speech and of thought. . . . Slovenly in dress. . . . Without any ability as a soldier. Utterly hopeless as an instructor or tactician, fails to appreciate soldierly qualities, possessing none himself. . . . Opinionated withal and difficult to teach. He has a very high opinion of his own worth. . . ."

Pershing favored those he knew best and eleven division commanders were from his own West Point class. Of the 474 generals to serve with the AEF, about thirty percent were from the West Point classes of 1883–89, men whom Pershing would have known when he was there. Sibert was replaced by Major General Robert Lee Bullard, class of 1885, a man so tough that he thought Pershing "soft." Returned to the United States, Sibert was named director of the Chemical Warfare Service.

To train his staff Pershing established a General Staff College with a three-month course. In organizing his own staff he followed the French system and this was emulated by lower units in his army and with some modification is still in use. A chief of staff was assisted by a deputy and five major offices: G-1 (personnel), G-2 (intelligence), G-3 (operations), G-4 (supply), and G-5 (training). At the regimental and battalion level the staff functions were the same except that the letter G was replaced by S.

To provide logistical support he established a line of communication, officially named Services of Supply (SOS), with depots and ports, docks and trains, all under a single commander (originally General Francis J. Kerman), responsible only to him personally. The difficulties in putting this supply line in place and making it work were compounded by the necessity of dealing with French bureaucracies where differences in language, customs, and methods made every action trying. Pershing later wrote: "Although our own departments at home were considered rather adept in the use of red tape, yet . . . the art of tying things up in official routine was in swaddling clothes as compared to its development in France." Supply officers soon found themselves in competition with the French and British for the purchase of scarce resources.

Pershing was fortunate to have as a friend fifty-two-year-old Charles Gates Dawes, a lawyer, financier, and politician. In 1917 he was president of the Central Union Trust Company in Chicago, but he was commissioned a lieutenant colonel in the Corps of Engineers and sent to France to inspect French harbor facilities. Although he knew absolutely nothing about the army, General Harbord called him "the most outstanding civilian in the American uniform." Pershing considered him the most unmilitary of men, but knowing his abilities, he snatched him and made him his chief procurement officer. Dawes, his unmilitary manners forgiven, enjoyed wide discretion and enjoyed his work: "I feel as if I were exercising the powers of one of the old monarchs. To negotiate singlehandedly with governments comes to but few men." He managed to purchase ten million tons of supplies in Europe, saving that much cargo space on ships sailing from the United States. Except for small arms, almost all of the army's needs were supplied by Britain and France at exorbitant prices. Dawes paid whatever was necessary to get what Pershing needed. Later, when taxed with extravagance by a congressional committee, he exploded: "Damn it all, the purpose of an army is to win the war, not to quibble about a lot of cheap buying. We would have paid horse prices for sheep if they could pull artillery to the front. It's all right now to say we bought too much vinegar or too many cold chisels, but we saved the civilization of the world. . . . Hell and Maria, we weren't trying to keep a set of books. We were trying to win a war."

Dawes was one of the few men who seems to have had a genuine affection for Pershing, always referring to him as "a dear fellow." Most men who knew Pershing found him "easy to admire, but hard to like."

The War Department maddened Pershing by quibbling over his requisitions for supplies, or worse, simply ignoring them. When he warned that he would not have sufficient ammunition for the French 75 mm and 155 mm guns with which his division artillery was equipped, he was shocked and angered to be told, "the French Government must furnish it, for there is no other way of getting it. At the present time there is not in this country any actual output of ammunition of the types mentioned. None has been expected."

He had no more success when on 12 January 1918 he cabled the War Department of the need for forage for the 21,000 animals in service, saying that "35 percent of the animals have been on less than half rations of oats for 10 days and also on short rations of hay and some have died of starvation." The French refused to help, pleading their own shortage; many animals died as a result.

Added to its other problems was the necessity of coping with the French telephone system with its French-speaking switchboard operators. This proved a near impossible task. Before the war was over the Signal Corps was forced to string 22 miles of new wire and to recruit more than 200 young American women who spoke French to man the switchboards at major headquarters. The switchboard operators soon came to be known as the Hello Girls.*

Although the AEF suffered a shortage of all needed weapons, clothing, accoutrements, trained commissioned and noncommissioned officers, and much else, it was plentifully supplied with chaplains and Bibles. Chaplains were provided from the top echelons to the battalion level and, as Private Elton Mackin in France wrote bitterly: "We all had Testaments. A loving people back home in God's country issued them to us with many blessings—and sent us out to fight the Germans. They had not cared to see that we had the tools of war. We borrowed most of those. Christians are such charming people."

In the army's highest ranks dissension was in the air. Generals Pershing and March clashed frequently. In his memoirs Pershing wrote: "Up to this time we had been handicapped in our efforts by lack of aggressive direction of affairs at home. Whether this was due to inefficiency or failure to appreciate the urgency of the situation, the War Department General Staff, as the superior coordinating agency, must take the greater part of the blame." On 17 August 1918, writing directly to Secretary Baker, Pershing suggested that March should be replaced by an officer from his own staff. Baker ignored him.

French and British commanders entertained misgivings about each other. After meeting with Pershing, Haig wrote in his diary: "I was much struck with his quiet gentlemanly bearing—so unusual for an American. Most anxious to learn, and fully realizes the greatness of the task before

*See Appendix B.

him. He has already begun to realize that the French are a broken reed." Reflecting on this meeting, Pershing said: "His remarks entirely confirmed that I had long since held that teamwork between the two nations was almost totally absent."

However, the relations between the French and the British were not of primary concern to Pershing. On 21 October 1917 the infantry battalions of the 1st Division began their move, a battalion at a time, into trenches in the Sommerviller sector, east of Lunéville, about ten kilometers northeast of Nancy. Only a few days earlier the lion cub acquired in Paris, unable to withstand the rigors of winter in Lorraine, died of pneumonia.

There had been no fighting in the sector since the first days of the war. Captain Sidney C. Graves, commanding Company F, 16th Infantry, remembered that, "You could have stood on the parapet and hung up your laundry and so could the Germans when we came." But the Americans were not there to rest, nor merely to exist, difficult as this was. They were there to fight. "We really made them mad," Graves said.

Many men on duty for the first time as sentinels were understandably nervous as they stared across the dark no-man's-land. Private Quincy Sharpe Mills wrote home: "I shot six Germans sneaking up on me one night, and when daylight came they were all the same stump."

As Henry J. Reilly, the division's historian recalled: "The trenches were not quite like what the officers and men had expected to find. The front line was not always continuous." The French usually formed a *Groupe de Combat* (GC), commonly a self-sufficient combat unit surrounded by barbed wire. It was covered by machine guns and supported by artillery. Behind the GC was a *Poste d'Appui* (PA) that could support the GCs with machine gun, rifle, and mortar fire. Two or more PAs were supported by a *Centre de Resistance* (CR).

Throughout the war much was made of "firsts." On 22 October the 6th Field Artillery passed through what had been Lunéville, once one of the most beautiful cities in Lorraine, and took up positions near the now ruined town. From a former French gun position "one kilometer due east of the town of Bathelemont and 300 meters northeast of the Bauzemont-Bathelemont road" at 6:05 the next morning red-headed Sergeant Alexander L. Arch from South Bend, Indiana, pulled the lanyard of a French 75 in Battery C, firing the first AEF shell of the war at the Bavarians in the German lines. Journalist Floyd Gibbon, who was there, claimed the shell casing as a souvenir. The gun itself along with Sergeant Arch and his gunners was soon sent home to spur the sale of Liberty Bonds.

On 27 October 1917 the first German prisoner to fall into American hands was Leonard Hoffman, a handsome, blond, twenty-year-old mail orderly of the 7th Regiment of the 1st Landwehr Division, who was shot when he stumbled into the area of Company C, 16th Infantry. Although he survived an operation, he died in the hospital the next morning. His operating team realized belatedly that they should have had a photograph made of the historic occasion, so they wheeled his corpse back into the operating room, donned their gowns and masks, and a photographer exploded a tray of flash powder. The body was then buried behind the hospital.

On 28 October Lieutenant D. H. Harden, a reserve officer with the 26th Infantry, which was serving its first term in the trenches, was wounded in the knee by a shell fragment, becoming the first AEF officer to be wounded in the trenches. On the following day Private Ashburn of the 18th Infantry was hit by a shell fragment and was credited with being the first AEF enlisted man to be wounded, although that doubtful distinction probably should have gone to Sergeant Matthew Calderwoon and Private William Branigan of the 11th Engineers who were wounded by enemy artillery on 5 September 1917 while working with the British Third Army near the village of Gouzeaucourt.

Everyone knew that war meant men would be killed, but the AEF had not yet taken its place in the order of battle on the Western Front when Lieutenant William T. Fitzsimmons, a surgeon, became the first American killed in action. Tall and blond, the youngest in his class at Kansas University and at medical school, he was interning at Roosevelt Hospital in New York when the war began. He volunteered for the Red Cross and was shipped to a hospital at La Panne, Belgium, temporary seat of the Belgian government. His tour over, he had gone home to Kansas City and there set up practice as a surgeon, but on 14 June 1917, a Tuesday, he locked the door of his office in the Rialto Building and caught the 4:00 train to Chicago and thence one to Washington, D.C. He was soon on his way overseas as a "casual." Once in France he was assigned as adjutant of Base Hospital No. 5 south of Boulogne. He and a nurse, Louise McCloskey, appeared to be falling in love when he was killed at the door to his tent by a bomb from a German airplane. He was buried in the British Military Cemetery in the sand dunes between Dannes-Camiers and Étaples.

His family learned of his death when his sixteen-year-old sister opened the door of his parents' home to a reporter looking for photographs and "last letters."

In short order the first American shots had been fired, the first American had been wounded, an officer killed, and the first German captured. There had been, however, no serious fighting. It was the deaths in Artois of the first AEF enlisted men on the Western Front early in the morning of 3 November 1917 that brought the reality of war close to home. Within six hours of the arrival of the 16th Infantry the Germans laid down a barrage and 213 officers and men of the 7th Bavarian Landwehr Regiment made a lightening raid, killing three, wounding five, and taking eleven prisoner, the first of 4,434 to be captured.

The three who were killed were Corporal James Bethel Gresham, Private Merle D. Hay, and Private Thomas F. Enright, members of Company F, 2nd Battalion, 16th Infantry, the unit which had paraded in Paris on the 4th of July. It was the 2nd Battalion's first time in the trenches. The Bavarians lost two killed, seven wounded, and one man who seized the opportunity to desert.

Later that morning Captain George C. Marshall, then on the staff of the 1st Division, with French General Paul E. I. Bordeaux visited the battalion and talked with survivors and with the German deserter. General Bordeaux praised the Americans, saying they had "offered the utmost possible resistance."

Across the nation people took notice. The Chicago *Herald* carried an eight-column banner: HUNS KILL 3 PERSHING MEN. The engagement, it editorialized, was a little one. "The historians of the war will not notice it. It had no particular military significance." But in London the *Daily Mail* found it significant, for "never again will it be possible for Americans to think they have one set of interests and Europe another."

Every American seemed touched by the deaths of these three young men. In Indiana people struggled to find meaning in the life of Corporal Gresham: "He was an ordinary American with no distinction of high birth, scholarship, or social prestige . . . only an average American." *Life Magazine* published a poem by Christopher Morley:

> *Gresham and Enright and Hay!*
> *There are no words to say*
> *Our love, our noble pride*
> *For these, our first who died.*

The county commissioners of Allegheny County, Pennsylvania, asked that the body of Private Enright be repatriated so that he could be given a hero's funeral in his home town, but the War Department had determined that no bodies would be returned until after the war—not until 1921, in fact.

The Americans were learning their trade although the price was high. They, too, learned to make raids. A night patrol by the 167th Infantry from Alabama came to hand-to-hand fighting in the dark. Corporal Homer Whited was wrestling with a large German in the bottom of a German trench when Corporal Freeman came to his aid and raised his rifle to shoot, but in the struggle in the dark it was hard to tell friend from foe. "Homer, which is you?" he shouted.

10

☆

TRENCH WARFARE

THE FINAL STEP in training was actual experience in the trenches—ten-day tours on a quiet sector of the Front under French command. Not all of the fighting on the Western Front had been trench warfare, but most of it had been and continued to be, the trenches stretching in a great arc of about 470 miles from the North Sea to Bec de Canard on the Swiss border. They linked strong points, listening and observation posts, machine gun nests, snipers' pits, and each unit was connected with units on either side. Even the great forts at Verdun and Metz were supported by trenches.

There was, of course, nothing new about the use of field fortifications to defend positions, but in other wars trenches were, except in siege operations such as those at Sevastopol in the Crimean War, always temporary; slits in the earth to be used for a few days, possibly a few weeks. But even in siege operations men did not actually *live* in the trenches as was the case on the Western Front.

Trenches were dug, or ought to have been dug, at least five feet deep in a pattern resembling Greek fretwork or wavy lines. This limited the damage of a direct hit or, in case of an enemy attack, of an enemy machine gun firing down a trench. Each short section was called a bay. Duckboards covered the dirt floors. Although the narrower the trench the greater protection it provided, it had to be wide enough for at least two men to pass. Forward trenches had fire steps and parapets, usually reinforced by sandbags filled with earth. Behind the forward trenches—and these were in multiple lines with support trenches and then reserve trenches—were the communication trenches (underground roads, up and down which passed food, water, ammunition, medicines, supplies of all sorts, as well as the sick, wounded, prisoners, and dead), messengers, special patrols, staff officers, and wire layers. Near the trenches were aid stations where wounded received their first treatment, usually an antite-tanus shot and fresh bandages, perhaps a sedative.

These complexes in which millions of men lived and died have been compared to a vast underground city. Long-used trenches were often given names, complete with handmade street signs, some harking back to famil-iar places at home—Broadway or Piccadilly or Champs Elysées. Others bore names they had earned: Dead Dog Avenue or Suicide Corner.

Tens of thousands of miles of barbed wire, sometimes acres in depth, in concertinas and strung upon poles, protected the trenches. Metal poles resembling large corkscrews were developed so that they could be inserted into the ground without the telltale sound of pounding and without requir-ing men to stand erect. Often land mines were placed among the wire.

New wire had to be laid and old wire repaired at night. Even then, a flare might reveal the working parties to an alert enemy machine gunner. Before an infantry attack the enemy's wire had to be cut and gaps created in one's own wire.

The life of a soldier on the Western Front involved a vast amount of manual labor, mostly digging and carrying. Because trenches were living quarters, latrines had to be dug, provision had to be made for sleeping, and for some warmth in winter; dugouts had to be excavated for medical aid stations, orderly rooms, store rooms, etc.

The air was noisome. One soldier described it as "a reek of moldering rottenness." The wet and rotting sandbags of burlap had a pungent, unpleasant order. The stench of latrines was pervasive, and the effect of a high explosive (HE) shell making a direct hit upon a company latrine can be imagined. The most sickening of all was the odor of putrid corpses in the hot sun. The dead were a persistent presence. Many were buried where they fell, but were disinterred by artillery shells; others were left to rot in no-man's-land, it being too dangerous to attempt retrieval. The car-casses of dead farm animals often lay bloated and reeking. Worms and maggots grew fat on corpses. Vomiting recruits did not add to the plea-sures of trench life.

The infantrymen shared their quarters with other living creatures. Flies were thick in summer and rats knew no season. Corporal Adel wrote in a letter home: "Never in my life have I seen rats of such size as these are here. They don't run from us either, like any ordinary rat does. They will fight like good fellows when you fool with them." One veteran, years later, said: "Mud, lice and rats competed for pride of place in my memory." There were no facilities for washing and the unwashed, stinking soldiers acquired armies of lice and fleas, dubbed "cooties." They suffered from scabies and a liver ailment called Weil's disease for which rats were blamed, and from "trench fever," a kind of rickets transmitted by body lice and marked by fever and pain in joints, bones, and muscles. It was difficult for the simplest infection to heal. Gangrene was common.

Lieutenant Howard V. O'Brien wrote home: "The gilt chips off the glamour of soldiering pretty quick over here. Mail call and the quality of the mess become of deeper interest than the future of the world. . . ."

A great enemy, particularly in Flanders, was the all-prevailing mud, in places so deep that men actually drowned in it. Trenches filled with water, and men developed what was called "trench foot," a painful disorder resembling frost bite. Of every five men brought into casualty collection stations, three were unwounded but seriously ill. Even in relatively quiet sectors, battalions could expect to lose about thirty men per month from death or wounds and at least an equal number, usually more, through sickness.

Private Stephan Wildman of Thorndale, Texas, entered the trenches for the first time in August 1918 with the 360th Infantry; he found it "a real funny sensation . . . but I finally got used to it." The first two men in his regiment to die were killed by the accidental explosion of a hand grenade. Even in quiet sectors men faced desultory artillery fire. After only nineteen days in a quiet sector the 30th Division suffered ten dead, thirty-nine wounded, and one missing.

Regardless of the amount of training men received before going into the line, there was much that could only be learned in battle. For all it was mostly on-the-job training. It was not just the combat arms that had to learn how to cope with new weapons and tactics. Army doctors were presented with wounds such as they had never before seen and enlisted medical personnel had to learn how to evacuate wounded and gassed men under extraordinary conditions. In trenches it was difficult to maneuver a man on a stretcher. Walking wounded were sent back quickly to dressing stations, usually about a mile back, which could retain those not severely wounded. Others were sent back to field hospitals, many of them French, which, although most were still under German observation from enemy balloons and within enemy artillery range, could provide a higher level of care. A triage system took in those with the best chance of survival and made the rest comfortable. Many were sent to evacuation centers and from there to one of the base hospitals established throughout France and Britain. All now began to take in an increasing number of Americans and in the United States many more families learned of losses.

Lieutenant Hugh S. Thompson of Company K, 168th Infantry, in the 42nd Rainbow Division, always remembered his initial experience in the trenches. He reported to a captain in a dugout: "A muddy officer poured [*sic*] over papers on a candle-lit table. A chorus of snores came from a dark tier of bunks." The underground shelter "was heavy with sewer-like odors." He was told about the arrangements for distributing rations and water, about gas alarms and artillery barrages, then taken to his GC: "The sight that greeted us brought an immediate and positive reaction. 'Desolate' was the only name for it. A mass of rusty barbed wire was strung on crisscrosses of posts that seemed to grow from the ground. Ghost-like trees to the right were splintered with shell scars. Some had fallen into the mass of twisted wire and upturned earth. Others were broken off at various heights, like so many match sticks. The expanse of desolation stretched up a gentle rise. The German trenches were hidden behind the crest some 200 yards away." The sight of a French intelligence officer calmly rifling a reeking German corpse, examining its papers, proved too much. Overcome by nausea, the young lieutenant became violently ill.

Daily routine in the trenches began before dawn at a "stand to," when men stood ready to repel an attack, for dawn was a favorite time for attacks to be launched. Sometimes this was followed by a "morning hate," concentrated fire from each side. Breakfast followed. Food was usually plentiful, but canned and tasteless. (British officers sometimes had hampers of food sent to them from Paris or from Fortnum & Mason in London.) French soldiers were given an issue of cheap wine. After breakfast those off duty tried to sleep while others were occupied with fatigue duties. Some of the most grueling work was the mining and countermining, usually carried on during the day, but sometimes at night as well. One of the great fears of the infantryman was the possibility that at any moment he might be blown to bits in his own trench by the explosion of a mine. At dusk the "stand to" and "hate" were repeated. There was usually an attempt to serve hot food for dinner.

The main work of the trenches began at dark. Rations and supplies were brought forward, damages were repaired, wire was strung, sentries were posted, and scouts and patrols were sent out to examine the enemy wire or perhaps to make a raid to obtain a prisoner.

Prisoners brought in by combat patrols and air reconnaissance were the main sources of intelligence for both sides. The Alabama soldiers of the 167th Infantry, established a reputation as aggressive raiders. *Croix de guerres* were awarded to all the members of a patrol that captured two soldiers of the 77th Bavarian Infantry. Another hung a sign on the German wire: "Germans, give your soul to God for your ass belongs to Alabam."

To aid their chances for survival, soldiers were burdened, beginning in March 1916, with an unstable and uncomfortable steel helmet ("tin hat") and a gas mask, burdensome to carry at all times and uncomfortable indeed to wear.

After a tour of duty in the trenches, troops went back to billets behind the line for rest, more drill, training, and endless fatigues. Although threatened by long-range artillery fire and the occasional strafing or bombing from airplanes, there was frequently time for games and for drinking "plonk"* (white wine) at an estaminet. This was also the time when replacements for casualties arrived.

*"Plonk" was Cockney rhyming slang for *vin blanc*.

11

✩

FIRST BATTLES:

SEICHEPREY AND CANTIGNY

IN THE FALL of 1917 the Italian front was disintegrating following the disaster to Italian arms at Caporetto, where an Austro-German army crashed through the Italian line, killing or wounding 40,000, taking 275,000 prisoners, and capturing 2,500 guns. In Russia the Bolsheviks were about to seize power and make a separate peace with Germany, releasing dozens of German divisions to fight on the Western Front. The European Allies, watching these disasters begin to unfold with increasing panic, were finally driven to strive for greater cooperation.

In an effort to overcome their mutual distrust and to coordinate overall strategy, a Supreme War Council was formed at Rapallo, Italy, on 7 November 1917, composed of representatives of the governments of France, Britain, and Italy. It was supported by "Permanent Military representatives" and a secretariat. The council's stated mission was "to watch over the general conduct of the war," to prepare "recommendations for the decisions of the governments" and to "keep itself informed of their execution." It was, therefore, both a coordinator and an initiator of action, superior to the general staff of any individual nation. France appointed Foch as its permanent military representative; the British appointed Major General Sir Henry Wilson, an intelligent man but one much given to intrigue. The participation of the United States began with the Council's second session, held at Versailles, on 1 December. Wilson did not appoint a diplomatic representative, for he still considered the United States an associate rather than an ally, but he did appoint a military representative: General Tasker H. Bliss—a wise choice.

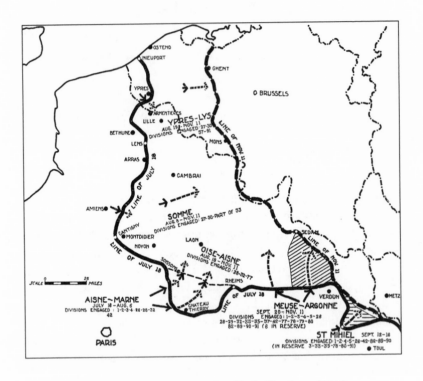

American participation in the allied offensives of 1918

CREDIT: *The War With Germany*

Bliss, sixty-four years old in 1917, was graduated from West Point in 1875 and commissioned in the 1st Artillery. He had taught at West Point and at the Naval War College, and had served as military attaché in Madrid. During the Spanish-American War he served as a divisional chief of staff in Puerto Rico. After the war he was appointed an advisor to Secretary of War Elihu Root in the formation of the first General Staff. In 1903 he became the first commandant of the new Army War College. From 1905 until 1909 he served in the Philippines and in 1910 until 1915, when he was named assistant chief of staff, he commanded several divisions and departments. He was for a time chief of staff and in that office supervised the rapid mobilization of the volunteer army. Like Baker, he was an exceptionally well-read man. Donald Smythe said of him: "Bliss's learning was tremendous. He would have ornamented any university faculty, provided the professors could get used to feeling second-rate in his presence. A scholar in uniform, he knew geology, French, Spanish, Italian, Latin and Greek, which he read as easily as his native English — a language he wrote with clarity and spoke with force." Writing after the war, Secretary Baker said: "Bliss had in a higher degree than anybody else with whom I have ever been in contact the habit of deliberate and consecutive thinking . . . [his] mind was a comprehensive card index."

Although Secretary Baker and General March usually complied with Pershing's wishes regarding senior commanders, when he once suggested that General Bliss be replaced on the Supreme War Council by General Liggett, the notion was quickly rejected.

Bliss landed in Europe in January 1918. Before his arrival the Council had determined that the Allied posture for that year should be defensive, and that it would not be until 1919, after the Americans had arrived in force, that they would go on the offensive. Given the facts as they then stood, this seemed like a wise decision.

Pershing thought the idea of a supreme war council was a bad one: "While the commanders-in-chief of the armies concerned were expected to attend, and usually did so and freely expressed their views, they were not members and had no vote." General James Harbord writing after the war agreed: "Its meddling possibilities were as dangerous as dynamite and were only thwarted by circumstances unforeseen at its inception . . ." British General John Charteris, Haig's chief of intelligence, gave a contemporary opinion: "It is utter rubbish as far as fighting is concerned. It will mean delay in any attack on the Germans and will break down at once if the Germans attack us." As it did.

On 21 March 1918 the first of the great German drives, sometimes called the Picardy offensive, began. Designed by the brilliant General Erich Ludendorff, who, it was said, was "never known to smile during the whole war," it encompassed a fifty-mile front in the area of the old Somme battlefield and opened with a brutal, successful assault upon the British 5th Army, preceded by a barrage by 6,473 guns and 3,532 trench mortars.

Ludendorff's success created a crisis which forced British and French soldiers and politicians to do what ought to have been done long before: create a generalissimo. On 26 March members of the Supreme War Council, including Haig, Pétain, Poincaré, and Clemenceau, with Lord Milner representing Lloyd George—no Americans were invited—met in the early afternoon at the village of Doullens, north of Amiens and appointed to the position sixty-seven-year-old Foch, signing their names to the following: "General Foch is charged by the British and French governments with coordinating the action of Allied Armies on the Western Front. For this purpose he will come to an understanding with the generals-in-chief, who are requested to furnish him with all necessary information." As the meeting broke up Clemenceau remarked to Foch: "Alors, you have the job you so much wanted."

"A fine gift!" Foch retorted. "You give me a lost battle and tell me to win it!"

On 30 March 1918 Lloyd George, and on the following day Clemenceau, dispatched messages to President Wilson urging him to send more American troops, even untrained and unorganized troops, as rapidly as possible. Infantry and machine gun units were requested before all others. As Churchill said, "The use to be made of all these great numbers of men, their organization, their training, their ammunition, their food and clothing—all were questions to be solved later on." Allied leaders, eager to use the Americans as a manpower pool for their own armies, failed to understand the American psychology and the need to create a separate army. The French had four black American regiments, a regiment of infantry had been sent to Italy, and Haig tried to hold on to troops sent to Britain for training, but Pershing, in compliance with his orders, was determined that the United States should have its own army.

When on 3 April the Supreme War Council met again, this time at Versailles with Pershing in attendance, it was at last agreed that "an American Army should be formed as early as possible under its own commander under its own flag." At the same time Foch's authority was extended. Pershing never thought highly of Foch, saying he "never seemed interested when I talked with him of our problems, and I doubt whether at the time ever thought, knew or cared much about our organization, or our questions of transportation and supply." Pétain was the French general Pershing most admired.

On 20 April the 26th (Yankee) Division first saw serious fighting. In late February it had moved into a quiet sector in the Woêvre Plain of Lorraine, near the La Reine Forest, and had occupied a front of 18,000 meters centered upon the ruined village of Seicheprey where German troops held the high ground. After a series of inconclusive raids the Germans assembled about 3,000 special storm troops (known as Hindenburg's Traveling Circus), and on 20 April, following a heavy bombardment, they advanced through dense fog along a two-mile front extending west from the Bois de Remières and caught the Americans by surprise.

Seicheprey was defended by two companies of infantry and a machine gun company of the 26th Division, but the village was quickly captured. Although retaken in an American counterattack the next day, the Germans had scored a point, for they had only intended a raid. They had inflicted 669 casualties: one officer and eighty enlisted men killed, 187 wounded, 214 gassed, 187 captured or reported missing. The first major action by an American division did not seem propitious. German propaganda made much of this raid on the Americans. There were radio broadcasts from Berlin and photographs taken during the raid were widely dispersed. Pershing was disgusted with General Edwards, whom he had never much liked, regarding him as a political general.

Ludendorff abandoned the offensive in this sector and, as he had planned, switched his attention to the British army in Flanders. There on 9 April he launched an attack upon the British armies lying east of the Lys River between Béthune and Armentières. A Portuguese division proved but a slight obstacle and soon the channel ports were endangered.

On 11 April Haig issued his famous "backs to the wall" order: "There is no other course open to us but to fight it out! Every position must be held to the last man; there must be no retirement. With our backs to the wall, and believing in the justice of our cause, each one of us must fight on to the end. The safety of our homes and the freedom of mankind alike depend upon the conduct of each one of us at this critical moment."

Pershing counted on his favorite 1st Division, under Major General Robert Lee Bullard, to wipe out the "stain of Seicheprey." On 25 April the division was posted on the ridge north of Montdidier covering the Paris-Calais railroad and elaborate plans were made for an attack upon

Cantigny, a small village in ruins on slightly rising ground three miles west northwest of Montdidier and eighteen miles south of Amiens. Lying at the tip of the German salient, it had been made into a strongly fortified observation point.

A mock battlefield simulating the terrain was laid out behind the lines where troops practiced their assault. Large sandtables reproduced the area over which the assault would be made. Aerial photographs allowed each trench and house to be studied.

The 1st Division attack, supported by French artillery and tanks, was begun on 28 May led by the 28th Infantry—122 officers and 3,757 enlisted men under Colonel Hanson E. Ely, widely regarded as one of the toughest senior officers in the AEF. Each man carried 220 rounds of ammunition, two grenades, and a rifle grenade; two canteens, a lemon, and a packet of gum to quench thirst; a shelter half, two iron rations— compact emergency food high in calories—and two slabs of chocolate.

After a two-hour barrage beginning at 4:45 A.M. the attacking force moved out behind a smoke screen and a rolling barrage. All went like clockwork. By 7:30 A.M. Cantigny was taken, its defenders killed or captured. Seven violent German counterattacks were repulsed. In all, 225 prisoners were taken and an estimated 1,400 killed or wounded, for a loss to the division of 1,607, of whom 199 were killed.

Pershing was elated. Visiting novelist Dorothy Canfield Fisher, a longtime friend who dined with him and his staff that evening, remembered their exultant talk of "the magnificent conduct of American troops." In truth it was a small victory, one that, in the words of George C. Marshall, was of "no strategic importance and of small tactical value," but in the prevailing climate of defeat it gave a lift to Allied morale, sorely in need of good tidings.

Pershing provided a further boost to morale. Although he had fought hard to keep his troops out of the hands of the British and French and to form an American army, in the crisis now facing the Allies he relented. According to Winston Churchill, on 28 May (actually 27 May) he and Bliss "presented themselves to General Foch . . . and spontaneously and in the finest manner, placed the whole of their resources in France for the time being at his disposal. Their plans for the development of the great American Army would be subordinated in the emergency wherever necessary. The American divisions, battalions if need be, would enter the line forthwith in spite of their inadequate training and incomplete organization. This decision was at the true height of circumstances, and in itself went far to repair the injuries of Ludendorff's inroads."

It was indeed a magnificent gesture, Pershing's exact words were: "Infanterie, artillerie, aviation—tout ce que nous avons est à vous. Disposez-en comme il vous plaira!" As Churchill later said, "To serve in one's national army, under one's own leader, amid a great mass of men animated by a common spirit is one ordeal. To serve in isolated divisions or brigades or even regiments under the orders of foreign generals, flanked on either side by troops of different race and language and of unknown comradeship or quality, is another."

In practical terms, however, Pershing's pledge had little effect upon the action. The 1st Division was ordered to Picardy from Lorraine and placed in reserve, but was not used. The 2nd Division extended its front. The 42nd and 24th Divisions relieved French divisions in quiet sectors. The only American troops seriously engaged were two companies of the American 6th Engineers building a railroad in the British sector. Although not equipped to fight in a major engagement, they commandeered machine guns from a nearby machine gun school, determined how they worked, and "fought their guns," suffering seventy-eight casualties.

But individual bravery could not stem the stunningly successful attack. The Germans inexorably advanced to within twelve miles of Amiens, a railroad center where the British had amassed enormous stocks of ammunition and supplies.

On 2 June 1918 the prime ministers of France, Great Britain, and Italy sent a cable to President Wilson, stating in part: "General Foch has presented to us a statement of the utmost gravity, which points out that the numerical superiority of the enemy in France, where 162 Allied Divisions now oppose 200 German Divisions, is very heavy, and that as there is no possibility of the British and French increasing the number of their Divisions (on the contrary, they are put to great straits to keep them up) there is danger of the War being lost unless the numerical inferiority of the Allies can be remedied as rapidly as possible by the advent of American troops. . . . He places the total American force required for this at no less than 100 Divisions, and urges the continuous raising of fresh American levies, which, in his opinion, should not be less than 300,000 a month. . . ."

Britain supplied the ships—finally—and it was the multitude of American troops, however ill-trained, that landed soon after which gave the Allies the mass to launch the offensive that won the war, although American aid never approached one hundred divisions.

12

☆

HOME FRONT

WAR OR NO war, the customary rituals of American life continued, but martial notes immediately crept into the national cacophony. On 11 April 1917 when the baseball season opened with the Boston Red Sox playing the New York Yankees, the Yankees put on an exhibition of military drill using their bats instead of rifles. An unkind critic noted that they drilled better than they played, losing to Babe Ruth's Red Sox 10 to 3.

To inform the nation and rally its citizens for war a Committee on Public Information (CPI) was established by executive order on 13 April 1917 with George Creel, a flamboyant, eager, impetuous, and energetic publicist as chairman and the secretaries of War, Navy, and State as members. It was popularly known as the Creel Committee.

The original purpose of the CPI was simply to oversee the release of government news. To do this Creel created the *Official Bulletin*, the first official daily newspaper in American history, naming as its first editor Edward Sudler, former managing editor of the Washington *Post*. By October 1918 it had reached a circulation of 115,000. The move from releasing news to creating and controlling it was an easy one. Creel's committee soon developed into the United States' first propaganda ministry, disseminating Wilson's political views to every village in the country and eventually throughout the world.

Writers, artists, teachers, photographers, cartoonists, historians, and entertainers were enlisted to "sell the war." It was "a war to end all wars." It was "a war to make the world safe for democracy." Experienced and imaginative, Creel invented new communication techniques and perfected existing ones.

A corps of 75,000 "Four Minute Men" was recruited to speak during theater intermissions, before clubs, or at any place an audience was available, lauding patriotism, sacrifice for the war effort, and "100% Americanism." New York alone boasted 1,600 speakers, some of whom gave their little talks in Yiddish, Italian, Serbian, or any language required. Creel enthusiastically called the program "a vast enterprise in salesmanship, the world's greatest adventure in advertising."

Traveling salesmen, of whom there were then many, were enlisted in the cause and supplied with pamphlets that enabled them to speak with a note of authority at country stores and farmhouses.

Between 1907 and 1917 more than 650,000 people a year had immigrated to the United States, mostly from southern and eastern Europe. *The Meaning of America*, a booklet provided by the CPI, urged its readers to press immigrants to "speak the English language . . . salute the flag . . . cultivate patriotism in children" and learn the words to the "Star Spangled Banner." Creel issued daily, sometimes hourly, press releases—in all, some 6,000—proclaiming the enemy to be "barbaric huns." He organized exhibitions of guns, ammunition, gas masks, steel helmets, and other militaria.

The committee produced in all thirty propaganda bulletins and distributed seventy-five million copies in various languages. A popular one, *How the War Came to America*, was published in Polish, German, Swedish, Bohemian, Italian, and Spanish, as well as English.

Creel persuaded renowned artist Charles Dana Gibson to form a committee of artists and urged them to "draw 'till it hurts," an admonition they took to heart, producing 700 poster designs, 122 streetcar advertising cards, 310 advertising illustrations, and 287 cartoons. The most famous to emerge was James Montgomery Flagg's poster of a stern Uncle Sam pointing directly at the viewer and barking "Uncle Sam wants YOU!" Used as a navy recruiting poster, it was an imitation of a British poster in which Secretary of War General Lord Kitchener did the pointing.

German and French authorities had encouraged artists to travel to the seat of war from 1914; Britain did so from 1917. In May of the same year the CPI recommended that America do the same. Eight artists were selected and in February 1918 were commissioned as captains in the Engineer Reserve Corps. Included were Harvey Dunn, Harry Townsend, and George Harding. They were charged with producing "oil paintings, portraits, sketches, etchings, etc., within the war zone for historical purposes." Their productions were sent to the Smithsonian Institution for a brief display, then placed in storage, where most of them languish today.

Magazines and newspapers sent their own artists to France to draw or paint the war. Between November 1918 and October 1919 the *Ladies Home Journal* ran "Souvenir Pictures of the Great War"—thirty-six images by thirteen artists. One of the most popular, Gayle Porter Hoskins' "The Greatest American Moment of the War," portrayed Pershing with open arms offering his troops to Foch during Ludendorff's Picardy offensive.

The fledgling motion picture industry, finding that the war was made for movies, issued a steady stream of hate-the-Hun films with titles such as *Outwitting the Hun* and *Claws of the Hun*. One of the most ambitious and popular films, *Hearts of the World* by D. W. Griffith, starred Lillian and Dorothy Gish. Its first scenes were shot in England, where Winston Churchill offered to write a script, Lady Paget opened her estate as a location, and the royal family and scores of the nobility served as extras. Later scenes were shot in ruined French villages just behind the front. Lillian Gish later recorded that, "Shells and shrapnel fell close enough to make us nervous." It was first shown to an enthusiastic VIP crowd in New York on 4 April 1918.

American news and propaganda was broadcast to the troops overseas and to countries around the world each night with the cooperation of the navy, which had erected the most powerful radio station in the world, the first to girdle the globe, at Croix d'Hins, near Bordeaux. Called Lafayette Radio Station, it contained eight towers, each 832 feet high—nearly 300 feet taller than the Washington Monument.

A bellicose national mood was fanned by Creel's propaganda. In San Antonio, Texas, when an old Confederate veteran failed to remove his hat "a sufficient length of time as the color passed" he was "hustled through the crowd" to the federal building where he was cautioned "to be careful the next time."

Many feared that the large immigrant population, the "aliens in our midst," were "the spies within." Those bearing German names were often molested, and in places lynched. Mrs. Hugo Heisinger, daughter of brewer Adolphus Busch, fell under suspicion when it was learned that she had a telegraph in her house. With some disappointment, it was found to belong to a servant who was taking a telegraphy course at the Young Men's Christian Association (YMCA). Some families with German names anglicized them. A number of towns bearing German names changed them: Berlin, Maryland, became Brunswick, the city fathers perhaps unaware that they had chosen the name of a former German state.

Many schools banned the teaching of German. In many places the

"Hun music" of Bach and Wagner was no longer played and actors and opera singers with German names found it difficult to get engagements. Even Vienna-born Fritz Kreisler was forbidden to give a concert in Jersey City, New Jersey. Libraries were purged of German literature. Sauerkraut became "liberty cabbage." Hamburgers became "Salisbury steak." Most curious of all, German measles became "Liberty measles." Zwieback lost its popularity; Hasenpfeffer and Wiener Schnitzel were banned from restaurant menus. Beer halls and saloons no longer offered pretzels. Owners of German shepherds were suspect until their breed's name was changed to "police dog"; in places dachshunds were stoned. Many admitted to *schadenfreude* when, during a Barnum and Bailey Circus performance, a Russian bear attacked an animal trainer of German extraction.

All aliens considered "dangerous" were ordered interned; sixty-three were arrested on the day war was declared. Patriotic organizations warned people to keep an eye out for "gloaters," those who smiled or expressed approval of German victories. Between April and November 1917 thousands of suspected citizens were arrested, often without a warrant, and their backgrounds checked by the Alien Enemy Bureau of the War Emergency Division of the Justice Department. While most were released, about 1,200 were placed in internment camps.

Among those arrested was Carl Muck, conductor of the Boston Symphony Orchestra, picked up just as he was about to conduct Bach's *Saint Matthew Passion*. Among the officials screening aliens at the Justice Department was twenty-two-year old J. Edgar Hoover, upon whose recommendation Ernst Kunwald, conductor of the Cincinnati Symphony Orchestra, was arrested. Mr. Kunwald had on the eve of war turned his back upon an audience demanding an encore of "The Star Spangled Banner." Hoover also recommended internment for a Mr. Otto Mueller who was reported to have called President Wilson "a cocksucker and a thief."

Creel was later blamed for the hysteria. One critic observed that, "Never have so many behaved so stupidly at the manipulation of so few." Americans grew suspicious of each other. Neighbor spied on neighbor and workers spied on their fellow workers. There developed a kind of national paranoia. Almost every aspect of American life was touched upon. The *Literary Digest* invited readers to send in clippings of newspaper articles they thought "seditious or treasonable." Some eight hundred industrial plants organized "Americanization Committees." Pay packets were stuffed with patriotic literature supplied by the American Chamber of Commerce.

Some factories established their own FBI. The head of personnel at the Winchester Repeating Arms Company in New Haven proudly announced that his company had "a factory Intelligence Bureau through which are reported disloyal utterances or actions." U.S. Attorney General Thomas W. Gregory worked with vigilante groups to uncover "disloyal Americans." The American Protective League, a Chicago-based business group, enrolled 250,000 members and supplied the FBI with information about leaders of groups suspected of disloyalty; these tended to be political and labor leaders of immigrant organizations.

Gregory boasted that he had "several hundred thousand private citizens," most of them members of "patriotic bodies" assisting "heavily overworked Federal authorities in keeping an eye on disloyal individuals and seeking reports of disloyal utterances." Boy Spies of America, the National Security League, founded before the war to plead for preparedness, and the American Defense Society joined the hunt.

The Free Speech clause of the Bill of Rights was trampled under patriotic feet. In violation of the law and the Fourth Amendment to the Constitution, federal troops were used to put down strikes, raid union premises, and arrest labor leaders. Captain Omar Bradley, sent to Butte, Montana, deployed his company with loaded rifles and fixed bayonets to cow strikers at the Anaconda mines.

In September 1917 the national leaders of the Industrial Workers of the World (IWW), and other "Wobblies," were arrested by the FBI for protesting America's entry into the war and later attempting to discourage enlistments with such slogans as "Sherman said 'War is hell!' Don't go to Hell in order to give the capitalists a bigger place in heaven!" Under the Espionage Act, 113 were tried, found guilty, and sent to prison; the fifteen top leaders were sentenced to twenty years.

The War Department established a list of seventy-five books, surmised to be "vicious German propaganda," "morbid," or "salacious." They were banned from army camp libraries, and throughout the nation librarians removed them from their shelves, sometimes burning them.

On 6 April 1917 Wilson authorized the seizure of radio stations. Congress passed the Espionage Act signed by the president on 15 June 1917, the Trading with the Enemy Act on 6 October, and the "Sedition Act," actually an amendment to the Espionage Act, on 16 May 1918.

The postmaster general was authorized to refuse mail advocating "trea-

President Woodrow Wilson.
Credit: National Archives.

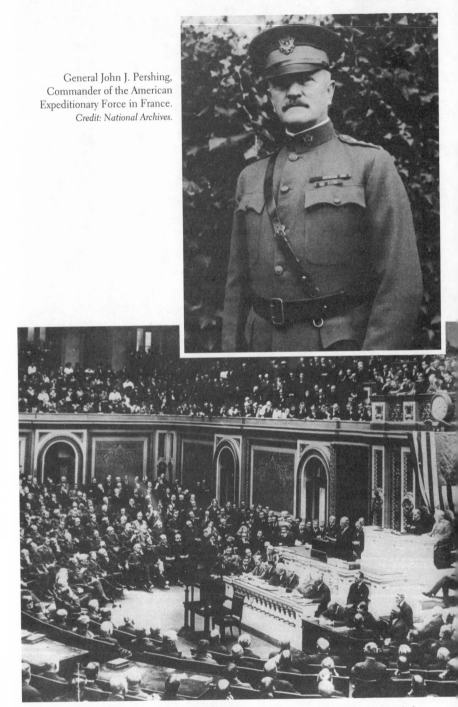

General John J. Pershing, Commander of the American Expeditionary Force in France.
Credit: National Archives.

On 2 April 1917, President Wilson announced that the world must be made safe for democracy and called on Congress to declare war on Germany.
Credit: Warder Collection.

Conscription came in the form of lottery with prominent figures, including
President Wilson, drawing numbers from a glass bowl.
Credit: UPI/Corbis-Bettmann.

At a camp near San Antonio, Texas, civilian draftees file into a barracks and
emerge at least looking like soldiers. Unfortunately, shortages of clothing and
equipment did not always make this transformation possible.
Credit: National Archives.

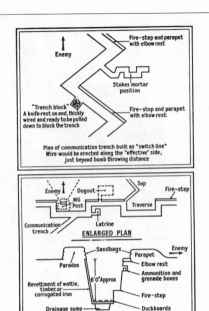

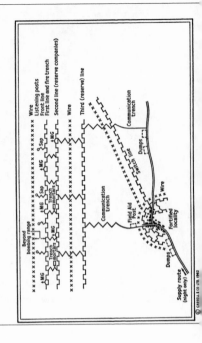

Trenches could appear neat and
geometrical on paper. In practice
they were usually wavy and disorderly.
Credit: Morgan-Wells

General Henri Philippe Pétain,
the "Hero of Verdun."
General Pershing found him
the most congenial of the
senior French commanders.
Credit: Morgan-Wells.

Marshal Ferdinand Foche, generalissimo of the Allied force, with whom General Pershing clashed.
Credit: U.S. War Dept. General Staff. Credit: Imperial War Museum.

One of the many postcards that helped sell war bonds to civilians.
Credit: U.S. War Department General Staff.

The most popular song of the war was undoubtedly "Over There" by George M. Cohan. Some two million copies of sheet music and a million phonograph recordings were sold.
Credit: Corbis-Bettmann.

Some of the soldiers of the 369th Infantry who fought in the French army and earned the *Croix de Guerre*. *Credit: National Archives.*

Although the YMCA was charged with providing services to blacks as well as whites, they usually provided less than equal facilities. Some black women opened clubs to "care for their men in the service," such as this one in Newark, New Jersey.
Credit: National Archives.

Lieutenant Colonel George S. Patton commanded the First Tank Center in France.
Credit: National Archives.

The use of poison gas by both sides added to the horrors of combat in the Great War. Those who did not or could not wear their protective mask paid a terrible price. *Credit: Corbis-Bettmann.*

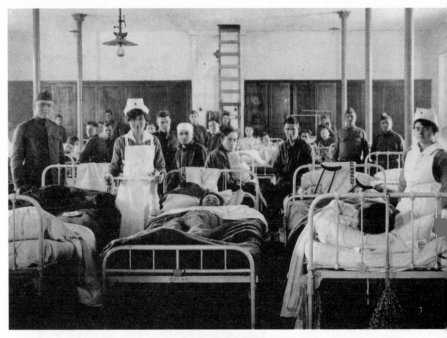

All military hospitals were overcrowded and lacked sufficient personnel and equipment. Shown above is a ward in an American hospital at Blois, France. *Credit: Library of Congress.*

son, insurrection or forcible resistance to any law of the United States."
Postmaster General Albert Sidney Burleson used this power to cut off the
second-class mailing privileges of assorted foreign language newspapers
and magazines, bankrupting many. More than four hundred periodical
issues were censored. Many were forced to submit English translations of
any articles they carried concerning the war. Publications such as the
Internationalist Socialist Review, The Masses, and the *Milwaukee Leader*
were suppressed.

It was under the provisions of Title XI of the Espionage Act that a
motion picture, *The Spirit of '76,* was seized in Los Angeles. Produced by
Robert Goldstein, a respected filmmaker who had been associated with
D. W. Griffith in making *The Birth of a Nation* (1915), it was begun
before the United States entered the war and after a year and a half in
production it was released in 1917 just before America's entry into the
war. Bad timing. A patriotic film about the Revolutionary War, it seemed
unobjectionable, but the villains of the piece were British soldiers who in
one scene ran amok, massacring women and children and carrying off
nubile maidens. The idea of British soldiers—even eighteenth-century
British soldiers—committing atrocities was now decreed offensive. It was
whispered that Goldstein had sought funds for his production from
German-American Anglophobes. The film was seized, the company was
bankrupted and Goldstein was tried, convicted, and sentenced to ten
years in a federal penitentiary, a verdict upheld by the United States
Circuit Court of Appeals.

In New York City Jacob Abrams, thirty-one, a Russian-born American
bookbinder, protested American intervention in Russia and wrote two
pamphlets asserting it was a crime for American workers to fight a workers' republic in Russia. On 23 August 1918 he and his friends, including
Hyman Rosansky, a hatmaker, and Mollie Steimer, barely twenty years
old, a small, round-faced seamstress, scattered the pamphlets from a
rooftop on Broadway. The Department of Justice collected some and
rounded up five of the protesters. They were tried and sentenced to twenty years in jail, a sentence upheld by seven justices of the Supreme Court
in October 1919, but denounced by Justice Oliver Wendell Holmes, in
whose opinion the defendants "had as much right to publish [the pam-
phlets] as the government has to publish the Constitution of the United
States now vainly invoked by them."

Never before in American history had the government attempted such
a near total control over the freedom of expression. Curiously, prior to

1917 the Supreme Court had never applied or interpreted the First Amendment. There were, therefore, no guidelines for courts to consider in free speech cases. By the time of the Armistice the government had the potential to exercise total control of the American press. The Creel Committee remained active until 30 June 1919.

Senator Robert M. La Follette of Wisconsin, who opposed the entrance of the United States into the war and was persistently critical of Wilson's war policies, became a target of the new patriots. A federal judge declared he should be shot by a firing squad. Dr. Nicholas Murray Butler, president of Columbia University, thundered: "You might just as well put poison in the food of every American boy that goes to his transport as permit this man to talk as he does." (In 1931, jointly with Jane Addams, Butler was awarded the Nobel Peace Prize.)

The four Liberty Loan Campaigns, launched by Secretary of the Treasury Williams Gibbs McAdoo, President Wilson's son-in-law, added more slogans to a country which, thanks to Mr. Creel, was already overburdened with them: "Buy Bonds Till It Hurts," "The Soldier Gives—You Must Lend," "Liberty Bonds or German Bondage," "Come Across or the Kaiser Will," and "A Bond Slacker is a Kaiser Backer." Pressure was put on American Indians and the foreign born to prove they were "100% Americans" by buying the bonds. The widow and son of Geronimo became liberal purchasers. The bonds paid only three and one-half percent.

Bond rallies were held throughout the country. One of the most notable was a noon-hour rally on the steps of the New York Public Library. Top entertainers performed, among them the musical comedy star, Elsie Janis, whose English actor fiancé had just been killed on the Western Front. Some $85,000 was raised.

Movie stars such as Douglas Fairbanks, Mary Pickford, and Theda Bara went on tour, giving countless speeches that brought in millions of dollars for Liberty Bonds. John Philip Sousa composed a "Liberty Bond March." The great tenor, Enrico Caruso, not only donated money, but lent his magnificent voice to the cause. His rousing rendition of George M. Cohen's "Over There" helped to make it the most popular of wartime songs. Recorded in 1918 it became a best-selling phonograph record.

Part of the success of the Liberty Bond drives was the result of a relaxation of controls on credit. Bond holders were allowed to use the bonds as collateral for bank loans, but as the banks in the Federal Reserve System used them as collateral for their own borrowing, the government was in effect printing money to lend to itself. The natural result was inflation. The cost of living increased by nearly twenty percent between 1914 and 1916 and by nearly seventy-four percent in the following four years.

It was so widely believed that German soldiers had cut off the hands of countless Belgian boys that Ora Buffington, a Philadelphia attorney, urged the Creel Committee to import some of the boys for public exhibition as an aid to war bond drives. Insensitivity and bad taste aside, this was impossible, for no such handless Belgian boys could be found, then or ever. When a wealthy American offered a large sum to anyone who could supply proof of this atrocity, André Gide, who with Edith Wharton was deeply involved in the Foyer Franco-Belge, a society to assist refugees, made a determined but fruitless search, finally concluding that, "Not one of these statements could be proved."

Enthusiasm for the war swept through almost all classes. Towns and cities held loyalty parades, marchers shouting slogans: "On to Berlin!" "Keep the flag flying!" and "Down with the Kaiser!" The New York Federation of Churches declared Sunday 11 March 1917 to be "War Sunday." Many churchmen preached pro-war sermons. The Rev. George A. Gordon in the Old South Church in Boston thundered from the pulpit: "Was Jesus a pacifist?" and answered himself with a resounding "No!" Passion reached such a height that even fifty-nine-year-old William Jennings Bryan, a lifelong pacifist, tried to enlist.

Capitalizing on the mood of the country, Flo Ziegfeld—who saw no reason to change his German-sounding name—staged an elaborate tableau featuring an attractive actress with one breast bared (What patriot dared protest?) as a live Statue of Liberty and introducing a song by Victor Herbert, "Can't You Hear Your Country Calling." When the *Ziegfeld Follies of 1918* opened in June at the Amsterdam Theatre on 42nd Street audiences found inserts in their programs pointing out that none of the chorus boys or other healthy-looking young men in the show were slackers; all had been excused military service for unspecified reasons.

Aided by the popular victrola, America became a singing nation. It was said, and many believed it, that "a Singing Army, whether it be a fighting army or a working army, cannot be beaten." Everybody sang. General Leonard Wood declared that "It is just as essential that a soldier knows how to sing as that he carry a rifle and shoot it." A film, *Keep 'Em Singing and Nothing Can Lick 'Em,* enjoyed considerable popularity. Four-minute sing-along sessions in which the words of patriotic songs were thrown up on the screen became a feature in movie theaters. Audiences sang with gusto songs such as "Over There," "Battle Hymn of the Republic," "Good-bye Broadway, Hello France," "If You Don't Like Your Uncle Sammy, Then Go Back to Your Home O'er the Sea!," and "Keep Your Head Down Allemand."

Service men in the United States put on their own shows. The Pelham Bay Naval Station's *Biff-Bang* played in legitimate theaters, and the 27th Division's musical comedy, *You Know Me, Al*, played for ten days in New York. At Camp Upton, near the village of Yaphank on Long Island, Private (later Corporal) Irving Berlin wrote for a musical, *Yip, Yip Yaphank*, a song that began "Oh how I hate to get up in the morning," which was to rank just behind "Over There" as the most popular song of World War I. Other Berlin songs followed: "Goodbye Broadway, Hello France," "Where Do We Go From Here Boys," "When Yankee Doodle Learns to Parlez-Vous Français."

Some units had their own songs. The 77th Division, made up largely of the multicultured young men from New York City, lustily sang:

> *Thirty dollars every month, deducting twenty-nine*
> *Oh, the army, the army, the democratic army.*
> *The Jews, the Wops, and the Dutch and Irish cops*
> *They're all in the army now!*

Contributions to the war effort took many forms. Schoolchildren rolled bandages and collected tin cans, used paper, old toothpaste tubes, and apricot pits. Knitting needles clicked in churches and parlors. Herbert Hoover, now chief of the United States Food Administration, urged grocery stores to pass out voluntary pledges to conserve food and some fourteen million families bothered to sign them and mail them to Washington, D.C. At his urging, many adhered to wheatless Mondays and Wednesdays, meatless Tuesdays, and porkless Thursdays and Saturdays. A coarse-grained bread called Victory Bread appeared, as did Over the Top Bread (heavy on bran). On 8 September 1917 the making of whiskey was banned to conserve grain. In 1918 in the northwest schoolboys over sixteen were released from school to help put in the wheat crop and were given credit for the full school term. Families planted victory gardens in backyards, vacant lots, and sometimes even in front yards. One was planted in the White House lawn under the supervision of Mrs. Wilson.

Not everyone was driven by patriotism. It was noticed that some people were making more money than they had before the war, some a great deal more. "Paytriots," Secretary Daniels called them. Pierre DuPont offered to manufacture much-needed smokeless powder—for a price. Secretary Baker was outraged by the proposal: "On the basis of a ninety million dollar investment, this would have yielded them gross profits of twenty to forty million." The War Department made a counterproposal, but Dupont refused, saying, "We cannot assent to allowing our patriotism to interfere with our duties as trustees."

Dupont was not alone. At the beginning of the war there was a great demand for flags; prices rose dramatically, leading the assistant secretary of the Treasury to denounce, of all people, the makers of American flags as unpatriotic profiteers.

There were more serious examples of people making exorbitant profits from the war. Secretary of the Treasury McAdoo looked over the tax returns of a number of coal mining companies and found "as fine a specimen of war profiteering as I have ever seen." Two companies had profits of more than a thousand percent in one year. Bethlehem Steel increased its profits by more than eight hundred percent in the war years. "The law of supply and demand has been replaced by the law of selfishness," said Herbert Hoover. The number of millionaires increased by 7,925 to 22,696—8,000 more than in 1916, noted the New York *Sun*. "War riches," explained the paper. "Blood money," said others. Labor took note and strikes for more pay hampered the production of war materials.

Although the United States had declared war on 6 April 1917, the actual fighting was delayed so long that the war took on a far away, romantic, exuberant quality. Reality did not begin to set in until the first enlisted combat deaths on 3 November, the large casualty list for the Battle of St. Mihiel in September 1918, and the even greater number of casualties immediately after in the Meuse-Argonne.

The voices of pacifists—many now calling themselves "noninterventionists"—began to be heard. One such was Mr. W. H. Beutterbaugh, who hectored evangelist William Ashley ("Billy") Sunday in Atlanta while in full flow of delivering a patriotic sermon. Sunday invited him to come up on the stage and, when he did, knocked him down. The two were soon rolling about the stage flailing away at each other while the congregation yelled, "Sock him! Kill him! Lynch him!" Mayor Asa Candler was himself decked before he could separate them. The belligerent Rev. Sunday, a former pro baseball player who believed in "muscular Christianity, strong-arm religion," emerged from the fray with a torn shirt. The peace-loving Mr. Beutterbaugh sported a black eye.

The war was not long in progress before it began to change long established ways. Cigarettes, previously thought unmasculine, became popular. They were easy to light and the cigarette pack fitted neatly into a uniform pocket. As there was no watch pocket in an army uniform, a wristwatch soon became a popular going away present. Famed war correspondent Richard Harding Davis wore one and so did dancer turned Royal Flying Corps (RFC) flying instructor Vernon Castle. Wearing one took a bit of adjustment; it felt strange. One officer candidate complained that, "it feels like a wart."

An increasing number of women entered the work force, replacing the men gone off to war. The YWCA offered training courses for young women, and many began to replace elevator operators and Western Union delivery boys, and to work in factories and on farms, where they were known as "farmerettes." Their presence in the workforce was resented by some, but the war had created a sharp drop in immigration and women's hands were needed. Feminist ideas were fermenting, and women were demanding political rights and social status.

When financier Bernard Baruch suggested that it would aid the war effort if less material was used in the manufacture of clothes the American fashion industry patriotically responded by abandoning forever shoe-length women's skirts. It became patriotic to wear simpler and shorter dresses. When General March declared that an army fights and moves on steel, elaborate steps were taken to reduce civilian use of metals, and the old-style corset was abolished forever as women donated to scrap drives their metal stays—enough, it was said facetiously, to build two battleships. Production of trunks was drastically reduced, baby carriages were standardized, tin toys for children were forbidden, and metal was even saved in the production of caskets. New York City ripped out 5,000 of its 35,000 lampposts and shipped them to arsenals needing steel and iron.

Some pockets were removed from uniforms to save material. "The great mailed fist of government, now fully war conscious, was slowly squeezing out waste of every kind," March boasted, but some waste March was helpless to control. In the AEF officers wore Sam Browne belts with a strap going over the right shoulder. Pershing thought that they made the uniform look more snappy and military, which they did; March forbade their use in the United States because the belts were a waste of leather and an unneeded financial burden on young officers, which they were. (The belts had to come off when officers returned to the United States, but when Pershing was named chief of staff on 1 July 1921 he at once ordered all officers to wear the Sam Browne. They continued to be worn until World War II.)

In spite of all the grass-roots efforts of civilians and the military, American industry failed to provide the support necessary to prosecute the war. The nation was outraged by a manufacturer whose army rain-coats dissolved in the rain. There were demands that the owners be shot as traitors and the New York *World* raged: "An Army contractor who robs or defrauds the government is the meanest and most detestable of all the by-products of war."

Outright corruption was rare, at least in comparison with earlier wars, but incompetence and inefficiency flourished. The AEF fired about nine million shells, of which only 208,000 were American made. Of 2,250 artillery pieces, only 130 came from United States steel and processing plants. Of the 23,000 tanks on order, only ten were manufactured and accepted. American-built planes did not fight in European skies. As General Halsey Dunwoody, in charge of airplane procurement, admitted: "We never had a single plane that was fit to use . . ."

Even before the United States entered the war, American industry had been strained providing for the needs of the Allies. American exports rose from $691 million in 1913 to well over a billion dollars in 1918. By the end of the war the United States held most of the world's gold.

One of the most serious shortcomings of American industry was the failure of the railroads to meet the needs of a war-time economy. Before the war they had produced handsome profits by paying low wages and operating antiquated equipment. An estimated 115,000 new freight cars were needed and the president of the Pennsylvania Railroad admitted that, "The conditions of the railroads presents a menace to the country." Railroad employees had just won the right to an eight-hour day, but many were disaffected. Wages were so low that disgruntled workers left to take jobs in war industries where they could sometimes make as much as $5.00 a day.

The United States had 397,014 miles of track owned by 2,905 compa-nies who found it impossible to cooperate with each other. Owners failed to shift from profits to patriotism. As they refused to coordinate the trans-portation of war matériel, by late 1917 some 180,000 loaded railroad cars sat idle; conditions were chaotic at eastern terminals. Ships lay idle in ports for lack of coal, AEF soldiers received no letters from home, and Pershing's desperate call for men and matériel went unheeded. There were shortages everywhere, even on the home front.

On 12 December 1917 Republican Senator George Earle
Chamberlain of Oregon, chairman of the Military Affairs Committee,
launched an inquiry into the conduct of the war. After three weeks of listening to tales of failures with unconvincing excuses attached, he exploded in rage in a talk before the National Security League, declaring: "We
are still unprepared, without a definite war program and still without
trained men. . . . The military establishment of the United States has broken down. It has almost stopped functioning."

Two weeks later the railroads were taken over by presidential proclamation and Secretary of the Treasury McAdoo became, in addition to his
other duties, tsar of the rails. "The system is utterly lacking in coordination," he said and he set about to put things right. But putting things right
took time and no sooner had he taken the reins than the northeast was hit
by bitter cold weather with blizzards and fifty-mile-an-hour winds. The
railroads were frozen to a standstill. Even so, McAdoo had them operating efficiently and their labor force pacified by summer.

On 20 May 1918 the Overton Act became the law of the land. This
was the most extraordinary and potentially dangerous law ever passed by
the United States Congress. The legislation, introduced by Senator Lee
Overton, a conservative Democrat from North Carolina, gave the president dictatorial powers for the duration of the war and for six months
after. It permitted Wilson to disband, add to, or reorganize any executive
or administrative agency without the approval of Congress and transformed the six existing war agencies—fuel, food, shipping railroads, war
trade, and war industries—into a virtual war cabinet. Fortunately for the
nation, Wilson used his great powers sparingly.

13

☆

ARMY WELFARE

WHEN THE UNITED STATES entered the Great War Secretary Baker formed a Commission on Training Camp Activities (CTCA). Raymond B. Fosdick, thirty-three, a lawyer and social worker, formerly an investigator for the Rockefeller-supported Bureau of Social Hygiene, and brother of the well-known Rev. Harry Emerson Fosdick, was appointed chairman and charged with "the responsibility for cultivating and conserving the manhood and manpower of America's fighting forces" by providing a "clean and wholesome environment." The war was seen as a great crusade; its warriors must have knightly virtues. President Wilson insisted that the new army be protected from the evils of whiskey and painted women. Under the Military Draft Act broad vice-free zones were established around all army camps; houses of ill repute were placed off limits and merchants and bartenders were forbidden to sell liquor to soldiers.

Training camp sites in the United States were selected on the basis of climate, sanitary conditions, accessibility to railroads, and sufficient space for maneuvers. The general moral tone of the nearest town as determined by the accessibility to prostitutes and liquor was also a factor. Eager to have the business that training camps brought them, cities and towns made an effort, not always successful, to polish their image.

When Fosdick sent a regional official of his commission to investigate San Antonio, then a town of about 133,000, he reported that conditions were unquestionably bad: "houses of ill-fame were being operated, gambling was going on, disorderly houses conducted by whites and blacks were in operation and selling liquor to soldiers was not uncommon." The

town was compelled to reduce to acceptable levels its flow of liquor and
sales of sexual favors, but after the war, in response to questionnaires submitted to veterans who had served in nearby Camp Travis, gambling,
liquor, and prostitutes were listed as favored diversions.

Another Fosdick representative, pulling no punches, reported in
November 1917 that "The worst place in Kansas City is the Jefferson
Hotel at 6th and Wynadotte. It is owned and controlled by Tom
Pendergast and is headquarters for his wing of the Democratic Party."
The city's 12th Avenue was known as Woodrow Wilson Avenue because it
offered "a piece at any price." Lieutenant Truman, writing from Camp
Doniphan, confided to Bess that Edward Jacobson, an enlisted man in
his company, "says he would go into the guardhouse for thirty days for
one night on Twelfth Street."

City brothels attracted a new type of customer: members of a horde of
young men cast adrift for the first time from their usual moral moorings and
the attention of neighbors. Ell Kimball, who owned and operated a brothel
in New Orleans, later wrote: "Every man and boy wanted to have one last
fling of screwing before the real war got him. Every farm boy wanted to have
one big fuck in a real house before he went off and maybe got killed."

Fosdick's agents sometimes crossed the lines of the law and propriety in
their efforts to stamp out vice. The CTCA closed down civilian dance
halls near camps and in some towns suspected prostitutes, their right of
habeas corpus ignored, were confined before trial in detention houses
operated by the CTCA and treated without their consent for venereal diseases whether they needed the treatment or not.

A strong bloc of prohibitionists in the Senate attempted to extend the
laws forbidding the sale of liquor to soldiers to a prohibition against giving
them a drink under any circumstance, contending that they needed clear
heads to shoot, a theory quickly dropped when it was suggested that, as senators also required clear heads, the ban should also apply to legislators.

The CTCA built forty-two Liberty theaters providing a wide variety of
entertainments in the hope of keeping young men from habituating low
bars and consorting with women of negotiable virtue. Marc Klaw, a
Broadway producer, aided by twenty-three others prominent in the theater, organized lectures, films, shows given by touring companies, and
entertainment by such stars as Harry Lauder and Elsie Janis. Part of this
effort was financed by the sale of "Smileage Books." Bought by patriotic
citizens and distributed to soldiers, they contained coupons used as tickets
to the shows. More than three million dollars was raised in this fashion.

Pershing wanted relief and humanitarian efforts to be supplied by the Red Cross and all recreational activities and amusements supplied by the YMCA with all other organizations interested in soldier welfare—such as Knights of Columbus, Salvation Army, Jewish Welfare Board, War Camp Community Service (the wartime branch of the Playground and Recreation Association of America) placed under the general supervision of the Red Cross.

Throughout the United States and in France the YMCA constructed "Y huts," each in charge of a "Y secretary" charged with providing athletic, religious, educational, recreational, and social programs, including motion pictures, organized sports, talent contests, plays, recreational singing, and vaudeville shows as well as pool tables, pianos, and victrolas with records, offering hundreds of thousands of men from lower economic classes unprecedented access to middle-class culture. "Separate but equal" facilities were supposed to be supplied to black troops, but these were usually much inferior and in France the Y frequently failed adequately to allocate supplies and equipment.

In the United States the YWCA operated 124 "Hostess Houses" for women visiting soldiers; and opened eighty in France to house women working for the army or navy.

For those in France the YMCA published a pamphlet with such helpful French expressions as, "I should like very much to see the periscope of a submarine," "Do not stick your head above the trench," and "I have pawned my watch." After the war the YMCA claimed to have performed ninety percent of all welfare work for the AEF in Europe.

The entertainment offered by the YMCA varied from the amateur to the professional. Margaret Wilson, daughter of the president, toured with a YMCA entertainment troupe as a singer. During the Meuse-Argonne Campaign popular comic actress, singer, and song-writer Elsie Janis, née Bierbower, entertained the troops, sometimes singing from the back of a wagon. She was twenty-nine years old in 1918 and, while not particularly pretty, possessed seemingly boundless energy and, all agreed, knew how to entertain.

Chaperoned by her mother, who accompanied her everywhere, she was able to reach wartime France because of a prewar contract with a French impresario. Once there she persuaded a reluctant YMCA to sponsor her. At first restricted to training camps and billeting areas far behind the lines, she announced herself with a large sign that read simply ELSIE JANIS and attracted thousands. At Chaumont she met General Pershing, whom she called "Boss General," and he, recognizing her value as a morale builder, presented her with a camouflage-painted Cadillac, a chauffeur, and a pass to travel wherever she chose.

She chose to entertain troops in the combat area, going as close to the front as she could. Father Duffy spoke of her as a "joy producer by coming up to us in our mud and desolation and giving a Broadway performance for an audience which was more wildly appreciative than ever acclaimed her on the street of a million lights." One near-incredulous soldier described her visit: "And into the middle of this filthy backyard of war with its sickening smells and sights and its unkempt, lousy men there bounded Elsie Janis—fluffy, beautiful, piquant—not at all unlike a goddess just stepping out of the clouds for a bit to see what it was all about here below."

Working without pay and without benefit of microphones or amplifiers, she always began by calling out "Are we downhearted?" and voices, often thousands of them, roared back "No!" Hers was a one-woman show; no one else was needed. She told stories, did impersonations, turned cartwheels, and danced. She sang vaudeville songs, patriotic songs, and led in the singing of soldiers' songs such as "All We Do Is Sign the Payroll" (*And we never get a goddamn cent*) to the tune of "Glory, Glory Hallelujah." She kept to a busy schedule and Captain Harry Townsend marveled at how "she keeps it up, day after day." She justly earned her title of the "sweetheart of the AEF."

The *Stars and Stripes* (3 May 1918), comparing her to the usual YMCA fare, called her "an oasis of color and vivacity in a dreary desert of frock-coated and white-tied lecturers who have been visited upon us." One of the paper's reporters described a performance she gave in a railroad shed: "Then came a signal to clear the track and with a great toot-tooting and a still greater roar of men, the locomotive trundled in. On the cow-catcher was Elsie, waving her hand and laughing as if she was having the time of her life, as she probably was. The locomotive made its way to the stage till it was near enough for the agile actress to make it in one jump. She did. With her black velvet tam perched on one side of her head, and her arms held high, she cried: 'Are we downhearted?' They were not and said as much at the top of their lungs."

In her diary for 2 May 1918 Miss Janis wrote: "Gave my afternoon show up back of the lines in what is called a *rest camp*. I imagine it is so called because the mud is so deep that if you once step in it you *rest there*. The fellows had just come out of the line. The show was out of doors—

the stage two tables 'wished' together. The boys seemed rather shocked to see me at first. I don't wear a uniform, and I'm the only girl I've met that does not. They were fine though. They gave me souvenirs they had picked up, pins, medals, German coins, etc. . . ."

At the beginning of the war Pershing had asked the YMCA to take over the task of providing post exchanges for the AEF and the YMCA unwisely agreed to do so. Pershing stipulated that goods and food be paid for; he did not want the soldiers to become "objects of charity." They were not to be "pauperized," he told Secretary Baker. It was an idea that did not occur to the doughboys, who grumbled, as they parted with their money, that YMCA stood for "You Must Come Across," meaning a soldier had to "come across" with cash for what the YMCA provided. Sweet Caporal cigarettes were sold for as much as a quarter a pack. Many soldiers came to believe that the Y was selling what had been sent to them as presents. And it did not look good when the Knights of Columbus passed out free cigarettes and candy before the Y came with goods to sell.

The YMCA received much criticism from those it was intended to help. Larry Collins of the 165th Infantry stood in line at a YMCA to buy a box holding tobacco, cigarette papers, and a pipe. When he opened it he found a handwritten note from the contributor, a girl's club in Augusta, Georgia.

Private Charles MacArthur of the 149th Field Artillery and some of his buddies found a YMCA secretary trading chocolate for the buttons and medals of German prisoners of war. "We hadn't had any chocolate since Somant bit the dust, so we knocked the secretary loose from his triangle and returned with his wares."

Leslie Langille, speaking of two YMCA men who visited his battery, said: "Those two birds had apparently gone broke in Paris and were out on a selling campaign to recoup their fortunes. After picking up a few francs, they would then be able to return to Paris and their harems, and live like kings again."

Men complained that the YMCA representatives refused to sell their limited supplies in quantity or to men outside the units to which they were assigned. Those at home received a flood of letters criticizing the "Y". In a letter (dated 6 July 1918) to E. C. Carter, the YMCA director in Paris, Raymond Fosdick presented a number of complaints: some secretaries permitted card playing in their huts and some did not; some refused to cooperate with Sunday athletics, which the army strongly favored; and soldiers objected to the use of a motion picture or a vaudeville act as bait for religious services. "The army needs strong men to serve it," wrote

Fosdick, "and it does not care if they are evangelical or not, whether they go to church or not . . . providing they are men of character and force. The army is using the YMCA as an instrument of public service."

The YMCA was accused of catering to officers, and its female workers were accused of "spending too much time with officers and too little with the men." But Greayer Clover, a Yale student who lost his life in the war, wrote in his diary that "a YMCA girl is the only one here allowed to talk to men. Nurses and Red Cross-ers are forbidden to converse with [us]."

General Peyton March believed there should not be "any organization serving in the field that is not militarized." When he was chief of artillery in the AEF he noted that the YMCA contained many "huskey young men, fully capable of joining the fight," and that the venereal disease rate among them was higher than in any unit in his command. Some sprang to the organization's defense, but its reputation suffered for years after the war.

The Red Cross came in for its share of criticism. In 1917 the American Red Cross unceremoniously swept into its maw the more than 130 small American charities engaged in war relief work. Its bureaucratic ways repelled many. Edith Wharton (the novelist), who tried to work with it, soon noted "daily evidence of neglect and indifference" and finally declared, "it is impossible for me to collaborate with the Red Cross in any branch of my work." In a letter to her sister-in-law fourteen months after America entered the war she wrote that "the feeling against the Red Cross is not only as strong as it was but far stronger within the last two or three months . . . and apparently their purpose is to strangle all the independent war charities."

There seems to have been only admiration for the Salvation Army, which passed out coffee and doughnuts close to the front. One soldier wrote: "In every advanced zone you will always find this organization. It is always in the places where the boys need help and the closest hut to the line you'll find is the Salvation Army."

In addition to the organized national institutions, a general desire to "help the boys" swept the nation and civilians who would do good abounded. When it was reported that a soldier in a training camp in Chillicothe, Ohio, never received mail, he was flooded with 1,200 letters, 19 special delivery messages, and 54 packages. Unable to read or write, he was, in fact, not even a soldier. The local postmaster reported to Washington: "He is not just right and was not accepted by the army but refuses to leave."

14

☆

VENEREAL DISEASE

THE LEADING CAUSE of disability during the war in every army in the western hemisphere was the great influenza epidemic of 1918–19. In second place, far ahead of battle wounds and injuries, were venereal diseases. The problem was an old one in all societies and in all armies. In 1913 the American Social Hygiene Association had been founded, but despite support from John D. Rockefeller, Jr., its efforts to inform the public about venereal diseases foundered, the victim of a prevailing indifference. But a surprising fact revealed by the draft was its prevalence. Of those inducted, 259,612 were found to be infected, about five percent of all conscripts.

The armed services took venereal disease seriously—as well they should, for it was "the greatest source of noneffectiveness." Pershing, who had himself contracted gonorrhea in his youth, called venereal diseases a "menace to the young manhood in the armed forces and to the health and future well-being of our people." Even before the war the army had taken steps to protect its men. Between 1911 and 1915 through mandatory sex lectures and punishment for those infected, the army had reduced its syphilis rate by one-third.

To educate recruits, lectures, films, pamphlets, and posters were employed. "Sexual Hygiene for Young Men," a pamphlet published in a variety of languages by the Illinois Vigilance Society, was widely distributed. A film, "Keeping Fit to Fight," followed Billy Hale and four buddies through back alleys, fist fights, and encounters with fast women. In the end, Billy, having resisted all temptations, sailed to France, leaving his errant companions behind, languishing in venereal wards. Shown to immigrant soldiers with scant knowledge of English, it was usually enjoyed as a "smutty exhibition." A simpler version was shown to black troops.

Camp newspapers circulated a poem by Ella Wheeler Wilcox:

> *Whatever the dangers waiting*
> *In the lands I have not seen*
> *If I do not fall—if I come back at all—*
> *Then I will come back clean.*

More effective, perhaps, were the prophylaxis stations established in and around camps and the regular inspection of penises, known as "short arm inspections."* The procedure to be followed at prophylaxis stations was set forth by Major Deane C. Howard of the Army Medical Corps in 1912: the external genital organs were first to be thoroughly washed with a solution of bichloride of mercury and then 4 cc. of argyrol was injected into the urethra with "an ordinary penis syringe," the solution to remain "for *full five* minutes"; finally, the entire penis was smeared with two grams of calomel ointment and "allowed to remain undisturbed."

Although generally effective in the army, Secretary of the Navy Josephus Daniels saw the prophylaxis stations as "an invitation to sin," and even when venereal disease rate rose alarmingly, he could not bring himself to authorize them. Acting quickly during Daniel's temporary absence, the assistant secretary, Franklin D. Roosevelt, less prudish, ordered them installed.

Progressing beyond his "vice free" zones around military camps, Raymond Fosdick turned his attention to red light districts across the nation. By the end of 1917 he claimed to have closed 110 of them. By the end of the war 15,520 prostitutes were imprisoned in detention homes or reformatories. In May 1918 special Development Battalions were formed for "unfit and venereal soldiers."

The campaign against venereal diseases in the United States proved a spectacular medical success. Controlling it in France proved more difficult. In May 1917 three conferences on the prevention of venereal diseases were held in France and one in Britain, but without positive results.

---

*In December 1944 men were no longer punished for acquiring venereal disese, and inspection of enlisted men's penises was discontinued after World War II.

The Allies took a relaxed view of the problem. In Britain the official attitude was to ignore the threat, although in one British division some twenty-five percent of its men were disabled by venereal disease. The French simply refused to regard it as a problem. Prostitution was legal and women were licensed and inspected, usually weekly, but unlicensed prostitutes were believed to outnumber the licensed by five to one in peacetime and to exceed that during the war.

As the venereal rate climbed, Pershing watched it carefully. Reducing it became almost an obsession. James Harbord, Pershing's chief of staff, later remembered: "There was no subject on which more emphasis was laid, throughout the existence of the American Expeditionary Force." In his first six months in France Pershing issued three general orders on the subject. Unit commanders were held responsible for the rate in their units, and at inspections Pershing's first question always addressed the number of venereal cases. When one proud commander replied, "Only one," Pershing snapped: "One is one too many." Officers whose command had more than half of one percent disabled were admonished and their fitness to command questioned.

Pershing later wrote, "Venereal disease was destined to give us considerable concern because of the difference between the French attitude and our own regarding the suppression of the source of infection." In February 1918 Premier Georges Clemenceau wrote to Pershing, criticizing the American policy of placing brothels off limits as repressive and suggesting an alternative: The French government would provide licensed brothels. Pershing passed this letter on to Raymond Fosdick, who showed the letter to Secretary Baker, who after reading it twice, exclaimed, "For God's sake, Raymond, don't show this to the President or he'll stop the war."

Pershing requested the French minister of war to declare a state of siege (similar to American martial law) at ports of entry used by the Americans, and in a letter to Secretary Baker on 13 November wrote that, "Such a state practically exists in St. Nazaire." "Stench Nazaire," as the doughboys soon dubbed it, was the principal port of debarkation for American troops. During the summer and early fall of 1917 some 200,000 American troops passed through it. As a port St. Nazaire had always had a surplus of prostitutes, and the night before the first American troops of the 1st Division arrived, three new brothels opened.

The venereal disease rate was particularly high among the black troops who were employed there as stevedores. In the months after their arrival the rate soared to 625 per 1,000 simply because they viewed prophylaxis with "horrified suspicion" and refused to report for treatment. When orders were given that all blacks be given prophylaxis treatment on returning to camp whether they admitted exposure or not, the rate fell in three months to 110 per 1,000; eventually it was reduced to 35 per 1,000.

Dr. Hugh Young, a distinguished urologist from Johns Hopkins who was commissioned a major and placed in charge of the antivenereal disease program, investigated the examination of prostitutes in legal brothels and found it "thoroughly inadequate and insufficient." When he reported that prostitutes welcomed foreign troops because they had more money, Pershing wired the War Department to withhold a portion of each soldier's pay, the first of his measures to keep his command free of venereal disease.

When the American authorities demanded that all known brothels in St. Nazaire be closed, they were informed that this was impossible, but they were assured by the French chief of mission attached to the AEF medical department that unlicensed prostitutes would be "relentlessly suppressed." However, licensing was a delicate matter, he said, explaining that "a careful distinction must be made between professional debauchery and passing shortcomings, and efforts must always tend to safeguard family honor." A young woman who wished to earn a few extra francs should not be exposed as a harlot by the forced issuance of a license.

Pershing responded by placing every brothel in town off limits and posting military police at their doors, a measure to which the mayor and police officials strongly objected. The female population, they declared, would be endangered if black stevedores were not allowed to use the brothels. Either they must be open to them or the Americans must import black prostitutes. If neither suggestion was approved, then the stevedores must be sent back to the United States. The AEF headquarters found none of these options feasible.

In mid-January 1918 American troops began to use Blois, a manufacturing town on the Loire thirty-five miles southwest of Orléans, as a training area. When the provost marshal there placed all brothels off limits, the French authorities protested and the houses were reopened. On 10 February, on the recommendation of an American medical officer, the army took over one and ran it for the exclusive use of the American troops: open from 5:00 P.M. until 9:00 P.M. for enlisted men and until 10:00 P.M. for officers. No French civilians allowed. An American medical officer examined the women two or three times a week. In six weeks it was peremptorily shut down on orders from AEF headquarters. Military police were then stationed at railway stations, where women suspected of prostitution were reported to the French authorities, and about 150 unlicensed women were forced to leave town. Dr. Young's report on Blois was marked "Strictly Confidential."

In other towns, too, the American authorities tried to part soldiers from prostitutes. In Brest, which became a major debarkation port, soldiers were forbidden to be seen on the street with a French woman, apparently on the assumption that no respectable woman would consort with an American soldier. After a series of embarrassing incidents the order was rescinded. At La Rochelle military police took the names of soldiers seen with women so they could be questioned later.

The American attitude was incomprehensible to the French who, said Dr. Young, "believe our attitude to be founded upon a prudery of which they feel themselves incapable and to be essentially a matter of morals . . . [but] the matter of the AEF is essentially a matter of hygiene."

Contracting a venereal disease was a court-martial offense and many were tried. The distribution of condoms was discussed and rejected. Explaining the opposition of AEF headquarters, urologist Dr. H. L. Sanford, said: "I don't think you should hand them out a license to cohabit, and the condom pretends to represent an absolute guarantee against infection."

From a medical point of view the antivenereal disease program was a dramatic success with the exception of venereal diseases among officers. The rate for officers, negligible in the United States, soared to 27.7 per 1,000 in France. The lowest rate was among the infantry, who probably had the least opportunity; it was highest among the military police, who, posted as guards at the brothels, had the greatest occasion for sexual contact.

It was hard to separate soldiers and whores. Private Albert Ettinger, a dispatch rider with the 165th Infantry, who agreed to help out a bordello near the town of Deneuvre in exchange for a free session, passed out a local madame's business cards to his buddies. A lieutenant wrote in his diary: "Wandering through dark streets. Ever-present women. So mysterious and seductive in darkness. . . . A fellow's got to hang on to himself here. Not many do."

In the 42nd Division several officers, out of the line for a time, were discovered to have rented rooms in Baccarat and Badonviller which they shared with local women or prostitutes. They were court-martialed, deprived of pay, and given a stern lecture by Douglas MacArthur, who after the war was to do exactly the same thing himself—without, however, receiving reprimand or punishment.

While it was recognized that men could not be permanently confined to their camp, furloughs presented serious problems. In January 1918 the army began the practice of sending men to designated leave areas where the YMCA and other service organizations provided recreational facilities. The first such area opened on 15 February 1918 at Aix-les-Baines. Eventually nineteen areas in France that included thirty-nine towns were designated as well as five in the Rhine Valley, two in Italy, and one in England. Two areas, Chambery and Challes-les-Eaux, were designated for black troops. AEF headquarters considered the program a success, although not all areas were equally popular. Men complained that three in the Pyrenees offered nothing but magnificent scenery; it was noted that the incidence of venereal disease was low in these places. Nice was the least satisfactory from the medical standpoint: 45,000 men visited the town; 30,000 prophylactic treatments were given.

Although Paris with its estimated 75,000 prostitutes was not a leave area, it was not off limits. Dr. Joseph E. Moire, who studied the incidence of venereal disease in the city, reported with seeming incomprehension: "Many soldiers, although thoroughly instructed in venereal disease matters and fully provided with the opportunity of Y.M.C.A. and Red Cross entertainments, were obstinate in preferring the society of women of the Paris streets."

Still, at the end of the war, General March, speaking of the venereal disease rate, proudly boasted that the United States had "a smaller loss of man power to the Army, and a smaller number of permanently disabled and invalided men than was recorded in any other army or than had ever before been recorded among our troops." Lauding the handling of the problem "in a common-sense open manner," he wrote: "There is no question but that this medical treatment of men afflicted with venereal disease, during the progress of the war, has increased the virility and strength of their descendants."

In January 1918 an incensed Pershing, having learned that an American magazine had charged his soldiers with immorality and drunkenness, shot back a cable denying the charges, adding: "American mothers may rest assured that their sons are a credit to them and the nation, and they may well look forward to the proud day when on the battlefield these splendid men will shed a new luster on American manhood."

To make sure that as many young men as possible would live to shed their luster on American manhood, Dr. Young established venereal treatment centers in each regiment and provided medical services to French females in troop areas. He used posters and lectures and even established an antiprostitution spy ring of mothers and housewives. His efforts, strongly supported by Pershing, held the rate down until in September 1918 there was only one case per thousand, a remarkable performance.

Pershing maintained to the last his war against venereal diseases. Speaking to officers at Brest in January 1919 he told them: "It is my very great ambition that not a single case among the American Expeditionary Forces shall arrive in the United States. I think this is a goal we all ought to work for." Consequently, no man with a venereal disease was allowed to board ship for home.

15

☆

BLACKS AND INDIANS IN

THE AMERICAN ARMY

BLACKS HAD NOT been permitted to enlist as regulars in the United States Army until 1866 when Congress authorized their enlistment in six segregated black regiments led by white officers. These were soon reduced to four: the 9th and 10th Cavalries and the 24th and 25th Infantries. Integration was suggested by General Ambrose E. Burnside in 1877, when he was a United States senator; other generals recommended it as well. All were ignored.

During the Indian fighting period, from 1866 to 1891, eighteen blacks, eleven of whom were troopers in the 9th Cavalry, won the Medal of Honor. On the Mexican border black troops under Brigadier General John Pershing had generally done well, although there had been one disgraceful failure: On 21 June 1916 units of the 10th Cavalry broke under fire during a skirmish with Mexican forces at Carrizal, a village in Chihuahua State, eighty-five miles south of Juárez.

In spite of their generally good performance—a lower desertion rate and a higher percentage of reenlistments than in white regiments—most of their junior officers came from the bottom of West Point classes until 1887, after which some graduates of higher class standing, attracted by their rising reputation, chose the 9th or 10th Cavalry. General Pershing served as a first lieutenant in the 10th Cavalry from 1892 to 1898 and for his championship of black soldiers was called "Black Jack" Pershing.

Later he was to write: "My earlier service with colored troops in the Regular Army had left a favorable impression on my mind. In the field on the frontier and elsewhere they were reliable and courageous and the old

10th Cavalry (colored), with which I served in Cuba, made an enviable record there. Under capable white officers and with sufficient training, negro soldiers have always acquitted themselves creditably."

Pershing did not, however, favor black officers. In his memoirs he wrote: "It was well known that the time and attention that must be devoted to training colored troops in order to raise their level of efficiency to the average were considerably greater than for white regiments. More responsibility rested upon officers of colored regiments owing to the lower capacity and lack of education of the personnel. In the new army, with hastily trained colored officers below white officers in general ability and in previous preparation, the problem of attaining battle efficiency for colored troops was vastly more difficult. It would have been much wiser to have followed the long experience of our Regular Army and provided these colored units with selected white officers."

The lack of education was indeed a handicap. John Green, a soldier in the 92nd Division, described how he became a noncommissioned officer. He and other conscripts were asked by a regular army sergeant if any of them had had any previous military experience. None had. He then asked, "How many of you boys can read and write?" Only Green raised his hand. "Well, Green," said the sergeant, "you, too, are now a sergeant."

The Wilson presidency was not sympathetic to black interests. Wilson himself and half of his cabinet came from the south and the administration was supported by southerners. Racists bills were introduced in Congress and no steps were taken to prevent abuses or even lynchings. Nevertheless, many black leaders, including the strongly pacifist Dr. W. E. B. Du Bois, supported American entry into the Great War and the enlistment of black soldiers: "Our country is at war. . . . If this is *our* country, then this is *our* war. We must fight it with every ounce of blood and treasure." But blacks were slow to enlist.

Of the 367,710 blacks who served in the army and the 5,328 who served in the navy, about ninety percent were conscripted. Blacks constituted ten percent of those who registered, but made up thirteen percent of those drafted. More than half (51.65 percent) who registered for the draft were placed in Class I (subject to immediate call). Only 32.53 percent registered whites were in this category. However, as the provost marshal general pointed out, there were 650,000 white volunteers and only 4,000 blacks.

Many blacks objected to conscription. A military intelligence report in June 1918 noted that "at no time have the colored people resented the discrimination as keenly as at present." William M. Kelly, a black from Brooklyn conscripted in the summer of 1918, wrote to Secretary Baker: "I go forth to battle, not as a patriotic soldier eager to defend a flag that defends me and mine, but as a prisoner of war, shackled to a gun that shall spit fire in the defense of a humanity that does not include me." But Private Kelly's chances of seeing combat were slim.

Black troops fell into three categories: the four regiments of black regulars, none of which was sent to France; National Guard units in seven states and the District of Columbia in which 10,000 served; and by far the largest category, draftees and a few volunteers who were mostly organized into labor units.

Blacks were excluded from regular service in the navy, Marine Corps, and certain branches of the army. The Air Service banned blacks and on 16 July 1918 General Frank McIntyre recommended to the chief of staff "not to commission colored men in the Field Artillery as the number of men of that race who have the mental qualifications to come up to the standards of efficiency of the Field Artillery officers is so small that the few isolated cases might better be handled in other branches."

In May 1917 at a conference of 700 leaders of organizations with black interests the army was urged to place blacks in combat units led by black officers. The following month the first camp for training and commissioning black officers, a Colored Officers Training Camp, was established at Des Moines, Iowa, to train infantry officers.

The Des Moines camp opened with 1,250 candidates, of whom 250 were noncommissioned officers (NCOs) from the black regular regiments. About half of the remainder had business or professional training. Many were disappointed that Colonel Charles Young, the third black to be graduated from West Point (Class of 1889) and the ranking black officer in the army, was not given the command he himself wanted, but Young had been forced to retire because of high blood pressure. To demonstrate his fitness, he rode on horseback from his home in Ohio to the War Department in Washington, but to no avail. He did have kidney problems and in 1922 died of nephritis.

Instead, the school was commanded by Lieutenant Colonel (soon Major General) Charles Clarendon Ballou, a West Pointer, class of 1886, who had served on the Frontier against the Sioux and had won distinction in the Philippines. He had recently been second in command of the 24th Infantry and was known to support the commissioning of black officers, but he disapproved of the use of black units in combat.

Twelve other West Pointers, some from the deep south, were appointed instructors. During the course 372 candidates failed. After ninety days those who remained were not commissioned, as were white candidates, but were given another month of training, which most resented. The first class was graduated on 15 October 1917 and commissions were given to 439 at different grades: 106, mostly former regular NCOs, were made captains; 129 were commissioned as first lieutenants; and 204 as second lieutenants. After a furlough all were appointed to the 92nd Division, where Ballou, a newly promoted major general, was given command. Most of those commissioned as captains were soon dismissed as incompetent. (The leap from sergeant to captain would be difficult for any man.) Although all were trained as infantry, some were assigned to other arms or services.

The 92nd Division, with its mix of white and black officers, was regarded as something of an experiment, and originally 82 percent of its officers were white—58 percent at war's end. Ballou's adjutant soon issued Command Bulletin No. 35 in which he cautioned that in cases of conflict between white soldiers and blacks, the later would always have to prove their innocence, ending grimly with the warning that, "White men made the Division, and they can break it just as easily if it becomes a trouble maker."

In the summer of 1918 Pershing began receiving cables complaining that black soldiers were always placed in the most dangerous positions, that they were being sacrificed to save white troops, and that they were often left on the field to die without medical attention, even though up to this time the 92nd, the only black division serving in Pershing's army in France, had served only in quiet sectors. Others complained of the use of black soldiers as laborers and a dearth of black combat units. It was true that most black troops—about 150,000 out of the 200,000 sent to France—served in labor battalions, many as stevedores.

The American blacks used as stevedores did not always perform satisfactorily. W. W. Atterbury, the AEF Director General of Transportation, complained that, "We have experienced considerable difficulty in getting the proper amount of work out of the negro stevedores at the various ports." In England police and citizens asked that they be removed. One officer described his stevedores as "without exception the most worthless aggregation of humanity that was ever collected in one unit."

WAR DEPARTMENT GENERAL Order No. 109 of 31 August 1917 directed that the 1st Provisional Infantry Regiment (Colored) be formed at Camp Jackson, near Columbia, South Carolina. It was made up entirely of conscripts, most from the south. It trained at Camp Jackson without incident and without overt hostility from local citizens. All of the officers were white and Colonel Perry L. Miles, a West Point graduate of the Class of 1895, who had seen service in the Spanish-American War and in the Philippines, was its commander. The lieutenant colonel and some first lieutenants were also regulars; the remainder were National Guard and reserve officers. Many were disappointed at being sent to a black regiment. The draftees who appeared seemed to be mostly farm laborers and unpromising material for making soldiers. But Captain Chester Heywood, a company commander, recorded: "Clean clothes, well-cooked food in quantity, systematic exercises and drill, regular hours, plus strict but intelligent and helpful discipline, soon worked wonders."

The men took to soldiering enthusiastically and, wrote Heywood, "took pride in their uniforms and equipment. . . . We were all proud, not only of our individual companies, but of the regiment as a whole." In December the regiment's designation was changed to the 371st Infantry. It distinguished itself in France and Private Junius Diggs returned to his home in Columbia, South Carolina, with the *Medaille Militaire*, the *Croix de Guerre* with palm, and the Distinguished Service Cross.

The 371st with three National Guard black regiments—the 369th, 370th, and 372nd—formed an infantry brigade in the 93rd Infantry Division (Provisional). The division was designated provisional because it had no artillery, engineers, ordnance, or train and, in fact, never consisted of more than the four regiments of infantry.

On 6 April 1918 the 370th sailed for France. It had lost its black colonel, but most of its officers still were black. It fought in the Oise-Aisne offensive and suffered 665 casualties, of whom 105 were killed or died of wounds. The regiment developed a reputation for ferocity and was said to take few prisoners. By the war's end the 307th had suffered 147 officers and men killed in action or died of wounds. In addition, 900 officers and men were wounded.

The 15th New York, a National Guard regiment which became the 369th Infantry in the 93rd Division (Provisional), was raised in the fall of 1916 by William Hayward, a prominent white New York lawyer and politician who was its colonel. During the Spanish-American War he had volunteered and served as a captain in the 2nd Nebraska. After service in the Philippines he left the army as a colonel and married eighteen-year-old Sarah Ireland. He was serving as Public Service Commissioner in

New York when in 1915 he resigned to devote himself full time to his regiment. He could afford to do this after his first wife divorced him, for he
then married a widow who was said to be the richest woman in America.

The regiment consisted of ten understrength companies, each with
about sixty-five men, all of whom had had prior service. Raised to
wartime strength, it expanded to 1,378 men, although it had fewer than
fifty officers, some black and some white. Instead of the authorized six
officers, most companies had only two. It had no bayonets, not enough
uniforms, and its drill hall was a dance hall over a cigar store, but it did
have a magnificent forty-four-man band under the direction of
Lieutenant James Reese ("Jim") Europe (a black musician of note who
played the Cotton Club and was the pianist and arranger for Irene and
Vernon Castle). Noble Sissle, a well-known black singer and composer,
was its drum major and every member of the band was a professional
musician; their pay was augmented from a special fund. John D.
Rockefeller, Jr., an admirer, sent several checks for $500, telling Hayward
to "buy another musician," and Daniel Reed, the "Tin Plate King," when
asked to write to forty friends requesting contributions to a $10,000 fund,
wrote instead a check for the full $10,000, saying it was "a damn sight eas-
ier than writing a lot of letters."

Mustered into service in May 1917 and sent to Camp Whitman, near
Peekskill, New York, the regiment still lacked uniforms, individual equipment such as mess kits, and had only 250 rifles. Hayward asked that it be
made part of the Rainbow Division, but was told that "black was not one
of the colors of the rainbow." In the fall it was sent to Camp Wadsworth,
near Spartanburg, South Carolina, a move unpopular with the citizens of
the town. In a speech to the Chamber of Commerce, the mayor
announced that "they will probably expect to be treated like white men. I
say right now they will not be treated as anything but Negroes. We shall
treat them exactly as we treat our resident Negroes."

Although the regimental band was an instant success and was invited
to play at the country club, most merchants refused to sell to the soldiers.
After several incidents the camp commander, General Charles L.
Phillips, suggested that Hayward go to Washington and persuade the War
Department to send his regiment to France. While he was gone Drum
Major Sissle was cursed and kicked in a hotel lobby. Hayward's mission
was successful and in December his regiment embarked for France, the
first of the 93rd to sail.

The four infantry regiments which constituted the 93rd Division

(Provisional) were given to the French. This was believed to be a temporary measure, but they remained with the French for the duration of the war. Organized as French infantry, they were issued French arms and equipment and served as integral parts of French divisions. The men found ready social acceptance even though white Americans, without great success, attempted to impose their own racial prejudices upon the French.

The 369th Infantry spent 191 days—perhaps more than any other regiment—at the front, serving in the Champagne-Marne offensive and suffering a loss of some 1,500 men. Colonel Hayward boasted that although his regiment had been engaged in some of the heaviest fighting, it had never lost a prisoner or a trench. More than one hundred of its men earned the *Croix de Guerre* or the even more prestigious *Medaille Militaire*.

THE FIRST TWO men to earn the *Croix de Guerre* were Private Henry Johnson, a former New York Central red cap from Albany, New York, and Private Nedham Roberts. During the regiment's second tour in the trenches they were together manning a forward observation post when at 2:00 A.M. on 14 May 1918 they were attacked by a twenty-four-man German raiding party. Roberts, although wounded, doggedly threw grenades. Johnson, also wounded, after using up his ammunition, fought with his clubbed rifle and killed one German with a bolo knife. The raiding party retreated.

In America a number of racially related incidents, great and small, flared between black soldiers and white civilians, particularly in the south. On 29 July 1917 members of the 1st Battalion, 24th Infantry, who had been sent to guard the construction site at Camp MacArthur near Waco, Texas (then a town of about 33,000), flouted the city's Jim Crow laws, and when threatened with arrest, engaged in a shootout in a Waco street. In the resultant courts-martial seven soldiers were given dishonorable discharges and sentenced to five years in prison.

On 28 July 1917 the 3rd Battalion, 24th Infantry, arrived at Houston, Texas, to protect the construction site of Camp Logan, a mile and one-half from western Houston. From the beginning there were apprehensions on the part of the military authorities of racial violence. In an effort to keep his troops out of town, the colonel of the regiment arranged for social events to be held at the camp, but inevitably men went into town and many complained of abuse.

On 23 August 1917 Private Alonzo Edwards tried to protect a black woman being beaten by a white policeman who had arrested her for gambling. He was pistol-whipped and arrested for drunkenness. Later that day when Corporal Charles Baltimore of the military police inquired about him, he, too, was struck with a pistol, shot at, beaten, and arrested. Although Corporal Baltimore was soon released, word spread in the camp that he had been killed. A group of his fellow soldiers stole some ammunition and, bent on vengeance, made for the city, some firing as they went. At Filipo Street they were met by police and armed citizens and gunfire was exchanged. Three black soldiers and seventeen white men, including five policemen and one army officer, apparently mistaken for a policeman, were killed.

Two companies of Coast Artillery and a battalion of infantry, all white, were rushed to Houston. The battalion of the 24th was disarmed and sent to its regimental headquarters in Denning, New Mexico. There courts-martial were held for 156 "mutineers," as they were officially declared. In the first, held on 8 December, a Sunday, sixty-three soldiers were tried, thirteen were condemned to death, and forty-one were sentenced to life imprisonment; five were acquitted. Those condemned to death were hanged before dawn on Wednesday, 11 December. In subsequent trials sixteen more were sentenced to death and more were imprisoned for life. Six of the sixteen were hanged. President Wilson, on Secretary Baker's advice, had the sentences of the others commuted. One of those given life imprisonment committed suicide, as did a white company commander before he could testify. It was the bloodiest racial encounter in American military-civilian relations since the Civil War.

This affair had an impact on the wartime role of blacks. The number of black combat units was reduced and blacks were trained in small contingents in areas where they easily could be outnumbered by white troops.

The 370th Infantry of the 93rd Division, originally the 8th Illinois National Guard, was the only National Guard regiment with an all-black officer corps, including its commander, Colonel Franklin A. Dennison. It entered Federal service in July 1917. En route to Camp Logan, Texas, the men tore down Jim Crow signs in train stations along the way and looted a store that refused them service.

In 1918 a battlefield catastrophe had a profound and long-lasting effect upon the employment of blacks in combat in the American army. In General Ballou's 92nd Division, the only fully formed black division in the army, its 368th Infantry regiment, composed of conscripts from

Tennessee, Pennsylvania, and Maryland, was commanded by Colonel Fred R. Brown, a West Pointer (Class of 1899) with nineteen years' service. All of the company officers were black; many had been trained at Des Moines under Ballou.

In the Meuse-Argonne offensive on 25 September the 368th took its position in the line between the dismounted French 11th Cuirassiers on its left and the infantry of the American 77th Division on its right. Its officers had no maps and its men had insufficient wire cutters, rifle grenades, and signal flares, but this also was true in many other regiments.

On 26 September Colonel Brown placed his 2nd Battalion in the front with the 3rd in reserve; the 1st Battalion, turned over to the French, served as divisional reserve. The 2nd was ordered to advance through a heavily wooded area laced with barbed wire. For the first four hours of the morning all went well, but the battalion commander lost contact with some of his men in the woods, there was a breakdown in communications, and German resistance stiffened. In the resulting confusion the troops responded sporadically. At dusk the battalion commander, perhaps in hope of regaining control, ordered his men to pull back to their starting point, but not all units received the order and some spent the night where they were.

The French 11th Cuirassiers on the regiment's left had not advanced, but the American 77th Division had moved ahead on the right. The next morning Colonel Brown brought back the 1st Battalion and divided the nearly two kilometer front in half with a battalion covering each half. An advance was made against stiff German resistance, but again the commander of the 2nd Battalion lost control; one company drifted back to its original position.

On 28 September the regiment received some artillery support: a half-hour bombardment. The 2nd Battalion made two unsuccessful attacks and after the second failure fell back in some confusion. Brown relieved the battalion commander. The 3rd Battalion then twice attempted to attack, but the men broke and ran to the rear.

On 29 September the two battalions were replaced by the French 9th Cuirassiers and the 1st Battalion of the American 368th Infantry, commanded by Major John N. Merrill, a soldier of fortune and a nongraduate of the West Point Class of 1902. He claimed to have served as an enlisted man in the American army, as an officer in the Philippine Constabulary, in the Persian gendarmerie and the Persian army, and as a captain in the British Indian Army. In the Argonne he pushed his men forward, sometimes threatening them with his pistol. Although he kept control of his men and maintained liaison with the units on his flanks, he later stated that "not a single officer of the battalion has shown any anxiety to get to close quarters with the Germans" and that "the cowardice shown by the men was abject," a statement echoed by Major B. F. Norris of the 3rd Battalion. On 30 September the 368th was relieved. It had suffered comparatively few casualties in the Argonne: forty-two killed, sixteen later died of wounds, and some 200 wounded. On 5 October the entire 92nd Division was ordered out of the area.

After being withdrawn, the division was turned over to the French, but the French found the black officers, most of them former career NCOs, "very mediocre," and the division soon was sent back and posted in the rear. Colonel Brown and the other white officers placed the blame for the debacle on their black officers, whom they called incompetent cowards. Lieutenant Colonel Robert P. Harbold (United States Military Academy, 1904, near the bottom of his class) reported to Pershing that while black soldiers were submissive, faithful, and subordinate, black officers were lacking in initiative and self-control; they were, he said, unable to exercise control over their troops. Thirty officers were relieved of command. The commander of the 3rd Battalion court-martialed five of his officers for cowardice in the face of the enemy. Four were sentenced to death by firing squad and one to life imprisonment. All five were later freed. Lieutenant General Robert Bullard recommended clemency, writing that "these Negroes could not be held as responsible as white men."

The commander of the 2nd Battalion, Major Max Elser, appears to have had a nervous breakdown. First Lieutenant Howard H. Long, a black who held a Master's degree in experimental psychology from Clark University was at Elser's headquarters during the battle and twenty-five years later wrote: "Many of the field officers seemed far more concerned with reminding their Negro subordinates that they were Negroes than they were with having an effective unit that would perform well in combat." Colonel Ballou concurred and in a letter written in 1920 said: "It was my misfortune to be handicapped by many white officers who were rabidly hostile to the idea of a colored officer, and who continually conveyed misinformation to the staff of the superior units and generally created much trouble and discontent. Such men will never give the Negro the square deal that is his just due."

In 1919, soon after the war, there was a special investigation into the affair and a board concluded that the failure of the regiment was due to lack of sufficient artillery support, inadequate maps, not enough wire cutters, and the inexperience of the troops. It also concluded that "the operations would have been more successful had the majority of company officers shown more individuality and personal resourcefulness." The battalion commanders were not censured.

The war's most highly decorated black American did not serve in the American army. Eugene Jacques Bullard was born in Georgia in 1894 and from an early age he watched his family suffer at the hands of white neighbors. Still an adolescent, he sold his pet goat and set off to find freedom in Europe. He made his way to England and a few years later crossed the channel to France where on 19 October 1914 he joined the French Foreign Legion. He served in the infantry in four major campaigns and was severely wounded before he was finally sent to flight school. In the spring of 1917 he became a pursuit pilot. He was credited with shooting down two enemy planes, a Fokker and a Pfalz, near Verdun in November. By the end of the war he was a Chevalier of the Legion of Honor and had won, among other decorations, the *Croix de Guerre* and the *Medaille Militaire*.

Bullard returned to the United States after the war and lived until 1961. He was buried in the Federation of French War Veterans Cemetery in Flushing, New York.

THE FIRST PEOPLES in the New World to declare war on the Central Powers in Europe were the Onondaga and Oneida Indians in 1914. Since the days of William "Buffalo Bill" Cody, touring Wild West shows had been popular in Europe. Among the 70,000 Americans caught stranded there when war broke out in August 1914 were two such shows, one in Berlin and the other at Trieste, then a part of the Austro-Hungarian Empire. Before they could make their way out of the warring countries they were assaulted several times by mobs, some of whom apparently thought them Serbian or Russian spies. In response to this mistreatment of their tribesmen — and to assert their tribal sovereignty — the Onondagas and Oneidas unilaterally declared war on Germany. When the United States eventually entered the war, ways and means opened for them and other Indians to strike back.

About a third of all Indians were noncitizens and these were exempt from the draft. In some cases, as with the Eastern Cherokees, their status as citizens was ambiguous. However, 17,313 Indians registered for the draft and 12,000–12,500 Indians served in the army, of whom 6,509 were conscripts. Less than two percent claimed deferment. Not until the last months of the war were they allowed to enlist. Fourteen tribes were involved in combat operations and Indians pledged more than thirteen million dollars in Liberty Loan drives.

Enthusiasm for the war varied by tribe. Very few Navajo enlisted, but forty percent of the young men in the Osage and Quapaw tribes from Oklahoma volunteered. Many had to make personal concessions. An Oklahoma circus rider, Baby Lone Kickapoo Brave, twenty-six, sacrificed his "thick black locks" that "dangled to his waist," and submitted to a "doughboy haircut" to enlist.

While the ability of black soldiers successfully to serve as combat soldiers was often contested, a prevailing belief, fostered further by the press, glorified Indian soldiers. The Indian was a natural warrior, it was said, possessing an exceptional sense of direction, great powers of endurance and a delight in battle. Provost Marshal General Enoch H. Crowder spoke of their "zeal for the great cause."

Dr. Joseph K. Nixon, Secretary of the National American Indian Memorial Association, lobbied Congress to establish segregated Indian units, believing that this would help preserve Indian culture. But most reformers sought to "Americanize" the Indians and hoped that military service with white soldiers would hasten their adoption of "civilized behavior." The matter was debated in Congress in 1917, but neither the War Department nor Cator Sells, Commissioner of Indian Affairs, wanted to see segregated units.

Many Indians served in regiments from the southwest. Since 1912 Company L of the 142nd Infantry had been an Indian company in the 36th Division, a National Guard division from Texas and Oklahoma. This was soon changed, but the 142nd retained a high proportion of the 600 Indians in the division.

Although Canada refused to enlist blacks, Asians, or Eskimos until the end of 1915, a number of American Indians, particularly in the northwest, crossed the border to enlist in the Canadian army before American entry into the war. About 3,000–4,000 served.

Indian casualties were high: At least five percent were killed in action compared to one percent for the AEF as a whole. This was undoubtedly due to the fact that almost all served in the infantry and very few served on the line of communication. Their reputed prowess as warriors further increased their chances of being killed, leading, as it did, to their officers assigning them to dangerous positions as scouts, snipers, and messengers.

As the war progressed the value of their languages, unknown in Europe, was recognized and many were used as telephone operators, speaking in their native tongues. The 142nd Infantry had two Choctaw soldiers who transmitted telephone messages. When words had no Choctaw equivalent, they paraphrased them. Casualties became "scalps"; poison gas, "bad air"; and the 3rd Battalion, "three grains of rice."

The Germans had such a high opinion of the fighting abilities of the Indians, their impressions drawn from Wild West shows and from highly popular German books about them, that German newspapers tried to conceal the fact that their soldiers were fighting against them. During the St. Mihiel offensive the commanding officer of the German 97th Landwehr ordered snipers to pick off Indians when they could be recognized.

Overall the Indians lived up to their reputations. Ten received the *Croix de Guerre* and 150 received other decorations, including the Distinguished Service Cross.

16

☆

SECOND BATTLE OF THE MARNE:

ON THE AISNE RIVER

ALTHOUGH THE BRITISH and French were eager to acquire the services of the fresh young American soldiers sent to Europe, their opinion of Pershing and his senior officers dropped ever lower. Lloyd George even went so far as to suggest that Pershing relinquish his command of American troops in Britain and let Haig decide when they were ready for battle. In late May 1918 Jan Christiaan Smuts, the former Boer leader who now was a British general, made the extraordinary suggestion in a confidential letter to Lloyd George that the American army be taken away from Pershing and given to someone more competent—like himself. "Pershing is very commonplace," he wrote, "without real war experience, and already overwhelmed by the initial difficulties of a job too big for him. It is also doubtful whether he will loyally co-operate with the Allied Higher Commands. He could not get together a first class staff either. I fear very much that with the present Higher Command the American Army will not be used to the best advantage; and victory for us depends on squeezing the last ounce of proper use out of the American Army."

Faced with the apprehensions of the French and British, a feeling grew among some in power in Washington that Pershing was incapable of handling his vast responsibilities. On 3 June 1918 Colonel House suggested to the President that Pershing "be relieved from all responsibility except the training and fighting of our troops." Marsh wrote to the same effect and privately expressed his belief that Pershing had more work to do "than any one man in this world can accomplish."

On 6 July, while the Second Battle of the Marne was in progress, Baker

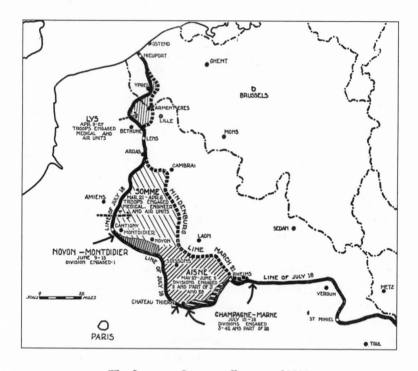

The five great German offensives of 1918

CREDIT: *The War With Germany*

wrote to Pershing suggesting that General George W. Goethals, the builder of the Panama Canal and number-two man on the General Staff, be sent to handle the AEF's supply system, which was indeed in trouble. He would be, Baker explained, a coordinator and not a subordinate.

When Pershing read Baker's letter he sprang into action. He knew that his supply situation was not as well in hand as it should be, but he did not want this important segment of his command taken from him. Although he respected and admired Goethals, he did not want him in France. In a confidential telegram to Baker marked RUSH RUSH RUSH RUSH he responded that the whole supply system "is intimately interwoven with our whole organization. The whole must absolutely remain under one head. Any division of responsibility or coordinate control in any sense would be fatal." Within the next forty-eight hours he followed up with another cable and two letters. Moving quickly, he put in charge of the Services of Supply (SOS) his best and most loyal subordinate, General James G. Harbord, and with Harbord and a number of staff officers he made a week-long inspection of the supply line. Although not happy to be relieved of a fighting command, Harbord brought great energy and imagination to his task and efficiency was achieved. Tonnage unloaded increased by twenty percent.

Pershing's independent American army was still unrealized. Strategically the French still called the tune. It was not until 1918 that American troops in numbers fought the Germans, first on the defensive to blunt the great Ludendorff offensives—the so-called *Friedstürmes* (Peace Offensives)—that were expected to end the war. In the provinces of Aisne and Marne nearly nine American divisions were in action in support of the Allied offensive of Marshal Foch, and in August two corps under American commanders occupied abutting sectors. It was Foch who set the time and place and gave overall direction to the battles. But as the Americans in the hundreds of thousands arrived in France, reaching well over a million by August, American influence on the battlefield became a decisive factor, and the independent army of Pershing's dreams drew closer to reality.

The Second Battle of the Marne began on 28 May with the third Ludendorff offensive, sometimes called the Third Battle of the Aisne River or the Chemin des Dames offensive. It was the final thrust of the German spring campaign and was the most threatening of all the German drives.

The Chemin des Dames, a highway constructed for the journeys of the daughters of Louis XV in the eighteenth century, ran about four miles north of and parallel to the Aisne River with its east end near Craonne and its west end at Malmaison. This area already had witnessed severe fighting in phases of the battles waged in September 1914, April, May, and October 1917, and May 1918.

Three distinct sectors lay in this part of the front: the Craonne Plateau itself, a steep-walled bulwark extending from east to west; a low area stretching from the eastern end of the Craonne Plateau to the hills on the south bank of the Aisne; and the Sapigneul Heights, crowned by Fort Brimont, a German-held fortification which French General Robert-Georges Nivelle had tried unsuccessfully to take in 1917.

Foch, assuming that the Germans believed the French defenses to be impregnable, persuaded Haig that the area was so safe he could send five completely crippled divisions to rest there. By late May it held eleven divisions, including three British, spread out over ninety-two kilometers, thus about five and one-quarter kilometers of front per division.

The Germans made their preparations for an offensive with great care and secrecy. Security officers kept a careful eye on civilians in the area and monitored the talk of soldiers in the canteens. Aircraft swept over bivouac areas to make sure no telltale sign could be seen from the air. The chorus of frogs in the Ailette marshes helped conceal the sounds of engineers nightly bringing forward bridging materials. So well were the preparations for the attack concealed that as late as 25 May, three days before the blow fell, French army headquarters suspected nothing.

Even with the advantage of surprise, the German task was formidable. Their attacking force had first to cross the Ailette marshes and climb 300 feet up a bare glacis raked by machine gun fire to reach the main Allied positions on the Craonne Plateau. If successful there, they would then need to cross the Aisne River, which at this point was some sixty yards wide, and seize the south bank. And all this had to be accomplished before any strong Allied resistance could be organized.

The front here was controlled by French General Denis "Tiger" Duchêne, commanding the French Sixth Army. An arrogant man of a brutal disposition, he scorned all plans and discouraged initiative in his subordinates. Well satisfied with his defenses, he failed to prepare them in depth.

Two weeks before the German attack Captain Samuel T. Hubbard, Jr., a young American intelligence officer in charge of the order of battle section, predicted that it was impending. Seven years out of Harvard and a cotton broker, he had enlisted in the New York National Guard in 1911 and had been commissioned just before the war. Laying his information and conclusions before his superiors, including Brigadier General Dennis E. Noland, the AEF's brilliant chief of intelligence, he convinced them. Noland, with Pershing's permission, informed the French that the Germans were massing troops to break their lines on the Chemin des Dames. The French, unimpressed by the word of inexperienced American intelligence officers, assured Noland that he was mistaken. No extra defensive measures were taken. Thus was the scene set for the greatest Allied disaster since the German drive to take Paris in 1914, when German armies had overrun Belgium and northern France, and had reached the Marne and threatened Paris before being brought to a halt.

The Allied attitude changed swiftly when on 26 May a German *Unteroffizier* (noncommissioned officer) and a private were captured by a French patrol. Under interrogation the private revealed that preparations were being made for an attack; the *Unteroffizier*, for his part, denied there were any such preparations, but threatened with being shot as a spy for giving false information, he divulged the full extent of the German plans. At this late hour all that could be done was to warn the units destined to be struck and to send urgent preliminary orders to eight divisions in the northern reserves to hurry toward them. General Duchêne, unconcerned, was "visiting the ladies" in Paris when the blow struck.

The German attack was not only the most thoroughly prepared, but also the best executed of the war. Ludendorff assembled 3,719 guns in the Aisne region and at 1:00 A.M. on 27 May began a barrage that lasted for one hour and five minutes. Tons of gas and high-explosive shells landed upon the trenches of three British and three French divisions while trench mortars worked on Allied protective wire. Then, suddenly shifting their fire, light and medium guns sought out Allied headquarters, road junctions, and artillery positions. After a second brief but overpowering barrage on the front-line trenches, selected German storm troopers armed with light machine guns overran them, dashing past dead, wounded, gassed, and dazed French and British soldiers.

Then with seventeen divisions in the first wave and thirteen in reserve the Germans stormed the Chemin des Dames and the area beyond on a nine-mile front. Intact bridges over the Aisne, left unblown by the French, were quickly taken. By nightfall the Germans, having crossed three rivers—the Ailette, Aisne, and Vesle—were in the village of Fismes, sixteen miles west-northwest of Rheims.

German artillery had practically destroyed the six Allied divisions, and, thanks to Duchêne's incompetence, there were no backup units behind the lines. By evening the Germans had created a twenty-five-mile-wide breach in the Allied line and penetrated twelve miles.

Foch gave XXI Corps under fifty-two-year-old General Jean Marie Joseph Degoutte the near-impossible task of stemming the tide. Reserves were rushed immediately from railhead to battle and, as one French officer observed, "evaporated immediately like drops of rain on a whitehot iron." Foch, too, later wrote that the "divisions sent by the Sixth Army melted away as fast as they were flung into battle. . . ."

On 29 May General Jean-Henri Mordacq, a staff officer, found a badly shaken General Degoutte at his headquarters so out of touch that he had difficulty indicating the location of the rapidly spreading German infantry. On leaving, Mordacq glanced back and saw Degoutte "silently weeping over a tattered remnant of a map." On his return to Paris Mordacq wrote in his diary: "I left him with no hope of ever seeing him again."

By 30 May the Germans had reached the Marne at Château-Thierry, less than fifty miles from Paris, occupying the high hills stretching for ten miles along the north bank of the river and establishing outposts south of it. In three days they had advanced forty miles, captured nearly 60,000 prisoners, 650 guns, 2,000 machine guns, immense quantities of supplies, munitions, airdromes, depots, and a wealth of railroad rolling stock. Theirs was the longest advance made by any army on the Western Front since the beginning of trench warfare. A huge bulge now loomed between Rheims and Soissons, and both cities were threatened. Even Ludendorff was taken aback by such a spectacular success. He had intended this attack to be merely a strong diversion to draw Allied troops away from the north where Crown Prince Rupprecht of Bavaria was preparing the main German attack. Now he was tempted to pursue his good fortune. His victorious troops had reached country as yet untouched by war's devastations. Before them were large stretches of arable land; unfinished new houses indicated how safe the French had felt.

On 30 May Pershing despatched his 1st and 3rd divisions to the French. The first Americans to reach the battlefield, two companies of the 7th Motorized Machine Gun Battalion of the 3rd Division, arrived late in the afternoon of 31 May and took up positions guarding the bridges crossing the Marne near Château-Thierry. The following day, they covered the retreat of the remnants of a Senegalese division. Second Lieutenant John Ter Bush Bissell, who had been graduated from West Point only nine months before, rushed across a bridge with two machine guns and their crews—thirteen men in all—and took up positions on the north bank. They fought off all German attacks until at 10:30 P.M. French pioneers prematurely blew the center span of the bridge, killing a remnant of the Senegalese rear guard and the leading Germans. Bissell and his machine gunners were cut off, but in the dark they made their way to a railroad bridge and retreated across it, carrying their wounded. That bridge, too, was blown a few hours later. (Bissell later served as a brigadier general in World War II.)

Pershing had intended to use the 2nd Division to relieve the 1st Division, but at Pétain's request, it was simply added to the fray. French *camions*, driven by Vietnamese,* carried the infantry forward at a breakneck pace. One lieutenant remembered thinking, "Lucky if we don't get killed before reaching the front," but as they moved forward their progress slowed for they had to push against a sea of refugees. Brigadier General Harbord, then still commanding the brigade of marines in the 2nd Division, reported he had never seen a more pathetic sight: "Little flocks of sheep, occasionally a led cow, sometimes a crate of chickens on a cart. Everything that a frightened peasantry fleeing before a barbarian invader would be likely to think of bringing from among their little treasures was to be seen on that congested highway."

French morale was plunging. Mixed with the refugees were French soldiers fleeing the battle. As they passed they called out to the Americans that they had come too late, that they could only delay the inevitable end. "They were tired and demoralized," said Harbord. "It was a beaten, routed army."

On the road he encountered a French general of division who, when Harbord asked where the Germans were, said he didn't know. He gave the same response when asked where his own command was. Asked where he was going, he smiled and replied, "La soupe."

Harbord made his headquarters in the recently deserted village of Bremoiselle, and was shocked to see that it had been sacked, not by the Germans, but by retreating French soldiers: "The houses had been looted, not forgetting the wine cellars. The contents of chests and cupboards

*The French imported tens of thousands of men from French Indo-China, whom they employed as laborers and truck drivers.

had been thrown on the floor, dresses were torn in strips, dead chickens and pigs were lying on the streets. With Germans close behind, the *poilus* were salvaging for personal account." A peasant who protested the vandalism, was tied to a chair and beaten.

The plummeting French morale was not limited to the *poilus*. At Pétain's forward headquarters despairing staff officers performed their duties with long faces. But one of Pétain's aides, Jean de Pierrefeu, described the rejuvenating effect of the arrival of the closely packed trucks of American infantry,

> almost all bare headed and bare chested, singing American airs at the top of their voices. . . . The spectacle of these magnificent youths from overseas, these beardless children of twenty, radiating strength and health in their equipment, produced a great effect. They contrasted strikingly with our regiments in their faded uniforms, wasted by so many years of war, whose members, thin, their sunken eyes shining with a dull fire, were no more than bundles of nerves held together by a will to heroism and sacrifice. We had the impression that we were about to see a wonderful transfusion of blood. Life was coming in floods to reanimate the dying body of France.

Amid confusion and conflicting French orders, on 1 June the 2nd Division infantry struggled to find its place in the line. Soldiers and marines were hungry and tired. The machine gun battalion, the artillery, and the mobile kitchens were still fighting road traffic. However, by 3 June the infantry was largely in place, occupying defensive positions north of the Marne on the main highway to Paris west of Château-Thierry, where it repelled all German attacks. The remaining troops followed, among them the 4th Marine Brigade, made up of the 5th and 6th regiments. For the first time marines were to see active service in the war. On 4 June General Degoutte assigned the new arrivals a nine-mile stretch of the front centering upon the village of Lucy-le-Bocage.

As the German offensive began to run out of steam Foch counterattacked with twenty-five French divisions and the American 2nd and 3rd divisions. As its part in this massive operation the 2nd Division on 6 June attacked at Belleau Wood, a relatively small section of the Château-Thierry sector, striking at Bouresches and Vaux at dawn.

Belleau Wood was a kidney-shaped timbered area of dense trees with a tangle of undergrowth about a thousand yards across at its widest northern sector and three thousand yards long from north to south. It had once been the hunting preserve for the ancient Château de Belleau which, with its village, lay about a half mile north of the wood.

This was the first United States offensive operation of division strength in the war. The Marine Brigade, with support from the army's 6th Engineers and the semitrained 7th Infantry, launched two attacks against the wood and the nearby village of Bouresches. Opposing them was the German 10th Division, rated a first-class combat unit, that was part of General Oskar von Hutier's Eighteenth Army, the southernmost of the three German armies involved in the Ludendorff offensive along the Aisne.

West of the wood was Hill 142, a key German position attacked by the 5th Marines. The attack began, one participant recalled, on "a warm and sunny day. The air was sparkling. Millions of poppies flared among the grain; the fields glowed like crimson carpets."

The German positions at Belleau Wood should not have been attacked until the artillery had built up a supply of gas shells, but the Americans had no accurate maps and little information about the wood or the strength and disposition of the Germans inside it, an intelligence failure due in large part because orders to reconnoiter the area had been neglected.

The marines attacked in waves, lines of men sometimes moving shoulder to shoulder, almost like a Civil War attack, without benefit of mortars or grenades, and German Maxim machine guns scythed them down. Marine Captain John W. Thomason described the attack: "Platoons were formed in four waves . . . a formation proved in trench warfare, where there was a short way to go, and you calculated on losing the first three waves and getting the fourth to the objective. The Marines never used it again. It was a formation unadapted for open warfare, and incredibly vulnerable. It didn't take long to learn better, but there was a price to pay for the learning." First Sergeant Daniel "Pop" Hunter, a thirty-year veteran, lined up the 67th Company, the platoons in four waves, blew his whistle, and pointed forward with his cane. He was one of the first casualties as the German machine guns sprayed them. Twice he went down and twice he got up, only to be killed when shot a third time. Floyd Gibbons wrote: "I never saw men charge to their death with finer spirit."

Writing five weeks later, Joyce Lewis, serving in the 5th Marines with his brother William, described what he saw and did:

Brother "Billy" and I were of the first 1,250 to go "over the top." Eight hundred of these were either killed or wounded almost before we got started. I saw Major [John] Berry killed,* and shortly thereafter "Billy" went down. He was about 200 feet from me. The boys were charging into machine-gun nests and Billy was running along the edge of a wheat-field toward a wood where the Germans were concealed. The first bullet hit him in the top of the head and others lower down as he fell.

In the charge I got within fifty feet of the machine-gun nests when a bullet plowed through the top of my skull. It was a bad wound. . . . As I lay there I could plainly see the German gunners and hear them talk-ing. They could see I was not dead and I watched them as they prepared to finish me. They reloaded their gun and turned it on me. The first three bullets went through my legs and hip and the rest splashed up dust and dirt around my head and body. Evidently thinking they had done a good job the Boches turned their gun to other parts of the field.

The charge at dawn across fields of red poppies and golden wheat was successful. The marines took the hill, but suffered 1,087 casualties.

During the height of the battle for Bouresches a battered Ford truck named Lizzie gained distinction. The truck originally had been fitted out as an ambulance and donated to the 6th Marines by Mrs. Elizabeth Pearce of New York City, but it was now serving as a supply truck. Bouresches had been taken and the southwest portion of the woods was penetrated, but the men holding the village were running short of ammu-nition and rations. At this critical moment Lizzie, driven by Private Morris Fletz, was seen careening toward them at breakneck speed across a wheat field, shrapnel bursting overhead. She gained the village in a close-run race. Private Fletz was unhurt, but Lizzie was found to have been hit by twelve lead balls. On the spot the marines awarded her a *Croix de Guerre* and later painted the insignia on her hood.

Gunnery Sergeant Dan Daly, already the holder of two Medals of Honor—one won in the Boxer Rebellion in 1900 and a second in the occupation of Haiti in 1915—was said to have urged his men forward by calling, "Come on, you sons of bitches! Do you want to live forever?" Daly piously denied ever using such language, but during the war he continued to distinguish himself, earning the Distinguished Service Cross, the Navy Cross, the *Medaille Militaire*, and the *Croix de Guerre* with palm.

A battalion surgeon described the hideous wounds of those carried to

---

*The marine battalion commander was not killed but he had been shot in the left elbow, the bullet traveling down his arm and lodging in the palm of his hand.

his aid station: "The character of the wounds encountered here fall chiefly into the tearing, lacerating crushing and amputating types, accompanied by all degrees of fractures, hemorrhage and destruction of soft tissue."

The American medical services could not handle the flood of wounded. Evacuation Hospital No. 6 at Juilly had 250 beds, two surgeons and twenty nurses, but from 4 to 8 June it was swamped by more than 2,000 wounded. Many were felled by mustard gas; particularly hit was the 2nd Battalion of the 6th Marines. Private Frederick Pottle later remembered seeing hundreds of men "nearly all blinded, many delirious, all crying, moaning, tossing about."

Pershing visited the American wounded in French hospitals after the battle. Stopping by one cot, he asked the young man where he was wounded. The soldier earnestly replied: "Do you remember, sir, just where the road skirts a small grove and runs to the left across the wheat field and then leads up over the brow of the hill? Well, right there, sir."

A young soldier who had lost an arm apologized because he could not salute. Pershing ran his hand lightly through the boy's hair and said, "No, it's I that should salute you."

On 12 July the New York *Times* headlined a story with a dateline of the day before: OUR MEN TAKE BELLEAU WOOD, 300 CAPTIVES. This was not so. It was not even close. The marines had not even entered the northern part of the wood. Belleau Wood proved a hard nut to crack. Fourteen days later it was indeed taken, but the marines sustained nearly 5,200 casualties, including 750 killed, more than fifty percent of its strength. One mile had been gained. It was the costliest battle in Marine Corps history and would remain so until the Battle of Tarawa in November 1943.

Southeast of Belleau Wood was Hill 192, for which the army's 23rd Infantry fought on 6–7 June. Soldiers in the 3rd Infantry brigade of the 2nd Division and soldiers of the 7th Infantry also fought bravely; they encountered heavy resistance and suffered heavily. A Private Hebel wrote home: "We are having very heavy days with death before us hourly. Here we have no hope ever to come out. My company has been reduced from 120 to 30 men." Nevertheless, it was the marines who received the lion's share of the laurels, being credited with winning the entire battle around Château-Thierry.

War correspondents were eager to report on American battles, but censorship was strict and any who refused to obey the rules, even star reporters such as Westbrook Pegler, Heywood Broun, and Reginald

Kauffman, had their credentials revoked. Newsmen were told where they could go and when, to whom they could speak and when; they were forbidden to give the name or number of any unit or even to say if a division was regular army, National Guard, or conscript. Reporters were, however, allowed to mention marines, an incongruity that Floyd Gibbons, thirty-one, of the Chicago *Tribune*, perhaps the best-known and best-liked of the war correspondents, took full advantage of. He had filed a skeleton story of the attack before joining the marines at the front, intending to fill in details later. It began: "I am up front and entering Belleau Wood with the U.S. Marines." On 6 June he was severely wounded in an oat field while attempting to rescue Major John Berry.

Gibbons later described the sensation of being hit in the head: "Then there came a crash. It sounded to me like someone had dropped a glass bottle on a porcelain bathtub. A barrel of whitewash tipped over and it seemed that everything in the world turned white. That was the sensation." He had been lying on the ground when a German machine gun bullet struck the ground under his left cheekbone and "ricochetted upward, going completely through my left eye and then crashing out through my forehead, leaving the eyeball and upper eyelid completely halved, the lower eyelid torn away, and a compound fracture of the skull." He also took two bullets in his shoulder, one of which ran down his arm. He lay fully conscious for an hour and one-half with his shattered eye on his cheek until assisted to safety by Lieutenant Oscar Hartzell, one of Pershing's press officers, formerly of the New York *Times*.

He was first reported dead and sympathetic censors quickly passed his "last story." American newspapers headlined: U.S. MARINES SMASH HUNS and GREAT CHARGE OVERTHROWS CRACK FOE FORCES. The New York *Times* reported that "The United States Marines are the toast of New York. . . . Everywhere one went . . . the one topic was the Marines, who are fighting with such glorious success in France." Belleau Wood was, as Marine Corps historian Allan Millett has noted, a "stunningly successful public relations coup for the Corps." Historian Robert Moskin observed that, "By such a fluke came glory." Other members of the Second Army, notably the 3rd Infantry, which had performed equally well, were understandably bitter. Correspondent Don Martin, who filled the New York *Herald* with paeans of praise for the marines but could make no mention of the 3rd Infantry, was particularly reviled.

On the morning of 26 June the Bois de Belleau was finally cleared of Germans by the marines and the Second Army engineers, after what

Private Hiram Pottinger of the 6th Marines called "days of hell." The French honored the marines by changing the name of the wood to Bois de la Brigade de Marine.

Two marines and two navy medics won Medals of Honor at Belleau Wood. But not all men were valiant and not all the wounds were the result of enemy action. Private Carl Brannen of the 6th Marines was shocked to see a man near him shoot off his own trigger finger.

A few weeks later, in August, Assistant Secretary of the Navy Franklin D. Roosevelt visited the battlefield: "In order to enter the wood itself we had to thread our way past water-filled shell-holes and thence up the steep slope over outcropping rocks, overturned boulders, down trees, hastily improvised shelter pits, rusty bayonets, broken guns, emergency ration tins, hand grenades, discarded overcoats, rain-stained love letters, crawling lines of ants and many little mounds, some wholly unmarked, some with a rifle stuck bayonet down in the earth, some with a helmet, and some, too, with a whittled cross with a tag of wood or wrapping paper hung over it and in a pencil scrawl an American name."

A German intelligence officer rated the American 2nd Division "very good," adding: "The spirit of the troops is high and they possess an innocent self confidence." A German private writing home described the Americans as "terribly reckless fellows." The Americans, particularly the marines, had indeed been "terribly reckless fellows," and they paid dearly. The marines and soldiers had fought beyond what is normally considered the level of endurance. In all, American casualties were 9,777, including 1,811 dead, more casualties than any comparable American unit had suffered since the Civil War.

In striking contrast to the reckless bloody marine assaults at Belleau Wood was the army attack by the 9th and 23rd Infantry regiments of the 2nd Division upon Vaux, just outside Château-Thierry, on 1 July. Artillery was used effectively to soften up the enemy and the assault was well-planned and well-conducted. Using aerial photographs, prewar tourist post cards, and information from the old village stone mason, American intelligence officers made maps of Vaux and the inside of most of the houses. Each attacker was given an individual map and assigned a house to secure. Thanks to such careful planning the town was taken in twenty minutes at a cost of forty-six Americans killed; about four hundred Germans were killed. Colonel Leroy Upton, commanding the 9th Infantry, reported, "The whole thing came off like a dress rehearsal and I regret we did not take a motion picture of it."

The Americans had captured a wood and the remains of two insignificant villages. Historian S. L. A. Marshall was to describe Belleau Wood as "not a key position but a blind alley." But although Belleau Wood was of no great consequence strategically, it was nevertheless important in ways that civilians often find difficult to understand. German General von Böhm, commanding the 28th Division, explained in an order to his troops on 6 June that the importance of the coming battle was psychological, a test of wills. The significance, he said, was that, "An American success along our front, even if only temporary, may have the most unfavorable influence on the attitude of the Entente and the duration of the war. In the coming battles, therefore, it is not a question of the possession or non-possession of this or that village or woods, insignificant in itself [sic]; it is a question of whether the Anglo-American claim that the American Army is the equal or even the superior of the German Army is to be made good."

Atrocities were committed on both sides in this bitter campaign, as in others. A company commander in the 5th Marines described the bitter fight: "Germans fought their machine guns with desperation and courage. . . . There were absolutely no prisoners taken during the heat of the attack and anything on the ground received a bayonet thrust to make sure of death." Marine John C. Geiger, who was in an attack on 10 July, later confessed that after he and others surrounded a German machine gun nest the crew wanted to surrender: "But there's not much use taking as prisoners men who fire at you until they see they are overpowered. I don't remember any prisoners walking back from that crowd."

Private Carl Brannen of the 6th Marines claimed that, "Machine gunners were never taken prisoner by either side." In a letter to his aunt in Washington, D.C., Lieutenant van Dolson wrote that the soldiers from Alabama "did not take many prisoners, but I do not blame them much for that."

A Georgia soldier wrote home: "All of you can cheer up and wear a smile for I'm a little hero now. I got two of the rascals and finished killing a wounded with my bayonet that might have gotten well had I not finished him. . . . [H]ow could I have mercy on such low life rascals as they are?"

The Senegalese in the Moroccan Division had a reputation for barbarities committed upon prisoners. Marine Captain John Thomason, who saw them in action, later wrote: "These wild black Mohammedans from West Africa were enjoying themselves. Killing, which is at best an acquired taste with the civilized races, was only too palpably their mission in life. . . . They were deadly. . . . They took no prisoners." Marines of the

2nd Division escorting some German prisoners to the rear encountered a party of Senegalese who tried to rob them of their prisoners, but were fought off by the marines with the help of the prisoners, who looked about for weapons and joined the fray. In this melee none of the three nationalities understood the language of either of the other two.

German newspapers carried accounts of Allied atrocities and Brigadier General Dennis E. Noland wrote to Major General Menoher, commanding the Rainbow Division, asking that he investigate. An inquiry was duly held and twenty-three officers were asked to give testimony. All denied any knowledge of atrocities. A report of the inquiry was written and filed at AEF headquarters and that was an end to the matter.

Private Elton Mackin was scornful of those who tried to "fight fair," and wrote: "It's revolting business for an educated man. He must divest himself of nonessentials and tear down to basic things. They were pitiful sometimes, these men who took clean sportsmanship and decency to France. It's such a poor way of preparation."

Although the German offensive had driven a salient forty miles deep into the French line, its armies were served by only one railroad and the salient's flanks were vulnerable. The primary concern of Ludendorff was to widen the entrance to the salient and the main concern of Foch was to prevent this from happening.

While the fighting raged on the Marne, on 9 July Ludendorff launched a new attack a few miles north with fifteen divisions under General Oskar von Hutier, to broaden the salient by attacking south of Noyon to carry the German line forward to Compiègne and then to Villers-Cotterêts. Hutier destroyed three French divisions, captured 8,000 French prisoners, and advanced six miles. On this day "Tiger" Duchêne was relieved of his command of the French Sixth Army and replaced by General Degoutte, who had by this time recovered his composure.

The fighting continued into the night of 10 July, when the Germans discovered that five French divisions and 144 tanks were on their flank. Hutier was thrown on the defensive and his troops were pushed back in a bloody battle involving both tanks and air support. Lieutenant Colonel George S. Patton was an interested observer; he had not as yet had a chance to lead tanks in battle.

When Pershing received reports of the behavior of the routed French soldiers he feared that his own men might be infected by their defeatism; this was all the more reason to keep his troops from being amalgamated with French and British units. He need not have worried. The Americans remained optimistic and confident. Only the day before elements of the 1st Division had scored a hard-won victory just south of the Somme River at Cantigny. Their morale was high. A war correspondent spoke with admiration of the "long procession of singing slangy Americans, still in the strange headgear of the days of service in the plains." Brand Whitlock, who had been United States Ambassador to Belgium when the Germans invaded, also saw them: "I watched them with a lift in my heart, with a lump in my throat, with moisture in my eyes, and an almost personal affection for each of them."

17

☆

SECOND BATTLE OF THE MARNE:

FINAL PHASE

IN MID-JULY the Germans occupied a front parallel to but north of the line held by General Alexander von Kluck in 1914. Ludendorff's final offensive—sometimes known as the Fourth Battle of Champagne—was launched on 15 July in the area of the Western Front that ranged from Chalons in the east to Soissons in the west. It essentially duplicated von Kluck's action in August and September 1914, and for the same reason. While the French populace feared for Paris, this was not the goal of the German commanders. Both von Kluck and Ludendorff knew that the destruction of the Allied armies must be their major objective.

Ludendorff, like von Kluck, dared to march his armies between the French garrisons protecting Paris and those defending Verdun, ignoring the danger of an attack on his flank from Paris. Like von Kluck, he believed the Allies incapable of an offensive thrust. Aiming to drive a wedge between the British and French armies, Ludendorff struck between Château-Thierry and the Argonne Forest. He took greater care than had von Kluck, but neither took enough.

Although the Germans had taken elaborate precautions to preserve security, the French learned all about it. By 11 July French military intelligence knew the axis and width of their advance, the size of the German force, and, soon after the lucky capture in a raid by Gouraud's troops of 127 German soldiers (including a German major with papers detailing the plan of attack), Foch knew even the date and hour it was to begin. The plan was to start with an artillery bombardment at mid-

night on 14 July, when it was hoped that French troops would be inebri-
ated at the end of their celebration of Bastille Day.

On 7 July General Henri Gouraud issued a Gallic call to arms to his
Franco-American army: "We may be attacked at any moment. You know
that a defensive battle was never fought under more favorable conditions. You will fight on terrain that you have transformed into a
redoubtable fortress. . . . The bombardment will be terrible. You will
stand it without weakening. The assault will be fierce. . . . In your breasts
beat the brave and strong hearts of free men. None shall look to the rear;
none shall yield a step. . . . Each shall have but one thought, to kill. . . .
Your General says to you 'You will break this assault and it will be a glorious day.'"

Gouraud emptied his forward trenches of men and filled them with
mustard gas and land mines. He has been credited with creating the
"elastic defense," sometimes referred to as the "Gouraud maneuver," but
in fact it was Pétain's idea. It employed a defense in depth with the front
line thin, a "sacrifice line," and the strongest defenses further back so that
the preliminary bombardment would have little effect. This was not an
entirely new concept—Hannibal had used it against the Romans at
Cannae in 216 B.C.—and it worked as well for Pétain and Gouraud as it
had for him.

Shortly before midnight on 14 July, just minutes before the German
bombardment was to begin, Allied artillery opened a heavy bombardment of German gun positions, ammunition dumps, and infantry assembly areas with more than 2,500 French and American guns. As the
German batteries answered, watchers in Paris could see the reddened sky
and could hear the roar of the guns.

The German infantry, twenty divisions, attacked in the early hours of
the morning, but although they fought skillfully and desperately—there
was hand-to-hand fighting with the 42nd Division near Souain—they
were rolled back all along the line. Their only breakthrough occurred
west of Rheims where General Degoutte, having ignored orders to pull
his front line back, suffered heavy casualties in the fierce preliminary
German bombardment.

Colonel "Billy" Mitchell, flying low over the area, saw some of the
fighting: "The opposing troops were almost together. This was the nearest
to hand-to-hand combat than anything I had ever seen."

The worst disaster to Americans was sustained by four rifle companies
of the 28th Division, a National Guard unit from Pennsylvania that had

been integrated into a French unit which retreated without warning, leaving them to be killed or captured. Only a few managed to fight their way free, slowly retreating, fighting all the way. Lieutenant W. M. A. Crossman brought out a corporal with two broken legs, carrying him on his back for two miles, putting him down from time to time to fight a one-man rearguard action.

In the center, the easternmost flank of the French Fifth Army held fast, but the left flank fell back, leaving Degoutte's right flank in danger. In this sector was the American 3rd Division which included the 38th Infantry, commanded by a colonel who gloried in the name of Ulysses Grant McAlexander. The 38th was positioned just west of the point where the Surmelin River flows into the Marne. On either side of the river were roads leading to the main highway to Paris. It was down these roads that the Germans planned to move their artillery. McAlexander deployed his men with care. Even after French units on his right had retreated and the regiment was surrounded on three sides, the 38th held fast for forty-eight hours, earning its *nom de guerre*: "Rock of the Marne." No German unit penetrated its position.

Company G, commanded by Captain Jesse W. Wooldridge, repeatedly counterattacked through the day. When finally ordered to fall back, he was unhit, but found fourteen bullet holes in his uniform. His company lost three lieutenants and 147 enlisted men.

McAlexander reported in his after-action report: "This regiment fought the German 10th and 36th Divisions to a standstill and captured prisoners from each of their six attacks." The German 6th Grenadiers was virtually destroyed; its officers could find only 150 survivors by day's end. Of some 1,500 men engaged, 1,087 were killed or wounded. In his *Final Report*, Pershing declared that the 38th Regiment "wrote one of the most brilliant pages in our military annals."

Earlier, Colonel McAlexander had narrowly escaped being sent home in disgrace. He had graduated near the bottom of his class at West Point in 1887 and had served for four years on the Western Frontier and in the Spanish-American War. It was eleven years before he became a regular army captain. In France he commanded the 18th Infantry until a staff officer in the Sommerviller Sector found him asleep in his dugout at 9:00 one morning. He was saved thanks to the pleading of his brigade commander, George Duncan, who appealed to Pershing, explaining that McAlexander habitually spent his nights in the front-line trenches with his troops. McAlexander emerged from the war with the unusual distinction of having earned both the Distinguished Service Cross and the Distinguished Service Medal.

The wounded were pouring back to aid stations and hospitals. Major William E. Boyce, the surgeon of the 30th U.S. Infantry described some of the shell shocked cases: "Some of them cursed and raved and had to be tied to their litters; some shook violently . . . some trembled and slunk away in apparent fear of every incoming shell, while others simply stood speechless, oblivious to all surroundings."

Hospitals were again swamped. One field hospital with 200 beds was inundated by more than 3,000 wounded. "The scene was indescribable," said Dr. Hugh Young. Men lay in the streets outside in the wet and cold; many who might have been saved died from exposure, shock, and lack of care.

Beginning with an attack by four German armies—forty-seven divisions and perhaps the densest concentration of artillery in the war—Ludendorff carved out a salient, thirty-seven miles wide at its base, from six miles west of Soissons to just west of Rheims, and bulging twenty miles to Château-Thierry. But then the offensive ran out of steam.

Foch at once planned a counteroffensive. The French Tenth Army, under General Charles Mangin—containing Italian and British troops as well as the American 1st and 2nd divisions—with 746 tanks (mostly Renault FTs) was placed on the left of the line. The Americans had a relatively small but dramatic part to play as the spearhead of the attack. In the center, west of Rheims, was the French Sixth Army, now under General Jean Marie Degoutte, the Americans' least favorite general, and on the right, east of Rheims, between the Ourcq and the Marne rivers, was the French Fourth Army under General Henri Joseph Eugène Gouraud, which contained the American 26th Division and, south of the Marne, the 3rd Division. The French Fifth Army, under General Henri M. Berthelot, took its place on the far left. In reserve was the Ninth Army under General M. A. H. de Mitry. The western face of the German salient, near Soissons, was attacked by General Charles Mangin's Tenth Army, whose most vital mission, seizing the heights below Soissons, was assigned to a corps under General Pierre E. Berdoulat.

By this time more than a million American soldiers were serving in France. The United States 4th, 26th, and 42nd divisions served in Major General Hunter Liggett's I Corps with the French Sixth Army under General Degoutte; the 3rd, 28th, and 32nd divisions in General Robert

Lee Bullard's III Corps of the French Ninth Army under General Gouraud, which moved into line between the Sixth and Fifth armies.

In 1918, at the age of forty-six, the red-bearded Gouraud was the youngest general in the French army. He had made his reputation in North Africa and walked with a limp from a wound received in Algeria. He had commanded the French troops at Gallipoli where both of his legs had been broken and he had lost an arm. Major Henry J. Reilly of the 42nd Division said of him: "The mere sight of this bearded general, with his alert eyes, his gold braided kepi, worn jauntily on one side of his head, his empty right sleeve and lameness inspired liking and confidence. . . . The men were one hundred percent for him and proud to serve in his army."

In June when several American units had been first placed under his command he had sped off to see them in his chauffeured car. Rounding a corner in the village of Tilloy his car struck Private C. W. Burnett from Macon, Georgia, who was serving with the 151st Machine Gun Battalion in the 42nd Division, breaking his leg. "General Pershing entrusts me with a division for reinforcements and *voilà*, the first man to fall is knocked senseless by my own automobile!" Gouraud said ruefully. Happily, Private Bennett survived the accident and the war.

Foch's deployment for his first counteroffensive has been described by historian Frank Simonds as using Pershing's Americans to deliver a right-hand blow, Haig's British to deliver a left-hand blow, and Pétain's French army to supply the kick, the *savate* (then allowed in French boxing).

Foch's first objective was to cut the highway between Soissons and Château-Thierry, the main supply route for the Germans in the Marne salient. On the east end of the Champagne bulge General Mangin assembled twenty-four divisions for an attack. The main assault was to be made by three of his best divisions: the American 1st Division under General Charles P. Summerall, the 2nd American Division under James G. Harbord, and the 1st Moroccan Division. General Harbord had been an excellent chief of staff for Pershing, but Pershing, alone among Allied commanders, believed that staff officers also should understand the problems of command and that commanders must personally go forward to understand what their troops were facing.

The two American divisions flanked the 1st Moroccan Division, which included units of the French Foreign Legion, Moroccan *goums*, and three battalions of Senegalese *tirailleurs*. On 15 July, in great secrecy, the Americans were moved to the XX Corps area just southwest of Soissons. On the night of 17 July the units moved in the midst of a severe thunderstorm and with much confusion to their forward positions through the Forêt de Retz, a forest of mostly oak and beech trees, "very old and of almost primeval growth." At 4:00 A.M. on the 18th, the 9th Infantry and the 5th Marines arrived on the double at the starting line, hungry, exhausted, and almost out of breath. Thirty-five minutes later the Allied barrage of 108 guns in each division opened up. Marine Sergeant R. M. Ganoe described it as "a grand, glorious, terrific, ear-gouging explosion." Nearby he heard someone say, "I never want to have a grander feeling or I'd just naturally die of joy."

"Billy" Mitchell described the scene at the front from the air: "The whole sky was lighted up by the artillery on both sides. Rockets and signals were appearing everywhere; searchlight beams were sweeping the sky; the buzz of airplanes going and coming; and the noise of their bombs dropping covered the whole of the line."

The Americans went over the top at 4:35 A.M. behind a rolling barrage which advanced one hundred meters every two minutes. Leading the attack behind the rolling barrage were nearly 350 new French whippet tanks with Mangin's Tenth Army and more than 150 supporting Degoutte's Sixth Army. For many Americans these were the first tanks they had seen: there were only forty-eight with the 1st Division and twenty-eight with the 2nd Division. Attacking with great élan, the Americans achieved their first objective within an hour.

By 7:00 A.M. they had advanced four kilometers, but the Moroccan Division failed to keep pace, leaving exposed American flanks. Marines in the 2nd Division moved left to take out German strong points in what ought to have been the Moroccan area. In carrying out this mission two marine sergeants from the 66th Company won Medals of Honor: Louis Cukela and Matej Kocak, both immigrants, captured machine gun nests at the point of the bayonet near Villers-Cotterêts (once the home of Alexander Dumas *pére* and later a resort area).

The Germans were taken by surprise but withdrew in good order, fighting desperately from position to position, trying to save what they could of the enormous quantities of supplies and equipment they had brought into the salient. The Allied tanks and infantry followed close behind them. One group of Americans captured a 4-inch gun, some prisoners and, most welcome to hungry men, bread and coffee. A group of marines found sauerkraut and grabbed handfuls as they moved forward through fields of growing crops. Thousands of Germans raised their hands in surrender, many of them, said Sergeant Ganoe, were, "Nothing but rosy-cheeked, red-lipped, bright-eyed boys." Indeed, Mangin's twenty-four divisions faced only eleven mostly low-rated German divisions filled with young boys and old men. But the American 1st Division faced what one man described as "sheer hell."

Private First Class James Rose, a machine gunner, saw a German shell land on a group of men: "We were transfixed as we watched the holocaust. Some of them fell and never moved again, some flew through the air and miraculously walked away, others just disintegrated before our eyes. Private Lewis got it behind the ear and Oleson in the hip. Lewis went wild and I had to tussle trying to head him to the rear. Many were dazed but still on their feet." Rose was untouched, but his machine gun was disabled.

When a 1st Division battalion commander reported that he had been stopped, General Summerall corrected him: "You may have paused for reorganization. If you ever send a message with the word *stopped* in it, you will be sent to the rear for reclassification."

By noon the 1st Division was established on a plateau within three miles of Soissons; Berzy-le-Sec was captured the following day. But in spite of generally good progress, the men were exhausted, famished, and much disorganized. Nevertheless the attack was sustained into the evening. The 2nd Division made the deepest penetration. Advancing 8.2 kilometers, it occupied a plateau, some 1,200 meters east of the village of Vierzy and approaching the highroad between Soissons and Château-Thierry. The two divisions took 4,000 prisoners and by 21 July had cut both the Soissons-Château-Thierry highway and the Soissons-Paris railroad.

Criticism of the AEF and doubts as to their fighting ability faded. Even General Walther Reinhardt, chief of staff of the German Seventh Army which opposed the Americans in this battle, praised their élan and will to attack. "They may not look so good," he said, "but hell, how they can fight!"

Corporal Pierre Teilhard de Chardin, thirty-seven, Jesuit priest, philosopher, paleontologist, and future Asian explorer, was a stretcher-bearer in the 1st Moroccan Division and a witness to the fighting. He wrote his sister of "the sound of continuous light crackling, and it was a shock to see among the ripening crops little blotches that lay still, forever. Here and there a tank slowly made its way through the tall corn, followed by a group of supporters, like a ship sailing the seas."

The Americans impressed him: "We had the Americans as neighbors and I had a close-up view of them. Everyone says the same: they're first rate troops, fighting with intense *individual* passion . . . and wonderful courage. The only complaint one would make about them is that they don't take sufficient care; they're too apt to get themselves killed. When they're wounded they make their way back holding themselves upright, almost stiff, impassive, and uncomplaining. I don't think I've ever seen such pride and dignity in suffering. There's complete comradeship between them and us, born fully-fledged under fire." He exaggerated.

After the battle he tried to describe it to a friend: "There was something implacable about all this; above all, it seemed *inanimate*. You could see nothing of the agony and passion that gave each little moving human dot its own individual character and made them all into so many worlds. All you saw was the material development of a clash between the huge material forces."

General Joseph Hellé, Mangin's chief of staff, said of the Americans: "We were quite unprepared for such fury in an attack." So were the Germans. General Walther Reinhardt, chief of staff of the Seventh German Army, agreed with Hellé and compared the fervor of the Americans to the German volunteers in 1914.

Pershing referred to the Battle of Soissons, as this phase of the Second Marne often is called, as "the Gettysburg of this war." George C. Marshall agreed. He saw it as the "turning point of the war." The Germans lost more than 35,000 men and more than 700 guns. The French recovered some 200 villages and towns, including Soissons and Château-Thierry, and were able to reopen the Nancy-Paris railroad. Georg Hertling, Chancellor of Germany, later recorded: "At the beginning of July, 1918, I was convinced, I confess it, that before the first of September our adversaries would send us peace proposals. . . .We expected grave events in Paris for the end of July. That was on the 15th. On the 18th even the most optimistic of us knew that all was lost. The history of the world was played out in three days."

The units of the German Seventh Army struck by the Allied attack were battle-weary, understrength divisions which had lost many men to influenza. Nevertheless they resisted stoutly and, using the several ravines in the area for shelter and placing machine gun nests in woods, they exacted a heavy toll.

In the first five days fighting objectives were reached, but in every advance the French had left American flanks uncovered, and the cost had been high. The poor performance of the French did not prevent their generals from criticizing the Americans, claiming that they were poorly trained and led and that they suffered such heavy casualties because they bunched too close together.

During 18 and 19 July the 2nd Division lost about 5,000 men (either killed or wounded), before it was relieved on the night of 19 July, but it had captured sixty-six officers and 2,810 other ranks, nine pieces of heavy artillery, sixty-six field guns, two trench mortars, and hundreds of machine guns. The 1st Division fought on for two days longer and lost 7,200. The British suffered 13,000 casualties and the French lost 95,000.

After Mangin's attack, Degoutte launched his attack between the Marne and the Ourcq rivers. His army included the American 26th and 42nd Divisions with elements of the 4th Division. The two American divisions were soon relieved by British and French divisions, but as the offensive continued the 3rd, 4th, and 28th Divisions and eventually the 32nd, 42nd, and 77th Divisions, joined the fray.

On 26 July at Croix Rouge Farm the 42nd became engaged again and experienced some of the hardest fighting of the war. There had been scant ground or air reconnaissance and the usual lack of maps. A heavy rain reduced roads to treacherous seas of mud. Most of the men had received no food for more than twenty-four hours. Ammunition soon began to run low and Lieutenant Colonel Frank Travis, commanding the 117th Ammunition Train, was not energetic in pushing his men forward. His division commander pronounced him "unfit to command the Ammunition Train" and said he gave the "appearance of timidity for his personal safety."

By 8:00 P.M. the farm was taken, but the cost was high, particularly among the National Guardsmen from Iowa and Alabama. The rain and the bad roads prevented the removal of the wounded and the woods near the farm were filled with piteous cries, German and American.

The day before, Leo Cuthbertson had written a letter but had not had time to mail it. In it he wrote: "Last night I witnessed a truly pitiful sight—the burying of our boys. The sight of our comrades being laid away for their final rest, garbed in a U.S. uniform, makes one's blood run cold and increases a passionate desire to deal out misery to the enemy— and I believe before this war is over he will have had more misery than he bargained for." A soldier picked up the crumpled, stained letter on the field and mailed it.

On 30 July poet Sergeant Joyce Kilmer of the 165th Infantry, 42nd Division, was shot through the forehead by a German sniper while on a reconnaissance. The poet had been a professor and poetry editor of the *Literary Digest* before the war. At thirty-two years of age and with a wife and three children he had been exempt from conscription, but with his wife's permission he had enlisted and had refused a commission.

By 4 August the Americans had taken Fismes, where large quantities of supplies had been built up by the Germans, who retired in good order behind the Vesle and Aisne rivers with their backs to the Chemin des Dames (positions they could and did hold). They were henceforth on the defensive. This marked the end of Ludendorff's hopes for victory; the initiative had now passed to the Allies. Hindenburg and Ludendorff harbored no illusions as to the far-reaching effects of this offensive. After the war Hindenburg wrote in his memoirs: "From the purely military point of view it was of the greatest and most fateful importance that we had lost the initiative to the enemy."

The failure of the German offensive to accomplish all its aims was the most considerable German defeat in the west since September 1914. French intelligence estimated German losses at 168,000, including 29,000 captured. Also captured were 793 field guns and 3,723 machine guns.

On 6 August Foch was made a marshal of France, Pétain was awarded the *Medaille Militaire*, and Pershing was given the Grand Cross of the Legion of Honor. President Poincaré came to Pershing's headquarters at Chaumont to present the decoration and the entire headquarters staff turned out to witness the ceremony. When Poincaré, standing five feet four inches, attempted to kiss the six-foot tall Pershing on both cheeks, he had to stand on tiptoe while Pershing was forced to lean slightly forward, a tableau greeted by the staff with half-smothered laughter. Not long after, Pershing was presented with the Grand Cross of the Order of the Bath by King George, but the award was made privately, without fanfare, the king simply handing Pershing the decoration with a few words of appreciation for American help.

Two days later, on 8 August, Brigadier General Robert Brown, commanding the 84th Brigade of the Rainbow Division, was relieved of his command by Pershing. He was later reduced in rank to colonel. Although a West Pointer who had been graduated in the top third of his class in 1885 and had served ably in the cavalry, he had failed the test of battle in France. He protested his demotion, but an inquiry confirmed that he had panicked. Under stress he had cracked, making frequent demands that his brigade be taken out of the line. Brown remained in the army until he retired in 1923, but he was never again promoted. His place was taken by Colonel Douglas MacArthur.

While the battle was in progress arrangements had been made for the formation of the American First Army. Field Marshal Haig thought it a "stupid" idea, but on 24 July Pershing issued the necessary orders, to take effect on 10 August.

Although forced by the Allied need for support during the Ludendorff offensives to commit American forces piecemeal, on 10 July Foch told Pershing: "Today, when there are a million Americans in France, I am going to be still more American than any of you. . . . An American army must become an accomplished fact." It was decided that within the next three weeks the American army would assemble near Château-Thierry. On its formation Premier Clemenceau wired Pershing: "History awaits you. You will not fail it." Its first big assignment was the reduction of the St. Mihiel salient.

One of Pershing's best corps commanders, later commander of the First Army on the Meuse, was Major General (soon Lieutenant General) Hunter Liggett, who soon demonstrated that he was one of Pershing's most brilliant subordinates. A West Pointer of the Class of 1879, he had served on the western Frontier and in the Philippines during the Spanish-American War. He was better read than most officers and had been president of the War College. Retired Major General Frank D. Baldwin, two-time winner of the Medal of Honor, said of him that he "has no equal in professional ability or noble character among our American generals." And Billy Mitchell, who seldom met an army general he didn't dislike, declared he was "one of the ablest soldiers I was ever brought in contact with." But Liggett suffered what was then as now a major handicap for a professional American officer: He was obese. He loved good food and drink and carried with him a splendid Greek-born chef, a conscript who before the war had been a candy manufacturer in Seattle. Although, he said, quite correctly, there was no fat above his collar, he admitted that front-line troops he inspected probably asked, "What's that fat-assed bastard doing up here? What does he know about the hell I'm undergoing?"

At sixty-one he was no longer young. In the autumn of 1917 when he had been sent to France to look around and be looked at, the commander of the British Guards Division reported that he was "very much too old to command a division in the field."

He narrowly missed being rejected. Pershing had his doubts about this aging gourmand general who arrived in France in March 1918 in command of the 41st Division, until it was reported to him that when thrown from a horse, he had, despite his bulk, nimbly remounted before anyone could help him.

Liggett had soon proved his worth and was given command of a Corps in the Aisne-Marne offensive. On the night of 20 July he ordered each of his divisions to "push forward at all cost" and "without waiting for its neighbors if they should be delayed." His objective was to "place the main body of the army along the line of the railroad Nanteuil–Château-Thierry." Major General Clarence Edwards, commanding the New England 26th Division, was told that "every human effort must be made" to achieve his objective "as quickly as possible." Colonel (later army chief of staff) Marlin Craig on Liggett's staff pressed him "to drive forward to the limit of endurance of every man and animal." For whatever reason, Edwards ignored these injunctions. Although the enemy was slowly retreating before him, he fell back, even withdrawing his advanced posts of command, and lost contact.

Although a West Pointer, he had absorbed, in the opinion of many regulars, too much of the independent spirit of his New England National Guardsmen and Pershing thought him "contentious." Many of the field officers, most of whom were politically well connected, and his personal friends, were too old and unfit for the rigors of battle and he, unlike Pershing, lacked the will to retire them. It was misplaced affection, which battle cruelly punished. In the course of the fighting many junior officers and sergeants had simply taken over commands from their superiors' inept hands. Edwards and his staff failed to maintain proper liaison, left dead unburied on the ground, frequently had no idea where their infantry were and one brigade could not be located for three days. In its first week the division suffered more than 4,000 casualties. On 25 and 26 July infantry of the 42nd Division with some additions took over from the 26th Division.

Liggett did nothing while the battle was on, but afterwards he made a thorough investigation and forwarded a stinging report to the AEF adjutant general at Chaumont. On 22 October, Pershing, having studied Liggett's report, relieved Edwards of his command. He was replaced by Major General Frank E. Bamford. (Pershing's generals did not get second chances.) Adored by his men, who called him "Daddy" Edwards, he was known for his "effusive magnetism and charm." He was perhaps the best known division commander in the AEF, both in France and in New England, and his relief became a *cause célèbre*. One historian suggested that Germans bombing the White House would have been less sensational news. The controversy over the dismissal raged for a decade.

18

☆

THE WAR IN THE AIR

IT WAS DIFFICULT in the emerging mechanical age to envision the effect of all the new machines being developed so rapidly. This was especially true of the airplane. Orville Wright said, "We thought we were introducing into the world an invention that would make future wars practically impossible." As historian Albert Marrin wrote, "Seldom has so intelligent a person been so wrong about something so important."

The American contribution to the war in the air was almost insignificant. Pershing, reviewing the state of American military aviation at the beginning of the war, wrote: "The situation at that time as to aviation was such that every American ought to feel mortified to hear it mentioned. . . . Looking back over the period immediately prior to our entry into the war, the very primitive state of our aviation still gives me a feeling of humiliation." The United States never did catch up with the Allies. According to British historian John Terraine, "The American Air Force was only effective in the last weeks of the war, and in order to be so acquired 2,676 planes from the French."

But war in the air caught the American imagination. The daring aviators were lionized in the press and like young gods they wore wings. In the biased opinion of Billy Mitchell, "The only interest and romance in this war was in the air." Many agreed.

Pershing's General Order No. 1, issued on 26 May 1917, appointed Major Townsend F. Dodd, a flyer who had served with him on the Mexican border, as the aviation officer on his staff, but he was soon replaced by Lieutenant Colonel Billy Mitchell, one of the leading

American airman in Europe. Handsome and dashing, flamboyant and self-assured, he tended to quarrel with his superiors. He was born in Nice, France, of American parents in 1879; his father became a senator. During the Spanish-American War he enlisted as a private in the Signal Corps, but within six weeks was commissioned, and, as early as 1906, writing in the *Cavalry Journal*, he predicted that "conflicts no doubt, will be carried out in the future in the air." He served in the Philippine insurrection and on the Mexican border. In France he was soon a colonel and appointed Pershing's aviation officer. Although the AEF had neither pilots nor planes, he established an air headquarters at 49 Boulevard Haussman in Paris.

In May 1917 the French had 1,700 planes at the front; the United States army possessed only fifty-five, of which fifty-one were obsolete and four were obsolescent; none was fit for combat. In all, when the United States entered the war, the Air Service Section of the Army Signal Corps had only 131 officers and 1,087 enlisted men. Of these, only twenty-six were considered fully trained and were rated as Junior Military Aviators. The service had not been popular. Fliers were accepted only from among unmarried officers under the age of thirty, and a career as an army airman appeared to offer no future.

Pershing said that "in no other service was unpreparedness so evident and so difficult to overcome. The Air Service had five officers in Europe, but none had acquired any advanced technical knowledge of aerial photography, air gunnery or bombing techniques." Soon after becoming chief of staff, on 4 March 1918, General March took the Air Service out of the Signal Corps and made it a separate corps, a fourth fighting arm of the army.

The first American airmen to land in France were naval aviators— seven officers and 123 enlisted men under the command of Lieutenant Kenneth W. Whiting. They arrived on 9 June 1917 at Pauillac on the Gironde River, the port from which Lafayette had sailed for America. Naval air stations were eventually operating all along the French coast, and in England, Ireland and Italy, forty-four in all. Naval aviators flew 5,691 combat missions, attacked forty-three enemy submarines and claimed to have sunk two. Before the end of the war the naval air service had 18,736 officers and men in France and a total force of almost 40,000, including 1,656 qualified pilots.

The army was slow getting off the mark. Douglas Campbell, from Mt. Hamilton, California, a graduate of Groton and Harvard, was one of the first to respond to posters urging young men to BE AN AMERICAN EAGLE! but he had difficulty enlisting. After spending an entire day in Washington, D.C., unsuccessfully searching for the Signal Corps' Aviation Section, he stumbled upon it by accident the next day. It was manned by a captain and a secretary, to whom he gave the requested information, and one month later he was in training in a ground school to be a pilot.

Cadets were trained in the Curtiss JN4-D, known as the "Jenny." France and Britain both sent over instructors, one of whom was Vernon Castle (the most famous dancer of the era; he and his wife, Irene, introduced the wildly popular Turkey Trot, Fox Trot, Castle Step, and the One-Step). Serving in the Royal Flying Corps he had shot down two German aircraft. He was killed in a mid-air collision with a cadet at Taliaferro Field, near Fort Worth, Texas, on 15 February 1918.

Most of the real training was done in France, but among the problems faced by the American Air Service in France was the difficulty in obtaining airfields, or airdromes as they were called. A typical American field covered about 250 acres and included about 600 separate parcels of land owned by seventy-five or more landowners. The 1st Air Depot, established near Colombey-les-Belles, covered 575 acres, including a thousand parcels of land owned by 250 different landholders. Acquiring the use of this land involved working with French engineers, submitting maps and tracings of cadastral plans (some of which were drawn in the Napoleonic era), the posting of notices by the local authorities, and the formal cession of land. By the time the armistice was signed almost none of the thirty-six separate fields chosen had been definitely leased. However, the largest United States flying school was established seven miles outside Issoudun in central France, nineteen miles northeast of Châteauroux and 60 miles south of Orléans.

Construction was begun on 17 August 1917 and on 21 September it was still under construction when the 26th Aero Squadron—formerly the 1st Reserve Aero Squadron of the New York National Guard—arrived: 200 enlisted men, under Captain James E. Miller, to be trained. Miller was a banker in private life, and later was given command of the 95th Aero Squadron.

At Issoudun those who had learned to fly the Curtis "Jennys" had to relearn their trade on French Nieuports. Charles R. Codrington, a student there in the winter of 1917–18, tersely described the place: "A sea of frozen mud. Waiting in shivering line before dawn for the spoonful of gluey porridge slapped into outstretched mess kits, cold as ice. Wretched flying equipment. Broken necks. The flu. A hell of a place, Issoudun."

For several months the school's commanding officer was Major Carl Spaatz, who in World War II was to command the Strategic Air Force. For a short time "Eddie" Rickenbacker was the engineering officer; Douglas Campbell, destined to become the first American ace in the United States Signal Corps Aviation Section served as adjutant; and the post quartermaster was Quentin Roosevelt, the twenty-one-year-old youngest son of Theodore Roosevelt. He was, said his father, "a rolly polly person, the brightest of the children." Eddie Rickenbacker described him as "Gay, hearty and absolutely square in everything he said and did." He was shot down and killed over the German lines on 14 July 1918 near the tiny village of Chamery, by Sergeant Johannes Thom—or so a German radio message reported a few days later. (German records credit Sergeant Christian Donhauser, who ended the war with fifteen victories.) The German airmen buried young Roosevelt with military honors and set his plane's wheels and propeller over his grave.

Pershing wrote to Roosevelt's father: "Quentin died as he had lived and served, nobly and unselfishly, in the full strength and vigor of his youth, fighting the enemy in clean combat. You may well be proud of your gift to the nation in his supreme sacrifice."

German propaganda crowed: "The greatest of living Americans sends his sons to fight against us, yet even they go down before the might of the Fatherland." Counterpropaganda answered, "Quite true, but where are the sons of the Kaiser?"

After learning the basics, American pilots went on to specialized French schools. Those, like Campbell, destined to be pursuit pilots, were trained in aerial gunnery by French instructors at Cazaubon, twenty-one miles east of Mont-de-Marsan. Other schools prepared pilots for observation and bombardment.

Several hundred Americans were trained at British airfields after ground studies at Oxford. In addition, 10,500 American mechanics were trained at British aircraft factories and air service stations. On 16 March 1918 the first flight of Americans was posted to France to serve with British squadrons. At war's end 284 British-trained American pilots were serving in British units at the front; others served in American squadrons.

Some 500 American cadets received training at the Italian school at Foggia, the first arriving to a tumultuous welcome on 28 September 1917. In all, 121 students completed their training and ninety-six served at the front in Italian squadrons. In August 1918 Captain Fiorello La Guardia, an Italian-born United States Congressman from New York who later became mayor of New York City, took charge of combat pilots on the Italian front where he piloted a Caproni biplane bomber and was promoted to major. The American aviators suffered only three casualties on the Italian Front: two killed and one taken prisoner by the Austrians.

On 12 November 1917 military aviation pioneer Brigadier General Benjamin Delehauf Foulois landed in France with a large number of officers to take charge of the American Air Service there and at once made plans for a vastly expanded organization. Foulois had been an enlisted infantryman in the Spanish-American War and had been commissioned in 1901 in the Philippines. In 1908 he was detailed to aviation duty and in 1909 he had flown as navigator-observer with Orville Wright on the final acceptance flight of the army's first airplane, ordered from the Wright brothers with the stipulation that it must be capable of being packed into a wagon to be transported.

Foulois flew the first reconnaissance mission for Pershing on the Mexican border in 1916, one of only a handful of men who gained flying experience while serving in the 1st Aero Squadron seeking Pancho Villa. In the course of this abortive campaign Pershing's pilots crashed the entire army air force—all six airplanes.

The most experienced American pilots were the volunteers who flew with the French in the Escadrille Lafayette, originally known as the Escadrille Volontaires. The unit, the brainchild of Norman Prince, was formed on 20 April 1916 at Luxeuil-les-Bains with thirty-eight Americans, some transfers from the Foreign Legion, and four French officers who trained them to fly pursuit (fighter) planes.

The first American pilot killed in the war was twenty-one-year-old Edmond Charles Clinton Genet, a flyer with the Escadrille Lafayette who was shot down over St. Quentin and fell 4,000 feet. When retrieved, his body was said to resemble "a bag of bloody laundry." Norman Prince was mortally wounded when his plane crashed into high tension wires. Others survived to establish a distinguished record, flying some 3,000 combat sorties. Of the 224 Americans who served in the unit, eleven died of illnesses or in accidents, fifteen became prisoners of war, and fifty-one died in combat. Eleven of its pilots became aces.

An "ace" in the French and American view was an aviator who had shot down five enemy aircraft. A German aviator had to have destroyed ten to qualify. The British never officially recognized the system. Manfred von Richthofen, the German "Red Baron," achieved the highest score of any ace, having shot down eighty airplanes or balloons before coming to grief himself. René Fonck, a French flyer, was second with seventy-five. Seventy-one Americans became aces, of whom ten shot down ten or more enemy aircraft.

On 26 December 1917 the American pilots of the Escadrille Lafayette were transferred to the American service, but for a short time flew as civilians until commissioned in January 1918. On 18 February the Escadrille became the American 103rd Aero Squadron, its members the first flyers in action to wear the American uniform. Strictly American aviation operations did not begin until March 1918 when an American pursuit squadron began to patrol the front in French Nieuport 28s.

By April the United States had three squadrons in active sectors: two for observation and one for pursuit. Douglas Campbell and Eddie Rickenbacker, after completing the course for pursuit pilots at Cazaubon, were assigned to the 94th (known as the "Hat in the Ring" Squadron because its insignia, an Uncle Sam's hat in a loop, was said to symbolize the United States joining the war). It flew Nieuport 28s (later Spads) in the Toul sector and the fledgling pilots were aided in their first weeks by some experienced officers from the Escadrille Lafayette, including thirty-one-year-old Major Raoul Lufbery, son of a French mother and an American father, who was credited with seventeen victories. On 28 March Lufbery led the first patrol with Rickenbacker and Campbell.

Lufbery was killed on 19 May when he leapt from his burning plane, for he, like most pilots, scorned to wear a parachute. Perhaps from bravado or perhaps from the belief that the falling plane would hit the parachutes before they could fall clear, pilots did not carry them until the last months of the war. Father Duffy first saw a German pilot escape a stricken plane by parachute on 16 October 1918. Parachutes were, however, used by observers in balloons, who jumped 116 times with only one fatality. (Parachutes only became standard in the Air Service in 1919 and were made compulsory in fighter planes only in 1922.)

Sunday, 14 April 1918, a miserable foggy day, was the first day of operations for the 94th Squadron. That morning two German Pfalzes set out to shoot up the newcomers. Both were shot down within four minutes by twenty-two-year-old Douglas Campbell and Lieutenant Alan Winslow, flying Nieuport 28s. Campbell was credited with being the first American-trained pilot to down an enemy airplane. The battle was observed by those on the ground and Billy Mitchell declared that this

double victory "had a more important effect on American fighting aviation than any other single occurrence. It gave our men a confidence that
could have been obtained in no other way." The German pilots survived
and were taken prisoner. Campbell and Winslow were both awarded the
Croix de Guerre.

On 31 May Campbell became the first ace in the AEF by official
accreditation of his fifth victory. On 5 June he achieved his sixth victory
but was wounded by a bullet in his back. When he recovered, although
eager to be back with his squadron, he was sent to the United States,
where he was promoted captain and awarded the Distinguished Service
Cross with four oak leaf clusters (devices worn on the ribbon representing
additional awards of the same medal). He was not able to return to
France until after the Armistice.

On 29 April 1918 Eddie Rickenbacker and Captain James Norman
Hall downed a German plane, Rickenbacker's first victory and only the
fourth won by Americans in the Air Service. Twenty-seven-year-old
Edward Vernon Reichenbacher (the family name was anglicized in 1917)
had quit school at the age of eleven, but later studied engineering by correspondence. At the age of seventeen, he was a test driver, and soon
became a racer, making $40,000 a year by 1910. He had come to France
as a staff sergeant and Pershing's chauffeur. His ambition was to fly, but
Pershing rejected his frequent requests for transfer, telling him: "War flying is for youngsters just out of school. It's not for mature men." Only the
intercession of Billy Mitchell persuaded Pershing to release him. He was
finally commissioned in January 1918 and, after a tour as engineering
officer at Issoudun, he qualified as an aviator. On 4 March 1918 he
joined the 94th Aero Pursuit Squadron, and ten days later flew his first
mission. On 30 May he shot down his fifth enemy plane, becoming the
second American ace. During the St. Mihiel offensive he shot down two
more, but he did not score another victory until September, for during
the summer he underwent a mastoid operation after being twice hospital-
ized with a severe pain in his ear.

It was during the Meuse-Argonne campaign that he rose to the height
of his fame. On 25 September he was appointed to command the 94th
Aero Squadron and in his first day attacked seven Fokkers and two
Halberstadts, shooting down two of them. For this he was awarded the
Medal of Honor—but not until 1931. He had already earned the
Distinguished Service Cross with nine oak leaf clusters, the French
Legion of Honor, and the *Croix de Guerre* with four palms. Called the

"ace of aces," he ended the war credited with sixty-nine victories, of which twenty-six were credited to him personally.

Rickenbacker was not a rash devil-may-care pilot. A perfectionist, he approached his work with deliberation and caution and strove constantly to improve his fighting skills. Although he was twice forced to crash-land injured planes, he was never wounded. Not a bloodthirsty man, he once said that "the pleasure of shooting down another man was no more attractive to me than the chance of being shot down myself."

One of the most daring pursuit pilots was handsome, blond twenty-one-year-old Second Lieutenant Frank Luke, Jr. Vain, boastful, undisciplined, and unpopular, his specialty was shooting down observation balloons. These were always surrounded by machine guns and anti-aircraft guns and protected by pursuit planes flying above them. Aside from the danger, it was not easy to destroy a balloon. To bring one down it was necessary to fly low and place machine gun bullets in a tight pattern at the top of the bag, where the hydrogen was concentrated, thus opening a large enough leak to create a hydrogen-oxygen explosion.

Flying a Spad (the name was derived from the initials of the *Société pour l'Aviation et ses Dérivés*), a single-seat, single-engine fighter plane renowned for its ruggedness and high performance, although not for its speed, Luke shot down his first balloon on 12 September in the St. Mihiel sector. Two days later he shot down two more. On 15 September he shot down three. On 18 September he destroyed five enemy aircraft and became, briefly, America's top ace. On 29 September, after downing three balloons and two Fokker pursuit planes, he disappeared. A graves registration officer later found his grave in the village of Murvaux. Villagers reported that even after he had crash-landed, he had held off German soldiers with his pistol until he died of his wounds. Captain Rickenbacker proclaimed him "the greatest fighting pilot in the war." He was awarded a posthumous Medal of Honor, the first such medal ever awarded to an airman.

From the beginning the Germans had a technological superiority in the air, for they concentrated on making small numbers of the best airplanes. The Allies countered by making large numbers of good planes. The French developed and manufactured sixty-four types of observation, pursuit, and bombing aircraft. The British developed sixty-seven types, the best known and most successful of which was the Sopwith Camel, a one-seat, single-engine pursuit plane whose pilots scored 1,294 victories; it was noted for its maneuverability, though not its speed.

On 23 May 1917 the French government had, with an overly optimistic opinion of the capabilities of American industry, asked the United
States to provide 4,500 airplanes, 5,000 pilots, and 50,000 mechanics for
the 1918 campaigns. In response, General George Squier, chief of the
Signal Corps, called on the United States to "put the Yankee punch in
the war by building an army in the air, regiments and brigades of winged
cavalry on gas driven flying horses." In mid-July Congress enthusiastically
passed a huge appropriations bill, $600 million for aviation, and on 24
July Wilson signed it. But money alone could not create an air force. In
that month American industry delivered only seventy-eight planes.

Curiously, the Germans, too, believed the United States capable of
bringing a great air armada to Europe. In the summer of 1917 it
launched a major manufacturing effort called the *Amerikaprogramm* to
field an air force large enough to counter it.

The only American-built aircraft to see action at the front was the
DeHavilland-D.H.4, designed by British Army Captain Geoffrey
DeHavilland and equipped with a 375-horsepower engine. Originally
made by Rolls Royce, it was manufactured in the United States by the
Dayton-Wright Aeroplane Company and the Fisher Body Company.
Because the gas tank was located between the pilot's seat and the observer's, it was the most vulnerable military aircraft ever built and it soon
came to be known as the "Flying Coffin" or "Flaming Coffin." Eddie
Rickenbacker spoke of its "criminally constructed fuel tanks." In addition
to its flawed design, those built in the United States revealed a number of
defects indicating construction problems, and inadequate inspection
standards. Nevertheless, 417 American-made planes reached the front,
the first in August 1918. In one fight Rickenbacker saw three shot down
in flames, their pilots and observer-gunners "dying this frightful and
needless death."

On the first day of the Meuse-Argonne offensive, a flight of seven
DeHavilland-4s sallied forth to bomb Dun-sur-Meuse. There were to
have been eight, but one failed to get off the ground and both pilot and
observer were killed. Led by future dramatist and journalist Sidney
Howard, they dropped their bombs and were at once jumped by German
Fokkers. Of the sixteen men who set off to bomb Dun-sur-Meuse, only
three, including Howard, returned alive.

Even when successful, bombers seldom did much damage. General
Hunter Liggett later wrote: "Our experience demonstrated that aerial
bombardment of towns, railroads, bridges, etc., produced little material

effect; it has a moral however, if constantly repeated." After the war General Bullard commented: "Day after day for almost a year the Allied Communiqués told of the 'successful bombing' of Metz-Sablons railway station, which to the day of the armistice calmly went on functioning."

On 10 July 1918 the American Air Service lost its entire daylight bombardment ability in the most humiliating loss ever suffered by American aviation. The only American day bombardment squadron, the 96th Aero, had spent the early summer of 1918 at Amanty, making sporadic raids on supply depots and railroad centers in the Metz-Conflans area. It was scheduled to raid the railroad yards at Conflans, but dawn revealed a rainy day with low clouds and it appeared that the mission would have to be cancelled. Aviators sat playing poker or talked of going to nearby Nancy for "a bath and a good French meal." However, late in the afternoon the weather seemed to clear a bit and the clouds lifted. Major Harry Brown, the squadron commander, decided to fly.

At 6:05 A.M. Brown led six bomb-laden Breguets aloft and was immediately swallowed by lowering clouds. Nevertheless, he pushed on northeast at 100 mph. After about an hour he shook his ailerons to signal that he was lost and, followed by the rest of the squadron, made a 180-degree turn, unaware that a southwest wind had carried him well over the German lines. Gas was running low so after working their way below the cloud layer pilots were relieved to see an airfield near a large city. All landed safely, but the city was Prussian Koblenz. All were quickly captured.

The Germans found this capture of six uninjured, fully loaded bombers hilarious and they signaled Air Service headquarters: "We thank you for the fine airplanes and equipment which you sent us, but what shall we do with the Major?"

Billy Mitchell was furious. He wrote in his diary: "This was the worst exhibition of worthlessness that we have ever had on the front . . . needless to say we did not reply about the major as he was better off in Germany at that time than he would have been with us."

AIR-TO-AIR COMBAT was almost nonexistent until Anthony Fokker, a Dutch inventor who worked for the Germans, developed a gear that synchronized machine gun fire with the turning of the propeller blades, permitting guns to be mounted in front of the pilot's cockpit. (Actually Fokker was not the first to invent a synchronizing device; other Europeans had done so but no armed service had ever accepted their efforts.) When a member rose in the British Parliament to ask why British planes were not using this device the War Department replied that as Herr Fokker was a neutral Dutchman it would not be cricket to appropriate his invention. Instead the authorities attempted to acquire the rights, only to discover that Fokker had sold the rights to all his inventions to the Germans and was producing their best airplanes. Until this nonsense was played out—it took four months—German pursuit planes ruled the skies and Allied pilots referred to themselves as "Fokker fodder."

Fokker's synchronizing mechanism was highly intricate and those made in the United States were unsatisfactory. After a few propellers were shot off airplanes in mid-air the gears made in America were rejected as "entirely useless," one of the many failures of American aircraft production.

Americans did better in designing machine guns for aircraft. The Marlin machine gun, Model 1918, manufactured by the Marlin-Rockwell Corporation, was one of the best and 38,000 were manufactured before the Armistice. But as in the case of the Browning machine gun, the war was almost over before the guns could reach the front.

In July 1917 the country had begun production of the recently designed 8-cylinder Liberty engine, but Pershing asked for a 12-cylinder engine instead and 13,574 of the 12-cylinder Liberty engines were built. A British expert called it "about the most reliable power plant that the world had seen up to that date," but it was too heavy for pursuit planes. In May 1918 Pershing demanded the 8-cylinder plane again.

Even after three and one-half years of war the combined construction of planes by all the Allies was behind that of the Germans. Planning and organization remained in a state of flux. General Henry H. "Hap" Arnold, a major in the war, recalled that, "Until the spring of 1918 our situation, despite constant minor changes, was more a state of affairs than a chain of events." Much of the difficulty was the result of Pershing's continual changing of specifications. General March complained: "We never knew from day to day where we stood. As soon as we got going on the construction of a type which he had stated was necessary, a cable would come in from him, saying that he did not want that type and asking for something else. . . . He did not seem to have the faintest conception of the effect on production of all this vacillation. Thousands of changes in the details of planes were cabled by him, until manufacturers simply threw up their hands . . ." Production was so limited that in the spring of 1918 the Air Service had more airmen than aircraft. Some flyers were parceled out to the French and served with French squadrons.

Pershing recognized aviation as "an important auxiliary arm," but, as far as is known, he never went aloft. He was perplexed and irked by his Air Service. He found the personnel "careless in dress and none too strict in discipline." Nor was this all: "Differences in the views of the senior officers of the corps were not easily reconciled. Jealousies existed among them, no one had the confidence of all the others, and it was not easy to select from among the officers of the corps an outstanding executive." He finally selected as the head of the AEF Air Service Major General Mason M. Patrick, an army engineer who had been one of his classmates at West Point. Patrick was taken aback. "I have never before seen an airplane, except maybe casually. . . ." Nevertheless, he proved a sound administrator and exercised a steadying hand on the fledgling air force.

Pershing had hoped to have 120 squadrons at the front by December 1918 and at one point plans were made to have an American Air Service of 296 service squadrons in France by June 1919, but it is highly unlikely that either of these goals could have been achieved. At its peak, just before the Armistice, the United States had only forty-five squadrons at the front, and of its 740 flyable planes—ten percent of the Allied air strength—only twelve were American made. Still, during their relatively short existence these squadrons shot down 781 enemy airplanes and seventy-three balloons and dropped 140 tons of bombs.

In June 1917 Mitchell was placed in charge of AEF aviation at the Front—the "Zone of Advance." There he was remarkably successful in supporting ground troops, but he constantly railed against the AEF staff and in 1917 he wrote in his journal: "The general staff is now trying to run the Air Service with just as much knowledge of it as a hog knows about skating. It's terrible to fight with an organization like this."

General Patrick sent Pershing an evaluation of Mitchell: "He thinks rapidly and acts quickly, sometimes a little too hastily. He is opinionated, but I have usually found him properly subordinate. . . . While he has worked well with the men and material which it was possible to furnish, his own ideas of what was necessary to accomplish his task I have found sometimes exaggerated. . . . He has some tendency to act on his own initiative. . . . He is at all times enthusiastic and full of energy." Mitchell emerged from the war a much-decorated brigadier general.

Air battles were often fought at such low levels that foot soldiers could follow them closely. Sometimes convoys of trucks stopped and men arranged themselves along the roadside to watch the spectacle. Private Charles MacArthur of the 149th Field Artillery, who saw a German pilot go down in flames, wrote: "Later in the war they were dropping like flies; but nothing ever equalled the thrill that poor devil gave us." Father Duffy also spoke of these "melodramas of war." He once saw four Allied balloons attacked by German airplanes while French airmen maneuvered to protect them. One German plane dashed through the anti-aircraft fire "swift as a hawk at its prey" and brought down a balloon. "We saw something drop suddenly from the balloon, which rapidly developed into a parachute with two observers clinging to it. A thin wisp of smoke which we could detect from the balloon then burst into flames, and the blazing material began to drop towards the parachute." In an instant the automobile to which the balloon was attached began to move, pulling the fiery mass away.

Although the airmen sometimes provided theater, ground forces often disparaged them. Ground officers resented the bonus that flyers received—twenty-five percent of their base pay. Both March and Pershing thought they should be paid no more than infantry platoon leaders and strongly objected to the extra pay. Secretary of War Baker agreed, but Congress, enamored by the exploits of the aviators, refused to change the pay scale.

A song of many verses set to the tune of "Homeward Bound" made the rounds. One verse ran:

> Way back in the rear where there's no guns to hear
> Our aviators tune up their planes,
> Then they go out and flirt with the janes.
> But when danger's hovering about
> You bet your elbow they're never found.
>
> Because they're homeward bound
> They're flying fast and near the ground.
> And while the shot and shell are flying
> For the S.O.S.* they're sighing.
> It's good they get high pay.

General March maintained that the "Air Service from its inception, has been the stormy petrel of the army." When the British formed the Royal Air Force on the same level as the Royal Navy and the army, pres-

---

*The Service of Supply area in the rear of the front lines.

sure was applied to form such an entity in the American armed forces. March strongly protested. Already "the effect of the special favors granted the Air Service was to make that arm feel that they were entitled to special consideration in other things; particularly that they should be freed from the discipline and control which applied to all the rest of the army."

Private MacArthur was mad at aviators—on both sides: The Germans for bombing and strafing him and the Allied flyers for doing nothing to prevent them: "Every morning our bully boys sailed over the line, fifty at a time, saw the sights, and came back." He recorded one instance when Allied planes strafed American troops: "Two of the doughboys were dead; several were wounded, and two more missed death by an eyelash. Their clothes were ripped by the bullets. Some of the horses were nicked."

In July 1918 when the Germans launched their great offensive at Chemin des Dames and swept to the Marne, their airmen were flying a new Fokker superior to the French planes flown by the Americans. The commander of the 3rd Division complained that "hostile aircraft flew over our troops with impunity, observing for the enemy artillery, bombing, and firing upon all concentrations with machine guns. Many of our casualties were due to the work of these planes . . . our planes put in their appearance only very tardily and never for any extensive period of time."

Artillery Captain Harry S. Truman told Bess: "The easiest and safest place for a man to get is in the Air Service. They fly around a couple hours a day, sleep in a featherbed every night, eat hotcakes and maple syrup for breakfast, pie and roast beef for supper every day, spend their vacations in Paris or wherever else suits their fancy, and draw 20 percent extra pay for doing it. Their death rate is about like the quartermaster and ordnance departments and on top of it all they are dubbed the heroes of the war."

However, contrary to Truman, air losses, while not to be likened to infantry losses of fifty-five officers and forty-six enlisted men per thousand, were nevertheless heavy, at least among officers. Thirty-one per thousand officers and one percent of enlisted men were killed in combat. On 26 September 1918 the Air Service at the front had 646 planes; three weeks later it had 579.

Much of the friction between fliers and ground forces was caused by mutual ignorance. The infantry had no understanding of the capabilities and restraints of the Air Service nor did the pilots and observers understand the needs of the infantry. The infantry wanted close support, but because it was difficult for the airmen to distinguish friendly from enemy trenches they preferred to bomb and strafe well behind the enemy lines. Although the infantry was supplied with panels to lay out as markers, they were reluctant to use them, having seen that this drew the attention of enemy aircraft. In an attempt to foster mutual understanding, some infantrymen and artillerymen were taken up in planes and some airmen served for a time with the infantry. Still, the problem of ground–air relations was never satisfactorily resolved.

The value of the work of observers and photographers on reconnaissance planes was never disputed. General Robert Alexander pointed out that while the activities of the pursuit ace were more spectacular, "the trained observer who can orient himself even over difficult country, who knows what he is looking at and who can tell where it was when he saw it" was far more valuable. "The single combat of the 'ace' can exercise but little influence on the outcome of a campaign, an intelligent report from a trained observer may be decisive."

A shortage of commissioned observers led to the use of enlisted men and beginning with the St. Mihiel campaign they were raised to flying status. Sergeant Fred Graveline shot down three enemy aircraft and was awarded the Distinguished Service Cross. Two other enlisted observers were credited with kills.

Tethered observation balloons were a feature on the Western Front, for they were well suited for the stagnant warfare that prevailed for most of the war. An observer could keep watch upon about five miles of enemy lines, prepare sketch maps of enemy positions, and direct artillery fire.

When World War I began there were no practical corps of balloonists in any army. The United States entered the war with one winch and one obsolete balloon. In June 1917 the Balloon Service was established and five army captains were sent to Omaha, Nebraska, to establish a balloon school. A British major and a sergeant gave theoretical instruction and the French sent over a few balloons until a source of supply could be established in the United States. About fifty-five reserve officers were sent to France and given practical training with French balloon companies. By the end of the war 751 balloon officers had been trained.

The balloon used was the Caquot, named after Albert Caquot, a French engineer. It was egg-shaped, filled with hydrogen, and equipped with three stabilizing fins by means of which it was possible to maintain a constant direction and stillness under normal conditions. From its basket one or two officer-observers telephoned information or dropped weighted messages.

Eventually squadrons were formed of four companies each. The 2nd

Balloon Squadron under Major John A. Paegelow left Fort Omaha for France on 27 November 1917 and debarked at Le Havre on 28 December. In March 1918 the first American-trained unit at the front was Company B (later designated 2nd Balloon Company) of the 2nd Balloon Squadron, commanded by Captain William O. Butler, an artillery officer. During the St. Mihiel Offensive, Paegelow, then a lieutenant colonel and balloon officer of the First American Army, commanded fifteen American balloons, the most under one officer at any time during the war.

Pershing, among his many complaints of shortages, complained about balloons: "A shortage of balloons always existed in our forces and as usual we sponged on the French." But he was flatly contradicted by General March: "In no field did American manufacturing capacity achieve a greater success. We not only produced all the balloons demanded by the AEF, but constructed so many besides that we were able to give the French and British 45. Up to the Armistice we provided 642 observation balloons." March was right. At war's end the United States had 574, the French seventy-two, the British forty-three, and the Belgians six; the Germans had 170 on the Western Front. The manufacture of balloons was one of the United States' few production success stories.

The first American to experience the hazards of ballooning at the front was Lieutenant J. B. Wallace, who was in ascension with a French officer while on duty with the French 26th Balloon Company when his balloon was set afire by a German airplane. He parachuted, it was said, "with perfect coolness." Lieutenant D. M. Reeves, while a student observer with the 7th Balloon Company, spent a total of only four hours in the air but during that time he was forced to make three parachute jumps and twice had his balloon burned. One American first lieutenant successfully escaped five times from balloons burning above him.

At the beginning of the Meuse-Argonne campaign, Balloon No. 12 broke loose and with its two officer-observers went sailing over the German lines until it finally drifted down near Conflans and the observers were taken prisoner.

Only one American balloonist was killed. During the Meuse-Argonne offensive Lieutenant Cleo J. Ross delayed parachuting from his burning balloon to make sure his companion had jumped clear. His parachute caught fire and he fell one thousand feet to his death. In the course of the war thirty-four American balloons were burned at the front and American planes shot down seventy-one enemy balloons.

At the end of the war the army Air Service had 11,425 officers, of whom 4,307 were with the AEF. They had brought down in combat 755 enemy airplanes and suffered a loss of 357. The aircraft themselves proved deadlier than the Germans. Of the 677 pilots killed, 508 died in accidents—263 in the United States. A third of the pilots who reached France and fought were killed.

The United States Marine Corps air service, which at the beginning of the war totaled five officers and thirty enlisted men, had grown by October 1917 to thirty-four officers and 330 men, and increased by the end of the war to 282 officers and 2,180 enlisted men. The 1st Marine Aviation Force of 149 officers and 842 men under Lieutenant Colonel Alfred A. Cunningham made its first bombing raid in October 1918 and by end of the war had flown in fourteen raids and dropped 27,000 pounds of bombs. Between four and twelve enemy planes were destroyed by marines; four marine fliers died in air actions.

Airmen in every service served valiantly and their letters, like those of many ground troops, reflected an idealism seldom equaled in later wars. Lieutenant Kenneth MacLeish of Glencoe, Illinois, enlisted in the Naval Reserve Flying Corps in March 1917 and in October was flying with a bomber group in France. In a letter to his parents he wrote: "In the first place, if I find it necessary to make the supreme sacrifice, always remember this: I am convinced that the ideals which I am going to fight for are right, and splendid ideals, that I am happy to be able to give so much for them. I could not have any self respect, I could not consider myself a man, if I saw these ideals defeated when it lies in my power to defend them. . . . So you see, I have no fears, I have no regrets. I have only to thank God for such a wonderful opportunity to serve Him and His world." Soon after writing this his plane was shot down and he was killed. The navy named a destroyer after him.

19

☆

THE ST. MIHIEL OFFENSIVE:

12 – 16 SEPTEMBER 1918

THE ALLIES LAID plans for a gigantic triple offensive at the end of September 1918: toward Mezieres by the French and Americans; toward Maubeuge by the British; and toward Ghent by the Belgians and British with a French contingent. Meanwhile there began a forward movement of the Allied armies toward the new main fronts of assault. This involved important preliminary stages. Of these, the first was the attack by the newly formed American First Army on the St. Mihiel salient, a German finger pointed toward Paris that historian Captain B. H. Liddell Hart described as a "fang." It would be the first important mission of the nearly united and nearly all-American army of 61,061 officers and 1,354,067 enlisted men.

In 1914 after the First Battle of the Marne, the Germans had attempted a double attack upon Verdun. The Crown Prince tried to push south between the Argonne and the Meuse, cutting the Paris-Châlons-Verdun railroad, thus isolating Verdun from the west. At the same time an army emerged from Metz and pushed up the valley of the Rupt-de-Mad, a small stream, in an attempt to reach the Meuse and cut the Toul-Verdun railroad into Verdun. Its purpose was to isolate Verdun and then to surround and capture it. The Crown Prince's attack was quickly stopped, but the thrust from Metz reached the Meuse at St. Mihiel and captured Fort Camp des Romains, creating the St. Mihiel salient, which provided the Germans with an excellent assembly area for attacks on Verdun and at the same time helped secure the German hold on Metz. The French attacks the following winter and in the summer of 1915 failed to reduce the salients.

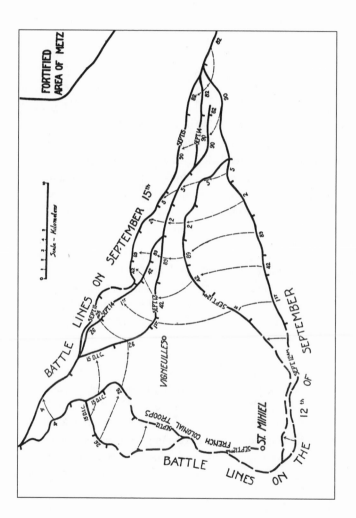

The battle of St. Mihiel

CREDIT: *The War With Germany*

The salient had played a passive but important role in the Verdun campaign of 1916, for it enabled the Germans to prevent the munitioning of Verdun by positioning heavy artillery to command the Paris-Verdun railroad. The French built a new and safer rail line via Gondrecourt, which diminished the value of the salient, but the Germans still controlled the main Paris-Nancy railroad, depriving France of iron ore from its best mines in the Longwy-Briey region and the Saar coal fields.

The town of St. Mihiel contained just under 10,000 inhabitants—"Sanmielians"—many of whom remained during the long German occupation. The area was occupied by Saxons, Bavarians, Hungarians, and Austrians, many of whom had settled down with gardens and French mistresses, content to serve in what had become a quiet sector.

The American plan of attack was simple: French units would keep the nose of the salient occupied while the Americans assailed its flanks. The preparations for the attack were meticulous. Pershing described the vast amount of planning and the many facilities that had to be constructed before the infantry went "over the top":

> We had 3,010 artillery guns of all caliber, none of which were of American manufacture. Of the total, 1,681 were manned by Americans and 1,329 by French. Before the attack 40,000 tons of ammunition were placed in dumps. Signal communication consisted of telegraph and telephone lines, radio and pigeons. The central switchboard was at Ligny-en-Barrois with 38 circuits with separate nets for command, supply, artillery, air service and utilities. There were 19 railheads for daily supplies such as food, clothing and equipment. In addition to our own limited road transport, we borrowed from the French trucks capable of moving at one time 2,000 ton of materiel and 20,000 men. The Medical Department provided 15,000 beds for the southern and 5,000 for the western attack and 65 evacuation trains for patients. Engineers provided material, including rolling stock and shops, for the reconstruction and operation of over 45 miles of standard gauge and 250 miles of light railways. A bridge of 200 feet at Griscourt was built and 15 miles of road reconstructed. Road rock used was over 100,000 tons. 120 water points were established, furnishing 1,200,000 gallons per day, replenished by night trips of railroad or truck water trains.

Because Pershing, in response to Allied pressure during the Ludendorff offensives, agreed that only infantry and machine gunners would be sent to France, his army had many deficiencies and was forced to rely greatly upon the Allies. Johnson Hagood, chief of staff of the SOS, later wrote: "We did not have the engineers, pioneers and labor troops to build the roads, the medical troops to attend the wounded, the ordnance troops to handle the ammunition, the signal troops to establish telegraph and telephone lines. We were short of chauffeurs [truck drivers] and auto mechanics. We did not have the supply trains nor the military police to regulate traffic. . . . In transportation we were short of wagons, horses, ambulances, trucks, locomotives, and railroad cars. We were lacking in replacements of all kinds, both personnel and matériel."

The attack was to be aided by five 14-inch naval railroad guns, the largest ever placed on mobile mounts. They and the trains to carry them were built in the United States and shipped to France. Although they were capable of throwing projectiles weighing 1,400 pounds for 42,000 yards, nearly twenty-five miles, in practice they were fired at targets from eighteen to twenty-three miles distant. They could be set up within a few hours and, if necessary, could be fired from the rails. Manned entirely by naval personnel under the command of Rear Admiral Charles P. Plunkett, each gun constituted a self-sustaining battery with all needed equipment.

When the first arrived at St. Nazaire on 9 June 1918, it was feared that the French railroad tracks could not handle the load, a fear which proved groundless. Nevertheless, the train carrying it moved glacially and was viewed by crowds along the way. Girls hung flowers on the guns and people cheered as if it were a triumphal procession. Secretary of the Navy Daniels proclaimed this deployment to be "one of the most successful operations in which the Navy ever engaged." The five guns fired 782 rounds (or 646, accounts differ) in the St. Mihiel and Meuse-Argonne campaigns, the last at 10:59 A.M. on 11 November, one minute before the Armistice took effect.

The guns had difficulty hitting small targets twenty miles away until Edwin P. Hubble, an infantry captain who knew something about the mathematics of moving objects through curved space and time, provided solutions. Dr. Hubble later won a Nobel prize and built the 200-inch telescope on Mount Palomar. His name was given to the first space telescope.

The British had promised to supply the Americans with some of their heavy tanks, but as Pershing later said, "not at all to my surprise . . . the British now said they could not spare any." The French provided 267 light tanks, of which 154 were manned by Americans commanded by

Brigadier General Samuel D. Rockenbach, under whom served thirty-two-year-old Lieutenant Colonel George S. Patton, commanding the 900-man 304th Light Tank Brigade. Four divisions of the French II Colonial Corps were provided to serve around the tip of the salient. The total strength under Pershing's command would be 550,000 Americans and 110,000 French.

Fearing that the massing of troops in the area and the preparations being made would alert the Germans to the plans, elaborate measures were taken to lead them to believe that the attack was to be from the Belfort region in the direction of Mulhouse, 125 miles south of the actual point of attack. Hints were thrown out to reporters; Pershing made a trip to inspect the 29th Division there, which was ordered to increase its raids; a few tanks were sent rumbling about the countryside. A VI Corps, largely a paper unit, was established under General Omar Bundy, with an active communications network sending fake coded messages. Colonel Arthur L. Conger of Pershing's staff was dispatched to Belfort, which had a large German-speaking population. Checking into a hotel there, he threw the carbon paper of typed counterfeit orders to VI Corps in the wastebasket of his room, then left on an errand. He was delighted to find it gone when he returned. German intelligence officers suspected a *ruse de guerre*, but the German high command, unsure, shifted divisions to the Mulhouse area.

The newly formed American army now faced its first test: the reduction of the St. Mihiel salient. Of the ten divisions with the most combat experience, only four—the 1st, 2nd, 3rd, and 42nd—had had as much as three full months in France prior to their commitment to battle. Staff officers were in short supply. Pershing had established an AEF staff college at Langres, but, as he told March: "Officers cannot learn the art of war in three months. . . . I cannot tell you how hard put we are for staff officers, and I need not tell you how important it is."

The Allies, too, worried about American staff work. General Sir Henry Wilson spoke darkly of the "incapacity and inexperience" of American staff officers and predicted disaster. Foch called the AEF "inexperienced and immature."

On 30 August Foch, influenced by Haig, paid a call on Pershing at his headquarters, then at Ligny-en-Barrois, and proposed a scheme to divide the American army between the French Second and Fourth armies. Pershing was shocked. "I realize that I am presenting a number of new ideas and that you will probably need time to think them over, but I should like your first impressions," Foch said.

Pershing replied, "Well, Marshal, this is a very sudden change. We are going forward as already recommended to you and approved by you, and I cannot understand why you want these changes."

The discussion grew heated.

Foch argued that there would not be time for Pershing to reduce the St. Mihiel salient and still take part in the huge offensive. Pershing said, "If you will assign me a sector I will take it at once."

"Where would it be?"

"Wherever you say."

Foch then reminded Pershing that his all-American army was equipped with artillery, airplanes, and tanks by the French and British; Pershing retorted that the United States had shipped only men—infantry, machine gunners, and artillerymen—at the urgent request of the Allies.

Foch pressed on until Pershing was provoked to say: "Marshal Foch, you have no authority as Allied commander-in-chief to call upon me to yield up my command of the American army and have it scattered among the Allied forces where it will not be an American army at all."

"I must insist upon the arrangement," said Foch as both arose from the table.

"Marshal Foch, you may insist all you please," said Pershing, "but I decline absolutely to agree to your plan. While our army will fight wherever you may decide, it will not fight except as an independent American army."

Foch made a veiled threat to go over Pershing's head to President Wilson, but this was ignored. Pershing was unthreatened. He ignored as well Foch's condescending offer, as Captain B. H. Liddell later put it, "to send General Degoutte to hold Pershing's hand and guide his tactical decisions."

In a follow-up letter to Foch the next day Pershing wrote: "I can no longer agree to any plan that allows the dispersion of our units. . . . Briefly, our officers and soldiers alike are . . . no longer willing to be incorporated in other armies. . . . The danger of destroying by such dispersion the fine morale of the American soldier is too great."

On 2 September Pershing, Foch, and Pétain met and some concessions were made. Pershing, given his choice of the Champagne or Argonne sectors, chose the Argonne. Foch pressed again for the abandonment of the attack on St. Mihiel, but Pershing was adamant. There would be two battles, one to be followed immediately by another in a completely new area.

Pershing made his decisions without consulting his superiors in Washington, Bliss, March, or anyone else. Opinions of his diplomatic skills varied. Writing after the war, James Harbord, who twice served as his chief of staff, wrote: "I regard General Pershing as one of the most successful diplomats of the World War period. Certainly he had no superiors among the military hierarchies. He knew exactly what he wanted and how to state it; he had excellent judgment as to essentials; he was patience personified when patience was necessary; his firmness tempered by tact was as the stone wall. In negotiating he never lost his temper unintentionally. He had great personal charm when he chose to exercise it."

The Germans had converted the St. Mihiel salient into what Pershing described as "practically a great field fortress," but like all salients it was vulnerable to attack from both flanks in converging operations, and this was what the Americans intended to do. It was also what the Germans expected. A German soldier wrote home: "We are expecting every day an American attack and when the bombardment starts we will get it from three sides. . . . What have we done that the whole world has designs on our lives?"

TO GAIN SURPRISE no preliminary bombardment was planned, but Pershing changed his mind at the last minute and a four-hour bombardment of 3,000 guns threw 1,100,000 artillery shells of all sizes on both faces of the salient in the largest single artillery bombardment of the war. George Tomek, an artilleryman in the 32nd Division, was enthralled and told his parents: "It was indeed a spectacle to behold!"

On the evening before the attack, scheduled for 5:00 A.M. on 12 September, Secretary Baker had visited the American headquarters and asked if he could help. "Pray for fog," Pershing replied. And there was indeed a heavy fog, preceded by a savage storm. After an intense four-hour barrage, the troops of two American corps, the IV Corps under General Joseph Dickman and the V Corps under George Cameron, slogged through a no-man's-land turned into a sea of mud and assailed both faces of the salient while the French Colonial Corps struck its nose.

Norman Roberts of the 168th Infantry later recorded in his diary: "Day had not broke and you could hardly tell where to go. Bullets, millions of them flying like raindrops. Rockets and flares in all directions. Shrapnel bursting and sending down its deadly iron. High explosives bursting on the ground. . . . A mad dash of 50 feet, then look for cover. A stop for a minute . . . Then another mad dash."

Private George A. Dennis, a medic in the Rainbow Division's 166th Infantry, set off in a mule-drawn medical cart to establish an advanced aid station in the village of St. Benoit. At one point an agitated group of infantrymen in the distance shouted at him unintelligibly and gesticulated wildly. He trotted on. He had set up his aid station in the deserted village when, a half hour later, the American assault troops arrived. He had passed through their advanced line.

The Americans, attacking with elan, penetrated at the first shock of their Eastern attack nearly six miles upon a front of eleven miles.

An Allied airforce of 1,481 Italian, American, French, British, and Portuguese aircraft under the command of Billy Mitchell supported the American attack upon both faces of the salient. Mitchell's superior, Major General Mason M. Patrick, reported that it was "the largest aggregation of air forces that had ever been engaged in one operation on the Western Front at any one time during the entire progress of the war." It was, in fact, the largest concentration of air power ever assembled up to that time. The American contribution was twelve pursuit squadrons, twelve observation squadrons, three bombing squadrons, and fifteen balloon companies—about one-third of the whole. The French supplied 749 planes and the British 130. Opposing this Allied aerial armada were fewer than 300 German aircraft. Although these were augmented on 15 September, the Allies retained air superiority.

Mitchell personally briefed his American pilots, telling them that "just as a boxer gives a right hook and a left hook successively to his opponent" he intended to strike both sides of the salient. Unfortunately, as one squadron reported, "September 12th, which opened the St. Mihiel offensive, was the worst flying day in many months." Nevertheless, the pursuit squadrons made 186 sorties and brought down five enemy planes; one was the sixth victory of Eddie Rickenbacker. Targets were attacked on the ground as well. Rickenbacker later described an attack upon a half-mile-long convoy of artillery: "Dipping down at the head of the column I sprinkled a few bullets over the leading team. Horses fell right and left. One driver leaped from his seat and started running for the ditch. Halfway across the road he threw up his arms and rolled over on his face. He had stepped full in front of my stream of machine-gun bullets! . . . The whole column was thrown into the wildest confusion. Horses plunged and broke away. Some were killed and fell in their tracks."

Lieutenant Harold of the 95th Aero Squadron was on a patrol that flew as low as fifty feet above the ground: "No enemy aircraft were encountered but we had an exciting day flying just over the heads of Germans, shooting into trenches, at retreating columns on the roads, troop trains, and whatever targets we could find."

Major Carl Spaatz, under orders to return to the United States to oversee pursuit training, arrived at the front and, at his own request, flew as "a lieutenant" in the 13th Aero Squadron and destroyed two enemy aircraft.

By the end of the campaign American planes had flown 3,300 sorties, fired 30,000 rounds of machine-gun ammunition, and shot down at least fifty enemy aircraft for a loss of forty pilots and observers killed, missing, or taken prisoner, among them David Putnam, an ace who had shot down twelve enemy aircraft, who was killed while leading the 139th Aero Squadron.

Fifteen American and six French balloons assisted the offensive. Ten of the American balloons were destroyed by enemy planes. Twelve enemy balloons were shot down.

Some of the war-weary Germans were more than willing to capitulate. At Bouillonville Sergeant Harry J. Adams of the 89th Division pursued a pair of Germans who dodged into a dugout. Firing his last two bullets through the door he called on them to surrender. To his astonishment, more than 300 filed out. Flourishing his empty pistol he herded them to the rear.

Here, as in most places where the Germans had been long in residence, German dugouts were elaborate. Many large ones had doors, were paneled, and wired for electricity. Some even had running water.

Lieutenant Colonel George S. Patton watched the advance from a hill in front of the main line: "When the shelling first started I had some doubts about the advisability of sticking my head above the parapet, but it is just like taking a cold bath, once you get in it is all right. And I soon got out and sat on the parapet." He saw his tanks getting stuck in the mud and finding this "a most irritating sight," he hurried forward on foot. Seeing a soldier, rifle in hand crouching in a shell hole, he stopped to "cuss him out" only to discover that the man "had a bullet over his right eye and was dead."

Pressing on, he came under shellfire and "probably" ducked at first, "but soon saw the futility of dodging fate, besides I was the only officer around who had left on his shoulder straps and I had to live up to them. It was much easier than you would think and the feeling, foolish probably, of being admired by the men lying down is a great stimulus."

Rickenbacker, flying low over the lines, watched the battle below: "I flew above this scene for many miles watching the most spectacular free show that ever men gazed upon."

Pershing, too, was watching the progress of the battle from an elevated position and later wrote: "The exultation in our minds that here, at last, after seventeen months of effort, an American army was fighting under its own flag was tempered by the realization of the sacrifice of life on both sides, and yet fate willed it thus and we must carry through."

Sergeant Charles Allen of the 357th Infantry, enraged by the death of his buddy, killed by a German machine gun, lay in a ditch until the gunners were forced to change their ammunition belt, then charged. Emptying his rifle on three, he killed three more with his bayonet.

Lieutenant Tobin Rote of the same regiment accidentally fell into a German machine gun nest. He fired the only five shots in his pistol at "about six Germans." One he missed came charging at him so overwrought that he beat Rote over the head with his cap three times, then turned and ran.

Rote was lucky this time but later in the battle he was hit by a grenade, pieces of which lodged in his right lung. "You can't imagine what I went through. I laid out on that battlefield for hours before they found me, for when I got hit I fell in some bushes on the side of a hill and couldn't move. My breath was coming shorter all the time but I finally pushed myself down the hill into a trench where they found me six hours later." Rote lived to tell his story to the *San Antonio Light* (published on 27 October 1918) and was awarded the Distinguished Service Cross.

Major Terry de la Mesa Allen, a nongraduate of the West Point class of 1911 who finally was commissioned in the cavalry in 1912, now commanded the 3rd Battalion of the 358th Infantry. Hit by shrapnel and stunned, he was carried to an aid station. When he regained consciousness, he ripped off his medical tag and set off for the battlefield. Gathering up some stragglers he stormed several machine gun nests as the Germans came out of hiding after the American assault wave had passed. In a hand-to-hand fight he expended all his ammunition and had several teeth knocked out. He was covered with blood and near to collapse when he was picked up and evacuated. He survived to command a division in North Africa and Sicily during World War II.

Not all were heroes. Private Guy Woodson of the 357th Infantry saw a man in his company who, on seeing his first dead American, dropped his rifle, cried "I can't stand it!" and fled.

By nightfall of the first day the two American forces converged at

Hattonchatel, a small village eleven miles northeast of St. Mihiel. By the 14 September the salient was taken, and entirely cleared by the 16 September. As Captain Liddell Hart dramatically put it, "the two sharp points of the American forceps, cutting into each side, met midway, and the ugly fang was removed." Pershing in his final report wrote:

> The material results of the victory achieved were very important. An American army was an accomplished fact, and the enemy had felt its power. No form of propaganda could overcome the depressing effect on the morale of the enemy of this demonstration of our ability to organize a large American force and drive it successfully through his defenses. It gave our troops implicit confidence in their superiority and raised their morale to the highest pitch.
>
> For the first time wire entanglements ceased to be regarded as impassable barriers. . . . Our divisions concluded the attack with such small losses and in such high spirits that without the usual rest they were immediately available for employment in heavy fighting in a new theater of operations.

The victory did not look glorious to cynical Private Charles MacArthur, who later wrote: "It was a mistake to win the battle of St. Mihiel. All it got us was a piece in the papers, three or four bum towns, and several thousand acres of marshy woods, worth five dollars an acre at the most."

But the German high command was shaken by their defeat at the hands of the Americans. Hindenburg called St. Mihiel a "severe defeat." "I refuse to believe that two German divisions are not a match for an American Division," an enraged Hindenburg told General Max Karl von Gallwitz, commander of Composite Army Group C, which was responsible for the St. Mihiel area. "It has rendered the situation of the Army Group critical." A German officer visiting Ludendorff on the evening of 12 September found him "so overcome by the events of the day as to be unable to carry on a clear and comprehensive discussion."

St. Mihiel was the largest American battle since the Civil War. Pershing's forces killed and wounded 2,300 Germans and captured 13,250 prisoners, 443 guns, and 752 machine guns. Two hundred square miles of French territory were liberated. A salient the Germans had held for four years and which the French had twice unsuccessfully attacked was taken by the Americans in forty-eight hours. American casualties were 7,000, but this did not include the French under Pershing's command.

Father Duffy reported that the battlefield proved "a great place for souvenir hunting—pistols, spurs, German post cards, musical instruments—all sorts of loot. Bill Schmidt with a long steel Uhlan's lance; while Tom Donohue . . . came by with no less than four violins." For most, however, German sausage and beer were the best finds. Private R. R. ("Mick") Wallace said: "We shot Germans, captured Germans and drank Dutch beer, eat [sic] straw bread and spent German money. I lost some mighty good pals . . . tho."

Pershing had originally envisioned the reduction of the St. Mihiel salient as a stepping stone in an advance through the Hindenburg line toward the Briey coal fields and the eastern end of the main lateral railroad near Metz, but this plan was changed to participate in Foch's big counteroffensive. Without pause, he shifted his army sixty miles west and began another offensive in the Meuse-Argonne sector.

THE REDUCTION OF the St. Mihiel salient was indeed a fine victory for Pershing and his new American army; President Wilson and every Allied headquarters sent their congratulations. But his success did not silence all his French and British critics, some of whom deprecated the American achievement, saying the Germans were leaving the salient anyway and the Americans should have captured more prisoners. There was some truth to this.

In view of the American buildup in the area and the Allied advances in Flanders, Ludendorff had ordered his forces in the salient to pull back to the Michel Stellung of the Hindenburg Line. On 11 September, the day before the attack, the Germans had begun to pull back; Pershing's drive had caught them off balance. And a more skilled and experienced army would probably have bagged more prisoners. Even some of the American generals conceded that the results were somewhat disappointing. General Bullard said: "St. Mihiel was given an importance which posterity will not concede it. Germany had begun to withdraw. She had her weaker divisions, young men and old and Austro-Hungarians. The operation fell short of expectations."

Still, it was an undeniable victory. American morale was high as the confident army turned to face the greatest battle so far in its country's history.

20

☆

THE MEUSE-ARGONNE OFFENSIVE:

FIRST PHASE
SEPTEMBER – OCTOBER 1918

WITH THE RALLYING cry, "Tout le monde à la bataille!" Marshal Foch opened his grand counteroffensive, the battle to break the Hindenburg Line.

The American army was to attack on a twenty-mile front in northeastern France about twenty-miles north of Verdun in the difficult Meuse Argonne sector. Pershing said later, "In my opinion no other Allied troops had the morale or the offensive spirit to overcome successfully the difficulties to be met in the Meuse-Argonne sector, and our plans and installations had been prepared for an expansion of operations in that direction. . . . The entire sector of 150 kilometers was accordingly placed under my command, including all French divisions in that zone."

Three important military features were contained in this sector: the heights above the east side of the Meuse River on the east; the Montfaucon Hills, 342 meters high, in the center; and the heavily wooded Argonne Forest on the west. All contained both manmade and natural obstacles. Colonel Leonard P. Ayres of the General Staff compared the Meuse-Argonne offensive with the Battle of the Wilderness in the Civil War: "both were fought over terrain covered with tangled woods and underbrush. The Wilderness was regarded as a long battle marked by slow progress against obstinate resistance, with very heavy casualties." General Hunter Liggett, commanding the American I Corps, pronounced it a "natural fortress . . . beside which the Wilderness in which Grant fought Lee was a park." For three years the Germans had been improving the defenses.

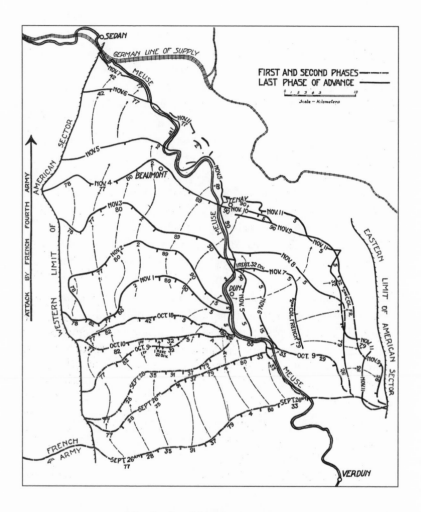

The Battle of the Meuse-Argonne

CREDIT: *The War With Germany*

Although the German lines were largely based on trenches, hundreds of machine gun nests were strategically placed on high ground, and behind these were mortar emplacements, all protected by barbed wire up to twenty feet in depth. The most formidable of the German defenses were at Barricourt, Cunel, and at Montfaucon ("Mount of the Falcon").

The three, and in places four, lines of fortifications, known to the Allies as the Hindenburg Line, were each named after a character in Teutonic mythology familiar to admirers of Richard Wagner's Ring Cycle: Hunding, Brunhilde, Kriemhilde, Giselher, et al. The Germans called it the Siegfried Line and deemed it impregnable. Actually not a line, but a dense defensive zone from three to a dozen miles in width, it used every possible natural obstacle.

The first of these, the *Giselher Stellung*, lay five miles behind the first battle positions on high ground just north of Montfaucon. Behind multiple strands of barbed wire, machine gun nests, and pillboxes were killing zones on which mortars and artillery were already registered.

The formidable *Kriemhilde Stellung*, was the second belt of defenses, of which General Hugh A. Drum wrote: "This was the most ideal defensive position I have ever seen or read about. Nature had provided for flank and crossfire to the utmost in addition to concealment. . . ." Lying behind other defensive lines, it crossed the Meuse north of Brieulles, through the Cunel Heights, and passed north of the Argonne near Grandpré. And about eight kilometers behind this lay a reserve position, *Streya Stellung*, a killing ground for this sector. General James Harbord referred to these as "the most comprehensive system of leisurely prepared field defense known to history."

Foch planned all-out attacks that made a giant pincer movement upon the Germans. He had at his disposal 220 divisions, of which he deployed 160 in the line and sixty in reserve. Forty-two of the total were the large American divisions, ten of which served in British and French armies.

On 21 September Pershing moved his headquarters to Souilly to be closer to the front. On 22 September Foch confirmed the dates and set the objectives for his great offensive: On 26 September French and American forces would attack between the Suippe and Meuse Rivers; on the following day two British armies would attack in the direction of Cambrai; on 28 September the armies in Flanders between the Lys River and the sea under the command of King Albert of Belgium would launch an attack; and on the 29th the British Fourth Army and the French First Army would attack in the center toward Busigny.

This final operation of the war, which Pershing called "the greatest, the most prolonged in American history," consisted of three phases for the Americans. On 26 September they drove forward and penetrated from three to seven miles and captured some 10,000 prisoners; the second phase from 4 to 14 October saw the center checked but advances made on the flanks; in the final phase, between 15 and 31 October, the *Kriemhilde Stellung* was penetrated; and on 1 November the First Army pushed north, pursuing a fleeing enemy. Pershing emphasized that "once started the battle was maintained continuously, aggressively, and relentlessly to the end. All difficulties were overridden in one tremendous sustained effort to terminate the war then and there in a victorious manner."

Many of the American divisions were still not fully trained or fully equipped. Some of their men, conscripted in July, had spent their six months in the army traveling. Some did not even know how to insert rifle clips and it was said that experienced soldiers were getting $5 apiece to instruct them. Four divisions had seen no action—not even experience in a quiet sector.

Most of the troops were unaware that they would so soon be going into battle again. Private Woodson learned it at a YMCA show: "We attended a sort of entertainment conducted by three YMCA men. They were not very good but they did tell us we were going to the front in the morning. This was the first we heard of it. One of the YMCA men with a tenor voice sang 'Somewhere a Voice is Calling' acappella [*sic*]. I asked him why he didn't sing 'Near[er] My God to Thee' but he didn't seem to get the idea of what I was trying to tell him."

George C. Marshall was taken aback to learn that the army that had fought at St. Mihiel was to be sent immediately to a new sector, for it was his responsibility to issue the orders for its transfer. "I could not recall an incident in history where the fighting of one battle had been preceded by the plans for a later battle to be fought by the same army on a different front, and involving the issuing of orders for the movement of troops already destined to participate in the first battle, directing their transfer to the new field of action. . . . This appalling proposition rather disturbed my equilibrium and I went out on the canal to have a walk."

Some 428,000 men, 90,000 horses and mules, 3,980 guns, and 900,000 tons of supplies and ammunition would have to be moved from the St. Mihiel sector to the Meuse-Argonne sector. The 200,000 men in the French units there would have to be relieved, and all would have to be accomplished in secrecy. Marshall later confessed it was the "hardest nut I had to crack in France." Only three poor roads were available. Marshall put motor vehicles on one road and horses and men on foot on the other two. He considered his plans for this movement represented his "best contribution to the war."

In ten days the movement was completed. The troops walked or were transported by buses and trucks about sixty miles west of St. Mihiel. The vehicles were driven by Vietnamese—the French called them Annamites or Tonkinese—from what was then French Indo-China. Many soldiers commented on them. Corporal Alvin York called them Chinamen; never having seen an Asian, he was fascinated by them. Father Duffy called them "sun-burned almond-eyed, square-cheeked Chinks." Marine Captain John W. Thomason called them "Annamitish heathen who smelt like camels and chattered like monkeys." Brigadier General Harbord spoke of them as "little yellow, dumb-looking Annamites." As truck drivers General Robert Alexander spoke of their "deserved reputation for speed." Private Ettinger said: "They were a crazy bunch, who drove those trucks like madmen, wrecked a couple on the way, and scared the hell out of us."

Sergeant Calvin Lambert, riding in a Dodge truck, long remembered the traffic congestion and the rain that fell so heavily: "Never have I seen such traffic," he later recalled. "It was a steady stream of trucks, guns and wagons, French and American. We went by jerks, a hundred yards at a time, then waited a half hour or so for the truck ahead to pull out. The mud was shoe top deep, the night was pitch dark and cold." He dozed off but was jolted awake when another truck skidded and crashed into his.

Through it all, the French officer in charge of the trucks insisted on counting the men in each and collecting receipts for their delivery, for the French charged the Americans by the head for transporting their soldiers to fight for them.

When Battery F of the 149th Field Artillery reached its position Private Charles MacArthur wrote, "We could see right off that the Argonne wasn't going to be any fun at all."

A total of 2,417 guns of various calibers, half supplied and manned by the French, were registered to support the attack. This was about one gun for every ten yards of front and in the campaign they were to fire about 4,214,000 shells. Also supplied by the French were 189 small tanks, of which 142 were manned by Americans under Lieutenant Colonel George S. Patton. The French manned 300, including twenty-nine heavy tanks. But this was not tank country and the Germans had cleverly constructed antitank mines from 5.9-inch shells. An Allied airforce of 821 aircraft, 604 piloted by Americans, supported the offensive.

As the 165th Infantry marched to battle their chaplain, Father Duffy, climbed a low hill and blessed them as they swung past lustily singing a ballad known as "Banging Away on Lulu." (*Bang away on Lulu / Bang away good and strong / Whatda yah going to do for your banging, / When Lulu's dead and gone.*) Private Albert Ettinger later saw a picture of the moment in the *Literary Gazette*. Its caption read: "Father Francis P. Duffy . . . blesses his troops as they march into battle singing 'Onward Christian Soldiers.'" Ettinger guffawed. "A Protestant hymn, no less!"

In the twenty-mile-wide American sector Pershing massed three corps: I Corps under Hunter Liggett, III Corps under Robert Lee Bullard, and V Corps, first under George H. Cameron, subsequently Charles P. Summerall. Each corps placed two divisions forward and held one in reserve. Pershing's advantages lay in superior numbers of men, about 8 to 1, and in guns, 10 to 1. His plan was bold and overly optimistic. He hoped to plow through the first three German lines, about ten miles, in one leap. His report of 20 November, nine days after the Armistice, gave a more realistic version of what his mission should have been and, in fact, what he accomplished. It was, he wrote, "to draw the best German divisions to our front and to consume them." At the end of forty-seven days of continuous combat the German divisions were indeed consumed.

After Major General Robert Alexander, commanding the 77th Division, finished briefing his officers, a French liaison officer asked to speak to him: "Sir, I have no doubt that your men are brave and that you have made every preparation that will give them a chance for victory tomorrow, but permit me to say that, in my opinion, the line in your front *will not move*. It has been in place for four years, is solidly established, well wired in, and the Boche is a good soldier. I fear that you will not be able to make the advance you hope far." A confident Alexander assured him: "The line *will* move."

At 11:30 P.M. on 25 September a preliminary three-hour bombardment began with long-range guns firing into back areas. Earlier that evening Lieutenant Colonel George S. Patton wrote to his wife: "Just a word to you before I leave to play a part in what promises to be the biggest battle of the war or world so far. . . . I am always nearvous [*sic*] about this time just as at Polo or Foot ball before the game starts but so far I have been all right after that I hope I keep on that way it is more pleasant."

In the 35th Division Harry S. Truman, now a captain, sat up all night with a lieutenant and his instrument sergeant, going over their final computations for the rolling barrage. Private MacArthur and his friends in the 149th Field Artillery sat up for much of the night trying to read a batch of mail which after many days had reached them. "We held matches for each other until all the mail was read. Most of it revealed that our girls were getting married to naval ensigns in droves, or giving lawn parties for second lieutenants."

Lieutenant Lansing C. Holden, flying over the lines, looked down on "the most gorgeous thing imaginable." Writing three years later in the New York *Times*, he remembered the "myriad of flashes extended in a line as far as one could see. The fire was incessant. Huge jets of flame from the big guns, with red pinpricks from the 75s, and then the enormous trench mortars bursting into a great fountain of sparks, leaving a glow in the white mist that was weird and ghostly."

Captain Eddie Rickenbacker with five other pursuit pilots took off in their Spads before dawn and flew toward Dun-sur-Meuse. Looking down he saw through the darkness "the whole western horizon . . . illuminated with one mass of jagged flashes." It reminded him of a switchboard on a giant telephone exchange.

On the ground the artillerymen furiously worked their guns. Private Paul Shaffer, who had been an apprentice blacksmith in Topeka, Kansas, was a runner with the 35th Division's 110th Field Signal Battalion. He was assigned that morning to carry a message to Captain Truman's battery. After the war he described the incident to the Whittier, California, Elks Club. He arrived at the battery's position, he said, "muddy as an alligator, all the skin off my nose." He found Captain Truman "standing there, his tin hat pushed on the back of his head, directing salvos. . . . He was a banty officer in spectacles, and when he read my message he started runnin' and cussin' all at the same time. . . . I never heard a man cuss so well or so intelligently, and I'd shoed a million mules. . . . The battery didn't say a word. They must have figured the cap'n could do the cussin' for the whole outfit." Shaffer never saw the "cussin' captain" again until he "voted for him in 1948."

At 2:30 A.M. on 23 September Allied guns began a rolling barrage which to General Bullard sounded like "the collision of a million express trains. Besides the noise there was the feel of concussion, quivering ground, livid [*sic*] skies—and that inevitable wait, while officers scanned luminous watch faces, and engineers and sergeants gazed at compasses with which, by dead reckoning, they were to lead through a No Man's Land where past shell fire and present fog eliminated landmarks." More powder was expended that morning than on both sides in the entire Civil War, at an estimated cost of a million dollars a minute.

The infantry began their attack at a walk one hundred meters behind the rolling barrage. The land over which they advanced was just within the area of the 1916 Battle of Verdun and for the first three miles the soldiers passed through the chaos created by one of the greatest battles of the war. No part of the field was more devastated than the left bank of the Meuse where in March and April of 1916 French and Germans had fought so bitterly. Private MacArthur described it: "The woods were splintered into small bits, green with mustard gas. There wasn't a live leaf in 20 miles."

As Colonel George C. Marshall was later to record, the first phase of the battle was "confusing in the extreme." Command and control of attacking forces was difficult if not impossible for senior commanders, but Marshall devised a system for discovering where the forward elements were. He sent young staff officers, each with six pigeons, to accompany the foremost assault troops with instructions to release three pigeons the first day and three the second. As soon as the birds arrived at the loft the messages they carried were telephoned to Marshall, who in turn relayed the information to corps headquarters.

Of the more than 15,000 pigeons trained to carry messages in France some 5,000 disappeared, perhaps some into French marmites. Marshall claimed that soldiers were enthusiastic about them because "there was always the chance of stealing one for a supper party." Still, not everyone enjoyed being a pigeon handler and one pigeon returned with the message: "I'm tired of carrying this God-damned bird."

The initial attack in the Meuse-Argonne sector was spearheaded by the 79th Division, consisting mostly of men from Washington, D.C., Maryland, and Pennsylvania and commanded by Major General Joseph E. Kuhn. It was a poor choice, for it had received the least training of any of the American divisions and in the United States it had been twice levied for men to fill other divisions.

Fog and a smoke screen obscured the field and it was nearly impossible to coordinate the movements of the assaulting infantry. Nevertheless, the troops initially made good progress. General Robert L. Bullard's III Corps plunged ahead five miles. The 77th Division's melting-pot New Yorkers, wryly described by their commanding general as "a group of hardy frontiersmen from the Bowery and the Lower East Side," were on the left of the American line. They were unrested from their exertions on the Aisne but on this first day of the battle they made a brilliant dash forward. General George H. Cameron's V Corps, consisting of the 35th, 79th, and 91st divisions, was halted by the elaborate defenses of Montfaucon on Cameron's left flank.

By the end of the bloody second day German opposition stiffened and the attack stalled. Cameron finally managed to take Montfaucon, but then was cut off and his men were virtually without food for three days, their only water scooped from filthy shell holes. All communication was cut off between the 79th and V Corps headquarters. Behind the American front line the support units dissolved in chaos as vehicles bogged down in mud. Trying to move artillery forward to support the new front line became a major problem and supplying the line with food, water, ammunition, and replacements became impossible. French and British officers scoffed that this chaos was exactly what they had predicted. British General Frederick Maurice swore the Americans had created the worst traffic jam of the war. General Cameron was relieved of his command and replaced by General Charles Summerall.

The 35th Division, a National Guard division from Missouri and Kansas, became badly disorganized and morale fell. When the Germans counterattacked, much of the infantry panicked. The war diary of the German Third Army told of the retreating soldiers: "Concentrated artillery fire struck enemy masses streaming to the rear with an annihilating effect."

The infantry brigades became entangled with each other. On the night of 27 September the commander of the 139th Infantry lost his bearings and wandered about the battlefield for twenty-four hours. His replacement could not find the regiment either, nor could he find the regimental command post. Neither brigade nor divisional headquarters knew the location of either.

General Peter E. Traub, commanding the division, lived on cigarettes and coffee between the 26th and 29th of September. Roaming around the battlefield, often out of touch with his brigades and even with his own command post, he was gassed, and nearly captured. As he himself admitted, he had "a hell of a time."

Much of the confusion in the 35th was caused by major shifts in commanders only a few days before the battle when the chief of staff, the colonel of one of the artillery regiments, the commanders of both infantry brigades, and other National Guard officers were replaced by regulars. The division historian blamed the poor performance of the division on "the United States Army system which replaces National Guard officers, however competent, with regular army officers, however incompetent." Whatever the reason the division took the heaviest casualties in the attack, somewhere between 6,000 and 8,000 (the record is clouded). An investigation later blamed "poor discipline, lack of leadership and probably poor preparation."

Casualties were heavy in all units. Charles MacArthur saw a young soldier of the 79th Division "on the ground dying with a bullet in his guts. He had been yanked from a stenographer's job in New York, trained (as they say) and exposed to his first fire—all in 37 days. He was slightly bewildered by it all."

Private Lawrence Stewart of the 168th Infantry watched an officer whose left arm had been blown off struggle to get his West Point ring off the severed hand.

Patton was seriously wounded. After experiencing only two days of combat a bullet passed through his upper left thigh just below the groin and came out two inches from his rectum, carrying away a sizeable chunk of his buttocks. War artist Captain Harry Townsend wrote in his diary: "Poor Colonel Patton. He was a most interesting man, and most enthusiastic and active and progressive as a Tank Commander."

On 27 September the poor, battered 79th Division finally captured Montfaucon, but American forces were stalled. On this day Foch sent a message to Pershing suggesting that another army be inserted between the Americans and the French Fourth Army, creating a new force which would place some American divisions under French command. It was the usual attempt to break up the new American army and Pershing promptly rejected it.

General Max von Gallwitz, commanding the army group facing the Americans, had called up reserve divisions and when the American attack stalled he felt he could relax: "On the 27th and 28th we had no more worries. . . ." But on 27 September, Ludendorff. looking at the larger picture of the entire Western Front, contemplated the failure of his armies and, seeing no hope for the future, fell to the floor in a convulsive fit, foaming at the mouth. On 28 September he conferred with Hindenburg and the two agreed that Germany must seek peace, but must not surrender. They shook hands "as men burying their dearest hopes." Six additional German divisions were sent to the Argonne and all the troops there were ordered to hold their positions at all costs.

The lull in the battle marked the end of the first stage of the Allied offensive. On 29 September Pershing was forced to admit that his forces must go over to the defensive while he reorganized.

After the war Pershing wrote: "The period of the battle from October 1st to the 11th involved the heaviest strain on the army and on me." On 1 October, under pressure from Foch, Pershing launched an attack on the *Kriemhilde Stellung*. German artillery and machine guns brought it to a halt. The 3rd Battalion of the 16th Infantry began the fight in the morning with twenty officers and 800 enlisted men; by 1:00 in the afternoon it was reduced to two officers and 240 men.

Not only had the attack failed but it had left a group of Americans trapped but still fighting behind the German lines. Repeated attempts to break through to them failed. The press soon dubbed them the "Lost Battalion." However, General Headquarters (GHQ) designed an intricate and daring plan that rescued the trapped men. It was in this endeavor that Corporal Alvin York earned his Medal of Honor by killing 25 Germans and capturing 132 more, including four officers.[*]

Another hero of this battle was Captain Frank Williams, who, like York, was in the 82nd Division. He had been a sheriff in Montana and Wyoming and had performed as a fast-draw shooter with Buffalo Bill's Wild West Show. Reconnoitering a hill north of St. Juvin on a foggy October morning he came upon five Germans escorting an American prisoner. Williams sauntered toward them, his pistol in its holster. Perhaps his empty hands put the Germans off guard, but when he drew near he pulled his pistol and shot four before they could raise their rifles. The survivor surrendered.

[*]For detailed accounts of the saga of the "Lost Battalion" and the remarkable feat of Alvin York, see Appendix B.

A contingent of "Hello Girls" in France. Recruited by the Army Signal Corps, they were trained by AT&T. *Credit: Corbis/Bettmann-UPI.*

Brigadier General "Billy" Mitchell, the army's foremost advocate of air power. *Credit: National Archives.*

Captain "Eddie" Rickenbacker of the 94th "Hat in the Ring" Squadron standing by his Spad at Rembercourt, France. He was officially credited with personally bringing down twenty-two enemy aircraft. *Credit: Corbis-Bettmann.*

Elsie Janis, the Sweetheart of the AEF, was the most popular entertainer in France, singing, dancing, telling jokes, and doing acrobatics on makeshift stages just behind the lines. She traveled in a chauffeur-driven car provided by Pershing, whom she called "Boss General." *Credit: Corbis/Bettmann-UPI.*

Cher Ami, the most famous of the Signal Corps pigeons. On the Verdun front he made trips averaging thirty kilometers in an average time of twenty-four minutes. He was best known for carrying the message from the "Lost Battalion" that they were being shelled by their own guns. Because he was badly wounded on this mission, he was returned to the United States by Captain John L. Carney and given an honorable retirement. *Credit: National Archives.*

The enemy. Field Marshal Paul von Hindenburg [*left*] and General Erid Friedrich Wilhelm Ludendorff [*right*]. *Credit: Imperial War Museum.*

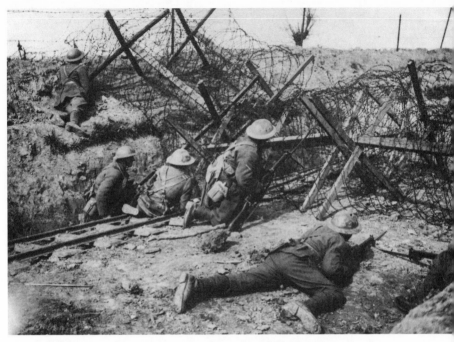

Front line trenches in a grim landscape.
Credit: Morgan-Wells.

Not all the dead were properly buried, and even those that were could not be counted to stay buried, for artillery shells often exhumed them.
Credit: Morgan-Wells.

The shattered church in the ruins of Neouilly was used as a temporary shelter for American wounded in September 1918 by the 110th Sanitary Train.
Credit: National Archives.

Sergeant Alvin C. York, 328th Infantry, who, with 17 men, captured 132 German prisoners in the Argonne Forest on 8 October 1918.
Credit: National Archives.

An American gun crew in action. *Credit: National Archives.*

General Pershing leads an American contingent through the Arc de Triomphe de l'Etoile in Paris for the victory parade. *Credit: Library of Congress.*

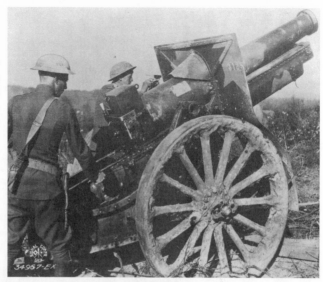

A gun called "Calamity Jane" in the 11th Field Artillery was believed to have fired the last round of the war. *Credit: Corbis-Bettmann.*

Micheline Resco, a French artist who painted portraits of Pershing and other generals. She became Pershing's mistress and eventually his second wife. *Credit: Corbis/Bettmann-UPI.*

Wall Street celebrates the armistice of 11 November 1918.
Credit: International News Photo.

21

☆

MEUSE-ARGONNE:

THE FINAL PHASE

NOT UNTIL 4 OCTOBER were the Americans able to resume their offensive. Their objective was the same as it had been on 27 September: to reach and penetrate the *Kriemhilde Stellung*, but the Germans had reinforced their position with nine divisions and portions of three others.

The attack was renewed without a preliminary bombardment at 5:00 A.M. The troops pushing through the Argonne Forest found the woods dotted with pavilion fortresses. Blockhouses of thick concrete were disguised as Swiss chalets and many served not only as strong defensive positions with large underground facilities, but as recreation areas. When the 77th Division overran the Bagatelle Pavilion on the second day of the attack the infantry were surprised to discover underground pavilions with music rooms, libraries, billiard rooms, and well-stocked bars. Men moved forward with long-necked bottles of Liebfraumilch and Johannisberger in their packs.

A surprise of a different sort awaited a scout platoon of Company K, 306th Regiment at the Saint Hubert Pavilion. German soldiers they encountered there readily raised their hands and called "Kamerad!" but as soon as the Americans lowered their rifles, the "prisoners" fell flat and an assault team burst through them and cut up the platoon. Lieutenant Dwight H. Shaffner, who ran to the sound of the firing, jumped on a parapet and cut down several men with his Chauchat, then drew his pistol and seized the German captain who had organized the ruse: Dragging him back, he forced him to divulge information about the German positions ahead. For his valor, and in spite of his disregard of the provisions of the Geneva Conventions, he was awarded the Medal of Honor.

The Germans retained strong defenses in the Bois de Romagne and the Bois de Bantheville, which had to be reduced before further progress could be made. West of the Romagne Heights along with other well-defended positions was the strongly fortified Côte de Châtillon, a razor-back ridge about a mile east of the Aire River near its confluence with the Aisne. Douglas MacArthur, commanding the 84th Infantry Brigade in the 42nd Division, described the Côte de Châtillon as "a series of trenches with dugouts and new wire with steel posts. It was strongly manned by both machine guns and infantry. One estimate put the number of machine guns at 200."

German fire from the Côte de Châtillon prevented all advances on the west bank of the Meuse. After the 83rd Brigade had tried and failed to take the hill, General Charles P. Summerall, commanding V Corps, directed MacArthur: "Give me Châtillon or a list of 5,000 casualties." MacArthur replied that he would take the hill or his name would head the list of the fallen. The hill was taken, but more than twenty-five years later MacArthur, reminiscing with General Robert Eichelberger, said, "I have hated him ever since."

MacArthur later wrote: "Officers fell and sergeants leaped to command. Companies dwindled to platoons and corporals took over. At the end Major Ross (Lloyd Ross, commanding an Iowa battalion) had only 300 men and six officers out of 1,450 men and twenty-five officers. That is the way the Côte-de-Châtillon fell."

Colonel "Wild Bill" Donovan (the sobriquet originated during his days as a star quarterback for Columbia University), wounded in the lower left leg by a machine gun and carried from the field, futilely tried to continue directing the wire-cutting efforts of his men. He described his wound in a letter to his wife: "Smash! I felt as if someone had hit me on the back of the leg with a spiked club. I fell like a log . . . but managed to crawl into my little telephone hole. A machine gun lieutenant ripped open my breeches and put on the first aid. The leg hurt but there were many things to be done . . ."

When he was finally brought out he was met by Father Duffy. Although in great pain he looked up from his stretcher and teased, "Father, you're a disappointed man. You expected to have the pleasure of burying me over there."

On this day Duffy was incapable of joking. "I certainly did, Bill," he said gravely. "And you are a lucky dog to get off with nothing more than you've got."

Private Thomas C. Neibaur, a National Guardsman from Sugar City, Idaho, who had recently been transferred from the 41st Division to Company M of the 167th Infantry, 42nd Division, carried a Browning automatic rifle. He and a group of other men were making their way up the hill when they were shot down. Neibaur was wounded in both legs and his companions were killed, but singled-handed he drove back a German attack. When rushed by four Germans he killed them all and he ended the day capturing eleven. He was awarded the Medal of Honor.

The military significance of the capture of Côte de Châtillon, according to Colonel Henry J. Reilly, was "that instead of the Germans looking down into the American position the Americans now looked down into German lines." Thus the American artillery observers were able to render the whole valley of the Rap de St. George, which formerly had been hidden entirely from them, unsafe for the Germans.

It was near Cunel on the right flank of the First Army that First Lieutenant Samuel Woodfill of the 5th Division, a former regular army sergeant who had seen service in the Philippines and Mexico, attacked single-handed a series of machine gun nests. Pinned down with his company by enemy fire in an open field, he dashed forward and jumped into a shell hole to assess the situation. The most serious threat seemed to come from a machine gun in a church tower about 200 yards away. He placed five accurate rifle shots into the tower and the fire ceased. Spotting another machine gun position in a stable, he put it out of action with another five rounds. Locating another that was giving grazing fire from a bushy area directly in front of him, he ran to a new shell hole and then crawled to an area on the flank of the gun and worked his way to within ten yards. He killed the partially hidden gunner and five of his replacements with rifle shots. Another he shot with his pistol.

Moving farther into the wood he shot a German officer who tried to disarm him. Two surprised soldiers surrendered and were sent to the rear with their hands up. After wiping out another machine gun nest and killing five more Germans, he called forward his company, but he was still far in the lead when he stumbled upon a position held by two enemy soldiers whom he killed with their own pickaxes. When the remnants of his company caught up with him he called for reinforcement but was told he was "too far out." Woodfill was forced to withdraw, but he had penetrated the Hindenburg Line. He was awarded the Medal of Honor.

Pershing reinforced the French XVII Corps east of the Meuse (under his command) and ordered it to attack. Two French Divisions, six battalions of Senegalese Tirailleurs and the 58th Brigade of the 29th Division began the attack early on the morning of 8 October. Three battalions and some machine gun units joined them and crossed the Meuse on footbridges.

That afternoon Company D, 124th Machine Gun Battalion was following the first line of infantry near Consenvoye when Private Clayton K. Slack saw on his left Germans carrying ammunition boxes. He pointed them out to his sergeant, who said he would tell the infantry about it. When Slack persisted that something should be done at once, the sergeant snapped, "If you're so damn brave go after them yourself." Slack did. Picking up a rifle from a wounded man—machine gunners only carried pistols—he maneuvered himself to the rear of the Germans. Seeing three of them and two machine guns, he shouted "Hands up!" To his astonishment, ten men stood up with hands raised. Slack marched his prisoners back, turned them over to an infantry officer, then hurried to catch up with his unit. At war's end he was awarded a Medal of Honor.

From the Meuse River to a position just north of the Argonne Forest the Americans confronted the formidable *Kriemhilde Stellung*. On the night of 9 October Ludendorff ordered the retreat of his left and center to form a new line running along a canal from the Dutch frontier to Ghent, thence behind the Scheldt to Denain, and then behind the little Selle to a point west of the Sambre, where it joined Germany's last defense, the *Hermann Stellung*, extending to the Meuse below Sedan. This meant giving up the Belgian coast, Bruge and Lille, but he ordered his right, facing Pershing and Gouraud, to hold fast.

Pershing and General Drum, then his chief of staff, believed that the key to the German position was a crescent-shaped ridge, just over a half-mile long with hills on the cusps, known as the Côte Dame Marie or Romagne Heights, west of the town of Romagne. On 9 October the 32nd Division, attacking to the right of the 42nd Division, reached Romagne. It penetrated the trenches on Côte Dame Marie on 10 October, but, unable to hold itsposition, it established lines on the southern slopes of the hill, from where the attack was pressed.

Pershing had ordered an attack by the 32nd Division, but it was not expected that the 32nd, although a fine division, would be able to capture the ridge; their attack would be considered a success if they could hold the enemy in place while the 5th and 42nd Divisions attacked the flanks and pinched off the ridge.

The 3rd Battalion of the 126th Infantry, 32nd Division, found a gap in the dense enemy wire, but it was well guarded by enemy machine guns. The battalion commander sent Captain Edward B. Strom and seven men forward to see what could be done. Strom and his men painfully worked their way through the wire up a steep slope. When about 150 yards from the guns, they fired rifle grenades and rushed the German position. They captured ten machine guns and fifteen prisoners. And they occupied the key to the Côte Dame Marie. Incredibly, this feat was accomplished without the loss of a single man. Incredible, too, was that Strom was not awarded a Medal of Honor.

Woes seemed to descend upon the commander of the AEF. "I feel like I am carrying the whole world on my shoulders," he moaned. Baker came to Europe and spent a month in England and France. He managed to pry 200,000 tons of shipping from the British, and to give some comfort and encouragement to Pershing, who needed both.

American casualties were so high, not only from battle losses but from influenza, that replacements could not arrive in sufficient numbers. Combat divisions were short nearly 80,000 men. The size of infantry companies was reduced from 250 to 175 men. Because there were no basic training camps and no replacement depots Pershing found it necessary to break up the 84th and 86th divisions to use their men as replacements; however, even this was not enough. Before the Armistice he was forced to break up or skeletonize four combat divisions and three depot divisions. He urgently cabled Washington: "If necessary, some divisions in the United States should be stripped of trained men and such men shipped as replacements at once." But the men were not there. On 5 November General March cabled Pershing: "Influenza not only stopped all draft calls but practically stopped all training."

It was during this period of heavy fighting that the influenza epidemic assumed its most serious proportions. More than a quarter of the army suffered from the disease in the course of the war. Many developed pneumonia and often died within a week. The scourge came in two waves. The first, which peaked in July 1918, was generally mild and caused few fatalities. The second, which began in September, was deadly indeed. There was no cure.

By September the epidemic had spread to twenty-four camps in the United States. The AEF suffered fewer cases, but in the damp, cold week that ended on 5 October, during the period of some of the hardest fighting, some 16,000 cases were recorded. By mid-October four out of every one thousand soldiers in the AEF had died of the flu. The death rate in some units rose to thirty-two percent and in at least one rose as high as eighty percent.

Nurses were in short supply and on 3 October Pershing asked that 1,500 be sent to France as soon as possible. The status of female nurses in the army was ambivalent: about 10,000 served in the AEF and 296 died in war service, but the army refused to uniform or equip them, leaving that to the Red Cross. The War Department designated them "officers without rank."

Some suspected the Germans of introducing germ warfare and it was rumored that German submarines had brought the disease to the United States. But the Germans also were stricken, and their soldiers fared worse than Allied soldiers. It has been estimated 186,000 German soldiers died of the disease. In the space of only eleven months influenza and pneumonia accounted for more deaths than did all the bullets, shells, and poison gas in the entire war.

On 11 October Pershing, himself ill with the flu, divided his large army of 1,031,000, including 135,000 French troops, into two armies: the First Army, to be commanded by Hunter Liggett, and the Second Army, to be commanded by Robert Lee Bullard. Liggett made his former aide, George C. Marshall, his chief of operations (G-3). Pershing then commanded an army group, but he retained immediate command of the First Army for another two weeks.

Pétain warned Pershing that Foch was "impatient" with the slow progress of the Americans, even "violent." On 13 October Foch sent General Maxime Weygand to Pershing with an order relieving him of his command and placing him in charge of a quiet sector. Pershing refused to comply and drove to Foch's headquarters at Bombon to confront him directly. He was ushered into Foch's drawing room by General Weygand, who was a witness to the scene and recorded the exchange. Foch asked Pershing how his forces were progressing. "We have met with hard fighting," Pershing replied. "The Germans are putting up a very determined resistance."

"On all other parts of the front the advances are very marked. The Americans are not progressing as rapidly."

"No army in our place would have advanced farther than the Americans."

"Every general is disposed to say the fighting on his front is the hardest. I myself only consider results."

"Results? In seventeen days we have engaged twenty-six German divisions."

This was an exaggeration and Foch said, "Shall I show you my figures on this."

"No," said Pershing crisply. "I shall continue my attacks until the Germans give way." Then, pausing, he added sarcastically, "provided, of course, that this is Marshal Foch's desire."

"By all means," said Foch and then, to Pershing's exasperation, the former War College professor began to lecture: "In order for an attack to succeed, a commander must go considerably into details. . . ." Orders must be issued in writing, etc."

Pershing replied that of course this was done the same way in the American army. "We are not advancing rapidly because the Germans are fighting by echeloning machine guns in depth."

"Ah, I judge by results."

Pershing mentioned the difficult terrain in the Argonne, but Foch replied coldly, "I am aware of the terrain. You chose the Argonne and I allowed you to attack there."

Weygand now interposed, presenting Pershing's plan to divide the American forces into two armies. Foch took the papers but did not look at them. "Ah yes. I am inclined to grant your request." But he then threw in another barb. Pershing, he said, should stay at the front and not move his headquarters back to Chaumont. An angry Pershing assured him that this would not be the case. Foch tried to end the interview, but Pershing pressed on. He wanted to be sure that Foch understood and accept that he, Pershing, as the commander of more than one army, was now on a equivalent level with Haig and Pétain.

Foch shrugged and agreed.

On 14 October, the day after Pershing's disagreeable encounter with Foch, the Americans captured Côte Dame Marie and Romagne. The main object of the American attack that had begun on 26 September had been reached. Pershing was elated: "The importance of these operations can hardly be overestimated. The capture of the Romagne heights, especially their dominating feature, Côte Dame Marie, was a decisive blow. We now occupied the enemy's strongest position on the front and flanked his line on the Aisne and on the Heights of the Meuse. Unless he could recapture the positions we held, our successes would compel him to retire from his lines to the north, as we were within heavy artillery range of his railroad communications."

The American line now ran from east to west roughly from Molleville Farm to the town of Grandpré, a citadel town located on steep slopes, protected by heavy fieldworks at Saint-Juvin. It was attacked on both flanks on 13 October by the 78th Division, commanded by Major General James H. McRae, a Pershing classmate whom his chief of staff, Colonel Charles Herron, described as a man who "Feared neither God, man, nor the Devil—or General Pershing either." The unblooded division went into the line on 16 October and, with the exception of a three-day lull, attacked every day until on 27 October. Grandpré was taken in a daring assault by Captain Julius Ochs Adler of the New York *Times* family with two men and a machine gun. The fight raged on for three more days as the Germans made a skillful withdrawal. The division suffered nearly 5,000 casualties.

George C. Marshall complained of the stream of visitors to the front, American and foreign, military and civilian, who then returned "to spread reports all over France and England to the effect that we had failed and proven incompetent to coordinate so large an undertaking." "The American army," said Marshall, was "accomplishing a miracle of achievement" while these "broadcasters furnished all the fuel possible to the flames of the Allied effort to subdivide our army and utilize its divisions in their own fashion."

French and British officers complained that by using too many troops at the front Pershing created transportation crises; that the Americans failed to maintain proper communication between units; and did not make proper staff reconnaissances. A French general appeared at Pershing's headquarters with a proposal from Foch that the Americans fighting in the Argonne be placed under a French commander with a French staff. Pershing, of course, refused to consider it.

British Field Marshal Henry Wilson wrote of Pershing in his diary: "The state of chaos the fool has got his troops into down in the Argonne is indescribable." In a later diary entry he called Pershing a "vain ignorant weak ASS." It was said that indiscipline was rampant and that Pershing had ordered deserters shot out of hand but that subordinates refused to obey.

Although General Liggett guessed that "perhaps there were as many as 100,000 stragglers," he did not mean 100,000 deserters. In the chaos of battle many units of one division frequently found themselves fighting in the area of another division and so were marked as absent from their own. As in all wars, there were some men who sought to escape combat and Pershing did indeed write to his corps and division commanders about them: "When men run away in front of the enemy, officers should take summary action to stop it, even to the point of shooting men down who are caught in such disgraceful conduct. No orders need be published on the subject, but it should be made known to younger officers that they must do whatever is required to prevent it." Pershing had no authority to shoot men court-martialed for purely military offenses, although he had vainly sought that power.*

There was, in truth, considerable confusion just behind the lines. Five American divisions were kept in line on the active front for an average of twenty-four days of continuous fighting. There was no time to make readjustments among the troops heavily engaged, without giving the enemy a respite in which to strengthen his defenses and bring up reserves. The battle could not be delayed while roads were being built or repaired and supplies brought up. The weather was cold and there was much rain, not an inspiration for energetic action on the part of troops now bloodied and mired in the mud in front of the formidable *Kriemhilde Stellung,* and unaccustomed to the damp, raw climate.

Transportation remained a problem, particularly the difficulty of moving food and ammunition across the wasteland of the old battlefield. Cars, trucks, and, above all, horses and mules were in short supply. No animals had been received in August and only 1,839 in September. The AEF was threatened with immobility. Desperate, Pershing pleaded with the French, but they claimed they needed animals themselves. Colonel Avery Andrews on Pershing's staff reported that "the animal situation will soon become desperate." Although every effort was made, day and night, to push forward supplies, back in Washington Secretary Baker received a petition "about a mile long" from Christian groups begging him not to move supplies on Sundays.

The AEF still confronted the *Kriemhilde Stellung* and the heights along the Meuse. Ludendorff had ordered German General Max von Gallwitz, the army group commander facing them, to "put into the fighting front every unit that is at all fit for use in battle." Thus elements of thirty-six German and three Austrian divisions fought in the Meuse-Argonne offensive, confusing American intelligence.

While the battle for *Kriemhilde Stellung* raged, Pershing faced a political crisis. On 21 October Premier Georges Clemenceau, against the

---

*Courts-martial in France could order the death sentence for murder or rape, but not for being AWOL or asleep on guard duty.

advice of President Poincaré, sent Foch a letter that sarcastically denigrated the American efforts. Clemenceau was particularly bitter about Pershing and he strongly urged Foch to appeal directly to President Wilson in what Foch interpreted as a move to have Pershing relieved of his command. "You have watched at close range the development of General Pershing's extractions. Unfortunately, thanks to his invincible obstinacy he has won against you as well as your immediate subordinates. The French Army and the British Army, without a moment's respite, have been daily fighting for the past three months . . . but our worthy American allies, who thirst to get into action and who are unanimously acknowledged to be great soldiers, have been marking time ever since their forward jump on the first day, and in spite of heavy losses, they have failed to conquer the ground assigned to them as their objective. No one can maintain that these troops are unusable; they are merely unused." He ended by saying: "If General Pershing finally resigns himself to obedience, if he accepts the advice of capable generals, whose presence at his side he has until now permitted only that he might reject their councils, I shall be wholly delighted." General Harbord later said of Clemenceau: "A politician with a Napoleonic complex is a dangerous nuisance in war."

Foch, more diplomatic than the politician, reminded Clemenceau that of the forty American divisions then in France, eight were with the French and two with the British. He also pointed out that after their victory at St. Mihiel the AEF had, from 26 September until 20 October, lost 54,158 men in battle "in exchange for small gains on a narrow front, it is true, but over particularly difficult country and in the face of serious resistance by the enemy." The Americans, he said, "have got to learn sometime. They are learning now rapidly." This seemed to end the matter, at least for the moment.

Pershing heard "rumors" of Clemenceau's complaints, but brushed them off: "It was clear the end was approaching," he said. "It was obvious, therefore, that any attempt on his part to discredit our accomplishments would be purely a political gesture designed to minimize America's prestige at the peace conference." On 22 October, after the American victories in the Meuse-Argonne, Pershing met Clemenceau in Paris and the French premier was "in fine humor . . . and was profuse in his compliments on the success of our army."

Pershing, like Foch, looked for results. George C. Marshall was impressed by his general's handling of this great battle: "At this time General Pershing gave hourly evidence of those qualities that make successful leaders of great armies. . . . As casualties and extreme fatigue wore down the organizations, and the strain of battle produced a form of nervous exhaustion, General Pershing increased his demands on subordinates and forced the fighting throughout every daylight hour. He directed his divisional commanders to move their personal headquarters forward . . . to overcome the difficulties of weather and terrain, to cast aside the depressions caused by fatigue and casualties, and to instil into the troops the determination to force the fight along every foot of the front."

Foch's main efforts were now made by Haig's army on his left and Pershing's on his right. Haig's army, which still included the 27th and 30th American divisions, fought the Battle of the Selle that began on 17 October and ended with an Allied victory on 23 October. Haig with twenty-six divisions fought against thirty-one weakened but determined German divisions. The British took 20,000 prisoners and 475 guns and turned to push their way down the valleys of the Sambre and the Meuse.

Just as the war was about to end, the AEF reached its finest fighting trim. On 31 October it numbered 1,867,623 and more men were arriving almost daily. Its staffs and troops had become veterans; American morale was high; French artillery, engineers and service troops had been largely displaced by Americans; the front line had been reorganized; inefficient commanders had been replaced by active, energetic ones; and large quantities of ammunition and supplies had been brought forward.

There was still the need to silence the German guns beyond the Meuse. Pershing now planned on deep penetration of the German line in the center of the front west of the Meuse River by the American First Army in conjunction with the French Fourth Army. Hundreds of tanks were sorely needed, but only eighteen were available. Pershing later remarked: "It seems strange that, with American genius for manufacturing from iron and steel, we could find ourselves after a year and a half of war almost completely without those mechanical contrivances which had exercised such a great influence on the Western Front in reducing infantry losses." The first American tank had arrived in October 1918 and only fifteen were ever built.

When the 33rd Division crossed the river it initially gained five kilometers, but then the attack stalled all along the line for a week. More than 2,000 men of the 33rd were gassed—more than in any other American division. This division had been on the front for more than a month when, on 21 October, it was withdrawn. The Germans tenaciously held their positions until the final week of the war. Pershing later paid tribute to his enemies: "It should be recorded that . . . the Germans defended every foot of ground with desperate tenacity and with the rare skill of experienced soldiers."

The 2nd Division, newly arrived on this front after being loaned to the French to fight at Mont Blanc, attacked and made a spectacular advance, cracking the *Kriemhilde Stellung* and the *Freya Stellung*, the German reserve fortifications, and destroying the two weak German divisions in its path. It spent the next few days consolidating the salient it had made in the German lines.

At 3:30 A.M. on 1 November the Americans began an attack with an enormous two-hour artillery bombardment that included fire from the 14-inch naval guns. For the first time the Americans used gas on a large scale, 41.1 tons of it. Nine of twelve German batteries hidden in the Bois de Bourgogne were destroyed.

The infantry advanced to the assault at 5:30 A.M. following an accurate rolling artillery barrage which, aided by machine guns, beat down the enemy's defenses over a zone 1,200 yards in depth. Pursuit planes drove the enemy from the skies and strafed German infantry. Bombers harassed key points in the enemy lines.

The attack continued on the 2nd and 3rd and I Corps hurled the enemy beyond the Meuse. The Americans advanced rapidly against heavy resistance on the fronts of the right and center corps. Artillery followed closely on the infantry and heavy guns were able to shell the railroad from Carignan to Sedan and the junctions at Longuyon and Conflans.

Heroes continued to perform. Captain Herbert Hilburn of Plainview, Texas, who had been commissioned after attending an officer training camp in August of the previous year, successfully led his Company H, 359th Infantry, in an attack on the village of Villers-devant-Dun and then beat off a determined counterattack. He was awarded not only the Distinguished Service Cross but the French Legion of Honor and *Croix de Guerre*. Asked to explain his achievement he said, "I was more afraid of my colonel than the Boche."

On the 4th and 5th German forces were retreating before the advance of the American First Army, but their retreat was not a rout. To slow the advance of their enemies they left behind scattered machine gun nests whose crews did their duty and died at their posts. American propaganda proclaimed that they were chained to their weapons, but this was not true. Private Mackin wrote of them: "We never really understood such men. The crews were small, seldom more than two or three, and always young. The young ones stayed and died because their orders had told them to." Floyd Gibbons wrote: "The German backed out of the Marne salient as a Western 'bad man' would back out of a saloon with an automatic pistol in each hand." F. Scott Fitzgerald later described the orderly German retreat, saying they "walked very slowly backward a few inches a day, leaving the dead like a million bloody rags."

The Battle of Meuse-Argonne was the largest yet fought by the United States Army. About 1,250,000 men in twenty-two divisions took part in it. Not until 1926 did the War Department publish a final tabulation of American casualties: 26,277 dead and 95,786 wounded in forty-seven days of continuous battle. From 26 September until 20 October the First Army captured 18,591 men. In the second and third weeks of October the Germans lost nearly 25,000 men.

Although the Meuse-Argonne offensive has been compared to the Battle of the Wilderness in the Civil War, the campaign in France lasted six times longer, engaged twelve times as many men as fought on the Union side, employed ten times as many guns, fired about one hundred times as many artillery rounds, and suffered casualties about four times heavier.

The tide was turning everywhere for the Allies. On the Italian Front on 29 October the Italians won the Battle of Vittorio Veneto, the Austrians losing 30,000 killed and nearly half a million taken prisoner. On 31 October Turkey threw in the towel. The AEF now had forty-two divisions in France, and more men were arriving almost daily. By the end of October the AEF numbered 1,867,623 men. The war was still one of attrition and generals on both sides knew it. General Drum, writing to his wife, told her: "The gaining of ground counts for little, it is the ruining of his army that will end the struggle." On the Allied side losses were also heavy, sometimes horrific. The 3rd Battalion of the 16th Infantry lost eighteen out of twenty officers and 560 out of 800 enlisted men. But it was now crystal-clear to the generals that the continuing arrival of the Americans made the Allies sure war-winners — if they could be supplied.

Between 1 and 7 November French and American forces had advanced twenty-four miles on either side of the Meuse River, the French on the left capturing Mézières and Charleville. Sedan lay just outside the American sector, but spurred by an "irrational sentimentality" the Americans tried to capture the city in one of the stupidest maneuvers of the war.

The seeds of this near disaster began on 6 November 1918 when AEF headquarters issued a pernicious order: "General Pershing desires that the honor of entering Sedan should fall to the American First Army." Colonel George C. Marshall drafted the initial order from First Army to corps commanders, but before it was transmitted General Hugh A. Drum compounded the evil by adding, "Boundaries will not be considered binding." The French were not informed of Pershing's order. Neither were most of the American commanders.

To understand the enormity of this order it must be remembered that in 1870, during the Franco-Prussian War, Sedan was the site of perhaps the worst disaster ever suffered by French arms. It was there that an entire French army was forced to surrender and it was there that Napoleon III was himself captured. The fiasco at Sedan hastened the collapse of the Second Empire and brought to France the humiliating Treaty of Frankfort in 1871. In a newly united Germany 2 September became Sedan Day, a national holiday. Now the city lay directly in the path of the advancing French, eager to wipe out the memory of this debacle. Pershing could not have been unaware of the significance the French attached to the capture of Sedan.

Drum's addition to the orders was a violation of common sense and of the doctrine senior commanders had always consistently preached. On the Western Front each unit was assigned its own section of the line and a defined area into which it was hoped it would advance. To stray from an assigned sector was to risk casualties from friendly fire and to disrupt battle plans.

The order also was ambiguous, leaving open which division was actually to cross the Meuse and take the city, and it was sent directly to the corps commander, bypassing Liggett, the First Army commander. The 42nd (Rainbow) Division was the closest to the city and to its right was the 77th Division and to the right of the 77th was the 1st Division. When General Charles Summerall received the order, he went to the headquarters of the 1st Division, which he had once commanded, and ordered its then commander, Brigadier General Frank Parker, to take Sedan regardless of the tactical and operational situation on the field. This meant that to reach the bridges across the Meuse Parker's Big Red One Division* would have to pass through the areas held by both the 77th and the 42nd divisions and into the French sector of General Gouraud's Fourth Army.

---

*The 1st Division, so called because of their shoulder patch of a large red "1."

Having been given the task of taking Sedan, Gouraud assigned the French 40th Division to move at all speed toward the city.

The 1st Division began its march of about fifty kilometers, using five routes through a pitch-black night in the rain, over winding, unfamiliar roads with no coordination with any of the American and French units whose space they were invading. Telephone lines were tangled, traffic was snarled, and Americans fired at each other. Most of the casualties were from friendly fire.

Early in the afternoon of 7 November the advance guard of the French 40th Division reaching the village of Checery discovered elements of the 29th United States Infantry Regiment of the 1st Division in its zone of action. The situation became increasingly chaotic. General Joseph Dickman, commanding I Corps, who had long quarreled with Summerall, was in a rage when he discovered what was taking place. Dickman instructed General Douglas MacArthur, now commanding the Rainbow Division, to take command of all American troops in his area. He told Summerall in no uncertain terms that he was to stop at once and withdraw his troops from I Corps' zone of action.

General James Harbord later wrote: "The division was sent on a futile errand in executing which it sustained about 500 casualties and marched itself to exhaustion. . . . As an illustration of lack of team work, and as an example of undisciplined inexperience, it justified much of what our associates [French and British] thought and said of us." General Liggett wisely allowed the French the honor of capturing Sedan. (It was not until 31 August 1944 that the Americans captured Sedan from the Germans.)

Ignoring his own culpability, Pershing essentially repudiated any mandate in the order that justified the march of the 1st Division. He later wrote: "Under normal conditions the action of the officer or officers responsible for this movement of the 1st Division directly across the zones of action of two other divisions could not have been overlooked, but the splendid record of that unit and the approach of the end of hostilities suggested leniency." And within two weeks he praised the division, still under General Parker, in a eulogistic order—the only division in the AEF ever to receive such signal honor.

In the last days of the war Pershing seemed to have lost all sense of proportion. The attempt to have an American division capture Sedan was clearly his fault. Cavalry was of no use at all in France, as had been frightfully demonstrated at Cambrai on 20 November 1917 when two cavalry divisions following behind British tanks to exploit the opening they made advanced about five miles before the Germans blew them off the battle-field. But in August 1918 Pershing had requested eight regiments of corps cavalry. Even though all senior people knew that an armistice was evident, he persisted in making what General March called "preposterous demands." On 30 October he submitted a scheme for the manufacture of 194 mm guns, when it should have been obvious that it would take more than a year for such a gun to reach him. On 1 November March directed a halt of all shipments of troops to France; on the following day Pershing demanded 140,000 replacements. During the last three days of hostilities the Second Army continued its advance along the entire front. Pershing "inferred" that Foch "wished to let the enemy know that there could be no further delay" in signing an armistice so V Corps was ordered to cross the Meuse on the night of 10 November and to launch an ill-advised attack that was halted by the Armistice.

In this final offensive the total strength of the American 1st Army, including 135,000 French troops, reached 1,031,000 men. It had suffered about 117,000 casualties, but had captured 26,000 prisoners, 874 guns, 3,000 machine guns and large quantities of materiel. German casualties were estimated at 100,000. The Meuse-Argonne offensive, said Pershing, "stands out as one of the great achievements in the history of American arms."

Captain Truman lost twenty pounds in the course of the offensive, but proclaimed it the "most terrific experience of my life."

In the forty-seven days of the offensive the men doing the fighting hardened. Sergeant Gerald C. Thomas of the 6th Marines, who rose to be a full general in the Korean War, said, "It was this period that made us tough. . . . We got tough and stayed tough." But twenty-year-old Private Elton E. Mackin in the 5th Marines disagreed: "Ours was not a real hardness. We were too young to be truly hard so soon. We became brittle, which differs from hardness in many degrees. We were not tempered. . . . We were just too damned young, and under fire too soon."

22

☆

AMERICANS UNDER EUROPEAN

COMMANDERS

PERSHING NEVER SUCCEEDED in collecting all the American troops into one army. They were scattered across the Euro-Asian land mass: the 332nd Infantry in Italy, the 339th in northwestern Russia and another expeditionary force of 9,000 men in Siberia, over which Pershing had no control. Even on the Western Front he was unable to pry all of his soldiers from the hands of British Field Marshal Haig and French Marshal Pétain.

Five American divisions were trained in Britain, but Pershing was not enthusiastic about the results. He believed that "due to differences in national characteristics and military systems, the instruction and training of our troops by them retarded our progress." For their part, the American troops were unhappy with the British; they talked funny, calling a wrench a spanner and a truck a lorry; above all, Americans objected to British rations and never learned to prefer tea to coffee. "We don't like their blooming tea or their blamed pet cats," wrote one soldier. "They said it was rabbit, but we used our own opinion. We had tasted rabbit in the states and we knew."

The Americans were exotics in Britain. Leslie Reade, a London schoolboy, remembered standing in a knot of boys in front of the statue of Eros in Piccadilly Circus staring silently at two American soldiers who were smoking cigars while having their boots polished. "They had 'U.S.' on the high collars of their uniforms, and the big hats. . . . Oddly enough, the Yanks also said nothing at all. . . . These two men from the West stood there in silence, as we of Europe stood staring silently back."

In the spring of 1918 when the five divisions were sent to France

Pershing established an American corps under General George W. Reed in command. It served under Haig and he wanted to keep it, but his first attempt to use the Americans aroused Pershing's wrath.

In the summer of 1918 Lieutenant General Sir John Monash, the commander of the Australian corps in France, planned an attack using sixty tanks, eight battalions of Australians, and eight companies of American infantry from the 33rd Division on a 6,000-yard front against German defenses along a ridge containing the Bois de Vaire and the town of Hamel. Monash, an Australian Jew, was an engineer in civil life, but in the words of military historian Basil H. Liddell Hart, he possessed "the greatest capacity for command in modern war among all who held command in the last war."

Monash believed that a battle plan should be much like "a score for an orchestral composition" and he made his troops practice every detail of a planned attack. On 30 June he held a final briefing of his subordinate commanders. The attack was to take place on 4 July. But abruptly Monash was ordered by Sir Henry Rawlinson, commanding the British Fourth Army, to cut the number of Americans in half. He reluctantly did so. Then on 2 July Pershing learned of the attack and ordered General Reed to withdraw all Americans from the battle plans. At this, Monash, who got the word less than twelve hours before the beginning of the attack, protested to Rawlinson that he could not attack without the Americans. The matter was referred to Haig, who told Monash to go ahead and use them.

The attack was a success. Monash later said: "No battle within my previous experience . . . passed off so smoothly, so exactly to timetable, or so free from any kind of hitch." In ninety-three minutes the objective was taken and two guns and 1,472 prisoners were taken. The Americans lost 176 men, mostly from Australian artillery whose rounds fell short. Corporal Thomas A. Pope in the 131st Infantry won the Medal of Honor for attacking a machine-gun nest single-handed and killing its gunners. Nevertheless, Pershing was furious and gave orders that Americans were never to be used this way again.

August proved a disastrous month for German arms. The British captured more than 63,000 prisoners and 870 guns, the French captured 31,000 prisoners and 890 guns. In his memoirs Ludendorff pinpointed 8 August as the "black day of the German army": "Our war machine was no longer efficient. Our fighting power had suffered, even though the majority of our divisions fought heroically. The 8th of August put the decline of that fighting power beyond all doubt and in such a situation as regards reserves, I had no hope of finding a strategic expedient whereby to turn the situation to our advantage." Nevertheless, he still entertained illusions of keeping Belgium and the territory torn from Russia. He knew his army could not win, but to lose was unthinkable. On 13 and 14 August he explained his views at a conference held at Spa (ironically, at the Hotel Britannique) and attended by the Kaiser, the Austrian Emperor, and Paul von Hintze, a former admiral who recently had been appointed head of the foreign office. Hintze wept when he learned the sad condition of the German army, but no plan of action was approved. On 28 September Ludendorff conferred with Hindenburg and they agreed that they must concede defeat. They shook hands "as men burying their dearest hopes."

In the famous British attack beginning on 8 August which led Ludendorff to conclude that he could not win, the American 131st Infantry, led by doughty sixty-one-year-old Colonel Joseph B. Sanborn, who had commanded the Illinois National Guard regiment since 1898, was in the reserve on the first day, but was at the front on 9 August. Fighting throughout the night, the regiment cleared the Bois de Gressaire and the Chipilly Ridge, which overlooked the Somme River.

The 131st was still at the front when on 12 August Pershing warned Haig that he might have to withdraw his divisions from the British. Haig, irritated, protested that although he had trained, equipped, and fed them, and had "done everything to help these units of the American Army and provide them with horses," he had had little opportunity to use them. In his diary Haig wrote: "What will History say regarding this action of the Americans leaving the British zone of operations when *the decisive battle* of the war is at its height, and the decision still in doubt!" In the event, Pershing requested only three and two National Guard divisions—the 27th, commanded by John F. O'Ryan, and the 30th, commanded by Edward M. Lewis—stayed with the British throughout the war, taking part in the British breaching of the Hindenburg Line in the vicinity of St. Quentin, the 30th earning more Medals of Honor than any other division in France.

In August the 27th Division fought on the British flank at the Battle of Mont Kemmel. In the same month the 30th Division had also fought beside the British near the town of Voormezele. These two American divisions fought at the Battle of the Bellicourt Tunnel on the Cambrai–St. Quentin canal. The tunnel, part of a canal system designed by Napoleon, was about 6,500 yards long and served as a shelter for German troops in that area.

The attack on a 3,000-yard front began at 6:00 A.M. on 29 September with the British 46th Division on the right, the American 27th on the left, and the 30th in the center. The 30th and the British division succeeded, the 30th cutting three lines of barbed wire, overrunning three trench systems, and blocking both ends of the tunnel. The 27th had a grimmer experience.

The British had failed to capture what was to have been the division's jumping-off positions. By the time the Americans seized them, the rolling barrage had gone too far ahead to protect them. The British were asked for a renewal of the barrage, but they refused to provide it. By the time the 27th attacked, the Germans had emerged from their deep shelters to attack them.

In this attack the 107th Infantry in the 27th Division charged with bared bayonets and the Germans turned to flee—all except one man who turned to fight with his bayonet. Actual fighting with bayonets always has been rare. In this instance the German's thrust was parried and an American bayonet was driven into him. Private First Class Raymond Williams was a witness: "The German gave a yell as he dropped that could be heard above the noise of battle. Everyone on the scene of the fight stood still and looked on with bated breath." Then the retreating Germans dropped their weapons and cried "Kamerad!"

The 107th lost fifty percent of its assault troops—227 killed and 658 wounded—the most Americans casualties suffered by any one unit in a single day in the war, a butcher's bill that stiffened Pershing's opposition to the amalgamation of American units with French and British forces.

In spite of Pershing's recalcitrance the Allies never ceased to clamor for American troops. When appeals and arguments failed to move him, political pressure was exerted. Lloyd George had written the British ambassador in Washington: "It is maddening to think that though the men are there the issue may be endangered because of the shortsightedness of one general and the failure of his Government to order him to carry out their undertakings." Baker and Wilson were asked to override Pershing, which, to their credit, they refused to do, regarding this as a military, not a political decision. Baker told Pershing of the British and French pressure, but cabled him: "The President, however, desires you to have full authority to use the forces at your command as you deem wise in consultation with the French and British Commanders-in-Chief."

WHILE POLITICIANS, STATESMEN, and generals debated, the war went on. The American 2nd Division and the newly arrived 36th Division, filled with Texas and Oklahoma National Guardsmen, were loaned to the French Fourth Army under General Henri Gouraud to attack a ridge in Champagne called Mont Blanc, between Rheims and the western edge of the Argonne Forest. It was part of a general Allied offensive across the entire Western Front, in an area where French attacks had repeatedly been thrown back. It was a maze of German trenches, machine gun nests, and bunkers, elaborately fortified over a four-year period. An officer in the 5th Marines, looking over the wasteland this once prosperous province had become, expressed his dislike of the locale, saying "it looks like it was just built for calamities to happen in."

The 2nd Division's plan for taking Mont Blanc was a good one, but it depended upon the French on its flanks, attacking on lower and less demanding ground, also advancing and taking their objectives.

On 3 October, the 2nd Division attacked the ridge on a three-mile front, the marines going over the top at 5:50 A.M. Two hours later, after suffering heavy casualties, they were astride the ridge, but one battalion of the 5th Marines was caught in the open without artillery support. German artillery soon had their range. Only about 100 out of 1,000 survived unscathed. The Americans took the ridge, but the French had failed to keep pace and the Americans were forced to defend their own flanks. As a result, 3 October 1918 was the bloodiest day in the division's history, but on the following day the French could with ease assume their places in the line. General John A. Lejeune, then commanding the 2nd Division, sent off an angry telegram to AEF headquarters saying he would resign his commission rather than again fight beside French units.

Even when faced with certain defeat, the Germans still fought skillfully and continued to hold large sections of the ridge, which was not taken until after four days of bitter fighting that cost the 2nd Division 4,075 casualties, among them ninety marine officers and 2,228 enlisted men. On 4 October the marines lost 1,100 men, its heaviest one-day casualties in the war. On the night of 6/7 October the Marine Brigade was relieved by a brigade of the 36th Division.

The Marine 5th and 6th regiments were awarded their third unit *Croix de Guerre*, entitling them to wear a green and red *fourragère*—braided cord worn about the left shoulder of every man in the unit so honored. Members of these units still wear the *fourragère*.

One of the heroes of the Mont Blanc fight was Private Frank J. Bart in the army brigade of the 2nd Division. A short man, he was assigned as a runner. When his unit was held up by German machine gunners at Médéah Farm, he was given a message to take back requesting artillery support. Instead, he picked up a Chauchat and, running ahead of the stalled line, wiped out the machine gun nest himself. An hour later he repeated this feat. His short legs were tired of running messages, he said. He was awarded the Medal of Honor.

A French résumé of the Mont Blanc battle noted that a detachment of marines had assisted the French of the XI Corps to clean out German trenches. In fact, the French had been two kilometers from the trenches mentioned, leading a wit from the Marine Brigade to compose some new verses for the immortal and ever-adaptable "Mademoiselle from Armentiéres":

> Oh, the general got the Croix de Guerre,
> Parley-voo.
> Oh, the general got the Croix de Guerre,
> Parley-voo.
> Yes, the general got the Croix de Guerre,
> But the sonofabitch wasn't even there,
> Hinky-Dinky, parley-voo.

In mid-October 1918 Foch demanded two good divisions from Pershing to fight in Flanders beside the Belgian and British armies pursuing German armies trying to break contact beyond Ypres and Ostend and hold a line on the Scheldt River. For reasons difficult to understand, Pershing agreed to the transfer and the 37th ("Buckeye") Division of Ohio National Guardsmen and the 91st Division, a National Army unit which called itself the Wild West Division, were sent to Belgium. His consent to this move seems particularly puzzling as they were to be placed under the command of General Degoutte, the least popular of French generals in the eyes of Americans, who always found him too ready to expend American blood.

The two divisions were under capable commanders, the 37th under Major General Charles S. Farnsworth and the 91st under Major William H. Johnston, but Degoutte managed to deprive both of tactical command and to put the divisions under separate French corps. On 30 October Degoutte sent them to capture the railroad line north of the town of Waereghem. The 37th advanced rapidly, destroying all opposition and gaining three miles; the 91st had a more difficult time.

The Germans were strongly entrenched in Spitaal Wood and the French on their flank refused to move until the Americans had made it safer for them. The fighting lasted all day, but the Germans withdrew at night and the following day the 91st moved up on line with the 37th. In Flanders, the fighting cost the 37th Division about 1,600 casualties and the 91st about one thousand.

In the spring of 1918 four infantry regiments of blacks—the 169th, 170th, 171st, and 172nd—were turned over to the French, becoming organic parts of French divisions and performing well. They were issued French gas masks, French Lebel rifles with three-round clips and long, thin 18-inch French bayonets, and for a time they even wore French helmets. They ate French rations, but were given a bit more sugar in place of the usual wine ration. They suffered 3,167 casualties—thirty-two percent of their strength.

The 371st Infantry, another black unit, was attached to the French XIII Army Corps and after trench warfare experience at St. Mihiel the 371st and the 372nd were made part of the famed French 157th ("Red Hand") Division. Both fought with distinction in the Meuse-Argonne offensive. In six days the 371st won thirteen Distinguished Service Crosses.

By the time of the Armistice fourteen of its officers and twelve enlisted men had won the Distinguished Service Cross and twelve officers had been awarded the Distinguished Service Medal. Two enlisted men were awarded the *Medaille Militaire*—described with some truth by Charles MacArthur as "the one incorruptible bona fide certificate of heroism in France"—and three officers received the Legion of Honor; forty-one officers and 110 enlisted men won the *Croix de Guerre* and the regiment was awarded the unit *Croix de Guerre* with palm.

There was a reluctance to give medals to blacks until after a reevaluation was begun in 1988. In 1991 a Medal of Honor was awarded posthumously to Corporal Freddie Stowers of the 93rd Division (Provisional) for leading an attack upon a machine gun nest.

Two pursuit squadrons, the 17th and 148th, flying Sopwith Camels, were trained by the British and fought under British command. On the night of 22 March 1918 the 148th suffered its greatest loss of the war before it had a chance to fire a shot. While camped near Chaules, waiting for their first assignment, German planes dropped three bombs, killing ten men and wounding eight others. On 13 July Lieutenant Field Kindley shot down a German Albatross D-3 over Ypres, the 148th squadron's first victory. Before the end of the war Kindley shot down eleven more planes.

On 13 August 1918 the 17th Aero Squadron took part in one of the most daring raids of the war, bombing and strafing the large German airdrome at Varssenaere, near Bruge, where there were five enemy squadrons. Ten German planes were put out of action and, it was said, thirty pilots and 120 soldier mechanics were killed. All the Americans returned safely, although many planes were badly shot up.

One flier who flew with the British was Elliott White Springs, scion of a wealthy textile tycoon in South Carolina, who after leaving Princeton went to England and joined the Royal Air Force (RAF). He shot down four enemy planes before joining the 148th in August 1918. When the war ended he was a captain and squadron commander with twelve victories.

Even after the United States entered the war, some Americans preferred to serve in the British or Canadian army. Among these was future novelist William Faulkner, who later said that he tried to join the American Air Service but was rejected. However, like much that Faulkner said of his 179 days, military service, this was probably not true. On 9 July 1918 he did enlist as a "cadet for pilot" in the Royal Air Force. From Canada he wrote his mother: "I am trying to learn to walk and salute nasty, like a British officer." He finished ground school on 13 November, two days after the Armistice, and never won the wings he nevertheless wore. Faulkner never flew solo or was sent to France or was injured in an airplane crash or was commissioned or did much else that he claimed; like Hemingway, he pretended to be what he was not and to have done what he did not do. (The real Faulkner family hero was his brother, Jack, a private who fought at Belleau Wood with the 5th Marines, where he was gassed and wounded.)

The most overlooked American regiment of the war was the 332nd Infantry in Italy, which saw little fighting until the end of the war. In October 1918 the Italians launched the Vittorio-Veneto drive and the regiment took part in the pursuit of the rapidly retreating Austrians. On 3 November it fought an Austrian rearguard defending a bridge on the Tagliamento River near Ponte della Delizia. The Austrians were driven off and the Americans pushed on, capturing large quantities of supplies at Codroipo. The next day at 3:00 P.M. the Austrian armistice took effect. The regiment's losses were only one killed and seven wounded.

23

☆

ARMISTICE

ON 8 JANUARY 1918 the morning was cold but sunny in Washington and President Wilson played a round of golf with his young wife. Returning to the White House at 11:30, he did a curious thing. Summoning his secretary, Joseph Patrick Tumulty, he told him to inform the speaker of the house and the vice president that he would speak to a joint session of Congress in thirty minutes. He had not consulted the Allies, any member of Congress, or any of his own Cabinet. Secretary of the Interior Franklin Lane declared this to be the "limit of humiliation as far as the Cabinet was concerned."

There was a mad scramble to assemble congressmen and cabinet members, not all of whom got the word. Introduced to scattered applause, Wilson proceeded to deliver the most momentous speech of his career, listing the Fourteen Points which he deemed necessary for world peace, chief among them were open covenants openly arrived at; freedom of the seas; free trade; impartial adjustments of all colonial claims; the evacuation of foreigners from Russia; Belgium and the Balkans evacuated by the Germans and restored; French territory restored, including Alsace and Lorraine; the Ottoman Empire to be dissolved; an independent Polish state erected; and, "A general association of nations must be formed." Clemenceau, a critic of the Fourteen Points, noted that God needed only ten.

The speech was greeted with wild applause. "Senators and representatives," according to John Dos Passos, "jumped on their chairs and waved their arms as if they were at a football game." It was applauded outside the

capital as well. The New York *Tribune*, not usually friendly toward
Wilson, called it a second Emancipation Proclamation and pronounced
that "Today, as never before, the whole nation marches with the
President, certain alike of the leader and the cause." Perhaps so. But
opposition soon developed in Congress where many demanded not nego-
tiation but unconditional surrender. Theodore Roosevelt telegraphed
senators urging them to repudiate the Fourteen Points: "Let us dictate
peace by the hammering guns and not chat about peace to the clicking of
typewriters."

Among liberals everywhere in the world Wilson's words resonated.
Izvestia thought the Fourteen Points "represent a great victory in the great
struggle for a democratic peace" until a few days later it changed its mind
when Lenin told his party: "The war with England and America will go
on for a long time; the aggressive imperialism of both groups has
unmasked itself finally and completely."

Wilson had not bothered to mention his Fourteen Points to the Allies
and the rulers of other countries were found to have other ideas. Britain
looked askance at the freedom of the seas clause; it was unthinkable that
Britain should not continue to rule the waves. The French, with colonies
of its own, sided with Britain, Clemenceau giving the curious argument
that, "War would not be war if there were freedom of the seas." Both
France and Britain wanted their own colonies untouched and a distribution of Ottoman territory and German colonies. In fact, the French wanted no part of Wilson's scheme; they were vindictive and wanted Germany
utterly crushed. Italy wanted to bite off parts of Austria for itself. Germany
at first refused to join a community of "peace-loving nations" but, eventually, recognizing in Wilson a more lenient national leader than could be
found among the other belligerents, clutched at his Fourteen Points.

In the initial stages of the discussion over peace terms, President Wilson
sent Colonel Edward House, his trusted confidant, to Europe. They com-
municated in a special private code, but unknown and unsuspected was
the fact that the British had broken both their code and the American
diplomatic code and regularly intercepted all communications between
Wilson and House and Wilson and Secretary of State Robert Lansing.
British Field Marshal Sir Henry Wilson found their cables "the most
amazing reading." In his diary on 9 November he wrote: "I believe Wilson
to be an unscrupulous knave and a hater of England and House to be a
poor miserable tool. Luckily I don't believe Wilson has any ability."

In June 1918 Richard von Kühlmann, the German foreign secretary, blurted out the truth: Military victory was impossible. He urged immediate negotiations for peace and was dismissed from office for his pains; he was replaced by Paul von Hintze, a former naval officer. On 8 August, after Haig smashed the German line on the Somme and Prussian soldiers cursed their officers and refused to fight, even Ludendorff saw that the war must be ended. On 29 September he sent a trusted officer to Berlin to lay out the true facts of the military situation to the German parliament. The government panicked. No one had realized how truly bad the situation was. A new ministry was put in place and Prince Maximilian of Baden, known as Prince Max, a second cousin of the Kaiser, was appointed the new chancellor of Germany. Finding it impossible to believe that the German army was in such straits, he asked Hindenburg why, if things were so bad, the army did not simply surrender. Hindenburg, nonplussed, could not reply. The surrender of the German army was unthinkable and, in fact, it never did surrender. On 1 October Kurt Riezler, the senior political councilor at the Wilhelmstrasse, wrote in his diary: "Slavery for 100 years. The dream of world power gone forever. The end of all hubris. The scattering of Germans throughout the world. Fate of the Jews." On 3 October Hindenburg sent a letter to Prince Max, demanding that he at once seek a peace: "There is now no longer any possibility of forcing peace on the enemy. . . . The situation grows more desperate every day and may force the High Command to grave decisions."

The exchange of notes between the German and American governments began on 6 October when Prince Max initiated a correspondence through the Swiss government with a note which read: "The German Government requests the President of the United States to take in hand the restoration of peace, acquaint all the belligerent states of this request, and invite them to send plenipotentiaries for the purpose of opening peace negotiations.

"It accepts the programme set forth by the President of the United States in his message to Congress on January 8 and in his later pronouncements, especially in his speech of September 28 [given at the opening of the Fourth Liberty Loan in New York City, memorable for his assertion: 'Militarism must go, root and branch.'].

"With a view to avoiding further bloodshed, the German Government requests the immediate conclusion of an armistice on land and sea."

This nonsense of an armistice without terms, leaving the Germans with all their gains, was quickly ended. The president conveyed in a message through the State Department on 23 October that "the nations of the world do not and can not trust the word of those who have hitherto been the masters of German policy," and that "the Government of the United States cannot deal with any but veritable representatives of the German people, who have been assured of a constitutional standing as the real rulers of Germany. If it must deal with the military masters and monarchial autocrats of Germany now, or if it is likely to have to deal with them later . . . it must demand, not peace negotiations, but surrender." On 5 November the Germans were advised to apply to Marshal Foch for terms of an armistice.

On 10 October 1918 a German submarine torpedoed a passenger ship off the coast of Ireland and with it almost torpedoed the peace talks. The ship went down with a loss of 292 lives; of 150 women and children on board, only seventeen were saved. On 17 October the "nonsinkable" *Lucia*, an army cargo transport fitted up with buoyancy boxes, was struck by what were believed to be torpedoes from the U-155. Although not unsinkable, the *Lucia* did stay afloat for twenty-two hours. On 9 November the *Saetia*, a cargo steamer from France bound for Philadelphia struck a mine ten miles southeast of Fenwick Island Shoals. On board beside the crew were eleven army officers and seventy-four enlisted soldiers. All were rescued. These German successes could not have come at a worse time for the German peace offensive.

A delicate problem faced by the new German government was the designation of a suitable person to tell Kaiser Wilhelm that his reign had ended and that he must abdicate. Prince Max was felled by influenza; no member of the royal family could be persuaded to do so. The unpleasant task finally fell upon Dr. Wilhelm Drews, the rather lowly minister of the interior. In a letter to a friend the Kaiser described his outrage. He predicted that if he abdicated there would be chaos, and he had told the unfortunate Drews: "All the dynasties will fall along with me, the army is left leaderless, the front line troops disband and stream across the Rhine. The disaffected gang together, hang, murder, and plunder—assisted by the enemy. That is why I have no intention of abdicating. . . . I have no intention of quitting the throne because of a few hundred Jews and a thousand workmen. Tell that to your masters in Berlin!"

Germany was indeed approaching chaos. Officers of the High Seas Fleet, sitting idle since Jutland, had tried to work up steam for a suicidal last attack upon the Royal Navy, but the sailors mutinied and by 29 October the fleet was immobile, the discontent spreading from the great naval base at Kiel to eleven northern cities, including Bremen, Hamburg, and other port towns. Troops sent to Kiel to suppress the mutineers joined them.

A workers and sailors soviet was established under the leadership of a stoker, Karl Artelt, and the mutiny became a revolution. In major cities throughout Germany other soviets were formed. Demands included abdication of the Kaiser and voting rights for all German citizens. A Bavarian republic was declared in Munich. Germany's allies deserted her: Bulgaria on 29 September, Turkey on 31 October, and Austria-Hungary on 4 November. It was the end of Imperial Germany.

The German Armistice Commission, headed by Matthias Erzberger, a Center Party delegate and minister without portfolio, with representatives of the navy and the Foreign Office and accompanied by a general who spoke perfect French, left Spa at noon on 7 November, but because of the chaotic conditions they met on the road did not cross the lines until 9:00 that night. In the course of their journey they witnessed the state of the German army in retreat: deserters, wounded, a despairing soldiery; stores of all kinds abandoned, loaded railroad cars standing without locomotives to move them, and clogged canals. They were taken by train to a siding in the Forest of Compiègne, arriving at 7:00 A.M. on 8 November. There they boarded Marshal Foch's railroad cars where French and British representatives awaited them. Foch presented them with nonnegotiable terms. In the armistice agreement a distinction was made between "the Allies and the United States of America." No American was present. In Foch's demands there was no hint of Wilson's Fourteen Points or of a "peace without victory." The terms were brutal and were meant to be.

On 9 November Germany declared itself a republic. The Kaiser reluctantly abdicated and on 10 November the Americans held the high ground overlooking Sedan. Had the war gone on the Americans and French were prepared to launch another offensive on 14 November. At the eleventh hour of the eleventh day of the eleventh month the war ended. It had lasted 1,568 days.

Pershing was alone in his office as the last minutes of the war ticked by. Major Lloyd Griscom, a staff officer, entered, thinking he would see his chief elated by victory. Instead, Pershing walked to a big map on his wall: "I suppose the campaigns are ended," he said, "but what an enormous difference a few days would have made!"

Pershing, like Theodore Roosevelt, Senator Henry Cabot Lodge, and others, felt that the Armistice was a mistake and that the Allies should have demanded unconditional surrender. He had conferred with Haig and Foch and he had cabled his views to Wilson. Although Wilson did not agree with him, he told him to "feel entirely free" to bring up any matters for consideration. Pershing misconstrued this and shocked all the political leaders when he presented the case for unconditional surrender to the Supreme War Council. Pershing, who had been America incarnate in Europe throughout the war, quickly learned that generals were fast becoming irrelevant and that now the politicians and diplomats would take center stage. He apologized to Wilson. But "We shouldn't have done it," he said of the Armistice. "If they had given us another ten days we would have rounded up the entire German army, captured it, humiliated it. . . . The German troops today are marching back into Germany announcing that they have never been defeated. . . . What I dread is that Germany doesn't know that she was licked. Had they given us another week we'd have *taught* them."

Pershing's point was bloody but valid. As Winfield Scott and Ulysses S. Grant knew, and Presidents Wilson and Bush did not, a political victory is not the same as a military victory and an army is not completely defeated until it has been forced to surrender—until it has been humiliated. The German army in 1918–19, as did the Iraqi army after the Gulf War, quickly regained its pride.

The Germans had signed their agreement to the terms Foch offered, but they had not admitted defeat and many Germans believed they had not been vanquished. Colonel General Karl von Einem, commander of the German Third Army, told his troops: "Firing has ceased. *Undefeated* [italics added] . . . you are terminating the war in enemy country." In Berlin the returning soldiers marched under triumphal arches wearing oak leaves on their helmets. The myth was soon current that the army had not been defeated but had been stabbed in the back by communists, liberals, socialists, politicians, profiteers, and Jews back home. This "stab-in-the-back" (*Dolchstoss*) legend was a myth Hitler was to exploit.

In the German navy, however, no doubt was left as to the war's victors. Scorning Wilson's plea for freedom of the seas, Britain demanded and received the complete humiliating surrender of the entire German fleet.

It has been estimated that in the five weeks of dithering about the terms of the Armistice at least a half million men were killed or wounded. American casualties in the war included 116,518 dead, 53,402 in battle, and 205,690 wounded. Casualties of the men in uniform of all nations engaged has been estimated to have exceeded 37,500,000, of whom more than 8,500,000 died.

Between 18 July and 11 November the Allies captured 385,000 prisoners and 6,615 guns. Of these the British captured 188,000 and 2,880 guns; the French took 139,000 prisoners and 474 guns; the Americans 44,000 prisoners and 1,423 guns; and the Belgians 14,000 prisoners and 474 guns. The American total would have been higher if the captures made by the two American divisions with Haig and the eight with the French had been computed.

Not until 6:00 A.M. on 11 November was Pershing informed of the cease fire that was to take effect at 11:00 A.M. that day. Although every effort was made to reach all the troops, a few did not get the word and in places the fighting continued after 11:00 A.M. Some fought to the last second. Captain Truman was one such. "I fired 164 rounds at him before he quit this morning," he told Bess. A battery of 155 mm guns nearby joined in. Many German guns, too, continued to fire that morning.

In the 26th (Yankee) Division the artillery was ordered to fire and infantry were ordered to advance until the final minute. War correspondent Frank P. Sibley was at division headquarters and reported: "The Yankee's line was concave and it was the desire of the commanding officer and the Corps to straighten out that concavity, therefore the worn out doughboys must make one final effort." Hundreds must have been killed or wounded in the final moments. It had been a bitter war.

Lieutenant Harry G. Rennagel of the 101st Infantry in the Yankee Division had been in the hospital, but returned to his unit, arriving at about 10:00. He and his men were "all talking, laughing and waiting for the gong to ring when orders came to go over the top. We thought it a joke—it was a grim one of Fate's, for we jumped off at 25 minutes to 11 and advanced but very slowly for we knew there were many machine gun nests ahead of us. At 10:55 a minenwerfer fell among my men and I was told one wanted to see me. I hurried over to where lay five of my best men. One fatally injured, hole near heart, two seriously injured and the other two badly hurt. We took care of the injured men and then I knelt beside the lad whose eyes had such a look of sorrow that my eyes filled with tears."

The last people to be killed on each side would appear to have been suicides.

Private Henry Gunther, in the 313rd Infantry, distraught because he had lost his sergeant's stripes, charged a German machine gun nest at one minute to 11:00. His buddies shouted to him to come back; the Germans waved for him to go back. He charged on and they shot him.

Perhaps the last German to die was Lieutenant Thoma of the 19th Uhlans advancing to inquire about billeting arrangements. At an 89th Division outpost men who had not received word of the Armistice fired, wounding him. Thoma must have snapped. He pulled out his luger and shot himself in the head.

General George C. Marshall and the officers who made up a headquarters mess in a private home in the village of Souilly were having a late breakfast on 11 November when a shell exploded about 10:30 just outside the room. Although the walls of the house were thick, they were all thrown from the table. Marshall found himself sitting on the back of his chair with his head against a wall. Except for a ruined breakfast, no damage was done. An American pilot, having made a final bomb run, was returning to base when a bomb that had failed to release over target did so over the officers' mess.

Tragedy came to Souilly later that day when a pilot, stunt flying over the village, crashed his plane and was killed.

Reactions to the Armistice varied. For most it seemed so sudden: "When the guns ceased all along the front line . . . [it] was so quiet it made me feel as if I had been suddenly deprived of my ability to hear," said one man.

"At eleven o'clock everything got so quiet that the silence was nearly unbearable," wrote A. R. Sunde of the 89th Division. "We were wet and cold, hungry and tired . . . we were allowed to build fires and could remove our shoes and stockings and dry them out and get warm. . . . It sure did seem strange. That night it was actually so quiet that I could not sleep until late in the morning, tired as I was, and I laid around the fire we had built until I finally dozed off for a few hours."

Lieutenant Broaddus, who had been spotting for the artillery of the 35th Division from a balloon, remembered how "people went so wild celebrating that they forgot to pull me down . . . and I sat there for two hours."

Although all squadrons had been ordered to stay on the ground, Eddie Rickenbacker "wanted to see the war end" and took off in his plane. "I was only up about a hundred feet over no-man's-land. I got out to see what I went out to see and went back home."

George S. Patton wrote in his diary: "Got rid of my bandage. Wrote a poem on peace."

In Moscow crowds cheered not for the Armistice but for the soldiers' and workers' revolutions taking place in Germany and Austria. Winston Churchill thought the time had come to destroy Bolshevism in Russia before it became too strong. But it was too late.

In Tokyo Japanese leaders made lists of the territory they hoped to gain by having joined the Allied side, notably the German islands in the Pacific: the Marianas, the Carolines, and the Marshalls.

Corporal Adolf Hitler was in a Pomeranian hospital recovering from being temporarily blinded by gas when an elderly pastor came by to tell the patients that the Kaiser had abdicated, the war was over, and Germany was now a republic. Hitler was devastated. "Again everything went black before my eyes; I tottered and groped my way back to the dormitory, threw myself on my bunk, and dug my burning head into my blanket." His misery was broken by a "supernatural vision." He could see again. Like Joan of Arc, he heard voices calling on him to save Germany: "That night I resolved that, if I recovered my sight, I would enter politics."

Throughout the belligerent countries there were somewhere between 6.5 and 8.5 million prisoners of war at the time of the Armistice. The Allies refused to repatriate German prisoners until at least the conclusion of the peace conference on June 1919. The Americans did not repatriate their prisoners until September 1919. The French were the last to release them for they wanted the prison labor. But all along the Allied lines on the Western Front, prisoners—Russians, Rumanians, Serbs, French, British, Italians, Americans et al.—released by the Germans tried to reach friendly lines. General George C. Marshall found that providing food and shelter and authorizing passes for these thousands presented new problems. The Italians, Marshall claimed, were particularly difficult. They talked a great deal; there were thousands of them; and they were exceptionally eager to go home.

Hearing rumors one day that released prisoners were molesting French peasants, Marshall drove out with his chauffeur to investigate. Near the ancient town of Stenay, the last town taken by Americans in the war, on the Meuse River twenty-six miles north northwest of Verdun, he encountered a mass of long-bearded, filthy Russians who, when he appeared, formed ranks and stood rigidly at attention. Thinking that in such a large group there would surely be at least one who spoke English, Marshall greeted them as he believed the Tsar had always addressed them. "Good morning my children!" Not a child moved. His chauffeur guffawed. With what dignity he could muster, Marshall pointed them toward the American lines and all marched off as if on parade. They were stopped at an outpost at the American lines by a lieutenant who, ordered to let no one pass, had no idea what he should do with 1,800 Russians. Marshall learned later that they had been captured at the Battle of the Masurian Lakes in the fall of 1914.

Not everyone greeted the war's end with joy. Captain Dwight D. Eisenhower, who had been forced to stay in the United States to organize the first Tank Corps Training camp at Gettysburg, Pennsylvania, achieved the rank of lieutenant colonel and in October was finally ordered to France, but to his intense disappointment, the war ended before he sailed and he was soon back to the rank of captain. Many of the troops who arrived in France immediately after the Armistice were disappointed that they were not even allowed to land; their ships were simply turned around and sent back. The peace was frustrating for Jerome Forbes and his friends in the 338th Field Artillery. After more than the usual training in the United States, the regiment had been dispatched to France in September 1918 and had completed specialized training at Camp de Souge on 9 November—two days before the Armistice.

Father Duffy knew that "throughout the world men were jubilant at the prospects of peace. But I could think of nothing except the fine lads who had come out with us to this war and who were not alive to enjoy the triumph. All day I had a lonely and an aching heart." Although nearly all were more than ready to return home, a few recognized that the war had provided the defining moments in their lives and that the comradeship formed of hardships borne together was about to end. Father Duffy had, in a sense, enjoyed the war: "When the orders finally came for our return to America I received them with a joy that was tinged with regret that the associations of the past two years were to be broken up. They had been years full of life and activity, and take them all in all, years of happiness. There never was a moment when I wanted to be any place other than where I was."

At war's end the American Air Service was just beginning to take shape and its pilots were developing their own elan. General H. H. "Hap" Arnold, speaking of Billy Mitchell, said, "For Billy the peace was an untimely interruption—as if the whistle had ended the game just as he was about to go over the goal line." Malcolm Cowley, who had served as an ambulance driver on the Chemin des Dames, wrote that the airmen had "lived more intensely than they would ever live again and felt in a vague fashion that something in them had died on the eleventh of November, 1918."

Lieutenant Bogart Rogers, an American pilot in the RFC who had shot down six enemy planes, felt something of this when on 11 November he wrote to his fiancée, Isabelle Young: "It's been a wonderful experience for the fellows who have come through with a whole skin. . . . Thank goodness I've seen a bit of the world and taken a chance. At least I'll have a clear conscience." With little expectation that being an ace would mean anything in the postwar world, he added: "After all I suppose what you did in the war won't buy any bacon for breakfast a year from now."

Many Allied sailors must have experienced feelings of relief at the Armistice, but Secretary Daniels described what may indeed have been the feelings of some: "For a year, every officer and man in the Grand Fleet had been waiting and hoping for a chance to get at the Germans. And, at last, when that fleet surrendered, without striking a blow, their disappointment was too deep for words."

Admiral Rodman describing the German surrender wrote: "Surely, no more complete victory was ever won, nor a more disgraceful and humiliating end could come to a powerful and much vaunted fleet than that which came to the German High Seas Fleet . . . the enemy ships were disarmed, ammunition landed, torpedo warheads sent ashore, breech-blocks and fire-control instruments removed, and every offensive utility rendered innocuous. Then, with reduced crews, under a German admiral in one long column, the heavy battleships leading, the Hun fleet sailed for a designated rendezvous . . . just outside the Firth of Forth in Scotland where the Grand Fleet lay at anchor."

The British Grand Fleet and the American squadron attached to it formed a double column six miles apart, the Americans in the middle of the northern line. A small British cruiser met the German ships and signalled "Follow me." It led the once proud fleet "between the columns where our battle flags were mast-headed, turrets trained toward the enemy, crews at battle stations, and all in readiness for any treachery. . . . Then came a signal from the commander-in-chief to the surrendered fleet: 'At sundown lower your colors and do not hoist them again without permission.' Surely no greater humiliation could have befallen them after their frequent and taunting boasts and threats." British Admiral Beatty later wrote: "It was a pitiful day to see those great ships coming in like sheep being herded by dogs to their fold, without an effort on anybody's part. . . ."

After inspection by British and American officers the ships were sent in groups under guard to Scapa Flow in the Orkney Islands. "They were," wrote Rodman, "corralled like wild and cruel beasts that had been hobbled, guarded by a single division of battleships." Seventy-four great gray warships of the German Imperial High Seas Fleet lay at anchor, still with their German crews, for seven months, until in June 1919 they were deliberately scuttled by their officers and men, sending 400,000 tons of steel to the bottom.

News of the cessation of hostilities was anticipated in the United States. On 7 November a report of an armistice sent New Yorkers into the streets to celebrate. Enrico Caruso stepped out on the balcony of his ninth floor suite in the Hotel Knickerbocker and before the largest audience of his life the world's greatest tenor sang "The Star Spangled Banner." Below him as he finished there was pandemonium.

Everyday duties were abandoned in the excitement, but not everyone reacted the same way. In New York a Fifth Avenue barber left a customer half shaved as he told his assistant: "Finish him and then close the shop. Me? I'm going home to cry with my wife."

News of the real Armistice reached Washington at 2:45 A.M. on 11 November. There were again jubilant celebrations in the streets. In New York the lights on the Statue of Liberty, off for the duration, were turned on again, and by dawn Fifth Avenue was chock-a-block with merrymakers. In San Francisco a huge bonfire blazed on Telegraph Hill.

President Wilson was asleep when the news arrived. No one awakened him, and he was not informed until breakfast. He then addressed his "Fellow Countrymen," telling them that, "Everything for which America fought has been accomplished. It will now be our fortunate duty to assist by example . . . in the establishment of just democracy throughout the world." He declared the day a national holiday, but as few workers had radios, many trudged to work as usual.

In Paris the church bells rang out and Prescott French from Arlington, Massachusetts, remembered the "singing, swinging, swaying, jolly jubilant mass of happy humanity" on the Champs Elysées. At the Place de Opéra lights blazed and Opéra stars sang "Madelon." A bugler blew the *Berloque*, the all-clear signal after an air raid, and all Paris laughed. A middle-aged woman kissed an astonished American soldier and told him: "You are the very image of my own son killed in this awful war."

In an address to his troops, Pershing wrote that it was "time to forget the hardships and the difficulties, except to record them with the glorious history of our achievements. . . . Your deeds will live forever on the most glorious pages of America's history."

President Lincoln had not waited for the end of the Civil War to visit the Gettysburg battlefield; President Wilson, attending the peace conference, made a grand tour of European capitals but, although Château-Thierry was only an hour away from Paris, the commander-in-chief did not find time to visit it or any of the fields where his soldiers had fought and bled, nor did he see any of the military cemeteries. His neglect was noted. Frederick Palmer, speaking on 14 March 1919 to the New York City Club, claimed that by this omission Wilson had lost the place he had "held in the hearts of the soldiers." Had he visited the battlefields, said Palmer, he could have spoken with greater eloquence, "he could have stirred the men of Europe and every mother and wife of the millions who have fallen." But he did not. His refusal, Wilson said, was based on his desire to remain dispassionate during the peace talks.

In the United States the Armistice found hundreds of trains streaming toward ships waiting in Atlantic ports while factories produced now unwanted war goods. The trains were sidetracked, the factory work halted, and soon a Liquidation Commission was getting rid of AEF assets. Surgical and medical supplies were turned over to the Red Cross and most of the assets in France were "sold" to the French government, which refused to pay for much of it.

More men died in this war than in all the wars of over one hundred years previously. Of the 2,084,000 American troops that reached France, 1,390,000 saw some action. Of every hundred American soldiers, sailors, and marines who took part in this bloodiest of wars, two died of wounds or disease. The best estimates of the number of American soldiers who died in the war is 122,500 men, of whom 48,909 were killed in battle. In this as in all previous wars, more men died of disease than from any other cause. The wounded numbered 237,135.

Included in the casualty figures are the killed and wounded who "deserted to the front": Men in the rear areas who went AWOL (Absent Without Leave) from their units and made their way to the battleline, where at least 3,170 were killed and 6,471 were wounded. The total number of men so eager to see combat is unknown, but the practice was so widespread that General Pershing made special arrangements for those men who had done good service in the rear to have the opportunity to go on the firing line.

Of the forty-two divisions sent to France, twenty-nine took part in active combat service. The battle record of the American army is the history of these combat divisions. Seven were originally regular army divisions, eleven were National Guard, and eleven were National Army, but conscripts filled the ranks of all. By war's end Americans held 101 miles or twenty-three percent of the battle line.

American losses were, of course, slight by comparison with the European combatants. Romania, with a much smaller population than the United States, lost 340,000, and the Italians 460,000. Britain and the soldiers from its empire lost 997,000 and France, which had mobilized the highest percentage of its population and suffered the greatest wartime death rate, lost 1,390,000 men. Allied deaths among the Portuguese, Japanese, and Serbians numbered about 14,650.

Among the Central Powers the Germans suffered 1,850,000 men killed, the Austro-Hungarian Empire 1,200,000, Turkey 350,000, and Bulgaria 95,000. Much unnecessary suffering was caused by the continuation of the Allied economic blockade after the Armistice, which was not raised until the signing of the Versailles Treaty on 28 June 1919. The medical effects of malnutrition being cumulative, most deaths in Germany in the eight months following the Armistice were among the very old and the very young, those most vulnerable to the effects of starvation.

United States unpreparedness and its subsequent loss of lives made no impression upon postwar politicians. Twenty years later, on the eve of World War II, the American army only slightly exceeded in size that of Portugal, was smaller than that of Bulgaria, and ranked 13th among the armies of the world.

24

☆

THE ARMY OF OCCUPATION AND
THE WAIT FOR SHIPPING SPACE

THE THIRD ARMY, with a strength of about 260,000, was activated on 7 November 1918 at Ligny-en-Pavois under Major General Joseph T. Dickman. Its mission was to serve as the American army of occupation after the war. On 2 May 1919 Dickman was replaced by Lieutenant General Hunter Liggett. On 2 July, after the signing of the Treaty of Versailles, the Third Army ceased to exist and the American troops in Germany were redesignated the American Forces in Germany (AFG) until withdrawn in January 1923. The commander was Major General Henry Tureman Allen, who had brought the 90th Division to France and led it through the Meuse-Argonne offensive.

On the morning of 17 November 1918, in unison with French, British, and Belgian forces, the Third Army began its march eastward, following the retreating German armies as closely as possible without coming into contact with them. Even the irreverent Private MacArthur found the Germans impressive: "Theoretically they were beaten to death, yet the only trace of their home run was an occasional neat pile of refuse burning beside the road. Remarkable because every American division we had followed was knee deep in rifles, picture books, Victrola records, water-color outfits, and blankets. It was not pleasant to think that the groggy Germans were still as disciplined as the order of their retreat indicated."

Marines, too, noted their discipline and one said, "perfect order and all that—not like a defeated outfit at all. . . . He wasn't licked enough, an' now he's goin' home like a peacock wit' seven tails!" sentiments the private shared with his commander-in-chief.

Following the orders of Marshal Foch, the American and Allied armies of occupation marched from France through Belgium, where they were greeted as heroes, kissed and feted, then on through beautiful Luxembourg, where Private MacArthur found the inhabitants "a sulky and suspicious bunch of bums." He complained of the high cost of food and proclaimed the City of Luxembourg "a night club without any of a night club's entertaining features." However, Captain Harry Townsend found that "the reception of the Americans had been almost too good to be true." People "threw open their houses to the fellows" and "treated them royally."

On 1 December the Americans entered the Trier region, where they were to occupy the Moselle area from the eastern end of Luxembourg to the western bank of the Rhine and the northerly half of the bridgehead of thirty kilometers radius east of the Rhine, centered on Koblenz. The area contained upward of a million civilians and an unknown number of disarmed soldiers.

Pershing established his headquarters at Treves [Trier] on the Moselle near the Luxembourg border, and there on 28 November he issued orders instructing his soldiers how to behave in Germany: "During our occupation the civil population is under the special safeguard of the faith and honor of the American army.

"It is, therefore, the intention of this order to appeal directly to your pride in your position as representatives of a powerful but righteous nation, with the firm conviction that you will so conduct yourselves in your relations with the inhabitants of Germany as will cause them to respect you and the country you have the honor to represent. While you appear among them as a conquering army, you will exhibit no ill will among the inhabitants . . ."

"Twenty-Eight Rules and Regulations" were drawn up for the civilian population. Identification was required and each head of a household was directed to post inside his front door the name, sex, and age of every resident. Passes were required for travel, and arms and ammunition were to be turned in.

Rule No. 6 caused the most trouble. It prohibited the sale of all liquor except light wine and beer to American soldiers and established drinking hours that ended at 7:00 P.M. It was widely disobeyed by everyone.

On the approach of the Americans many German families had sent their daughters to safety, but most were brought back when it became evident that the doughboys were not as dangerous as Berlin propaganda had portrayed them. Although at first forbidden to fraternize with the Germans, many could not resist giving the girls the "double O" (once over), and, as Americans in many places were billeted in private homes, fraternization occurred naturally and harmlessly. Nevertheless, a program was launched to persuade them that the Germans had "placed themselves outside the pale of civilized nations. They are not fit associates for the honest American soldier." But it was not in the nature of American soldiers to be aloof. As Private Ettinger said, "it was difficult to be formal and correct conquerors when confronted by smiling children and frauleins."

Relations between occupiers and the occupied were soon cordial. Many Americans found the Germans friendlier than the British or French. Clean and tidy German farms contrasted favorably with the manure-filled French farmyards; German wine was unpolluted with dead flies; German merchants were less venal; German girls seemed cleaner, prettier, and more friendly. Sergeant Alexander Woollcott, who wrote for the *Stars and Stripes*, claimed that the French never learned to use a toothbrush. A sergeant in a signals battalion wrote home: "The German people are treating us fine—so much better than some others we know—they are so clean and neat that it is very much like being at home."

The doughboys soon discovered the German passion for cleanliness could be turned to their advantage. The newly opened YMCA canteens had a run on soap and chocolate, for the doughboys had discovered their trading value. Soap had been in short supply for months and, as Private MacArthur discovered, to obtain a bar some young women "would do almost anything. Some would do anything."

German merchants appreciated the flood of new customers. A flourishing trade was soon established in German army helmets, badges, Luger pistols, medals, and insignia to satisfy the American mania for souvenirs. (It was said that the Germans fought for territory, the British for the sea, the French for patriotism, and the Americans for souvenirs.) Captain Harry Townsend, one of the first Americans to enter Metz, was surprised by what he found: "All the shops seemed full of supplies . . . one would never guess there was a pinch in Germany from the look of the shops and people in Metz. Prices tho [sic] are terrific in most all cases. We found iron crosses today at a fairly low figure, tho they will go up at once now that the Americans are coming!"

According to the *Stars and Stripes* correspondent in Koblenz, the living was easy for the troops, "stretching out at night in such billets as they never dreamed of in the days before the armistice. The officers and men are dwelling, all of them, in such comfort as they had not known since last their own front gates swung behind them. They are living, some of them, in such elegance as they had never known before in all their days, nor will again." Perhaps so, but the war was over and they wanted to go home. The army could not move fast enough. The statement erroneously attributed to Pershing—"Lafayette, nous somme ici"— was parodied to "Lafayette, we're *still* here."

A serious morale problem arose among men who did not understand why they were still in uniform at war's end. Soldiers were known to boo and hiss in movie theaters when Pershing's picture was shown. Donald Adair of the 42nd Division wrote to his family from Remagen on 5 March: "We expect our beloved (?) commander-in-chief, Gen. Pershing to come here soon to review the division. I hope he will make it snappy and shoot us along to the docks soon after. Most of the A.E.F. is hoping that Pershing will run for President on the Republican ticket next term so that we can show what good Democrats we are."

When drill and training courses were prescribed to keep the men busy, there were loud complaints on all sides. Although the orders applied to all troops, black and white, and were resented by all, black troops insisted that they were being discriminated against. The allegation persisted. In 1974 authors Arthur E. Barbeau and Florette Henri wrote: "The reason for the training courses was not that they were useful, but simply to keep the black troops busy and out of trouble until they could be put aboard ship for home." Expressing the sentiments of many, one man said, "Everybody had a bellyful of the damn army." Raymond Fosdick reported in January that the morale situation was "little short of desperate."

Morale fell to such an extent that some at Pershing's headquarters feared soldiers would "go Bolshevist." With the end of hostilities there was a natural relaxation of responsibility and the number of men going AWOL increased. Fifty-one additional companies of military police failed to stem the tide. A "morale conference" was called in Paris and from this sprang the American Legion. Pershing substituted sports for the hated drill, and on 24 January 1919 Liberty trucks pulled away from the YMCA Paris warehouses loaded with thirty-four tons of athletic equipment, including 10,000 baseballs, 2,000 footballs, 1,800 soccer balls, nearly 1,500 basketballs, and 600 sets of boxing gloves. Insel Oberwert, an island above Koblenz where the Germans once held Olympic tryouts, became an American army playground. And in the summer of 1919 Inter-Allied Games were held in Paris.

Bands substituted popular tunes for martial airs. "When Cooties have Cooties" and "Oh How I Hate to Get Up in the Morning" were in popular demand. Dances were held; men dancing with each other or with YMCA women, some of whom also gave dance lessons. A liberal leave policy was established. At Koblenz the YMCA took over an old multistoried grain warehouse capable of bedding 1,000.

At the army's request, the YMCA established an education program that allowed officers and enlisted men to study in French and British universities and in January 1919 the American Expeditionary Forces University, open to any American soldier in Germany who had graduated from high school, was established at Beaune with agricultural courses taught at Allery. Books and materials were furnished gratis and students continued to draw their regular pay. Colonel Ira Reeves, former president of Norwich University in Vermont, headed the program.

In spite of good works, the YMCA remained unpopular. Selling 5¢ candy bars for 20¢ enraged many. The mayor of Neuenahr, a Prussian town northwest of Koblenz, complained to the military authorities that the local YMCA people had confiscated pianos from seven private residences. When the army received complaints from several YMCA women that their superior, Mr. O. K. LaRoque, sexually harassed them, he was ordered out but refused to leave and went unpunished.

Leslie Langille, on leave in Annecy, found a swarm of YMCA workers, male and female, there. "Those babies know how to pick the spots all right. . . . I would much prefer to write about their merits, had they any."

In Germany there were continued attempts to maintain a morally pure army, and reduce the incidence of venereal disease. The 42nd Division, which had a high venereal disease rate, refused to grant passes for Cologne or Bonn, cities believed to have the most prostitutes. As contracting the disease was a court-martialable offense, some men sought out German doctors, but many refused to treat them, for they were threatened with loss of their licenses if they treated American soldiers.

When shipping orders finally arrived in April for the 42nd Division there were unit celebrations. The 149th Field Artillery rented the local opera house and staged a huge party, featuring what they called a "Rainbow Cocktail," a concoction of white and red wine, schnapps, lemon extract, and pepper. Drunken soldiers spilled into the street, released some prisoners from the guardhouse, descended upon Peter Schlemmer's bar, and wrecked it.

The 165th "Fighting Irish" got their shipping orders in Brest and they

celebrated their last night on French soil with a brawl that did not end
even after the arrival of the military police. The next morning, as Colonel
Donovan prepared to march his men to the dock, a military police captain and his men arrived to arrest the culprits. Donovan wasted no time
in argument. He threw out a platoon with bayonets fixed and escorted
every man to the ships.

Those selected to go home waited impatiently for shipping space. Most
doughboys had been brought to Europe in British ships, but Britain now
needed its transports to repatriate Canadians, Australians, South Africans,
and other empire troops. Most American troops had to be returned in
American ships and even warships were used to transport them.

The American soldiers were eager to leave Europe and the French
were glad to see their backs. The spirit that had animated the Parisians on
4 July 1917 was long gone.

Marshal Foch suggested that the idle American soldiers be used to
clear debris from battlefields, fill in trenches, and rebuild villages, but
Secretary Baker sent a resounding answer: "No soldiers of the United
States can be retained in France for any other reason than strictly military
purposes. No part of their duty to their country would justify . . . them to
perform such labor for such purposes."

Ambassador William Graves Sharp in Paris remarked that, "Many of
the French seem to have forgotten that but for us the Kaiser and his
nobles would be running France." Pershing complained that the French
"had never once said a word of thanks or complimented the American
troops on what they had done." According to Haig, Pershing told him that
Americans would never forget "the bad treatment which they had
received from the French and that it was difficult to exaggerate the feeling of dislike for the French which existed in the American army."

On 20 May 1919 Congress declared the end of the war. By 6 June 1919
all of the original National Guard and National Army divisions had left
Germany, leaving only regulars there. Separate peace treaties were ratified
with Germany and Austria-Hungary on 18 October 1919. The American
military presence in Europe was steadily reduced until by 1920 only 15,000
were left. By the end of 1922 there were only 1,200 American troops in
Germany. The last thousand troops left for home on 24 January 1923.

The army's 332nd Infantry regiment remained with the Italian forces for
four months after the war to occupy Austria. The war had ended in Western
Europe, but American troops were fighting Bolsheviks in Northern Russia
and an American Expeditionary Force was sent to Siberia.

25

☆

INTERVENTION IN
NORTHERN RUSSIA AND SIBERIA

ON 11 NOVEMBER 1918 the guns fell quiet on the Western Front, but in Northern Russia American troops serving under a British general were fighting Russian Bolsheviks. On 28 June 1919 the Treaty of Versailles was signed, but the fighting continued in North Russia and Siberia. Winston Churchill, the new British secretary of state for war, pronounced the Russian situation to be "part of the great quarrel with Germany," but this was difficult for American citizens to see. It was equally difficult for the fighting men to understand why they were there.

In his memoirs Pershing wrote: "There was a tendency on the part of the Allied Governments to send expeditions here and there in pursuit of political aims. They were prone to lose sight of the fundamental fact that the real objective was the German army. Once that was beaten, the political and naval power of Germany would collapse." For once Pershing, Bliss, and March were in complete agreement. In his memoirs March wrote: "President Wilson only interfered twice with the military operations of the War Department while I was Chief of Staff, and both times he was wrong. The first of these was the Siberian Expedition; the other sending American troops to Murmansk and Archangel, in northern Russia." In a letter to March, Bliss wrote: "As I have said before, if our Allies have any axes to grind in Russia, let them go and do it. I think the war has got to be ended on this Western Front. . . ." But the Russian revolution was a distraction seemingly irresistible to American, European, and Japanese political leaders, who found military, idealistic, or imperialistic reasons for intervention.

President Wilson, having decisively declared that "military interven-tion would add to the present sad confusion in Russia rather than cure it," then ordered American military intervention. He was persuaded by the Allies, and against the advice of his generals, to send men to Northern Russia and to join with Japan in each sending 7,000 men to Siberia. He based his decision to intervene upon spurious information, a misconcep-tion of the geographical and political realities, and on utopian dreams that were irrelevant to the situation.

LENIN WAS IN Switzerland when he learned of the Russian Revolution in February 1917. The Germans, correctly reasoning that his presence in Russia would add to the chaotic state of the country and speed the dissolu-tion of its army, facilitated his movements and he arrived by train at Finland Station in Russia in April. His Bolsheviki overthrew the moderate government of Aleksandr Kerenski in November and he became premier on 7 January 1918.

The first reaction in the United States to the overthrow of the Tsar had been favorable: The "freedom-loving Russian people" would join the world's great democracies. President Wilson, declaring that the United States would be "privileged to assist the people of Russia to attain their utmost hope of liberty and ordered peace," immediately authorized recognition of the provisional government. But when the Bolsheviks came to power and their goals became better known, this attitude quickly changed. To accomplish his aims Lenin needed to end the war with Germany and Austria-Hungary, and on 3 March he signed the humiliat-ing Treaty of Brest-Litovsk, a surrender document that not only gave enor-mous chunks of Russian territory to Germany, allowing the Germans to exploit the oil, food, and minerals of the Ukraine, but released some forty German divisions to fight on the Western Front. The Bolsheviks also revealed the secret tsarist treaties with the Allies, and cancelled all Russian debts. They no longer seemed friendly.

The treaty set free hundreds of thousands of German, Austrian, Hungarian, and Turkish soldiers whom the Russians had taken prisoner. In the chaos of the revolution their release was not an orderly process, and one of the most bizarre episodes of the Great War involved the anabasis of the Czech Legion, the most remarkable odyssey in twentieth-century military history.

The Czechs and Slovaks of Moravia and Slovakia had never relished being a part of the Austro-Hungarian Empire, feeling themselves more akin to the Russians. During the war, many had deserted. In the last days of the Tsar the deserters, Czech prisoners of war, and Czechs and Slovaks who had long lived in Russia, formed a legion of 50,000–70,000 men. When the Tsar was overthrown, Tomáš Garrigue Masaryk, a Czech philosopher and politician who had formed a central revolutionary committee in Paris, claimed the legion as the army of a future Czechoslovakia and offered it to France to fight on the Western Front if France would supply it and pay its soldiers. France agreed to the proposal, but the Czechs were in the middle of Russia, cut off from France by the German army.

The British hoped that they could fight their way to Northern Russia where a small Allied force, including an American regiment under a British general was fighting the Bolsheviks, but when the Bolsheviks made this impractical, the Czechs decided to make the 6,000-mile journey across Siberia to Vladivostok where they could be put on ships and sent to Europe.

On 18 August 1918, 9,014 American troops, including the 27th and 31st Infantries, then in the Philippines, and selected men from the 8th Division in California, were placed under Major General William S. Graves and dispatched to Vladivostok to join Japanese and other Allied troops—including eventually Canadian, Chinese, French, and Italian troops.

Siberia was in a chaotic state. On 23 July a Siberian Republic had been proclaimed, but an uncounted number of political entities laid claim to the right to rule. The country teemed with Red (Bolshevik) and White (anti-Bolshevik) Russian armies, bands of bandits, warlords, Cossacks of doubtful loyalty, freed German and Austrian prisoners of war, and foreign armies. It is difficult to imagine how anyone could believe that the puny American force could have any effect upon the events unfolding in Siberia, an immense region of nearly five million square miles—more than half again the size of the continental United States. The Japanese, with territorial acquisition in mind, sent not the 7,000 specified troops, but 72,000.

Major General Graves had been given only a ten-minute briefing on his mission at a secret meeting on 4 August with Secretary Baker in the Kansas City railroad station. Baker had pressed into his hands an *aide-mémoire* of President Wilson's and told him, "This contains the policy of the United States in Russia which you are to follow. Watch your step; you will be walking on eggs filled with dynamite. God bless you and goodbye!"

Graves, a West Point graduate of the class of 1889, had served most of his career on regimental duty, much of it in the Philippines. General March, who later wrote that his appointment was "peculiarly fortunate," described him as "particularly loyal, level-headed and firm" and added that "all of these qualities were strained to the limit during the period of the American occupation of Siberia."

Graves closely adhered to Wilson's *aide-mémoire*. The only reason for intervention, said Wilson, was "to aid the Czecho-Slovakians to consolidate their forces and to steady any efforts at self-government or self-defence." Graves soon learned that the Czechs had been so successful that they needed no help. His principal antagonists, he found, were the commanders of the British and Japanese military contingents and his own country's State Department, whose representatives pursued agendas at variance from those of the War Department. Following his instructions, he resisted pressures to intervene in the Russian civil war on the side of the White Russians under Admiral Alexsandr Vasilevich Kolchak and Grigori Semënov, the latter a Cossack hetman (leader) and general whom Kolchak had placed in charge of Transbaikalia. General Graves considered him to be a "murderer, robber and a most dissolute scoundrel." For his steadfastness he was attacked by newspapers, diplomats, and even the military. The British and French protested his position directly to President Wilson and even to General Pershing, who had nothing to do with expeditions to Russia.

American soldiers were not impressed by communism. Earl Thompson, an army medic wrote: "I wish some of the rank socialists at home could be here and live under conditions which now exist where socialism and Bolshevikism have been in power. I believe they would soon get some of their wild ideas out of their heads. . . . I do not think people in the states realize what a serious thing it would be if the Bolshevists gain power here in Russia."

When the war ended in Europe the Czech legionnaires expected to go home, but Masaryk, now the elected president of an independent Czechoslovakia, ordered them to stay in Siberia. Only about a thousand sick and wounded were evacuated to the United States.

The Legion, taking orders from Kolchak, was sent west to the Volga. They captured Kazan but lost it on 5 September 1918 and suffered a defeat at the hands of four Russian armies under the personal command of Leon Trotsky, the Bolshevik minister of war. The Czechs survived the fierce Siberian winter, but by August 1919 the Red Army had pushed them back to Omsk.

Conditions in Siberia rapidly worsened. White Russian soldiers, protected by Japanese troops, were, Graves later wrote, "roaming the country like wild animals, killing and robbing the people, and these murders could have been stopped any day Japan wished. If questions were asked about these brutal murders, the reply was that the murdered were Bolsheviks, and this explanation, apparently, satisfied the world."

Creel's Committee on Public Information sent Arthur Bullard, a journalist and author, to Siberia to distribute American propaganda, but the chaos there and the vagueness of American objectives led Bullard to question what he was supposed to be doing in Siberia: "We are rather in the position of advertising something and not knowing what it is. Buy it! Buy it! We don't know what, but we are sure it will do you good."

In January 1920 the Czechs, most of them west of Lake Baikal, again fought their way eastward and in the first six months of 1920 defeated a large force of Cossacks. By an Inter-Allied Railway agreement the Americans guarded the line from Lake Baikal to Vladivostok until the arrival and evacuation of the last Czech. Thus the United States became a participant in the Russian Civil War, for this favored the anti-Bolshevik forces. Allied forces supported the Siberian government of Admiral Kolchak until in December 1919 his government collapsed; the Czechs lost faith in him and turned him over to the Bolsheviks, who shot him.

When the Czechs again reached Vladivostok five American transports, joined by ships chartered by American Czechs and Slovaks and the Red Cross, carried the survivors to Europe where they formed the nucleus of the Czechoslovakian army. In April 1920 the last Americans withdrew as a Japanese band on the quay played "Hard Times, Come Again No More." The last Japanese could not be pried out until 1925.

American casualties in Siberia numbered thirty-five killed or mortally wounded, mostly by bandits, and 135 who died of diseases and other causes. Fifty-two others were wounded but survived and, curiously, fifty deserted, their fate unknown.

The American intervention in Siberia was futile as a military exercise, but its political consequences were many. It affected the dismemberment of the Austro-Hungarian empire, the founding of the Czechoslovakian state, and the first feeble efforts to curb Japanese imperialism.

ON 2 AUGUST 1918 when Allied warships steamed into the harbor at Archangel (Arkhangelsk)—a town of about 38,000 in normal times, but swollen now by refugees to about 50,000, sprawled along the Dvina River near its White Sea mouth—they were greeted by an enthusiastic crowd. Some 1,200 men were landed, including a battalion of the French

Foreign Legion, a detachment of one hundred British Royal Marines, and about an equal number of United States sailors and marines from the USS *Olympia*, Captain Bion Boyd Bierer. The force was commanded by Major General Frederick Cuthbert Poole, a forty-nine-year-old British artillery officer, who was ignorant of or ignored the American noncombatant role to protect the mountain of military supplies that had been ordered from the United States and the Allies by the tsarist government that now, it was feared, would fall into the hands of the Germans. The Reds had been driven out of the city, although they remained close by, and a White government had been formed under Socialist N. V. Chaikovsky.

General Poole established a defensive perimeter around the town. American Ensign Donald M. Hicks commandeered a wood-burning locomotive and some flatcars and with a group of seamen and marines pursued the Reds until they were stopped by a blown bridge. In a brief firefight two men were killed and three wounded, including Ensign Hicks who was wounded (in the leg), but the party returned with fifty-four prisoners: young Bolsheviki, hungry, dirty, and frightened.

President Wilson was prevailed upon by the Allies to add a regiment to the Archangel force and the 339th Infantry, 4,487 strong, with a battalion of engineers, a field hospital and an ambulance company for a total of 5,710 men—all of whom were in England en route to France—were diverted to Northern Russia. The little expeditionary force was commanded by Colonel George Evans Stewart, who was selected because he had once served in Alaska. On their way from England to Russia, packed into three British transports, only one lifeboat drill was held for, as one of the captains explained, the water was so cold that no one could live in it for more than five minutes anyway. "Wasn't that dandy" said one soldier.

On 4 September 1918 Colonel Stewart's expeditionary force landed in Archangel and the 339th infantry, mostly conscripts from Wisconsin and Michigan, were astonished to find themselves in Russia instead of France. Most had been conscripted in June and had received only about a month of training, during which they had fired twenty-five rounds on a rifle range; the rest of their service had been in transit.

Influenza had broken out on two of the troopships and 378 Americans were infected. Because the British said there was no room in their military hospital, the American and Russian Red Cross set up a makeshift arrangement for the sick in a barracks where, a medic later recalled: "They lay on stretchers without mattresses or pillows, lying in their O.D. uniforms, with only a simple blanket for covering. The place was a bed-

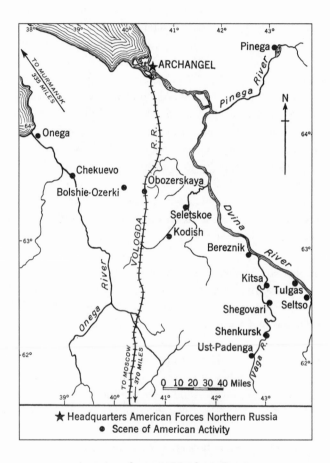

American forces in Northern Russia
September 4, 1918–August 5, 1919

CREDIT: *American Armies and Battlefields in Europe*

lam of sinister sounds of rasping, stertorous breathing, coughings, hack-
ings, moans and incoherent cries." There was no ventilation. The sewer
system consisted of ditches under the sidewalks whose contents emptied
into often-overflowing cesspools. Major Jonas Longley noted that
"human excreta was conspicuous and abundant both inside and outside
buildings." Seventy-two American soldiers died.

The Americans were not impressed with Archangel. Private W. C.
Butts wrote to his parents in Milwaukee: "It's the filthiest place I've ever
been in. The cooties keep us dancing every minute." Venereal disease was
rife and was soon a major problem. Although men were given prophylaxis
kits and warned to avoid the Café de Paris—and thus directed to it—by
the end of March 1919 the hospital had taken in fifty-four cases of
syphilis and 129 cases of gonorrhea, a toll that decreased only in February
after Colonel Stewart began to court-martial those who contracted a
venereal disease.

Stewart, who had been sent off with only vague instructions was at a loss
to understand exactly why he was in Russia and what he was supposed to
do there. He had been told to report to General Poole and although
British and American aims and interests did not coincide, he assumed, as
did Poole, that the Americans would serve under his command.

An attempt was made to establish a rail link at Vyatka, about 600 miles
from Archangel to offer an escape route for the embattled Czech Legion
and the United States was called on to supply railroad men. Volunteers
were sent to England to be outfitted for Arctic conditions, then dispatched to Russia. The American railroaders were appalled when they
arrived to find "obsolete rolling stock, rickety, tumbled down cars and
wood-burning locomotives." One railroad executive, John F. Stevens,
described the system as "strings of match boxes coupled with hairpins and
driven by samovars." Nevertheless construction began.

It met with considerable resistance from the Bolsheviks. In attempts to
drive them back men were sent forward ill-equipped for operations on the
tundra. One private wrote in his diary: "Spent the worst night ever, no
blankets, no fires, and soaking wet, could not even sit down. I have not
had any sleep since Saturday night. Nothing happened, however, but rain
and mosquitoes. I am just covered with bites."

In another operation, Poole packed four companies of infantry onto
coal barges pulled by wood-burning tugs on the Dvina to attack Beresnik,
a Bolshevik stronghold 140 miles upstream. Three soldiers died or were
killed en route. There were no beds and, as one soldier said, "The men

died on their blankets on the bare floor." The corpses were put in improvised coffins and Private Edwin Arkins wrote: "Blood from underneath coffins trickles across floor of barge while we eat our hard tack and black tea. Our faces and uniforms are black with moist coal dust."

Beresnik was occupied without opposition and in a few days a company was sent on foot to reconnoiter the banks of the Dvina. The inexperience of the soldiers was painfully evident. Private Arkins noted: "A little excitement when a scouting party mistakes runaway horse for an enemy attack. Several shots fired. No one hurt." A few days later he was on a patrol and recorded the result: "All we bring back is dead chicken after firing fusillade in error."

On 19 January 1919 Bolsheviks under General Alexandr Samoilo launched an attack on the Americans and Canadians at Shenkursk, their most advanced outpost, within 300 miles of the Arctic Circle. In spite of what was called "a gallant resistance," they were driven back nearly two and one-half miles to Spaskoe, suffering about 150 casualties. In one American platoon thirty-two out of forty-five men fell. "It's a real war now," wrote Sergeant John Crissman in his diary. In their retreat they abandoned large stocks of ammunition, clothing, equipment and two 18-pounder guns. One American soldier later told his mother, "We lost everything but the clothes on our back. It was a narrow escape. . . . It was just a big miracle."

Brigadier General William Edmund Ironside (chief of the Imperial General Staff in 1939–40) replaced Poole, but he seemed no more able to cope with the situation in Northern Russia than had Poole. After a month in Russia he reported two major difficulties: "The poor quality of the commanders" and the "poor quality of the troops." A detachment of the Royal Scots panicked and fled when attacked; the French were "demoralized" and refused orders to advance, their commander was, said Ironside, "weak and useless." But by far the worst were the American troops: "I have seen many American Regiments in France . . . but I have never seen anything quite so bad as this Regiment which consists of a very large proportion of Foreigners—Poles, Russians and Jews." Many came from Hamtramck, a city with many Polish emigrants completely surrounded by the city of Detroit, and could speak little English. "The Regiment had received absolutely no training and the officers were, one and all, of the lowest value imaginable. . . . There have been numerous cases amongst the American officers from living with women to selling the men's rations and embezzlement of funds. There have been cases of cowardice also." His only praise was for the battalion of engineers.

English soldiers developed a parody of "Over There" that included "The Yanks are running over there . . . everywhere" ending with "they didn't do a damn thing about it over there." The Americans in turn developed anglophobia. One soldier sent home a long letter of complaint: "We are under British control. Mind you the English own us; they can do with us as they please. Good God you can't believe how those English officers are hated around here . . . the God Damned fools are of more harm than good. They can't fight. . . . It's hell I'm telling you." Another declared that the British had "pulled the wool" over President Wilson's eyes and that the Americans are being used as "mere toys in the hands of Englishmen."

In spite of severe censorship, such letters got through and a number were placed in the *Congressional Record* by senators from Michigan and Wisconsin. Colonel Stewart was ordered by the War Department to tighten censorship of letters that were "most unsoldierly in tone and anti-British in sentiment."

In April 1919 Brigadier General Wilds P. Richardson arrived to take command of all American troops in Northern Russia, replacing Stewart, whom one soldier called "our very weak, half-assed commander."

A spirit of revolution seemed to permeate Russian life, affecting even some Allied and American troops. On 22 February troops in a Yorkshire battalion refused an order to go into front-line positions near Kodish; two of its sergeants were sentenced to be shot. A company of the French 21st Colonial Battalion refused to leave Archangel. A Polish unit led by its priest also refused to obey orders. Strikes flared among the Russian workers, who sabotaged and pilfered. On 1 March when the French infantry battalion, ordered to relieve the Americans at the front, "absolutely refused to go up," Ironside disarmed and imprisoned 113 of its soldiers. On 23 April 300 Russian volunteers in the Slavo-British Legion at Tulgas murdered their officers, five British and four Russian, sliced them open and smeared their intestines over their faces. The ringleaders were not identified, but Ironside executed eleven who attempted to desert.

On 30 March 1919, shortly before the arrival of General Richardson, there was a short "mutiny" among the troops in the 339th Infantry. Company I, which had been given a brief rest in Archangel, was ordered back to the front, but before they had finished loading their sleds and supplies on a train they sat down and declared they would not go. When they refused to obey the direct orders of their company officers, Colonel Stewart was sent for. He talked to the men long and earnestly, impressing upon them the seriousness of their action and reminding them of their duty to their country and of the shame of their friends and relations at home. He ended by saying that if any man intended to disobey orders he should step forward. None moved. The men resumed loading the train.

Although called a mutiny, the incident seems unworthy of all that word implies. As one soldier explained, "We kicked like hell, but we didn't mutiny." Major J. Brooks Nichols of Detroit said, "I have heard more 'bunk' about this mutiny than could be written in a dozen books."

No one seemed able to tell the troops why they were fighting Russians in Russia and many felt they had been forgotten and abandoned. Dr. Arthur Nugent, a battalion surgeon from Milwaukee, pointed out that those who fought on the Western Front knew why they were there, "But we were fighting a people against whom war had never been declared and we didn't know why we were fighting them."

The Allied rail line being pushed south was halted in mid-October when only half completed, but the conflict seemed to take on a life of its own and grew increasingly brutal. On 13 November a four-man American patrol was ambushed; only one man escaped. The three who fell were found "mutilated badly." Four days later Lieutenant Glen Weeks wrote in his diary that "we caught two spies trying to find out our position, outpost strength, etc. Lieutenant [Francis W.] Cuff, Lieutenant [J. W.] Winslow [a Canadian artilleryman], and myself took one of them out in the woods and shot him."

According to Ralph Albertson, a YMCA worker at Shenkursk, officers routinely instructed their men "to take no prisoners, to kill them even if they come in unarmed, and I have been told by the men themselves of many cases when this was done." Corporal John Toornman declared that prisoners were habitually shot by both sides. But this seems not always to have been the case. Ten American prisoners, eventually repatriated through Finland, reported that although in the hands of their captors they were beaten, robbed, starved, spat upon, and forced to listen to communist lectures, once they reached Moscow they were given the freedom of the city.

The American force in Northern Russia lost 144 killed in battle or died of wounds, seventy-eight who died of diseases or other causes; 305 were wounded. Of these, the 339th Infantry lost 139 killed and 266 wounded. The American expeditionary force began to withdraw in early June and by 27 June the withdrawal was completed.

One last battle, of a sort, was fought during a brief stopover in Murmansk when a ship carrying British reinforcements docked alongside a ship carrying returning Americans. The British began the altercation by calling the Americans "bloody hobos," cowards, and mutineers. The Americans replied by throwing coal and buckets of coal were soon being brought up from below "at amazing speed." The British replied in kind, adding bottles to the ammunition. There were casualties on both sides, but no fatalities.

The British left Northern Russia soon afterwards and by 27 September the little war along the railroad and the Dvina River was over. Their intervention cost the British 317 lives.

The survivors in the 339th Infantry reached Detroit in mid-July to a warm welcome, including a ticker tape parade down Woodward Avenue and a reception given by the Chamber of Commerce. Within a week the soldiers were discharged. Senator Hiram Johnson of California said of them: "They served under conditions that were the most confusing and complexing that an American army was ever asked to contend with, but they did their duty."

Americans have decided to forget the "interventions" and have successfully done so. President Ronald Reagan, his knowledge of history deficient, spoke of American-Russian relations in his 1984 State of the Union Address, telling an equally uninformed Congress and the American people: "It is true that our governments have had serious differences. But our sons and daughters have never fought each other in war." But the Russians remember. Premier Nikita Khrushchev expostulated: "We remember the grim days when American soldiers went to our soil headed by their generals to help the White Guard combat the new revolution. . . . Never have any of our soldiers been on American soil, but your soldiers were on Russian soil. These are the facts." Few Americans knew what he was talking about.

Secretary Baker had his only real disagreement with Wilson when the president ordered an expedition to Siberia. He later described the intervention as "one of those sideshows born of desperation and organized for the purpose of keeping up home morale rather than because of any clear view of the military situation." General March called the Siberian expedition a "military crime."

Both the Archangel and Siberian misadventures, said Secretary of War Baker, "will always illustrate the eccentricities of a remote and irrational emanation from the central madness of a warring world."

26

☆

RETURN OF THE LEGIONS

THE DOUGHBOYS HAD crossed the ocean and done their duty. To Winston Churchill it seemed a wonderful deed and he paid tribute to the Americans in *The World Crisis*: "To fight in defence of his native land is the first duty of the citizen. But to fight in defence of some one else's native land is a different proposition. . . . To cross the ocean and fight for strangers, far from home, upon an issue the making of which one has had no say, requires a wide outlook upon human affairs and a sense of world responsibility."

The doughboys had been eager to go and now were eager to return, but shortage of shipping space kept many waiting. The British, who had carried most of the troops to Europe, now needed their transports to carry home the Australians, New Zealanders, South Africans, and other colonial forces. American cargo ships were transformed into troopships and troops were even carried back in warships. The United States now had many more ships of its own, for American shipbuilding capacity had expanded enormously during the war, and 533 ships, more than three million tons, were built in 1918 alone, enabling eighty-four percent of the AEF to be returned home in American ships, but all could not leave at once.

Newsman Floyd Gibbons had assured Americans at home that they need not fear that "our soldiers will leave their hearts in France" for "every soldier overseas seems to have that perfectly natural hankering to come back to the girls he left behind." But this was not quite true. Although it hadn't occurred to any general or government bureaucrat that doughboys might marry European women, about 10,000 did. The army tried at first to avoid the problem, by neither consenting to the marriages nor forbidding them, but as usual, love prevailed, the marriages were sanctioned and arrangements had to be made to ship the brides to the United States. While the brides, mostly French and German women in their twenties from rural areas, waited for shipping space, the YMCA offered language lessons and tried to prepare them for their new life in America.

The French were glad to see the backs of the often turbulent American soldiers, but the Americans at home were overjoyed to welcome them back. Throughout the land victory parades were held as the boys came marching home. The War Department made every effort to cooperate with local committees, even arranging schedules to insure that cities and towns got a fair share of troops for parades. By 30 June 1919 men en route to demobilization stations had marched in more than 500 parades. No one heeded Will Rogers, who said: "We ought to let the boys sit in the grandstand and show our appreciation by marching past *them*."

The most splendid ceremonies were in New York where Mayor John F. Hylan had appointed an official welcoming committee headed by William Randolph Hearst. The appointment of Hearst, often accused of harboring a pro-German bias, raised a storm of indignation; Bishop W. T. Manning and Henry L. Stimson immediately resigned; a protest meeting was held in Madison Square Garden. Undaunted, Hearst greeted the first transports to arrive, but he was soon called to California where his mother lay dying and the furor subsided.

The 369th Infantry gave New York one of its grandest parades. Filled with pride, Colonel William Hayward led his black soldiers, marching behind their now famous "Harlem Hell Cats" band. It was the jazziest marching band in history, turning even "La Marseillaise" into ragtime with cakewalk licks so irresistible, it was said, that in offices along the route bosses seized their secretaries to fox trot among the files.

The men of the 369th, who had endured 161 days of combat, were wildly cheered as they swung along to their band's syncopated rhythm, changing their marching formation several times, even demonstrating the solid block formation they had learned from the French. But when they reached Harlem all order dissolved in an onslaught of young women and crowds that couldn't be restrained.

It was hoped that the 165th Infantry, New York's own "Fighting 69th," would reach New York in time for St. Patrick's Day. Although that hope was dashed, the city turned out en masse for its parade on 28 April. Stock markets and city schools closed. Led by Colonel William ("Wild Bill") Donovan, with Father Duffy close behind him, the men marched through hundreds of thousands of cheering, ecstatic men, women, and children from Washington Arch in Greenwich Village up 5th Avenue to 110th Street. They wore full battle dress and their steel helmets, for Donovan told them: "They'll never forget you in those helmets." The regiment, always glorying in its uniqueness, had designed its own medal, and on this day a well-deserved one was pinned on the breast of Elsie Janis, the "Sweetheart of the AEF."

The mayor conferred the freedom of the city upon Donovan and his staff. The regiment's "Board of Trustees," as Father Duffy called it, gave the entire regiment a banquet at the Hotel Commodore.

From May through June some 300,000 troops were returned from Europe. In August the 1st Division, last of the combat divisions to leave France, embarked. Not until 8 September 1919 did Pershing return home. He had enjoyed or endured victory parades in London and Paris and now his own nation turned out to honor him. As the *Leviathan*, carrying the victorious Iron Commander, neared New York, an airplane dropped on its deck a greeting from Mayor Hylan. On landing he mounted a horse and riding at attention, led a composite regiment of hand-picked soldiers, each at least six feet tall with an impeccable military bearing through streets of wildly cheering citizens. He halted on 57th Street in front of St. Patrick's Cathedral, where he dismounted to greet Belgium's Cardinal Désiré Joseph Mercier, who had come to the United States to thank Americans for their assistance to his country. Later he was welcomed home by 50,000 schoolchildren in Central Park. Wherever he went dignitaries and politicians paid court to him. Already a Pershing-for-President Campaign was taking shape.

The composite regiment, which had marched behind Pershing in Paris and London, as well as New York, marched for the last time in the final parade in Washington, D.C., on 17 September 1919. The day after that parade a joint session of Congress gave him the nation's thanks. Pershing replied with a ten-minute speech in which he assured the congressmen that the soldier-citizens were returning "in the full vigor of manhood, strong and clean. . . . They will bring into the life of our country a deeper love of our institutions and more intelligent devotion to the duties of citizenship."

War's end found 3,703,273 men in the army. Soon after the Armistice the War Department tried unsuccessfully to have Congress authorize a permanent regular army of 600,000 and a three-month training of conscripts. Pershing spent three days testifying before the House and Senate Military Affairs Committees, pressing for six-month universal military training. He told the congressmen: "We are now confronted with serious social problems resulting from the large masses [of] ignorant foreigners in our midst, who are highly susceptible to . . . Bolshevik proposals. . . . Universal military training is the only means I see available for educating the foreign element. . . ."

He could have saved his breath. The pulse of the people was not difficult for congressmen to find. Universal military training was as popular as a plague. Embedded in the many arguments against it was the dire warning that it would worsen the country's already disturbing race relations. A Virginia congressman declared, "I know nothing so irresponsible as a young negro boy rigged out in brass buttons and with a gun."

Demobilization proceeded rapidly. Within two months after war's end 818,532 of the army's war strength were discharged. Each was given a $60 bonus and allowed to take home his uniform, a coat, and a pair of shoes. Those who had served overseas could also take a helmet and gas mask. By the end of 1919 the regular army was reduced to about 19,000 officers and 205,000 enlisted men. By 1925 it had been reduced to 135,000 officers and men.

Some men sought to hold on to the exhilaration of war. Elliott White Springs, who had shot down twelve enemy aircraft while serving with the British, barnstormed around the United States and wandered the world in search of new challenges and adventures. He was in Paris recovering from stomach ulcers when he took up writing and successfully authored more than a half dozen books, mostly novels, about World War I aviation. He finally settled down to run the family business, Springs Cotton Mills, a major manufacturer of bedsheets. Becoming president on the death of his father in 1931, he expanded the company into a vast textile empire. During World War II he served as executive officer of an air base in North Carolina. After the war, back at Springs Cotton Mills again, he gained national attention with a series of catchy and often risqué advertisements for Spring Maid sheets. Until his death in 1959 he worked with the Civil Air Patrol.

Douglas Campbell, America's first ace, also succeeded in civilian life, in 1948 becoming general manager of Pan American Grace Airways (PANAGRA). He died in 1990 at the age of ninety-four. Eddie Rickenbacker, best known of American aces, organized the short-lived Rickenbacker Motor Company in Detroit and eventually became president of Eastern Air Lines. In 1942 the army plane he was flying went down in the Pacific Ocean and he endured three weeks on a raft before being rescued.

Charles G. Dawes, Pershing's unmilitary procurement genius, became in 1921 the first director of the Bureau of the Budget, in 1921 vice president of the United States, and in 1929 ambassador to Great Britain. In 1925 he was awarded, with corecipient Sir Austin Chamberlain, the Nobel Peace Prize.

There were jolts for some on their return. Men who had left aid stations prematurely to return to the fighting discovered that they had no credit for their wounds.

Noted sports writer Grantland Rice was overage (thirty-nine) and married with a baby daughter when the United States entered the war, but he left his family to enlist as a private in the 37th ("Buckeye") Division. Before signing up he had converted all his assets into cash, about $75,000, which he entrusted to a New York lawyer to invest for his wife and daughter. He returned home to find that the lawyer, having lost Rice's fortune, had shot himself.

Among regular officers, few in the AEF retained their wartime rank and there were hard feelings when they were reduced in rank while some who had stayed in the United States retained theirs. Charles D. Rhodes, who was at once reduced from major general to colonel, wrote: "Everywhere there was much discontent. . . . All of Pershing's generals, with but few exceptions, have been promptly demoted while all good army jobs continue to be filled with 'March adherents,' with officers of the field artillery 'running strong.'" The chiefs of staff of the three American armies were all reduced to their permanent rank of major. Presto Brown, who commanded the 3rd Division and whom Pershing had recommended for promotion to major general, and Brigadier General Dennis Nolan, Pershing's brilliant chief of intelligence, were both reduced to major.

Army units in time tend to seem like home, holding wherever they may be, buddies, leaders, familiar duties, and routines. A few pangs sometimes accompanied the dissolution of units with which men had been identified. Sergeant Hugh B. Griffiths condensed his homecoming:

> *We finally returned home — came back to our loved ones and friends.*
> *We paraded a bit.*
> *We ate some.*
> *We partied much.*
> *We were mustered out.*
> Fini *Machine Gun Company, 107th Infantry.*

The war had lasted less than two years, but much had changed since the doughboys went "over there." Even the time had changed when day-light saving was instituted on 31 March 1918—although the law was repealed over Wilson's veto the following year. And while the young men had been fighting the war or preparing to, those who abhorred liquor gained enough ground to insure a final triumph.

The "drys" had long been politically active. (The bar in the Capitol in Washington was shut down in 1903.) The war gave impetus to their movement. The great American breweries suffered from having German names such as Pabst, Busch, and Anheuser. Posters everywhere pro-claimed that "Liquor is the Kaiser's mightiest ally." Dr. William Herbert Perry Faunce, president of Brown University, declared that "Prohibition spells patriotism."

Not everyone agreed, of course, and H. L. Mencken, whose German-sounding name ought to have led him to keep his mouth shut, boldly char-acterized the prohibitionists as those who had a "haunting fear that some-one, somewhere, might be happy." Nevertheless, on 1 August 1918 the Senate voted sixty-five to twenty to submit the 18th Amendment to the Constitution to the states. In December the House of Representatives approved by a vote of 282 to 128. In January 1919 the 36th state ratified the amendment and it was embedded in the Constitution. Veterans faced a future in which joyous occasions could not legally be celebrated by a drink nor days of depression and grief alleviated by one. Theodore Roosevelt, Jr., wrote: "Over in France and in the occupied part of Germany the dough-boys feel peeved that Prohibition has been enacted in their absence."

As of 1 January income tax was increased so that many now had to pay what was billed as a "Liberty Tax." The number of American taxpayers rose to seven million in 1918 from only 500,000 the previous year.

A pleasant surprise was the change in women's fashions. "Peekaboo" blouses were now in style and hemlines had risen. Where it was once thought titillating to catch sight of a pretty woman's ankle, women's calves, covered only by silk stockings, were exposed.

The "women's movement" accelerated. The 19th Amendment to the Constitution, giving the right to vote to all citizens, had already passed the House of Representatives on 10 January 1918 and in the following June it passed the Senate.

More than any other event in American history the Great War marked the end of one era and the beginning of a new age. It was among history's clearest dividing lines. The soldiers and sailors returned to a land of boot-leggers, gangsters, "speakeasies," and bathtub gin, to women openly smoking cigarettes and bobbing their hair, to Freud, contract bridge, country clubs, golf, and the "Roaring Twenties." America danced to a different beat as the Jazz Age emerged to elate the young and horrify the old. The young found new and livelier dances to match the beat of "Ja-Da" and "Dardanella" and short-skirted young women danced the "shimmy," celebrated in the popular song: "I Wish I Could Shimmy Like My Sister Kate" (*She shakes like a jelly on a plate.*). "Over There" quickly changed to "How you gonna keep 'em down on the farm / After they've seen Paree." Many, like ex-captain and former farmer Harry S. Truman, never returned to the farm.

In 1920, for the first time, more Americans lived in cities than in the country. General March later wrote: "There has always been a pronounced tendency for returning soldiers to flock to the cities. Men from farms and rural communities, taken from their homes and shown something of the world, desire to go to the large cities to seek the excitement to be found there. This is a trait of human nature which cannot be overcome by legislation or War Department regulations. For a time there was anxiety in many communities lest the soldiers, suddenly released from the restrictions of discipline, might commit excesses." The fear proved groundless. It was, in the end, the government which committed the excesses.

The young men returning from the war had themselves changed. As F. Scott Fitzgerald put it, many had "grown up to find all gods dead, all wars fought, all faiths in man shaken." Most had seen more of the world than had their elders and had been exposed to beliefs and customs strange to them and to those they had left behind. Many had witnessed close and at first hand the horrors, fears, and excitements of an exceptionally brutal conflict.

For some, perhaps many, army service changed their lives for the better. An Oklahoma official on an Indian reservation reported that a Cheyenne, a "typical, no account, reservation Indian with long hair, went to France, was wounded, gassed and shell shocked" and returned a "square shouldered, level-eyed, courteous, self-reliant [man who] talked intelligently. A wonderful transformation and caused by contact with the outside world. He is at work." But not all Indians could find work.

Many soon found their homecoming disillusioning. Joseph Oklahombi, a Choctaw from the Ouachita Mountain region of southeastern Oklahoma, was said to be the most decorated Indian in the war. He had served in the 141st Infantry in the 36th Division and while on duty in the St. Etienne sector had won the *Croix de Guerre* for dashing under a heavy barrage and through wire entanglements to attack machine gun nests and taking dozens of prisoners. Illiterate and jobless, he turned to drink and was soon destitute. In 1932 he applied to the government for a pension of $12 a month.

As veterans donned civvies, admiration for their heroic conduct ebbed. Home was not the same. For many there was disillusionment. Some sweethearts had married men who stayed home and some wives had fallen in love with those they had worked beside. Returning soldiers found their former jobs in the hands of women or men who had escaped the draft. Work grew scarce as wartime contracts were abruptly ended.

Perhaps the greatest social change occurred among blacks. The gradual migration to the north of blacks seeking employment, education, and social services in the decade before the war increased dramatically during the war and immediately afterwards, when 350,000 black soldiers and sailors returned home. Some found in it a threat. The nation was plagued by racial disorders. There were bloody race riots—twenty-five in 1919. There were four nights of rioting in Washington, D.C. In Chicago, thirteen days of rioting left fifteen whites and twenty-three blacks dead. In Omaha a mob estimated at 20,000 burned down the courthouse, lynched a black man, and attempted to lynch the mayor who had tried to defend him.

In places in the south black troops were assaulted. Black officers who sought to retain their commissions were rejected. Captain T. Dent of the 368th infantry was denied a regular commission because of "the qualities inherent in the Negro race." The Ku Klux Klan resumed its activities and grew in numbers, vowing to unite "native-born white Christians for concerted action in the preservation of American institutions and the supremacy of the white race." Among those American institutions, it seems, was the lynching of blacks: thirty-eight in 1917; fifty-eight in 1918; and seventy, including ten veterans in uniform, in 1919. Ten blacks were burned at the stake. Norman Angell, author of *The Grand Illusion*, wrote that neither the Germans in Belgium and France nor the British in Ireland "burn alive, weekly, untried fellow-countrymen with a regularity that makes the thing an institution."

The newly rich war profiteers who had made fortunes producing and selling war supplies were bitterly resented. Attempts to recover war profits through special taxes failed, for they placed impossible burdens upon innocent businesses.

After the war the railroads, unrepentant, launched what William McAdoo described as "a frenzied attack on the United States Treasury." Although the government had, as McAdoo said, "put them on their feet, made them more efficient," they demanded what were then enormous sums for what they claimed was damage to their property during the war. Central Railroad of New Jersey demanded $22,546,000 and the Pullman Company $24,424,000. The courts disallowed about two-thirds of the claims, but the rapacious behavior of railroad owners and managers sickened many and damaged the reputation not only of the railroads but of big business in general.

Wilson's idealism did not survive the war and Congress refused to accept the League of Nations. The United States retreated into isolationism. Many succumbed to cynicism. The glow and excitement that for many characterized the war years seemed to be replaced by rancor and gloom. Newspaper columnist and commentator Mark Sullivan spoke of "an exaltation that had gone sour."

The hatred once directed at the Kaiser was turned upon "reds," "Bolsheviks," and "anarchists." Such sentiments in America generated suspicion of General Graves, who refused to fight Bolsheviks in Siberia. Throughout the country vigilantes and superpatriot groups sprang up. In Centralia, Washington, on 11 November 1919 a group of American Legionnaires attacked the IWW hall. They were fired upon and four were killed. Several "Wobblies" were lynched in the riot that followed.

President Wilson appointed Alexander Mitchell Palmer, a former congressman who during the war had served as alien property custodian, to be his attorney general, and Palmer, with the assistance of J. Edgar Hoover, inaugurated a witch hunt. On 2 January 1919 some 10,000 "radicals" were rounded up—all with foreign accents were suspect—and about 3,500 spent days or weeks incarcerated without due process of law. Several hundred, including anarchist Emma Goldman, were deported.

In the rising tide of discontent, bombs were indeed thrown at newspaper offices and the homes of politicians. One even landed on the steps of Palmer's Washington home. Two foreign-born, self-confessed anarchists, Nicola Sacco and Bartolomeo Vanzetti, were accused of murdering a shoe factory paymaster and a guard at South Braintree, Massachusetts, and stealing $16,000. They were convicted on 14 July 1921 and, in spite of growing worldwide support of their pleas of innocence, were electrocuted on 23 August 1927. Socialist leader Eugene Debs, after publicly speaking on the hypocrisy of waging a war to end wars, was seized by federal agents, tried and imprisoned in the federal prison in Atlanta, from which in 1920 he ran for president and won almost a million votes.

For many their few war months were the defining era of their lives.

Former soldiers organized themselves into veterans' organizations, seeking to preserve or rekindle the comradeships they had formed. The largest of these was the American Legion which aimed "to inculcate the duty and obligation of the citizen of the state." Like the Grand Army of the Republic formed after the Civil War, the Legion soon discovered its political clout and lobbied for a bonus. In 1922 Congress passed a bill authorizing one; President Harding vetoed it. The following year Congress again passed a bonus bill, but President Calvin Coolidge vetoed it. By 1924 the bill had enough congressional support to override the veto and about 3.5 billion dollars was appropriated to provide what were called Adjusted Compensation Certificates which had an average value of about $1,000.

The Depression brought further demands and in 1931 Congress overrode the veto of President Herbert Hoover to provide even more funds. In late May 1932 some 17,000 unemployed veterans from all parts of the country descended upon Washington and demanded immediate and full payment of the bonuses. The "bonus army" camped in ramshackle huts assembled by its members almost within sight of the Capitol. In June Congress voted down their demands and most of them returned from whence they had come. However, some 2,000 remained. When President Hoover ordered them removed, Chief of Staff General Douglas MacArthur, aided by Major Dwight D. Eisenhower, sent soldiers carrying bayoneted rifles to burn their shacks and move them on.

General James Harbord, who had toured a military hospital in France with Secretary Baker in 1918 and been touched by the good spirits of young men who had lost limbs, later wrote: "It would have taken a long vision to have looked forward eighteen years to see the difficulties these men would have in competition in the race of life with other men who stayed at home while they went to war. It would have been impossible that March morning to have convinced me that there would ever come a time when the American people would view such sacrifice with indifference."

27

EPILOGUE:

MEDALS   AND   OTHER   HONORS

COMPARATIVELY FEW AMERICAN medals were awarded during the war. The War Department failed to recognize their morale value and Pershing had originally believed that the knowledge a soldier had of a good job done and earning the respect of his comrades should be reward enough. When the war began only one medal existed: the Medal of Honor, instituted during the Civil War. This has remained the nation's highest military honor, but on January 1918 Congress approved the Distinguished Service Cross as a lesser medal. Of some 14,000 men recommended, only 6,153 received the award. Pershing ordered every headquarters to reexamine these awards in their unit to determine if any should be upgraded to the Medal of Honor, a review process that continued for years. Of the ninety-five Medals of Honor awarded to members of the AEF, only four were awarded before the Armistice. Eddie Rickenbacker did not receive his until 1930. Although the navy saw little action, sailors were awarded twenty-one.

The Rainbow Division submitted nine recommendations for the Medal of Honor, a list headed by Brigadier General Douglas MacArthur, one of only 111 to have won the Distinguished Service Cross twice. Pershing chose six, MacArthur was not one of them. He had not, Pershing said, reached the required standard of heroism. "The days for brigadier generals to rush forward in the firing line waving their hats and yelling 'Come on boys!' are in actual warfare at least a thing of the past," he wrote. He preferred awarding the medal to junior officers and enlisted men in the infantry.

Patton's wound in the buttocks, received in the Meuse-Argonne offensive, developed sepsis and by the time it had healed the war was over. He needlessly feared he would not receive the Distinguished Service Cross and considered resigning if he did not get it. Proud of his wound, he was later known to lower his trousers at parties to exhibit his scarred backside, and some ten years after the war he was evicted from a public beach at Narragansett, Rhode Island, for wearing a swim suit cut to reveal his wound.

At the same time Congress instituted the Distinguished Service Cross, it also instituted the Distinguished Service Medal for exceptional meritorious conduct in a duty of great responsibility. There was also considerable delay in awarding this medal. Not until ten years after the war did Eisenhower receive his.

The Silver Star medal was not instituted until 8 August 1932, but during World War I small silver stars were authorized to be worn on the campaign ribbons of those cited in orders for gallantry. Essentially these were what the British called "mentioned in dispatches." Douglas MacArthur, who earned seven of these in World War I, equated them with the new medal and awarded himself seven Silver Star Medals.

In 1919 a war medal was issued for all who had served in the war with clasps for those who had fought in major battles.

ON 3 SEPTEMBER 1919 Pershing was promoted general of the armies, the only officer, except possibly Washington, ever to hold this rank; on 23 September he was given the Thanks of Congress. Admiral Sims, who had been promoted to vice admiral in May 1917 and to full admiral rank in December 1918, was reduced to his permanent rank of rear admiral only three months later. In 1920 he wrote a lengthy report critical of the Navy Department's management of naval operations during the war and the same year published, with Burton Jesse Hendrick, *Victory at Sea*, which was awarded the Pulitzer Prize for history. He retired in October 1922.

James G. Harbord, who had begun the war as a major and Pershing's chief of staff, ended the war in the same position in the expanded army with the rank of major general. He had hoped to return to the United States with Pershing and to share in the glory, but President Wilson sent him as chief of a mission to Armenia and he did not return until November 1919 by which time everyone was trying to forget the war. He retired in 1922 to be chairman of the board of Radio Corporation of America.

After the war Billy Mitchell waged an unsuccessful campaign for the formation of a separate air service on the lines of the RAF. Thwarted by official opposition, he became increasingly truculent. In 1925 he publicly accused the army and navy of "almost treasonable neglect" of national defense. He was court-martialed, and when found guilty and suspended from rank and pay for five years, he resigned. In 1946 Congress voted him a special posthumous medal for his outstanding pioneer service and foresight in the field of military aviation.

ALVIN YORK'S FAME did not fade, at least not completely. Two biographies were published and in 1941 the immensely popular Warner Brothers film, *Sergeant York*, with Gary Cooper in the title role, firmly reestablished him as a national hero. The film also reflected the changed mood of the country, then on the verge of entering another world war; Cooper won an Oscar for his performance. Ten years earlier the Academy Award had been given to *All Quiet on the Western Front*.

On Sunday afternoon, 10 July 1921, newly elected President Warren G. Harding and his wife entertained guests aboard the presidential yacht *Mayflower*. Between poker hands and highballs Harding talked enthusiastically about plans for an international disarmament conference.

That same afternoon, while the president was socializing, a poignant ceremony was taking place on the docks at Hoboken, New Jersey. Stretching for a quarter of a mile along Pier 4, lay 7,264 coffins recently unloaded from the transports *Somme* and *Wheaton*. General Pershing, now chief of staff, spoke to the assembled parents, wives, children, and other relatives of the dead: "Only those who fought with them can ever know the height of religious devotion and patriotism to which they arose." Senator Henry Cabot Lodge, who was present, also spoke.

Directly in front of the speakers were three coffins on each of which Pershing laid a wreath after the speeches. Brass plates identified the remains within as those of Corporal James B. Gresham, Private Thomas F. Enright, and Private Merle Hay—the first from the ranks of the AEF to fall in France.

Not all the dead were returned. At war's end some 6,000 men of three black regiments—813th, 815th, and 816th Pioneer Infantry—were assigned the unpleasant task of collecting bodies to be buried at the Argonne National Cemetery at Romagne.

In 1923 Congress created the American Battle Monuments Commission to commemorate the services of the American forces in Europe during the Great War. General Pershing was its first chairman. The Commission improved and beautified the eight American cemeteries and at Montfaucon there stands today a 180-foot Doric column of Italian granite, the largest American war memorial in Europe. The Commission also made special studies of each division that served in combat on the Western Front.

Following an idea borrowed from other countries, three years after the war the United States decided to honor all the fallen soldiers whose identity was not known and a single unknown soldier's remains was chosen to represent them and be honored. In a ceremony in France a veteran selected one of four caskets, each containing a body from a different battlefield, by placing flowers on it.

Admiral Dewey's flagship at the Battle of Manila Bay in the Spanish-American War, the USS *Olympia*, was dispatched to France to collect the casket and on 25 October 1921 it was taken on board at La Havre after a brief ceremony. The *Olympia* was escorted for a part of its voyage home by a group of French destroyers, and throughout its passage it was saluted by every passing vessel. At the mouth of the Potomac it was joined by two American warships that escorted it to the Washington Navy Yard. There "with full and somber military honor" the casket was piped over the side.

With more ceremony the body was interred in the military cemetery at Arlington, Virginia, where a shrine was erected. As General James Harbord said, "We now worship at the altar of anonymity."

The end of the war did not mean the end of casualties. In addition to those which occurred in the fighting in Russia and Siberia, numerous civilian casualties were caused by unexploded shells, land mines, and other explosives. Indeed, tons of World War I debris are still being removed each year. Tens of thousands of mines still floated in the seas and the navy had the task of removing those it had laid, a dangerous proceeding in which several sailors lost their lives. The North Sea Mine Barrage was finally swept up on 30 September 1919.

In Britain, the United States, and the Commonwealth countries it was once the custom—and in some perhaps still is—to buy and wear paper poppies on Armistice Day, thus making a donation to provide comforts for disabled veterans. Poppies became identified with the Western Front when, to the surprise of most soldiers, they bloomed in Flanders amid the war-ravaged landscapes of no-man's-land. On 6 December 1915 *Punch* published anonymously a poem entitled "In Flanders Fields." Written by a Canadian medical officer, John McCrae, during the Second Battle of Ypres, it became the best-known poem of the war:

> *In Flanders field the poppies blow*
> *Between the crosses, row on row,*
> *That mark our place; and in the sky*
> *The larks, still bravely singing, fly*
> *Scarce heard amid the guns below.*

Most of the fighting men on the Western Front had seen all they wanted to see of France. The American artists and literati who took up residence in Paris and created their own subculture in the 1920s were not former combat soldiers. Some had driven ambulances or performed other social welfare work, but none had been infantrymen, artillerymen, or combat engineers.

Who won the War? No single weapon, nation, leader, or strategy won the war. Each nation tended to think its own contribution the greatest. The entry of the United States into the war was certainly an important one, and many have felt that other nations, whose losses were indeed far greater, did not sufficiently appreciate America's contribution. Of the eight billion dollars loaned to the Allies, little was repaid. Only Finland paid in full. British military historian Captain Basil Liddell Hart best summed up the American contribution: "The United States did not win the war, but without their economic aid to ease the strain, without the arrival of their troops to turn the numerical balance, and, above all, without the moral tonic which their coming gave, victory would have been impossible."

APPENDIX A

WORDS AND EXPRESSIONS FROM THE GREAT WAR

Ace: an aviator who had shot down five enemy planes or balloons. Its use first appeared in a French newspaper in June 1915 when Adolph Pégoud was dubbed *l'as de notre aviation*. A German aviator had to have downed ten enemy planes to be called an ace.

Ash Can: depth charge.

Archy: an antiaircraft gun.

Bangalore torpedo: a long narrow explosive that could be slipped under barbed wire and exploded to make a hole in entanglements.

Boche or Bosche: a derogatory term for a German. The origin of this word is obscure. Said to be French slang for rascal, or to be shortened from caboche, head, or *tête de boche* (obstinate person). It was first used in a newspaper article in the British *Daily Express* on 30 September 1914.

Bolo: a Bolshevik.

Bon Blighty: a French-British combination for a "good wound," meaning a wound bad enough to be sent to a safe hospital but not causing permanent injury.

Boys: an affectionate term for American soldiers. Often used in "our boys" by civilians and soldiers alike.

Brass or Brass Hat: high-ranking officers or staff officers.

Camion: a truck.

Chase Pilot: fighter pilot.

Communication Trench: a narrow trench connecting defense trenches permitting concealed access to forward trenches.

Concertina: coiled wire, usually barbed wire, used to make entanglements.

Cooties: body lice, fleas, and bed bugs. Also sometimes called seam squirrels or pants rabbits.

Corned Willie: corned beef: "dry, tinned, evil-smelling and equally bad-looking." Most often it was turned into a stew known as *Slum* or *slumgullion* to which vegetables were sometimes added.

Creeping Barrage: an artillery bombardment that advanced at timed intervals so that infantry advancing behind it would not be hit.

Dog Fight or Dogfight: aerial combat.

Dog Robber: an officer's orderly or personal servant, called a "batman" in British usage. The expression came from the privilege of the orderly to eat what was left over from the officer's table, thus taking food that otherwise would have been given to the dog.

Double O: the "once over" look given by doughboys to attractive girls.

Doughboy: an American soldier. Originally, a flour dumpling. Before the war the word was used to identify an infantryman, but during the war was applied to all soldiers, as "G.I." was used in World War II.

Doughnut Dollies: Salvation Army women who passed out doughnuts and other treats to soldiers.

Drachen: German observation balloons.

Flaming Onion: a type of antiaircraft shell that exploded in the form of flaming tentacles.

Ersatz: German reserve forces. The word was often used incorrectly to denote something artificial or substandard.

40 *et* 8: words on the side of every French boxcar indicating that it could hold 40 men or 8 horses (*Hommes 40, Chevaux 8*).

Frog: a Frenchman.

Goldbricking: malingering.

Goldfish: a cheap grade of canned salmon or sardines. Never popular with the soldiers.

Go West: to be killed.

Hash Marks: stripes on the sleeves of enlisted men indicating length of service by the number of enlistments.

Hun: a derogatory name for a German. A German contingent sent to China under Field Marshal Count Alfred von Waldersee during the Boxer Rebellion was addressed before its departure by Kaiser Wilhelm II, who exhorted them: "If you meet the enemy you ought to know: no pardon will be given, no prisoners will be taken. As a thousand years ago the Huns under their king Attila made a name for themselves that lets them even now appear mighty in tradition, so may the name of German be impressed by you on China in such a manner that never again will a Chinese dare to look askance at a German."
     Germans were also called heinies, boche, Fritz, and krauts.

Gyrene: slang word for a marine.

Jam Tin: a Mills bomb, a British hand grenade.

Kite Balloon: observation balloons controlled by cables on the ground.

KP: kitchen police. Soldiers assigned to work in the kitchen peeling potatoes, shelling peas, washing dishes, etc. This duty was usually rotated but could be assigned as punishment.

Landsturm: German and Austrian third-line militia.

Landwehr: German reserve units.

Limey: an Englishman.

Looie: a lieutenant. *See* Shave-tail.

Minnenwerfer: a German portable, muzzle-loading trench mortar.

Monkey Meat: a particularly odious ration of Argentine beef and carrots. A Marine Corps officer said, "Men ate it when they were very hungry."

No-man's-land: the space between the trenches of belligerents.

Observation Planes: two-seater airplanes used to take pictures or direct artillery fire. The observer in the rear cockpit operated a swivel gun. His insignia was a badge with a single wing.

Over the top: to leave the trenches and charge the enemy across no-man's-land.

Padre: military chaplain.

Poilu: affectionate name for a French soldier, as doughboy for Americans and Tommy for British. The original meaning was "hairy one."

Pond or The Big Pond: the Atlantic Ocean.

Potato Masher: a German hand grenade. It appeared to be a can on a wooden handle that made it resemble a potato masher.

Pursuit plane: a fighter plane used to attack enemy airplanes and balloons and to protect observation planes and bombers.

Read a Shirt: to hold up a shirt to look closely for body lice to pick off.

Red Leg: an artilleryman. Red is the service color of the artillery in the American army.

Riding the Gun: there were two metal seats on a French 75 field gun. On the left side sat the corporal who controlled the sight; on the right was the gunner who pulled the lanyard that fired the gun. To ride the gun was to remain on the seat while firing. It was then possible for the gunner to hook his toe under the axle and, leaning to his left side, throw open the breech, enabling the gun to be loaded again the second the tube returned to battery.

Sam Browne: a belt worn by officers in the AEF and by French and British officers. It was designed by a British officer, Samuel Browne, who lost an arm during the Indian Mutiny, to enable him to draw his sword more easily. It consisted of a wide belt that circled the waist and a narrower strap that passed diagonally over the right shoulder. Captain Harry S. Truman bought one just before sailing from New York. He noted that the belt had "a hook for a saber but I never expect to wear one." It later became universal in the American army and did not disappear until World War II.

Sammy: an American soldier. Presumably from Uncle Sam. This word, soon replaced by "doughboy," was used by some at the beginning of the war and often by French people.

Sausage: a captive balloon.

Selectee: a conscripted soldier.

Services of Supply (SOS): the American name given the line of communication and supply behind the Zone of Advance in France.

Shave-tail: a second lieutenant or a newly acquired army mule.

Shell Shocked: to break down under the stresses of battle conditions and become a neuropsychiatric casualty.

Shrapnel: the original shrapnel, invented by British Major Henry Shrapnel in about 1785, was an explosive shell filled with musket balls with a fuse that could be cut to time the shell to explode in the air, showering the target with lead balls. The balls themselves were often referred to as shrapnel. It was adopted by the British army in 1803 and was first used successfully in Surinam in 1804 and first used on land in Europe in the Battle of Vimeiro during the Peninsular War. During the American Civil War it was usually referred to as spherical case shot. Present usage, first used by misguided war correspondents in World War II, includes fragments from any munition, but this meaning was not attached to the word in World War I.

Slum: *see* Corned Willie.

Slum Gun: a mobile kitchen.

Stand to: the manning of a trench to repel an attack, or routinely at dawn and dusk when an enemy might attack in the half light.

Teddy Bear: the thick, warm flying suit worn by airplane pilots and observers.

Tin Can: a destroyer.

Tin Fish: a torpedo.

Tin Hat: the steel helmet worn in combat. Each nation had its own design, but the Americans wore the British style in this war.

Tommy: a British soldier.

Tracer: a phosphorescent bullet which glowed in flight, indicating its trajectory as an aid to aiming. It was usually used in machine gun belts, one per several regular bullets.

Trench Foot: a fungal infection of the foot caused by continued exposure to wet and cold.

Twirl a Dream: to roll a Bull Durham cigarette.

Whizz Bang: a shell from an Austrian 88 mm gun. Sometimes a reference to other large shells.

Wound Stripe: a small gold cloth V worn on the right sleeve of American soldiers who had been wounded or gassed.

Zone of Advance: the official American name for the forward areas on the Western Front.

APPENDIX B

THE "HELLO GIRLS"

NOT THE LEAST of the problems faced by AEF's headquarters was wrestling with the proverbially atrocious French telephone system, which had not been updated or changed by the war. Americans, more accustomed in their daily lives to the use of telephones and telegraphs, found that the Signal Corps had to string thousands of miles of telephone and telegraph lines and set up their own switchboards.

Instead of training Signal Corps men to work as telephone operators, Pershing decided that he would import French-speaking American women. From more than 7,000 who applied, 223 were chosen, then oriented and trained for six weeks by AT&T at Evanston, Illinois, to operate a "cable and plug" switchboard. They were then sent to New York to purchase their own required uniforms, which included blue Norfolk jackets, long skirts, hightop shoes, woolen underwear, and black sateen bloomers. Operators were paid $60 a month; $12 more for supervisors.

They sailed on board troopships, first class, two to a cabin, and at first were forbidden to associate with the troops. On board the *Baltic*, which sailed from New York on 25 April 1918, the women rebelled against their isolation. Their leader, Miss Nellie Snow, formerly chief telephone operator for the New England Telephone Company in Lowell, Massachusetts, led the protest that resulted in a lifting of the ban—after they had been properly introduced to a few selected officers and on condition that they were never alone with a man. As the *Baltic* entered the war zone the women were ordered to sleep with their clothes on.

The separation of the sexes policy appears to have been soon abandoned, for Louise Barbour, who sailed from New York on the S.S. *Aquitania* on 5 August 1918, wrote her mother: "There were some seven or eight thousand toops on board . . . so you may imagine that the girls had a gay time . . . we soon became acquainted with a number of officers who made the days pass pleasantly. All were obliged to wear life belts during the day and it was an amusing sight to see couples trying to dance in them."

Affectionately christened "Hello Girls," Pershing called them "switchboard soldiers." On 11 April 1919, after a crash course in close order drill, the operators at Neufchâteau took part in a parade where they were personally commended by Pershing, who in his memoirs wrote: "No civil telephone service that ever came under my observation excelled the perfection of ours after it was well established. The telephone girls in the A.E.F. took great pains and pride in their work and did it with satisfaction to all." A pretty tribute, even if not quite true.

On the afternoon of 6 November 1918, at the end of the Meuse-Argonne offensive, Brigadier General George C. Marshall, now an assistant chief of staff for operations (G-3) for the American First Army, became aware that heavy army and corps artillery were firing into an area occupied by American troops. He immediately placed a call to the chief of artillery, but the "Hello Girl" at the switchboard informed him that the line was busy. When he demanded the line for an urgent operational call, he was told firmly that only the army commander or the chief of staff could do this. At the moment he was acting chief of staff he insisted, but the girl was unimpressed. Desperately he asked to speak to the chief signal officer and was put through. Informed of what was happening, he immediately dashed next door to the chief of artillery with the news. The firing stopped.

The "Hello Girl," listening, became hysterical when she realized the cost of her obduracy. It was, said Marshall, "apparently the first time one of the women central at Army Headquarters had been brought into such immediate contact with the direction of the battle."

The "Hello Girls," wearing the uniforms required by the army and drawing army pay, had assumed they were in the Army Signal Corps. They discovered they were not only when they were discharged and informed that they had been merely employees and were ineligible for the status and benefits of veterans. Not until 1979, after a campaign led by former Hello Girl Mrs. Louise Le Breton Maxwell, did the army give honorable discharges, war medals, and veterans benefits to the few survivors.

A L V I N   Y O R K

WHEN WAR WAS declared, Alvin Cullum York was a twenty-nine-year-old conscientious objector who had spent most of his life in Fentress County, Tennessee, in the Cumberland Mountains. He was drafted after his pleas for a deferment on religious grounds were rejected. Unlike many other drafted conscientious objectors, he was not abused and he dropped his objections when his battalion commander, Major George Edward Buxton, persuaded him that the United States was fighting God's fight.

Born in a one-room log cabin on 13 December 1887, the third of eleven children, he attended school irregularly and reached only the third grade. Because game was necessary to provide food for the family, Alvin began to hunt at an early age. His father, he said, often "threatened to muss me up right smart if I failed to bring a squirrel down with the first shot or hit a turkey in the body instead of taking its head off." He was fascinated by firearms and regularly won prizes at rifle shooting events. His father died in 1911 after being kicked by a mule.

He worked as a blacksmith until a fire destroyed the shop, and then as a laborer. Standing six feet tall, he had red hair, weighed 175 pounds, and early acquired the traditional vices of mountain men—he "gambled, drank moonshine and rough-housed."

In 1915 he joined the Church of Christ in Christian Union, a small fundamentalist sect. After his reformation he said, "A feller does a heap of things he's ashamed of later, don't he." Before going off to war he engaged himself to Gracie Williams, a neighbor's daughter, one of thirteen children. At the age of sixteen, she was thirteen years younger than York but had passed the eighth grade.

He was inducted on 15 November 1917 and sent to Camp Gordon, Georgia. "Pretty flat country," he noted. There he was "throwed in with a lot of Greeks and Italians and New York Jews." On 1 May 1918 he sailed for England with Company G, 328th Infantry, 82nd Division, commanded by Major General William P. Burnham, a nongraduating West Pointer who had risen through the ranks in the regular army.

He first saw action in June 1918 when the 82nd occupied trenches on the St. Mihiel salient near Pont-à-Mousson, on the eastern side of the Allied line. Here he was promoted to corporal. His company went over the top at dawn on 12 September and was greeted by German gas shells and machine guns. "It was pretty heartbreaking for a simple mountain boy who believed in God to see all those good American boys lying around," he said later.

York earned his Medal of Honor during the Meuse-Argonne campaign in the operation designed to rescue the "Lost Battalion" on 8 October. His Company G was placed on the far left of the 2nd Battalion of the 328th Infantry. York was squad leader in the left platoon, led by Sergeant Harry M. Parsons. At 6:10 in the morning the attacking Americans moved forward down Hill 223, which had been taken the day before, and moved across a 500-yard valley toward the German positions opposite, held by three infantry regiments of the 2nd Württemberg Landwehr Division, including elements of the 12th Landwehr Infantry, the 210th Reserve Infantry, and the 7th Bavarian Pioneers commanded by Oberst Leutnant Vollmer, all of whom were protecting the Decauville Railroad. The German units were understrength and, suffering physical and mental exhaustion, their morale was low. Intelligence officers rated it a fourth (lowest) class division.

The attackers came under heavy fire and Sergeant Parsons decided to attack machine guns firing on them from a wooded area on the left. About sixteen men, including Corporal York, slipped around the German flank and stumbled upon two Germans with Red Cross brassards, one of whom surrendered while the other fled.

The events in the next few hours have been examined and reexamined by both Americans and Germans and the accounts of those who were present are conflicting. The fog of war has clouded all. What follows is perhaps as close an approximation of the action as can now be pieced together.

On the German side of the position being attacked, Oberst Leutnant Vollmer had lost contact with his flanks in the confusion of battle and was precariously isolated, but he had established a series of machine gun nests. Hearing a disturbance to his rear, he discovered a group of several dozen soldiers in a clearing. They had dropped their arms and equipment, claiming they were exhausted from a night of marching, and were having breakfast. As Vollmer tried to rouse them, several Americans, among them Corporal York, broke through the underbrush, firing.

There was little resistance. One man fired at York and York killed him. Suddenly a machine gun on a hill beyond opened fire. The Germans fell to the ground but nine Americans fell dead or wounded. York, unhurt, rolled to a sitting position, and fired at the head of any machine gunner that appeared. Knowing that York's American Enfield rifle had a five-round clip, five men and a lieutenant made a desperate charge.

York picked them off, beginning with the last man and working forward. He killed the German lieutenant with his pistol. As he later remembered, he shot him "right through the stomach and he dropped and screamed a lot. All of the boches who were hit squealed like pigs." York reloaded his rifle and called on the survivors to surrender.

While this was taking place Vollmer had been unsuccessfully shooting at York. He finally stood up and, speaking excellent English, having once worked in Chicago, called "English?"

"No, not English," York answered.

"What!"

"American."

"Good Lord!"

Vollmer offered to surrender his men and York, pointing a pistol at his head, said "Do it."

The surrenders began in an orderly fashion, but during the roundup one man lobbed a grenade at York; York shot him.

He was behind enemy lines, had only seven unwounded men with him, but he organized his prisoners into a column and forced them to carry the wounded Americans. As he worked his way back he gathered more prisoners. Ignorant of Geneva Conventions, he compelled Vollmer to call out to others to surrender. In this way he captured position after position. When one gunner refused to surrender, York shot him.

Safely into the American lines, he found that neither his battalion nor regiment had facilities to handle so many prisoners—four officers and 128 other ranks—so he marched them to brigade headquarters. His brigade commander remarked, "Well, York, I hear you've captured the whole damn German army."

"No," said York, saluting, "Only 132."

York emerged a hero. In addition to his prisoners he was credited with killing twenty-five and silencing thirty-five machine guns. He was promoted to sergeant and given the Distinguished Service Cross, later raised to the Medal of Honor. Marshal Foch presented him with the *Croix de Guerre* with palm and told him: "What you did was the greatest thing accomplished by any private soldier of all the armies of Europe." Other countries also hastened to award him medals, even Montenegro, a country York had probably never heard of.

When asked by General George B. Duncan how many he thought he had hit, York replied: "General, I would hate to think I missed any of them shots; they were all at pretty close range, 50 or 60 yards."

He spent the winter of 1918–19 receiving decorations, conducting prayer meetings, and appearing at events organized by the army. While in Paris Wilson summoned Sergeant York. The two disparate men, the polished, cultured president and the rough-cut hillbilly hero, came from different worlds and they found it difficult to communicate. However, it was the Christmas season and about dinner time, and York thought he might be invited to eat with the President, but after a few minutes an aide informed him that he must go as the Wilsons were expecting dinner guests. York walked back dinnerless to his lodgings.

York saw little of Paris until March 1919 when he arrived there for the organizational meeting of the American Legion. With time to visit the usual sights, he even went to the opera, although he was shocked by the price of nearly $4.00.

The army failed to make good use of York's amazing record. Although Pershing is said to have praised him, no such evidence can be found. (York was a conscript and Pershing's favorite soldier was Samuel Woodfill, the first American to penetrate the Hindenburg Line.) York's fame came from the press attention he received, especially in the *Saturday Evening Post*, which with its two million circulation was the largest periodical in the world. It was a *Post* journalist, George Pattullo, who stumbled on York's story while touring the Argonne area soon after the Armistice. His article appeared in the issue of 26 April 1919, scooping the newspapers. The response was enormous.

When York landed at Hoboken, New Jersey, on 22 May he was met at the dock by a throng of reporters and was soon driven through a blizzard of ticker tape to the Waldorf-Astoria. York said the cheering crowds "plumb scared me to death," and until it was explained to him, he did not realize it was all for him. That evening he was fêted at a formal banquet, but he was disheartened because he had failed to reach his mother by telephone.

He was ordered to Washington where he met with Secretary Baker and was given a standing ovation in the House of Representatives. When he was finally discharged, he hurried home to marry Gracie. The Yorks lived together for forty-five years and had eight children.

More than most returning doughboys, Alvin York found it difficult to readjust to civilian life. The transformation from Appalachian farm laborer to soldier to hero of the nation within eighteen months was a great deal for any man to accept. Only his innate dignity saved him from exploitation. Deluged with offers to trade on his fame, he refused them all. He did, however, accept a 400-acre farm presented by the Nashville Rotary Club. Sadly, the intentions of the donors fell short. The farm contained no house, had not enough stock, and the club fell behind in the mortgage payments. York was forced to borrow money but then suffered from the swift decline in prices in the 1920s. Later fund drives finally raised the needed funds.

With first-hand knowledge of the need of farmers for usable roads, York agitated for highway improvements. In recognition, Route 127, which passes through Fentress County, completed in the mid-1920s, was named Alvin York Highway. An Alvin C. York Foundation promoted education for mountainfolk, and the York Agricultural Institute was founded by local people in Tennessee, but religious and educational causes again led him into financial difficulties. He became entangled with political problems and lawsuits. The Internal Revenue Service, with its usual sensitivity, sued him.

In World War II he volunteered for service. He failed to pass his physical exam, but was nevertheless commissioned as a major. But to Americans he always remained "Sergeant" York. He died in 1964 at age 77.

THE "LOST BATTALION"

IN THE FINAL phase of the Meuse-Argonne offensive, Pershing ordered the 77th Division, which constituted the left wing of his army, to push ahead "without regard of losses and without regard to the exposed conditions of the flank." General James Harbord described the 77th Division, most of whose men came from metropolitan New York, as "made up of all the racial strains which characterize that great city." It was sometimes called the Times Square Division or the Melting Pot Division, for forty-two languages were spoken among its members. A battalion of the 308th Infantry was described as "practically a Jewish battalion."

On 2 October six companies of the 308th Infantry, one company of the 307th, and two companies of the 306th Machine Gun Battalion of the 77th Division (about 600 men in all), pushed ahead in a fog and light rain and were cut off and surrounded near Charlevaux Mill. Major Charles W. Whittlesey, a bespectacled, mild-mannered New Englander, in civilian life a New York lawyer, was the senior officer present.

The position occupied by the Americans was about 300 yards long and sixty yards deep on a steep and rocky hillside. Beginning at 1:15 P.M. on the second day of their ordeal American artillery laid down a massive four-hour barrage— that fell on Whittlesey's men, wounding his orderly and blowing Ben Gaedeke, the 1st Battalion sergeant major, to bits. One young soldier had both legs blown off and was heard calling, "Mamma, Mamma, Mamma."

Whittlesey's only communication was one way, by pigeon, and only two pigeons remained of the original six. In the carnage of the bombardment a nervous Private Omar Richards, the pigeon man, accidentally released one without a message. The last bird, a black checker cock named Cher Ami, carried the message: "Our own artillery is dropping a barrage directly on us. For heaven's sake stop it." When released he flew directly to a branch of the nearest tree and sat there. Thrown stones failed to persuade him to fly. Under fire, Private Richards climbed the tree and scolded him until he finally flew off. Men watched him disappear with little hope that he would get through. In the event, Cher Ami lost a leg and an eye en route but reached division headquarters about 4:00 P.M.

The barrage was stopped, but the men lay under persistent attack with no means of alleviating the suffering of the wounded. Hunger, thirst, cold, and pain were eating at morale. Whittlesey and Captain George G. McMurtry moved among them, trying to reassure them, but they were close to the end of their tether. When one soldier shot in the stomach groaned, McMurtry told him to keep quiet lest he bring on machine gun fire. "It pains like hell, Captain," he said, "but I'll keep as quiet as I can." He made no sound and died thirty minutes later.

The only water was a brook just below their position, but it was covered by a German machine gun. Zip Cepeglia, an Italian from the Bowery, proved adept at slipping down and getting water, but so many soldiers were hit making unauthorized attempts that Whittlesey had to post guards along the path leading to it.

Airplanes from the 50th Aero Squadron tried to drop supplies, chocolate, concentrated food—a prototype of today's dehydrated soups—and ammunition, but the parcels fell into the German lines and two planes and their crews were lost. As Billy Mitchell later wrote: "Our pilots thought they had located it [the surrounded group] from the panel that it showed, and dropped off considerable supplies, but later I found out that they had received none of the supplies we had dropped off. The Germans had made up a panel like theirs and our men had calmly dropped off the nice food to the Germans who undoubtedly ate it with much thanksgiving." Nine men who tried to recover air-dropped parcels were captured.

Repeated attempts to break through to Whittlesey failed. With the last pigeon gone, Private Richards ate the bird seed. Bandages were taken from the dead to use on those still alive. The Germans were unrelenting. A German assault with flame throwers on the fourth day was particularly demoralizing. A soldier ran to Whittlesey shouting, "Liquid fire!"

"Liquid hell!" Whittlesey snapped. "Get back where you belong."

The trapped men were soon described by the American press as the "Lost Battalion."

Leutnant Fritz Printz of the German 67th Reserve Division suggested to his major, who agreed, that one of the prisoners be sent with a note demanding surrender. Private Lowell R. Hollingshead consented to carry the note if the German commander would clear his name with Captain McMurtry and this was done: "The bearer of this present . . . refused to give the German Intelligence Officer any answer to his questions and is quite an honorable fellow. . . . The suffering of your wounded men can be heard over here in the German lines and we are appealing to your humane sentiments to stop. . . . Private Hollingshead is quite a soldier. We envy you." But the Americans had no thought of surrendering. Although Damon Runyon later embellished the story by saying that Whittlesey told the Germans to "Go to hell!" in fact, no reply was made. However, as news of the message was passed along, one wounded man rose on one elbow and shouted, "You Heinie bastards, come and get us!" This was followed by obscenities from other men. Lieutenant William Cullen remembered enough German to call the enemy sons-of-bitches in their own tongue.

GHQ designed a daring plan to rescue the battalion using the 82nd Division, which only two days earlier had received a new commander: Major General George Duncan, who had recently commanded the 77th Division. On 7 October the 164th Infantry Brigade of the 82nd under Brigadier General Julian R. Lindsay, supported by the 157th Field Artillery, was sent diagonally to attack the high ground on the northeast corner of the Argonne Forest. This maneuver exposed the brigade to enemy fire from three sides and uncovered its right flank, but it came in on the German flank and achieved its first objective, Hill 223 (west of the town of Châtel-Chéhéry), by nightfall.

The next morning an attack was made from the hill to the Decauville Railroad three miles beyond. It was in this attack that Corporal Alvin York earned his Medal of Honor.

The pressure of this attack forced the Germans surrounding the Americans to draw back, and on the afternoon of the 8th, after 104 hours without food or medical attention, Whittlesey and 193 other survivors, most of them wounded, limped out to safety and into the lines of the 82nd Division. They had suffered casualties of nearly seventy percent. One who saw them recorded: "I couldn't say anything to them. There was nothing to say, anyway. It made your heart jump up in your throat just to look at them. Their faces told the whole story of their fight."

From a hospital Lieutenant Maurice V. Griffin wrote his wife: "The picture I have of you has a hole in it from a piece of a shell. I have four bullet holes in my overcoat, and my trousers were torn to pieces by a grenade, but I only had my knee cut beside the bullet in the shoulder. . . . But they did not get me. The last . . . days we had nothing but tree leaves and roots. Most of our drinking water was rain water from shell holes."

The next morning General Alexander arrived on the scene. Asked if he wanted Major Whittlesey brought up, he replied: "By no means. I'll go to him." And he walked down to tell him that he was promoted to lieutenant colonel.

Many were cited for bravery. Whittlesey and McMurtry were each awarded the Medal of Honor; Lieutenant Harold E. Goettler of the Air Service, who lost his life in an effort to locate Whittlesey and his men, was awarded the Medal of Honor posthumously. Private Abraham Krotoshinsky, a barber from the Bronx who had managed to slip through the German lines with a message, was awarded the Distinguished Service Cross.

Cher Ami was given an honorable retirement from active duty and a year later died. He was stuffed and placed on exhibit in a glass case at the Smithsonian Institution.

Whittlesey found his laurels difficult to wear. After the war he said, "I used to think I was a lawyer; now I don't know what I am." On Thanksgiving Day, 1921, he boarded a liner to Cuba. After writing nine letters to relatives and friends and a note to the ship's captain regarding the disposition of his luggage, he jumped overboard. His body was never found.

BIBLIOGRAPHY

"There is more material on World War I than any man can possibly cope with."

— John Dos Passos,
Mr. Wilson's War

Ackerman, Carl W. *Following the Bolsheviki.* New York: Charles Scribner's Sons, 1919.

Alexander, Robert. *Memories of the World War, 1917–1918.* New York, Macmillan Company, 1931.

Asprey, Robert B. *At Belleau Wood.* Denton, Texas: University of North Texas Press, 1996.

Association of West Point Graduates. Child, Paul W., ed. *Register of Graduates and Former Cadets of the United States Military Academy.* New York: Association of Graduates, USMA, West Point, 1990.

Ayres, Leonard P. *The War with Germany: A Statistical Summary.* Washington, D.C.: Government Printing Office, 1919.

Baldwin, Fred Davis. *The American Enlisted Man in World War I.* Diss., Princeton University, 1964.

Ballard, Robert D., with Spencer Dunmore. *Exploring the* Lusitania. Ontario, Canada: Warner/Madison Press, 1995.

Barbeau, Arthur E., and Florette Henri. *The Unknown Soldiers: Black American Troops in World War I.* Philadelphia: Temple University Press, 1974.

Barnett, Corelli. *The Swordbearers: Supreme Command in the First World War.* New York: William Morrow, 1964.

Braim, Paul F. *The Test of Battle: The American Expeditionary Force in the Meuse Argonne Campaign.* Shippensburg, PA: White Mane Books, 1998.

Brannen, Carl Andrew. *Over There: A Marine in the Great War*. College Station, Texas: Texas A & M University Press, 1996.

Bristow, Nancy K. *Making Men Moral: Social Engineering During the Great War*. New York: New York University, 1996.

Britten, Thomas A. *American Indians in World War I: Military Service as Catalyst for Reform*. Diss., Texas Tech University, 1994.

Broun, Heywood. *The A.E.F.: With General Pershing and the American Forces*. New York: Harcourt, 1918.

Bullard, Robert L. *Fighting Generals*. Ann Arbor, Michigan: University of Michigan, 1944.

Churchill, Winston. *The World Crisis*. 5 vols. New York: Scribner, 1923–31.

Coffman, Edward M. *The War to End All Wars: The American Military Experience in World War I*. New York: Oxford University Press, 1968.

———. *The Hilt of the Sword: The Career of Peyton C. March*. Madison: University of Wisconsin Press, 1946.

Cole, Leonard A. *The Eleventh Plague: The Politics of Biological and Chemical Warfare*. New York: W. H. Freeman and Company, 1996.

Cooke, James J. *The Rainbow Division in the Great War, 1917–1918*. Westport, Connecticut: Praeger, 1994.

Crozier, William. *Ordnance and the World War: A Contribution to the History of American Preparedness*. New York: Scribner, 1920.

Daniels, Josephus. *Our Navy at War*. New York: George H. Doran Company, 1922.

Duffy, Francis P. *Father Duffy's Story: With an Historical Appendix by Joyce Kilmer*. Garden City, New York: Garden City Publishing Company, 1919.

Ettinger, Albert M., and A. Churchill. *A Doughboy with the Fighting 69th: A Remembrance of World War I*. Shippensburg, Pennsylvania: White Mane Publishing Company, 1992.

Ferrell, Robert H., ed. *Dear Bess: Letters from Harry to Bess Truman, 1910–1959*. New York: W. W. Norton & Company, 1983.

Ford, Nancy Gentile. *War and Ethnicity: Foreign-Born Soldiers and United States Military Policy During World War I*. Diss., Temple University, 1994.

Fredericks, Pierce G. *The Great Adventure: America in the First World War*. New York: E. P. Dutton, 1960.

Freidel, Frank. *Over There: The Story of America's First Great Overseas Crusade.* Philadelphia: Temple University Press, 1990.

Gavin, Lettie. *American Women in World War I: They Also Served.* Niwot, Colorado: University of Colorado Press, 1997.

Gibbons, Floyd. *And They Thought We Wouldn't Fight.* New York: George H. Doran Company, 1918.

Halpern, Paul G. *A Naval History of World War I.* Annapolis, Maryland: Naval Institute Press, 1994.

Hansen, Arlen J. *Gentlemen Volunteers: The Story of the American Ambulance Drivers in the Great War, August 1914–September 1918.* New York: Arcade Publishing, 1996.

Harbord, James G. *The American Army in France, 1917–1919.* Boston: Little, Brown, and Company, 1936.

Haverstock, Nathan A. *Fifty Years at the Front: The Life of War Correspondent Frederick Palmer.* New York & London: Brassey, 1996.

Hayes, John B. *Heroes Among the Brave.* Loachapoka, Alabama: Lee County Historical Society, 1973.

Haythornthwaite, Philip J. *The World War I Source Book.* London: Arms and Armour Press, 1992.

Herrmann, David G. *The Arming of Europe and the Making of the First World War.* Princeton, N.J.: Princeton University Press, 1996.

Herwig, Holger H. *The First World War: Germany and Austria-Hungary.* London: Arnold, 1997.

Hudson, James J. *Hostile Skies: A Combat History of the American Air Service in World War I.* Syracuse: Syracuse University Press, 1968.

Johnson, Hubert C. *Break-Through! Tactics, Technology, and the Search for Victory on the Western Front in World War I.* Novato, California: Presidio Press, 1995.

Lancaster, Richard C. *Serving the U.S. Armed Forces, 1861–1986: The Story of the YMCA's Ministry to Military Personnel for 125 Years.* Schaumburg, Illinois: Armed Services YMCA of the USA, 1987.

Leighton, John Langdon. *Simsadus London.* New York: Henry Holt & Co., 1920.

Liddell Hart, Captain B. H. *The Real War, 1914–1918*. Boston: Little, Brown, and Company, 1930; revised, 1964.

Longstreet, Stephen. *The Canvas Falcons: The Men and Planes of World War I*. New York: Barnes and Noble Books, 1970.

MacArthur, Charles. *War Bugs*. Garden City, New York: Doubleday, Doran & Co., 1929.

Mackin, Elton E. *Suddenly We Didn't Want to Die*. Novato, California: Presidio Press, 1993.

Markle, Clifford Milton. *A Yankee Prisoner in Hunland*. New Haven: Yale University Press, 1920.

Marrin, Albert. *The Yanks are Coming: The United States in the First World War*. New York: Atheneum, 1986.

Marsh, Peyton C. *The Nation at War*. New York: Doubleday, Doran & Company, 1932.

Millis, Walter. *Road to War: America 1914–1917*. Boston & New York: Houghton Mifflin, 1935.

Mock, James R., and Cedric Larson. *Words that Won the War: The Story of the Committee on Public Information, 1917–1919*. Princeton: Princeton University Press, 1939.

Office of the Adjutant General. *Histories of Two Hundred and Fifty-One Divisions of the German Army Which Participated in the War (1914–1918)*. War Department Document 905. Washington D.C.: United States War Office, 1920.

O'Shea, Stephen. *Back to the Front: An Accidental Historian Walks the Trenches of World War I*. New York: Walker and Company, 1997.

Paschall, Rod. *The Defeat of Imperial Germany, 1917–1918*. Chapel Hill, North Carolina: Algonquin Books, 1989.

Patton, Robert H. *The Pattons: A Personal History of an American Family*. Washington & London: Brassey's, 1994.

Perret, Geoffrey. *Old Soldiers Never Die: The Life of Douglas MacArthur*. New York: Random House, 1996.

Pershing, John J. *My Experiences in the World War*. 2 vols. New York: Harper & Row, 1931.

Reilly, Henry J. *Americans All, the Rainbow at War: The Official History of the 42nd Rainbow Division in the World War.* Columbus, Ohio: F. J. Heer, 1936.

Rhodes, Benjamin D. *The Anglo-American Winter War with Russia, 1918–1919: A Diplomatic and Military Tragicomedy.* Westport, Connecticut: Greenwood Press, 1988.

Simmonds, Frank H. *History of the World War.* 5 vols. Garden City & New York: Published for the Review of Review Company by Doubleday Page & Co., 1920.

Smith, Daniel M. *The Great Departure: The United States and World War I.* New York: John Wiley and Sons, 1965.

Smythe, Donald. *Pershing: General of the Armies.* Bloomington, Indiana: Indiana University Press, 1986.

Spiller, Roger J., ed. *Dictionary of American Military Biography.* 3 vols. Westport, Connecticut: Greenwood Press, 1984.

Stallings, Laurence. *The Doughboys: The Story of the AEF, 1917–1918.* New York: Harper & Row, 1963.

Taft, William Howard. [Chairman of the Editorial Board] *Service With Fighting Men: An Account of the Work of the American Young Men's Christian Association in the World War.* New York: Association Press, 1922.

Terraine, John. *To Win a War: 1918, the Year of Victory.* Garden City, New York: Doubleday Co., 1981.

Thayer, Lucien H. *America's First Eagles: The Official History of the U.S. Air Service, A.E.F. [1917–1918].* Mesa, Arizona: R. James Bender Publishing and Champlin Fighter Museum Press, 1983.

Toklas, Alice B. *What is Remembered.* New York: Holt, Rinehart and Winston, 1963.

Toland, John. *No Man's Land: 1918, the Last Year of the Great War.* New York: Smithmark, 1980.

Townsend, Harry Everett. *War Diary of a Combat Artist.* Niwot, Colorado: University Press of Colorado, 1991.

U.S. War Department. *The Official Records of the Great War.* New York: Parke, Austin and Lipscomb, 1923.

Venzon, Anne Cipriano. *The United States in the First World War: An Encyclopedia*. Diss., Garland Publishing, 1995.

Victory, James. *Soldier Making: The Forces that Shaped the Infantry Training of White Soldiers in the United States Army in World War I*. Diss., Kansas State University, 1990.

Walker, George. *Venereal Disease in the A.E.F*. Baltimore: Medical Standard Book Co., 1922.

White, Lonnie J. *The 90th Division in World War I*. Manhattan, Kansas: Sunflower University Press, 1996.

INDEX